HANDBOOK OF
THE INTERNATIONAL POLITICAL
SCIENCE ASSOCIATION

International Political Science Association
2000

D1446094

Published by the
International Political Science Association
with the financial assistance of the
International Social Science Council

Ordering information

Copies of this publication may be ordered from the
International Political Science Association
Department of Politics, University College Dublin
Belfield, Dublin 4, Ireland

fax: +353-1-706 17171
email: ipsa@ucd.ie
http://www.ucd.ie/~ipsa

ISBN 1-902277-27-9

CONTENTS

PREFACE

The *Oxford Dictionary* defines handbook as a manual or treatise that may be conveniently held in the hand; a manual of ecclesiastical offices or ritual; concise information on the art or occupation or voyage in question.

What the *Oxford* does not say but is well worth adding for social scientists is that you cannot have a handbook for an organization until that organization is mature enough to have a settled ritual, rules and offices.

The purpose of the *IPSA Handbook* is first and foremost to help guide current members and activists. A second purpose, also of immense importance, is to inform the larger community of political scientists throughout the world so that a maximum number will have incentive as well as opportunity to become members and activists. Growth is not a goal of business corporations only. However, for IPSA, growth is not an end in itself or even a measure of success. Our growth is important because the presence of a political science means the presence of at least one interest group with an organized selfish interest in freedom of thought, inquiry and criticism.

The *IPSA Handbook* is a sign of growth and also a promise of growth because neophytes and the seasoned but uninducted of all statuses are too often discouraged from joining because they lack the simple facts about procedure, etiquette, obligation and entitlement. This *Handbook*, like any good handbook or manual, provides "everything you wanted to know but were afraid to ask."

Theodore J Lowi
IPSA President
July 2000

ACKNOWLEDGEMENTS

In compiling this handbook, the IPSA secretariat has contracted a large number of debts. The first and most obvious is to our predecessors: to those who set up and maintained the databases that have formed the core of this volume. In recent years, these have included secretaries general John Trent in Ottawa and the late Francesco Kjellberg in Oslo, with their administrators Linda Vachon and Liette Boucher in Ottawa and Lise Fog in Oslo.

The second cluster to whom we are in debt comprises our colleagues: the current members of the IPSA executive committee and many others spread throughout the world who gave us careful feedback on earlier drafts of portions of this handbook. Their names are too numerous to mention individually, but IPSA's deep gratitude to them should be formally acknowledged.

The preparation of a publication of this kind is obviously not free of cost; in addition to printing and circulation, simple compilation of the material requires additional assistance. IPSA is grateful to the International Social Science Council, for long IPSA's close ally in disseminating information material in the social sciences, for generous financial assistance towards this publication.

But the penultimate word of thanks must go to those who bore the brunt of the work of preparation: to Louise Delaney, former IPSA administrator, who was responsible for maintaining our original databases; to Michelle Murphy of the IPSA secretariat, who assembled, edited and checked much of the material; to Nuala Ryan for her work in proofing the text; and especially to the administrator, Margaret Brindley, who played a central role in piloting this volume through to publication.

Finally, let the last word of appreciation go to the reader, who is invited to make allowance for the shortcomings that are, perhaps, an inevitable part of an undertaking on the scale of the present one. We hope that future editions will be an improvement, and it seemed appropriate to allow for this.

John Coakley
IPSA Secretary General
July 2000

1 / INTRODUCTION

1.1 OVERVIEW

The International Political Science Association (IPSA), founded under the auspices of UNESCO in 1949, is an international scholarly association. Its legal seat is in Paris, at the Fondation Nationale des Sciences Politiques. Its objectives are to promote the advancement of political science through the collaboration of scholars in different parts of the world; to organise world congresses and other academic activities; to provide documentary and reference services; to facilitate the spread of political science information; and to promote internationally planned research.

IPSA has more than 40 collective members (national and regional political science associations), approximately 100 associate members (political science departments and other institutions concerned with political science) and more than 1,200 individual members. It has consultative status with the Economic and Social Council of the United Nations and with UNESCO, and is a member of the International Social Science Council and of the International Committee for Social Science Information and Documentation.

The association's affairs are managed by a council, on which all collective members are represented, which meets once every three years; and, between meetings of the council, by an executive committee elected for a three-year term. The day-to-day affairs of the association are administered by its secretary general and by a permanent secretariat (see chapter 2 for a discussion of IPSA's structure).

IPSA's academic activities fall under three main headings. First, it organises a triennial world congress, which is typically attended by up to 2,000 political scientists. Its eighteenth triennial congress takes place in Quebec in August 2000. Second, it promotes research in the discipline and on the frontiers with adjacent disciplines, notably through a wide-reaching network of research committees. Third, it engages in an extensive publishing programme, one that includes the *International political science abstracts* (1951-), the *International political science review* (1980-), a book series and the association's bulletin, *Participation* (see chapter 3 for further details).

1.2 FOUNDATION AND GROWTH

IPSA's founder members in 1949 were four national associations: the American, Canadian, French and Indian political science associations. Since then, four more national associations joined in 1950 (Israel, Poland, Sweden and the United Kingdom), another four in 1951 (Austria, Belgium, Greece and Mexico), and six in 1952 (Brazil, Finland, Germany, Italy, Japan and Yugoslavia). By the mid-1950s a further five national associations had joined — Australia and the Netherlands (1953), and Ceylon, Cuba and the Soviet Union (1955).

Of course, not all of these associations survived as IPSA members (some, indeed, did not even survive as national associations). Those associations whose membership was discontinued were nevertheless fewer in number than newly affiliating associations, with the result that IPSA's collective membership has been expanding steadily.

Already at the very beginning two other categories of membership were introduced: individual and associate. Individual membership, open to political scientists who accept IPSA's objectives, has grown steadily from 1952 onwards. Associate membership, open to institutions engaged in research or teaching in the area of political science, grew steadily until the mid-1960s; since them it has hovered about an average of approximately 100.

The growth in IPSA's membership has reflected the range of services that it has provided for its members. Already in 1950 IPSA organised its first world congress, in Zurich, and in 1952 began a series of world congresses that has continued triennially since then. These continued to grow in size until the 1980s, and their academic significance has been steadily expanding. IPSA's publishing activities began in 1951 with the launch of what has become the leading source for bibliographical and abstracting information in the discipline, the *International political science abstracts*. The online and CD versions of the *Abstracts* are now the most widely used resources of their kind within the discipline. With the addition of a book series (which followed on from a large number of independent publications sponsored by IPSA) and the creation in 1980 of the *International political science review*, IPSA had attained an impressive stable of publications. But the vigour of IPSA's academic mission and its capacity to reach large numbers of political scientists, members and non-members alike, is arguably most visible in its network of research committees. The first research committee was recognised by IPSA in 1970; since then, the number has increased steadily, peaking at 50 by 1999.

1.3 CONTENTS OF THIS VOLUME

Given the range of academic activities in which IPSA is involved, and the complex nature of its organisational structure arising from the scale of its involvement in promoting the development of the discipline, there is clearly a need for a stock-taking review of the association in the context of disciplinary developments more generally. Since the end of the century and of the millennium coincide also with IPSA's fiftieth birthday, no more appropriate time than the present could be selected for such a review.

The objective of the present volume is, then, to provide a reference book for the International Political Science Association and thus to reflect the position in international political science more generally. It should not be seen as a definitive guide to the association, since by its very nature a publication of this kind will be out of date, in small ways, as soon as the ink on its pages has dried. Furthermore, this book breaks new ground in a number of ways and, as a first exercise of this kind, it will inevitably be victim of a range of errors, ranging from trivial misprints to serious factual misreporting. However, it is to be hoped that a broad overview of the kind of material covered here, however defective, will be preferable to no overview at all; and the present volume will at least serve as a basis from which it will be possible to plan future editions that will correct errors and fill gaps in the present one.

The structure of the book reflects this concern to provide a broad overview of the domains in which the association is active. Chapters 2 through 5 thus focus on IPSA itself: on its membership and structures of government (chapter 2), on the broad range of academic activities that it pursues and promotes (chapter 3), on its constitution and procedural rules (chapter 4), and on its network of research committees (chapter 5).

The four following chapters are also based on the work of IPSA, but less specifically. A list of national political science associations, with some general information and the coordinates of their secretariats, is provided in chapter 6; this includes associations which are not collective members of IPSA as well as those which are. Chapter 7 provides a list of IPSA's associate members and of political science departments world-wide, again with their coordinates. This is likely to be incomplete, especially for areas outside Europe and North America, but it is to be hoped that later editions will be able to supplement and amend this information. Chapter 8 lists a cross-section of political scientists world-wide: those who were IPSA members on the last day of the second millennium (31 December 1999), or who joined shortly afterwards, in early 2000. The last chapter lists the world's most significant political science journals, based on the list used by IPSA's *International political science abstracts*.

2 / ORGANISATION

The general provisions under which IPSA's affairs are conducted are outlined in full in chapter 4 of this volume. These include the text of the constitution, IPSA's fundamental law, as well as the texts of other documents governing IPSA's organs and activities. In this chapter we will consider four aspects of IPSA's make-up: its supreme decision making body, the *council*; the body charged with managing its affairs between meetings of the council, the *executive committee*; its most basic units, its *members*; and the body responsible for running its day-to-day activities, the *secretariat*.

2.1 THE COUNCIL

The IPSA council came into existence in 1950 shortly after the creation of the association itself. Since then it has met on 16 occasions, its meetings coinciding in each case with IPSA's triennial world congresses.

The council is responsible for determining the policy of the association, for approving its accounts, for reviewing its financial prospects and for electing the president of the association and the executive committee, to which it devolves power for the management of IPSA's affairs between meetings of the council. It also has the power to amend the constitution by a two-thirds majority, and it has used this power on eight occasions since its establishment.

Reflecting IPSA's membership base, the council comprises two classes of members. The largest group is made up of representatives designated by the collective members of the association (national and regional political science associations), each of which is entitled to between one and three members. Each collective member may also designate alternates to represent it at any meeting of the council. The second group is made up of individual members proposed by the president and ratified by the executive committee. These are selected from a number of constitutionally defined categories (individual and associate members of IPSA from countries or regions where there is no collective member, chairpersons and secretaries of IPSA research committees and study groups or their representatives, and boards of editors of IPSA official publications), subject to the restriction that their total number may not exceed 30% of the number of representatives of collective members.

In addition to its regular triennial sessions, the council may be summoned into special session by the secretary general upon request of two thirds of the collective members of the association. This provision of the constitution has never been invoked. The council is also authorised by the constitution to adopt its own rules of procedure. By 2000 it had not actually done this; but to mark the occasion of the fiftieth anniversary of its first meeting the executive committee drafted a set of proposed rules of procedure for presentation to and consideration by the council (see section 4.2)

The president is elected by the council on the basis of nominations from the executive committee and from the council itself. Since 1949, IPSA has had 17 presidents; their names and affiliations are indicated in table 2.1. The outgoing president chairs meetings of the council and then goes on to serve as a member of the executive committee for one more term.

2.2 THE EXECUTIVE COMMITTEE

In addition to the triennial meetings of the council, the president also chairs more frequent meetings of the executive committee. This was originally a smaller body, but the constitution now requires it to contain a minimum of 12 and a maximum of 18 members, including the president and the past president, who are members ex officio.

In practice, in recent years, the executive committee has adhered to its

---

Table 2.1: IPSA presidents, 1949-2000

Quincy Wright, University of Chicago (1949-52)
William A Robson, London School of Economics (1952-55)
James K Pollock, University of Michigan (1955-58)
Jacques Chapsal, FNSP, Paris (1958-61)
D N Chester, Nuffield College, Oxford (1961-64)
Jacques Freymond, IUHEI, Geneva (1964-67)
Carl J Friedrich, Harvard University (1967-70)
Stein Rokkan, University of Bergen (1970-73)
Jean Laponce, University of British Columbia (1973-76)
Karl Deutsch, Harvard University (1976-79)
Candido Mendes, SBI, Rio de Janeiro (1979-82)
Klaus von Beyme, University of Heidelberg (1982-85)
Kinhide Mushakoji, UN University, Tokyo (1985-88)
Guillermo O'Donnell, CEBRAP, São Paulo/Notre Dame (1988-91)
Carole Pateman, UCLA, Los Angeles (1991-94)
Jean Leca, FNSP, Paris (1994-97)
Theodore J Lowi, Cornell University (1997-2000)

maximum size. In addition to its 18 members, its meetings are attended, in a non-voting capacity, by the secretary general, the administrator, the programme chair and the editors of IPSA's publications (the *International political science abstracts*, the *International political science review* and *Advances in political science: an international series*). Other persons may, for particular purposes, be invited to attend all or part of a meeting.

The executive committee is required by article 22 of the constitution to meet immediately after the triennial congress, and thereafter it "shall regularly meet once a year". This practice was maintained literally by the first 10 executive committees. In 1982 the custom began of holding an additional meeting in the congress year, some months before the congress itself. In 1983 the practice began of holding a second meeting in the post-congress year, to plan for the following congress. The normal pattern of meetings is thus for each executive committee to meet six times:

- immediately after the congress
- in spring of the post-congress year
- in autumn of the post-congress year
- in spring of the pre-congress year
- in spring of the congress year
- immediately before the congress

IPSA marked the 80th meeting of its executive committee in Jerusalem

---

Table 2.2: IPSA executive committee, 1997-2000

Theodore J Lowi, Cornell University, USA, president
Jean Leca, FNSP, Paris, France, past president
Dalchoong Kim, Sejong Institute, Seoul, Korea, first vice president
Renato Boschi, IUPERJ, Rio de Janeiro, Brazil, vice president
Krzysztof Palecki, Jagiellonian University, Krakow, Poland, vice president
Helen Shestopal, Moscow State University, Russia, vice president
Ursula Vogel, University of Manchester, UK, vice president
Carlos Alba, Universidad Autónoma de Madrid, Spain
Mauro Calise, University of Naples, Italy
Gideon Doron, Tel Aviv University, Israel
L Adele Jinadu, Lagos State University, Nigeria
Max Kaase, Wissenschaftszentrum Berlin für Sozialforschung, Germany
Ikuo Kabashima, University of Tokyo, Japan
Guy Lachapelle, Université Concordia, Montréal, Canada
Paula McClain, University of Virginia / Duke University, USA
Yves Schemeil, Institut d'Etudes Politiques de Grenoble, France
Gunnar Sjöblom, University of Copenhagen, Denmark
Jan Škaloud, Prague School of Economics, Czech Republic

on 27 February 2000.

The principal duty of the executive committee, as defined in article 15 of the constitution, is "to carry out the programme and to direct the affairs of the association during the period between sessions of the council". Its functions are defined in section V of the constitution (articles 20-26). It has also recently adopted its own rules of procedure (see section 4.4).

Meetings of the executive committee are normally arranged to coincide with an academic event, such as the convention of a national association or a roundtable meeting on a specific theme. The local organisers normally cover local accommodation and subsistence costs; those attending are expected to raise their own travel funding. Members are expected to obtain any documentation necessary to support travel (such as visa applications) from the local organisers of the meeting.

A great deal of the work of the committee is carried out through sub-committees appointed by and answerable to it. These typically meet immediately before each plenary meeting of the executive committee. Their membership is normally confined to members of the executive committee, but in certain cases (most notably that of the committee on the congress programme) outside members may be appointed. The secretariat arranges provisional times for these meetings in association with the local organisers. The five standing committees of the executive committee are as follows.

Committee on organisation and procedure. The terms of reference of this committee are: "to advise on all aspects of organisational development, including procedures, membership policy and any other matter referred to it by the executive committee". Its members include, in addition to the president and the secretary general, Dalchoong Kim (chair), Carlos Alba, Serge Hurtig, Jean Laponce, Guy Lachapelle and Jean Leca.

Committee on the congress programme. The terms of reference of this committee are: "to advise on the structure of the programme and on all areas associated with the triennial world congress". Its members include, in addition to the president and the secretary general, William M Lafferty (chair), Renato Boschi, Mauro Calise, Max Kaase, Chung-in Moon, Krzysztof Palecki, Helen Shestopal, John Trent and Ursula Vogel.

Committee on research and training. The terms of reference of this committee are: "to advise on all aspects of the operation of research committees and study groups and on inter-congress activities". Its members include, in addition to the president and the secretary general, Ursula Vogel (chair), Renato Boschi, Gideon Doron, L Adele Jinadu, Max Kaase, Paula D McClain and Gunnar Sjöblom.

Committee on awards. The terms of reference of this committee are: "to advise on all aspects of IPSA awards and to evaluate candidates for these, including (1) Stein Rokkan fellowships, (2) the Karl Deutsch award, (3) the best paper award and (4) any other awards for which provision might be made". Its members include, in addition to the president and the secretary general, Helen Shestopal (chair), Asher Arian, Gideon Doron, Guy Lachapelle, Yves Schemeil and Jan Škaloud.

Committee on the status of women and diversity of participation. The terms of reference of this committee are: "to advise and take initiatives on all matters affecting the status of women in IPSA activities and programmes; and to build a broader base of participation by women scholars, younger scholars, and all scholars from countries and nationalities underrepresented for whatever reasons". Its members include, in addition to the president and the secretary general, Renato Boschi (chair), Nazli Choucri, L Adele Jinadu, Ikuo Kabashima, Paula D McClain and Jan Škaloud.

2.3 THE MEMBERS

IPSA recognises three categories of members: individual, associate and collective. Formal guidelines for accession to membership under each of these headings are contained in section 4.5. Members receive, free, four issues yearly of the *International political science review*, three issues of *Participation* and other information; they are also entitled to subscribe at a reduced rate to the *International political science abstracts* and the *International social science journal*. Individual members may register at a greatly reduced rate at IPSA's world congress.

Individual membership of IPSA is open to persons suitably qualified by their professional activity or general interest in political science. Persons employed as teachers or researchers in political science and related disciplines are eligible, and the executive committee may extend eligibility to other categories. Individual members of IPSA pay an annual or triennial subscription fee, fixed from time to time by the IPSA executive committee. Those joining in 2000 pay USD60 for one year or USD150 for three years. *Associate membership* is open to international or national associations, organisations, societies or institutions pursuing objectives compatible with those of IPSA in related fields of activity. They also pay an annual subscription fee, fixed from time to time by the IPSA executive committee (USD120 in 2000). *Collective membership* of IPSA is open to national and regional associations recognised by the executive committee as being representative of political science in their respective countries or regions; only in exceptional cases is more than one collective member per country admitted. They pay an annual subscription fee based on a table of payments approved by the IPSA council.

The general position regarding membership in each of IPSA's membership categories on 31 December 1999 is summarised in table 2.3. To facilitate comparison, this table also reports on membership on the same date in earlier years. Changes in the case of each category are commented upon in the subsections below.

Individual members. A listing of those individual members of IPSA on 31 December 1999 who consented to the publication of details about themselves, together with similar information on a number of members who joined subsequently, is contained in chapter 8, which also draws some conclusions about their general characteristics. We outline below the principal features of IPSA's membership base at the end of 1999, to the extent that this is permitted by our membership database (in a considerable number of cases important pieces of information were not supplied on the membership forms). A number of these are reviewed below: geographical distribution, involvement of women, age structure and research interests.

It will be clear that a breakdown of individual members by continent and country shows a rather distinctive pattern—clear dominance on the part of Europe and North America (62% of the total), but a strong showing on the part of Asia (26%), dating back to the 1997 Seoul congress.

As might be expected, the proportion of women is still small: of IPSA's 1,038 members whose sex is recorded, 827 (79.7%) are male and 211 (20.3%) are female. In the remaining 46 cases this information was not

Table 2.3: IPSA members by type, 1988-99			
Year	Individual members	Associate members	Collective members	Total members
1988	1,525	99	37	1,661
1989	880	83	37	1,000
1990	902	86	37	1,025
1991	1,150	88	35	1,273
1992	774	98	36	908
1993	980	127	37	1,144
1994	1,247	143	39	1,429
1995	1,062	102	41	1,205
1996	1,075	93	41	1,209
1997	1,430	91	41	1,562
1998	1,133	84	41	1,258
1999	1,084	78	42	1,204

Table 2.4: IPSA members by continent and sex, 31 December 1999

Continent	Men		Women		Total	
	no.	%	no.	%	no.	%
Africa	17	2.1	4	1.9	22	2.0
America, north	239	28.9	74	35.1	318	29.3
America, south	54	6.5	18	8.5	75	6.9
Asia	203	24.5	49	23.2	278	25.6
Europe, cent. & east.	34	4.1	12	5.7	49	4.5
Europe, western	254	30.7	49	23.2	309	28.6
Oceania	26	3.1	5	2.4	33	3.0
Total	827	100.0	211	100.0	1,084	100.0
(row percent)		(79.7)		(20.3)		(100.0)

Note: information on sex was missing in 46 cases.

supplied by the member, and it was not possible to infer it from personal names. Table 2.4 reports the distribution of members by continent, broken down by sex. Women members are proportionately strongest in North America, but even there the predominance of men is obvious. It should be noted that in tables 2.4-2.6 simply adding the columns relating to men and women will not give us the total figure, since the "total" column also includes those whose sex was unknown.

In terms of age, our data are less complete. For the members in respect of whom we have this information, the average age is exactly 52; for men

Table 2.5: IPSA members by age group and sex, 31 December 1999

Age group	Men		Women		Total	
	no.	%	no.	%	no.	%
under 30	11	1.4	6	3.4	17	1.8
30-39	89	11.7	33	18.4	122	13.0
40-49	209	27.5	58	32.4	267	28.5
50-59	251	33.1	59	33.0	311	33.2
60-69	149	19.6	17	9.5	166	17.7
70 or more	49	6.5	6	3.4	55	5.9
Total	759	100.0	179	100.0	938	100.0
(row percent)		(80.9)		(19.1)		(100.0)

Note: information on sex or age was missing in 146 cases.

the figure is slightly over this and for women it is 48. Table 2.5 breaks IPSA members down by age group and sex. The modal age group for men and women is now the 50s; and in both cases the clear tendency is for IPSA to be more successful in recruiting older than younger scholars.

The research interests of IPSA members have also been investigated. With a view to maintaining consistency with earlier data, the secretariat has retained on the membership application form a set of categories that it inherited from earlier questionnaires. This is not necessarily satisfactory for analytical purposes, and in table 2.6 an alternative classification is used. This regroups the categories on the application form to produce a classification system similar to that used in the *International political science abstracts*. The profile of women is strikingly similar to that of men, with even such topics as "women and politics", that might be expected to be of particular interest to women, accounting for a small proportion of women in terms of their primary research interests.

Associate members. A list of associate members broken down by continent and country is given in chapter 6. The dominance of Europe and North America in this category of membership also continues to be striking—87 per cent of the total come from these two continents, a relatively stable proportion since 1996.

Collective members. A list of collective members is given in chapter 5.

Table 2.6: IPSA members by broad research area and sex, 31 December 1999						
Research area	*Men*		*Women*		*Total*	
	no.	*%*	*no.*	*%*	*no.*	*%*
Methodology	3	0.4	3	1.5	6	0.6
Pol. theory/philosophy	110	14.5	32	16.0	142	14.8
Political institutions	114	15.0	28	14.0	142	14.8
Public admin. and policy	65	8.6	13	6.5	78	8.1
Local politics	6	0.8	2	1.0	8	0.8
Political behaviour	127	16.7	31	15.6	158	16.5
Comparative politics	185	24.4	46	23.1	231	24.1
Women and politics	2	0.3	8	4.0	10	1.0
International politics	97	12.8	26	13.1	123	12.8
Development politics	11	1.4	2	1.0	13	1.4
Area studies	39	5.1	8	4.0	47	4.9
Total	759	100.0	199	100.0	958	100.0
(row percent)		(79.2)		(20.8)		(100.0)
Note: information was missing in 121 cases.						

This interprets collective membership rather liberally, and includes certain associations that have been in arrears for many years. In each case, general information on officers, membership and activities is also given.

2.4 THE SECRETARIAT

From the outset, IPSA has had a secretariat which has been responsible for administering its routine affairs. This was based in Paris (1945-55 and 1960-67) and Brussels (1955-60 and 1967-76), before moving to Ottawa (1976-88), Oslo (1988-94) and Dublin (1994-2000). From 2001, it will be based in Concordia University, Montreal.

Given the range of tasks it is expected to undertake, the size of the secretariat is very small. It comprises only one full-time position, that of the IPSA administrator. In recent years, this post has been filled by Lise Fog (1988-94, Louise Delaney (1994-98) and Margaret Brindley (1998-2000). The secretary general acts in a part-time capacity in addition to his or her full-time academic position (see table 2.7 for a list of secretaries general). Additional part-time or temporary assistance is recruited as necessary. Thus Richard Fitzpatrick and Michelle Murphy have acted as full-time temporary research assistants, while Reggie Redmond and Nuala Ryan provide ongoing assistance in the maintenance of accounts and liaison with members respectively.

Because of the limited availability of resources, a reasonable and predictable division of labour between the secretariat and other bodies or posts answerable to the executive committee is essential to the effective functioning of IPSA. This arises from the increased range of activities in which the secretariat is engaged, flowing from changes in the nature of publishing (which now extends over electronic media), the growth of the world wide web, an increase in the number of research committees, and other developments — generally of a positive nature, but typically adding to the burden on the secretariat.

Table 2.7: IPSA secretaries general, 1949-2000

François Goguel, FNSP, Paris (1949-50)
Jean Meynaud, FNSP, Paris (1950-55)
John Goormaghtigh, Brussels (1955-60)
Serge Hurtig, FNSP, Paris (1960-67)
André Philippart, Carnegie Endowment, Brussels (1967-76)
John Trent, University of Ottawa (1976-88)
Francesco Kjellberg, University of Oslo (1988-94)
John Coakley, University College Dublin (1994-2000)

The work of the secretariat extends far and wide. Maintaining contact with individual, collective and associate members is an obvious task. In addition to other kinds of reports, from 1998 onwards the association has issued an annual report, and this, too is drawn up by the secretariat. IPSA's financial accounts have to be maintained and prepared for audit (the actual audit, of course, is carried out by an external auditor of international standing). One of the most demanding additional duties is the publication of the association's bulletin, *Participation*, which appears three times a year (or four times in a pre-congress year). This now ranges from 44 to 60 pages in length, and amounts to something approaching 100,000 words in all in a typical year. Each issue is divided into a maximum of ten sections, as follows:

1. Feature articles
2. IPSA news
3. News from national associations
4. News from research committees
5. Report (seasonal)
6. In memoriam (occasional)
7. Technology and political science (occasional)
8. Other news
9. Book corner
10. Forthcoming meetings.

The three seasonal reports each cover a special subject: individual and associate members (issue 1, spring); a directory of research committees (issue 2, summer) and a directory of national political science associations (issue 3, winter).

A number of other publications of one kind or another are also routinely produced by the secretariat. These include a *Directory of research committees*. The first edition of this booklet, covering the period 1991-94, appeared in 1992. From 1995 onwards, IPSA's policy has been to ensure that the directory appears annually, in the summer issue of *Participation*. In addition, a 48-page stand-alone version of the 1996 edition of the directory was produced for publicity purposes.

The first edition of a 48-page general information booklet entitled *The International Political Science Association: an introduction* appeared in 1997. The secretariat has also been working on other rather ambitious projects (such as this volume, and a 50-year history of IPSA). It also routinely produces a range of information leaflets in English and French, covering such areas as general information, research committees and the executive committee.

In the past, the secretariat also prepared a collection of congress papers for publication in microfiche form, and circulated these to a range of subscribing institutions. Taking advantage of technological developments, the 1997 congress papers were produced on CD-rom. In fact, the collection extends over two CDs: 400 papers on one, and the remaining 214 on another. The booklet describing the collection is also included in the CD, as well as being printed separately. The papers are listed in the descriptive booklet in formal order of the type of session in which they were presented and, within this, in alphabetical order. An alphabetical author index permits the location of individual papers. Also included is the programme chair's elaboration of the main theme.

Finally, the secretariat maintains IPSA's web pages (www.ucd.ie/~ipsa). These have retained the same overall structure since 1996, but the individual pages are updated periodically. The pages cover membership information (including an online membership application system that allows applicants who hold credit cards to join IPSA by filling the form in online), the constitution of IPSA and other procedural documents, links to national associations, research committees, other matters directly related to IPSA including its publications, and links to other political science resources.

By 29 January 2000 the secretariat was aware of permanent links to the IPSA pages from 439 other sites, signalling its very considerable value in publicising IPSA and its activities. The secretariat also maintains a permanent link to the web site of the programme chair (www.prosus.uio.no/ipsa/) and of the local organising committee for the XVIII congress in Quebec (www.ipsa-aisp.org/).

3 / ACADEMIC ACTIVITIES

IPSA engages in a wide range of scholarly activities. Some of these, such as the work of its research committees, are covered elsewhere in this volume (see chapter 5). The present chapter considers three other types of activity: IPSA's publications, its world congresses and its directly sponsored inter-congress activities.

3.1 PUBLICATIONS

IPSA issues three major publications: the *International political science abstracts*, dating from 1950 and published from the Fondation Nationale des Sciences Politiques in Paris; the *International political science review*, dating from 1980 and published by Sage of London; and a book series, *Advances in political science: an international series*, published since 1995 by Macmillan of London.

International political science abstracts. This is IPSA's longest-running publication. Dating from 1950, it has for long been edited by Serge Hurtig and published by IPSA from the Fondation Nationale des Sciences Politiques. Serge Hurtig was joined in 2000 by Paul Godt as associate editor.

The *Abstracts* appear six times per year and have a comprehensive annual index. They consist of abstracts of articles in political science drawn from a wide range of periodicals. By 1999 the number of abstracts published had reached approximately 7,500 annually, drawn from almost 1,000 journals. The enormous range of journals covered is indicated in chapter 9, which uses the *Abstracts* journals list as a guide to world political science periodicals.

Of the value of the *Abstracts* as a research tool there can be no doubt. Quite simply, the conduct of large-scale research in political science without consulting the *Abstracts* makes little sense — though, sadly, it remains the case that not all researchers have access to them. For many, the Social Sciences Citation Index (SSCI) is an essential tool. As its name implies, it spans the social sciences (very broadly defined), and it provides a unique mechanism for tracing cross-references within scholarly periodical literature. But its coverage extends to only a fraction of the universe of political science journals (as may be seen in chapter 9), and, although many abstracts are provided, even in the case of journals covered these are not nearly as comprehensive as those in the *International political science abstracts*. The reality is that the long-time editor of the *Abstracts*, Serge Hurtig, and his staff, have built up unrivalled expertise and an extraordinary network of contacts to facilitate them in maintaining this unique service – a huge collection of material assembled with professional dedication by specialists for specialists. The addition of Paul Godt to this team will ensure maintenance of the same level of quality for the future.

The editors of the *Abstracts* may be contacted at the following address:

Documentation Politique Internationale
27, rue Saint-Guillaume
75337 Paris Cedex 07
France
fax: +33-1-42.22.39.64
email: ipsa-aisp@sciences-po.fr

The usefulness of the *Abstracts* to political scientists has been greatly enhanced with the issue in 1995 of a CD-rom version. This collection is backdated to 1989, and contains an enormous and invaluable collection of material in easily accessible format. The publishers of the CD-rom version may be contacted at:

SilverPlatter Information, Inc.
100 River Ridge Drive
Norwood, MA 02062
USA
tel: +1-800-343-0064 / +1-617-769-2599
fax: +1-617-769-8763
web: http://www.silverplatter.com/

International political science review. Dating from 1980, the *Review* is a major international journal whose impact on the profession has been growing steadily. Published by Sage of London, it appears quarterly. It consists principally of guest-edited issues devoted to specialised topics, but numbers open to non-related articles are also published. It has been edited since 1995 by Nazli Choucri and Jean Laponce; they were joined in 2000 by James Meadowcroft as a third editor.

After its first 20 years, the *Review* has built up a formidable reputation in terms of its academic standing. Many of its thematic issues have become required reading in their areas, and in 1997 the *Review* was ranked among the top 20 political science journals in terms of its "impact factor" (this is a measure of a journal's impact within the profession, based essentially on the average number of times that articles in that journal are cited in other journals; the Social Sciences Citation Index is the source for this; see chapter 9).

The editors of the *Review* may be contacted at the following addresses:

Nazli Choucri
Department of Political Science
Massachusetts Institute of Technology
Cambridge, MA 02139, USA
email: nchoucri@mit.edu

or

Jean Laponce
Department of Political Science
University of British Columbia
Vancouver, BC
Canada V6T 1Z1
email: Jean_Laponce@mtsg.ubc.ca

or

James Meadowcroft
Department of Politics
University of Sheffield
Sheffield S10 2TU
England
email: j.meadowcroft@sheffield.ac.uk

From 1999, an electronic version of the *Review* has been made available to institutions subscribing to the print edition. Although the publisher makes no extra charge for this, the service providers typically pass on a small additional charge to users. This means that any library subscribing to the *Review* from 1999 onwards will have easy access to the electronic version. Subscription information about the print and electronic versions may be obtained from the publishers:

SAGE Publications Ltd
6 Bonhill St
London EC2A 4PU
United Kingdom

or

SAGE Publications Ltd
PO Box 5096
Thousand Oaks, CA91369
USA

A web-page for the *Review* is maintained by the publishers; it provides tables of contents and abstracts from vol. 18 (1997) onwards It may be found at http://www.sagepub.co.uk/journals/details/ j0034.html.

Advances in political science: an international series. This is a book series in which a number of volumes have already appeared. Under the general editorship of Asher Arian and published by Macmillan, the series aims to publish books which, in the view of the editorial committee, are likely to contribute to the advancement of political science. Many of these are drawn from IPSA's other activities, such as the output of the world congress and the work of research committees.

The goal of the book series is to promote publication of rigorous scholarly research by IPSA members and by affiliated groups. Simultaneously, this publication series promotes the association and its commitment to global political science, both in terms of the issues raised and the range of professional political scientists called upon to address these issues. In an era of unprecedented expansion of political science around the globe, the series was designed as a magnet for much of the new and exciting work taking place.

Volumes in the new series to date thus are:

- Klaus von Beyme, *Transition to democracy in Eastern Europe,* 1996
- Christa Altenstetter and James Warner Bjorkman (eds) *Health policy reform, national variations and globalization,* 1997
- Frank P Harvey and Ben Mor (eds), *New directions in the study of international conflict,* 1998
- Henry J Jacek and Justin Greenwood (eds), *Organized business and the new global order,* 1999
- Ofer Feldman, *The political personality of Japan: analysing the culture of Japanese Diet members,* 1999
- Klaus von Beyme, *Parliamentary democracy: democratization, destabilization, reconsolidiation, 1789-1999,* 2000.

Contracts were signed during 1999 for a further four volumes, bringing to seven the number of volumes currently under contract with IPSA. These are as follows:

- Asha Gupta, *The road to privatisation: a global perspective* (contracted September 1996)
- Renata Siemienska, *Gender and new challenges in Poland* (contracted February 1997)
- Luigi Graziano, *Lobbying, pluralism and democracy* (contracted January 1998)
- Mino Vianello and Gwen Moore (eds), *The sound of breaking glass: a study of gender and power in twenty seven countries* (contracted March 1999)
- William Zartman (ed.), *The universality of politics* (contracted April 1999)
- Asher Arian, David Nachmias and Ruth Amir, *Executive governance in Israel* (contracted July 1999)

- Malcolm Feeley and Setsuo Miyazawa (eds), *Controversies about the Japanese adversary system* (contracted September 1999)

In addition, a number of books have been brought to the series directly by Macmillan. In these cases, authors contract directly with Macmillan rather than through IPSA. The editor may be contacted at the following addresses:

> Asher Arian
> PhD Program in Political Science
> Graduate Center, City University of New York
> 33 West 42 Street
> New York, NY 10036
> USA
> fax: +1-212-642-1980
> email: cgraa-2@idt.net

or

> Asher Arian
> Department of Political Science
> The University of Haifa
> Mount Carmel
> Haifa, Israel 31095
> fax: +972-4-257-785
> email: cgraa-2@idt.net

To order books or for other information about sales, please contact the publishers at the following address:

> Macmillan Press Ltd
> Houndmills
> Basingstoke
> Hampshire RG21 6XS
> England
> web: http://www.macmillan-press.co.uk/

3.2 WORLD CONGRESSES

The principal non-publishing activities of IPSA have been its scholarly meetings. These began with a congress in 1950, and since 1952 world congresses have been taking place every three years. From a small beginning, they have developed into major international scientific occasions, typically attracting up to two thousand political participants.

Congresses consist of four main parts: sessions related to the main theme of the congress, sessions organised by research committees, special sessions organised by individual IPSA members and approved by the programme committee, and sessions of other types. The latter may include supplementary sessions (frequently with a regional dimension, or focusing on the state of the discipline) approved by the programme chair. In addition to a number of plenary sessions, then, there are typically several hundred panels comprising sessions of other kinds.

The academic organisation of the congress is planned by a programme committee that is made up predominantly of members of the IPSA executive committee and that functions under the presidency of a programme chair. All aspects of the physical organisation of the programme are managed by a local organising committee. This committee arranges meetings, organises accommodation, makes provision for a social programme and offers a range of tourism options to allow visitors to take advantage of their visit to the country in which the congress is being held.

Participation in the congress is open to all IPSA members, and to others who share IPSA's objectives. IPSA members receive full information on the planning of the congress through IPSA's newsletter, *Participation*, and through their national associations. Additional information is made available to members of research committees through their own newsletters and internal circulation media. Those wishing to present papers at the

N.	Year	Date	Location	Participants	Countries

Table 3.1: IPSA world congresses, 1950-97

N.	Year	Date	Location	Partici-pants	Coun-tries
1.	1950	Sep 4-9	Zurich	81	23
2.	1952	Sep 8-12	Hague	220	31
3.	1955	Aug 21-27	Stockholm	275	36
4.	1958	Sep 16-20	Rome	320	31
5.	1961	Sep 26-30	Paris	425	46
6.	1964	Sep 21-25	Geneva	494	43
7.	1967	Sep 18-23	Brussels	745	56
8.	1970	Aug 31-Sep 5	Munich	894	46
9.	1973	Aug 20-25	Montreal	1,044	56
10.	1976	Aug 16-21	Edinburgh	1,081	56
11.	1979	Aug 12-18	Moscow	1,466	53
12.	1982	Aug 9-14	Rio de Janeiro	1,477	49
13.	1985	Jul 15-20	Paris	1,763	66
14.	1988	Aug 28-Sep 1	Washington	1,265	74
15.	1991	Jul 21-25	Buenos Aires	*1,400	*55
16.	1994	Aug 21-25	Berlin	1,884	73
17.	1997	Aug 17-21	Seoul	1,470	72

*estimates

congress may contact panel convenors or chairs of research committees (information on these appears periodically in *Participation*). Proposals to convene special sessions may also be forwarded to the programme chair, who has overall responsibility for coordination of the academic programme. Convenors of main theme sessions are selected by the programme chair, in many cases on the basis of offers by IPSA members or others. The location of IPSA world congresses to date is reported in table 3.1, which also gives an indication of the levels of attendance.

Participation in the congress is also assisted by a generous programme of travel grants. Some of these are directly administered by IPSA, while others are offered by the local organising committee. The number of grants depends on the amount of funding that has been raised for this purpose. The grants are advertised approximately one year in advance of the congress. Formal applications are required. Priority consideration is given to participants from third world countries and countries with currency conversion problems. It is also the policy of the association to increase the active participation of women and young scholars in the congress. Applicants are required to show that they have made efforts to obtain other support from other sources, and presence on the congress programme is normally a precondition.

Also associated with the congress are a number of awards. These are as follows:

- **Stein Rokkan fellowships**: these are awarded to a small number of graduate students to allow them to attend the congress. The fellowships are advertised approximately one year in advance of the congress, and selection is based on academic merit.
- **Francesco Kjellberg award**: this is offered after each congress to the new scholar who presents the best paper. Nominations are made by panel convenors and chairs, and IPSA's committee on awards adjudicates on these.
- **Karl Deutsch award**: this is offered once every three years to a prominent scholars engaged in cross-disciplinary research of the kind of which Karl Deutsch, former IPSA present, was master. The recipient presents the Karl Deutsch lecture at IPSA triennial world congress or leads a special session of the congress
- **Gender and politics award**: initiated in 2000, this is offered after each congress to the scholar who presents the best paper in the area of gender and politics. Nominations are made by panel convenors and chairs, and IPSA's committee on awards adjudicates on these.

3.3 INTER-CONGRESS ACTIVITIES

In between congresses, IPSA organises meetings of other kinds. The longest-established of these are IPSA roundtables, of which several are normally organised between congresses. These consist of small groups of researchers who meet to transmit and compare the results of their research in specific sub-disciplinary areas, seek to address frontier areas of research and strive to develop new areas of political science and interdisciplinary topics. They frequently coincide with meetings of the IPSA executive committee.

A new initiative was developed in the later 1980s. This began under the name "travelling workshop", but is now referred to as an IPSA symposium. This is defined as a meeting at which selected speakers present a specialist theme to a non-specialist audience, which is typically regionally defined. Its objective is to internationalise approaches to the study of politics, to provide scholars from one country or region with insights into theories, methodologies and findings developed in other regions, and to contribute to the development of the discipline. Four of these have taken place so far: in Tallinn, Estonia, on 3-9 January 1993, Vilnius, Lithuania, on 10-15 December 1996, Durban, South Africa, on 26-29 January 1999, and Patiala, India, on 6-9 January 2000.

4 / CONSTITUTION AND RULES

IPSA's constutional and procedural documents fall into three main categories. The first and most formal is the set of fundamental documents approved by the IPSA council and comprising the association's most basic rules. Foremost among these is the constitution itself, adopted in 1949 and subsequently amended on eight occasions. Two other documents may be seen as falling into this category. One of these relates to procedure at council meetings. Up to now, procedures in this area have been confined to the area of elections, but in 1999 the executive committee drafted a set of more far-reaching rules for presentation to the council, with a proposal that the council adopt these as standing rules of procedure. The remaining document in this category deals with the fee structure of collective members, a matter much debated over the years by the council. The most recent document, approved in 1997, is the one reproduced here, together with the two other documents mentioned.

The second set of procedural documents, also reproduced here, consists of rules and regulations drawn up by the executive committee over the years to govern aspects of its own management of affairs. Six such documents are printed here. The first of these governs procedure at IPSA executive committee meetings, and was approved in 1999. Second, also during 1999 the executive overhauled and systematised its procedures for the admission of members to IPSA (of which the most important relate to the admission of new collective members). In the same year the executive committee also revised and codified procedures in two other areas: the responsibilities of the secretary general, and the organisation of world congresses. Finally, there were two areas where the executive committee recently placed its mark on older procedural documents by revising them radically: regulations regarding research committees, a revised version of which was finally approved after a five-year process of overhaul in 1999, and provisions for the organisation of inter-congress activities, revised in 1997.

The third category consists of rules and procedures followed within the secretariat or within such bodies as the congress local organising committee. Typically drawn up by these bodies themselves, they are not of sufficient significance to be included here.

4.1 CONSTITUTION

(As amended at the council meetings held in Stockholm, 19-26 August 1955; in Rome, 15-19 September 1958; in Geneva, 21-25 September 1964; in Munich, 31 August - 5 September, 1970; in Moscow, 12-18 August, 1979; in Rio de Janeiro, 9-14 August, 1982; in Buenos Aires, July 21-25, 1991; and in Seoul, 17-21 August 1997).

I. Name and legal address

1. There is hereby established, in accordance with action taken by the International Political Science Conference, held in Paris from the 12th to the 16th of September, 1949, an association which will take the name of "International Political Science Association" (hereafter referred to as the "association").

2. The association is constituted as an association with scientific objectives, in conformity with the provisions of the decree-law of the French Republic of 12 April 1939, amending the law of 1 July 1901.

3. The association is legally registered in the city of Paris. The secretariat is established at the location of the secretary general.

4. The council shall have the right to change the location of the legal address of the association. Prior to the first session of the council this right may be exercised by the executive committee.

II. Objectives

5. The general purpose of the association shall be to promote the advancement of political science throughout the world, by such means as:
   a) encouraging the establishment and development of political science associations;
   b) facilitating the spread of information about developments in political science;
   c) organising world congresses and round table discussions and providing other opportunities for personal contacts among political scientists;
   d) publishing books and journals and providing a newsletter to members;
   e) promoting internationally planned research.

III. Membership

6. The association shall be composed of three classes of members: *collective, individual,* and *associate.*

7. Collective members shall consist of national (and regional) associations recognised by the executive committee as being representative of political science in their respective countries (or regions).

8. There shall normally be only one collective member from a country, but if, in any country, two or more eligible groups are candidates for collective membership, the executive committee, at its discretion, may seek the establishment of a joint committee to which collective membership may be granted, or it may admit one or more of the groups as collective members.

9. Individual membership may be granted by the executive committee to persons suitably qualified by their professional activity or general interest in political science. Individual members may, but need not, belong to associations which are collective members.

10. Associate membership may be granted by the executive committee to international, or national, associations, organisations, societies, or institutions pursuing objectives compatible with those of the association in related fields of activity. An associate member may, at its own request, be invited to be represented without vote at the meetings of the council.

IV. The council

11. The council shall be composed of two classes of members:

    A) *Representatives designated by the collective members of the association* in such a number as may be determined by the executive committee, provided that no collective member shall be entitled to more than three representatives on the council; in case there should be two or more collective members from a country, the total number of representatives of such collective members on the council shall not exceed three. Each collective member shall be entitled to designate alternates to represent it at any meeting of the council.

    B) *Individual members proposed by the president and ratified by the executive committee.* The individual members, whose total number may not exceed 30% of the number of representatives of collective members, are selected from the following categories:

       a) individual and associate members of the IPSA from countries or regions where there is no collective member;
       b) chairpersons and secretaries of IPSA research committees and study groups or their representatives;
       c) boards of editors of IPSA official publications.

    The members of national associations which are more than two years in arrears with their fees are ineligible to sit on the council unless a successful appeal is made to the executive committee.

12. The council shall normally meet in regular session once every three years at such time and place as may be designated by the executive committee.

13. Half the members of the council constitutes a quorum.

14. A special session of the council shall be convened by the secretary general upon request of two thirds of the collective members of the association. The secretary general shall give reasonable notice of the date, place and object of any special session.

15. The council shall determine the policy of the association, approve the accounts, and review the financial prospects of the association for the succeeding three years.

16. Each member of the council shall have one vote.

17. The council shall elect the president of the association, who shall hold office until his or her successor is elected at the next regular session of the council. Should the president die, or resign, the vacancy shall be filled by the first vice-president.

The executive committee nominates a candidate or candidates for presidential elections one year before the election. Other candidates may be proposed during the council meeting.

18. Three months before the opening of each regular session of the council, the secretary general shall communicate to each member of the council the date, place, and provisional agenda of the session. The provisional agenda shall include:
    a) the report of the secretary general on the work of the association since the last session of the council;
    b) the accounts of the association for the preceding three years;
    c) a statement of the financial prospects of the association for the succeeding three years;
    d) items proposed by the executive committee;
    e) items proposed by any collective member;
    f) election of the president of the association;
    g) election of the executive committee for the succeeding three years.

19. The council, subject to the provisions of article 16, may adopt its own rules of procedure.

V. The executive committee

20. The executive committee shall consist of not less than twelve, nor more than eighteen members, or alternate members, of the council; the president and the past-president shall be counted part of this maximum. The executive committee shall be elected by the council at each regular session. There shall normally be only one representative of a collective member of the association on the committee and in any case no more than two representatives.

a) The retiring president is ex officio member of the executive committee with voting right for the period of three years following his or her retirement.

b) Editors of the association's official publications will normally attend the meetings of the executive committee without voting rights.

21. Each member of the executive committee shall have one vote.

22. The executive committee shall hold its first meeting immediately following the close of the session of the council at which the committee was elected. It shall then elect one or several of its membership to serve as vice-presidents. The executive committee shall regularly meet once a year. Special meetings may be convened when needed, upon the request of the president or of a majority of the membership of the committee.

23. If a member of the committee is unable to attend a membership meeting, the national or regional association or individual member of the association concerned may designate an alternate. In this event the secretary general shall be notified of the name of the alternate in advance of the meeting.

24. In addition to exercising those powers and duties specified elsewhere in this constitution, the executive committee shall:

a) execute the decisions of the council;

b) exercise general control over the administration of the association;

c) be responsible for the development of the programme and activities of the association between sessions of the council;

d) appoint the secretary general upon the proposition of a nomination committee selected by the executive committee. The secretary general is normally expected to serve for six years subject to his or her appointment being reviewed after three years. He or she may be reappointed for an additional three years;

e) establish such standing or temporary committees of the association as may seem desirable;

f) accept and expend moneys on behalf of the association;

g) submit reports as necessary to members of the council and invite and consider their comments thereon;

h) establish, subject to general directives adopted by the council, the annual budget of the association; and

i) ratify the appointment of the programme chair upon nomination by the president.

25. The executive committee may establish its own rules and regulations and may delegate authority to act on its behalf to the president or the

member acting for him or her, to the secretary general, or to sub-committees of its members.

26. The secretary general, with approval of the president, may appoint such staff as may be required and determines their salaries. The secretary general is authorised to handle the accounts of the association. The secretary general shall, at the end of his or her appointment hand over to his or her successor the audited accounts and assets of the association.

VI. Financial resources

27. The financial resources of the association shall include:
    a) annual dues to be contributed by collective members in accordance with such scale as may be determined by the executive committee prior to the first session of the council, and by the council thereafter;
    b) annual dues payable by individual and associate members, the amount which shall be determined by the executive committee, subject to any decision by the council;
    c) proceeds from the sale of publications of the association, after all expenses contracted have been met; and
    d) contributions and grants of public institutions and fees for special services the conditions of which are approved by the executive committee subject to any decision by the council, after all expenses contracted have been met.

28. The secretary general of the association shall be responsible for supervising:
    a) the receipt, custody, and disbursement of moneys on behalf of the association
    b) the archives of the association
    c) the publication of the association's newsletter.

29. The council reviews and approves, at each of its regular sessions, a financial report prepared by chartered accountants. The report covers the period between council meetings.

30. Members ceasing to belong to the association shall have no claim upon its assets.

VII. Dissolution

31. The dissolution of the association may be declared by the council at any time provided two thirds of the members of the council concur.

32. In the event of dissolution, the funds constituting the net assets of the association shall be transferred by the council to an international organisation or institution with objectives similar to those of the associa-

tion or shall be assigned to uses considered as corresponding to its objectives.

VIII. Amendments

33. This constitution may be amended by a two third majority of the members of the council present at any meeting, provided that the members present constitute at least half of the total membership of the council.

4.2 PROCEDURE AT COUNCIL MEETINGS

(Proposal to IPSA council prepared by the executive committee at meeting no. 78, Krakow, 25-26 April 1999, for presentation to the council under article 19 of the IPSA constitution, which authorises the council to "adopt its own rules of procedure"; based on existing documents and practices.)

I. Conduct of meetings

1. Meetings of the council shall be chaired by the president of IPSA; or, in his or her absence, by the first vice president; or, in his or her absence, by one of the other vice presidents designated by the president.
2. The secretary general shall act as secretary to the council.
3. Decisions of the council shall be by a majority of the votes of members present. In the event of a tie, the president shall have a second or casting vote.

II. Membership and attendance

4. Meetings of the council shall normally be attended, in a non-voting capacity, by the secretary general, the administrator, the programme chair and the editors of IPSA's publications (the *International political science abstracts*, the *International political science review* and *Advances in political science: an international series*). Other persons, including representatives of associate members, may be invited by the president to attend all or part of a meeting.
5. In proposing individual members for ratification by the executive committee as members of the council under article 11B of the constitution, the president shall take the following considerations into account:
   - in the case of chairpersons and secretaries of research committees or their representatives, the need to ensure circulation of representation from group to group between congresses;
   - in the case of other members, the need to maintain an appropriate gender and regional balance.

For purposes of rule 7, individual members appointed to the council under article 11B shall be seen as belonging to the collective member of the country or region in which they normally reside.

III. Elections

6. The election of the president of IPSA shall be governed by the following provisions.

   (i) In addition to the candidate or candidates nominated by the executive committee one year in advance of the council meeting, other candidates may be nominated by at least four members of the council. Any such nomination must be in writing, must contain the signatures of four council members, the assent of the candidate and a short biographical note, and must be handed to the secretary general by 17h00 at the latest on the day before the scheduled presidential election.

   (ii) If there is only one candidate, the sole candidate shall be declared elected unanimously.

   (iii) If there is more than one candidate, voting shall be held by secret ballot of members of the council (alternate members are not permitted to vote). The candidate obtaining a majority of valid votes is elected president. Should no candidate obtain a majority, a second ballot shall be held between the two candidates with the largest numbers of votes in the first ballot.

7. The election of the executive committee of IPSA shall be governed by the following provisions.

   (i) Subject to rule 7 (iv), the number of vacancies shall be 16, the maximum permitted by article 20 of the constitution.

   (ii) Any candidate must be a member or an alternate member of the council, and must be nominated by at least four members of the council. All nominations must be in writing, must contain the signatures of four council members, the assent of the candidate and a biographical note, and must be handed to the secretary general or to the administrator by a specified deadline, which shall be not less than 24 hours before the time for which the election is scheduled.

   (iii) The secretary general shall cause the list of candidates and their biographical details to be publicised appropriately as soon as possible after the close of nominations.

   (iv) If the number of candidates is at least 10 and no more than 16, all candidates shall be declared elected, provided there are no more than two candidates from any collective member. If there are more than two candidates from any collective member, a secret ballot shall be held to select two of them.

   (v) If the number of eligible candidates is less than 10, the president shall make provision for additional nominations.

(vi) If the number of candidates is greater than 16, voting shall be held by secret ballot of members of the council (alternate members are not permitted to vote). Each voter may cast up to 16 votes.

(vii) On the first ballot, candidates receiving an absolute majority of votes cast are elected in descending order of votes until all vacancies have been filled, subject to rule 7 (ix).

(viii)If fewer than 16 candidates are elected on the first ballot, a second ballot takes place among the remaining candidates. Candidates are declared elected in descending order of votes until all vacancies have been filled, subject to rule 7 (ix).

(ix) If more than two candidates from any collective member are placed within the top 16 candidates, only the two with the largest numbers of votes shall be considered eligible, and remaining vacancies shall be filled by remaining candidates in descending order of votes.

(x)   In nominating candidates and in voting, members of the council are requested to take into serious consideration the need for representation by world region and by gender.

8. All elections shall be subject to the following conditions.

(i)   The counting of votes shall be conducted by tellers appointed by the council, who shall normally include the president, the secretary general and the administrator.

(ii) In the event of a tie in the election of the IPSA president, the following provisions shall apply:
if, on the first ballot, two or more candidates tie for second position or three or more tie for first position, all of these candidates shall proceed to a second ballot, and a third ballot between the two candidates with the greatest numbers of votes shall be held if necessary;
if, on a later ballot, two or more candidates tie, the winning candidate shall be the one with the greatest number of votes on the first ballot.

(iii) In the event of a tie in the election of the IPSA executive committee, the following provisions shall apply:
if, on the first ballot, two or more candidates tie for the last position or positions, these candidates (and these alone) shall proceed to the second ballot;
if, on the second ballot, two or more candidates tie, the winning candidate or candidates shall be those with the greatest numbers of votes on the first ballot.

(iv) Should the provisions of rules 8 (ii) and 8 (iii) fail to break a tie, the issue shall be decided by lot.

IV. *Interpretation*

9. The meaning of these rules shall be determined by the president, subject to appeal to the council, whose decision shall be final.

4.3 FEE STRUCTURE FOR COLLECTIVE MEMBERS

(Adopted unanimously by the IPSA council at its meeting no. XVII, Seoul, 17-21 August 1997.)

I. *Calculation of payment capacity*

1. The fee of each collective member shall be based on an index of capacity to pay, which shall be defined as the average of (1) its proportionate share of the UN budget and (2) its proportionate share of the total individual membership of all collective members.

2. In the case of each collective member, *proportionate share of the UN budget* shall be calculated by dividing the share of the UN budget for the country represented by the collective member by the total share of the UN budget for all countries represented in IPSA by collective members. UN budget share shall be based on the UN table of payments for 1997. UN budget share shall be revised every ten years on the basis of the updated UN table.

3. In the case of each collective member, *proportionate share of the total individual membership* of all collective members shall be calculated by dividing the number of individual members affiliated to the collective member in question by the total number of individual members affiliated to all collective members; the number of collective members in each national association shall be the figure reported from time to time to the secretariat by that collective member.

II. *Normal payment categories*

4. The index of capacity to pay shall be converted into units of payment in accordance with the following provisions:

    - less than 1%   1 unit
    - 1-3.49%   2 units
    - 3.5-9.99%   4 units
    - 10-19.99%   6 units
    - 20% or more   16 units

5. The value of a unit of payment shall be determined from time to time by the IPSA council.

III. Reduced payment categories

6. A compensatory fund to assist poorer collective members whose resources do not permit them to pay their due fees shall be established. 10% of the revenue from collective members liable for at least four payment units shall be added to this fund. Collective members may also choose to pay more than the sum for which they are liable or may, at their request, be placed in a higher category than that to which they are allocated by the formula. The additional revenue raised by this means shall be added to a compensatory fund.

7. Collective members weighted at less than 0.5% of capacity to pay may apply for a reduced payment rate of one half of a unit of payment, and the executive committee shall be authorised to make further reductions in the membership fees of associations in this category, subject to the provision that no collective member shall pay less than one quarter of a unit of payment. The cost of such reduced payments shall be deducted from the compensatory fund.

4.4 PROCEDURE AT IPSA EXECUTIVE MEETINGS

(Adopted by the executive committee at meeting no. 78, Krakow, 25-26 April 1999, subject to agreement on article 7 at meeting no, 79, Naples, 6 October 1999)

I. Conduct of meetings

1. Meetings of the executive committee shall be chaired by the president of IPSA; or, in his or her absence, by the first vice president; or, in his or her absence, by one of the other vice presidents designated by the president.
2. The secretary general shall act as secretary to the executive committee.
3. Decisions of the executive committee shall be by a majority of the votes of members present. In the event of a tie, the president shall have a second or casting vote.
4. The executive committee shall meet immediately after the triennial congress, and thereafter at least once a year. It shall normally meet on six occasions between congresses, as follows:
   - immediately after the congress
   - in spring of the post-congress year
   - in autumn of the post-congress year
   - in spring of the pre-congress year
   - in spring of the congress year
   - immediately before the congress.

II. Membership and attendance

5. Meetings of the executive committee shall normally be attended, in a non-voting capacity, by the secretary general, the administrator, the programme chair and the editors of IPSA's publications (the *International political science abstracts*, the *International political science review* and *Advances in political science: an international series*). Other persons may, for particular purposes, be invited to attend all or part of a meeting.

III. Appointments and nominations

6. At its first meeting after the congress, the executive committee shall elect a first vice president and one or more other vice presidents. The list of nominees for these posts shall be presented by the president and the nominees shall be agreed by motion of the executive committee.

7. As soon as possible after the congress, the executive committee shall ratify the membership of subcommittees of the executive committee. The lists of nominees for these posts shall be presented by the president and the nominees shall be agreed by motion of the executive committee. Members of subcommittees shall normally be drawn from the membership of the executive committee and from others who regularly attend meetings of the executive committee. Each vice president shall normally chair one committee. Each subcommittee shall comprise the president and the secretary general as ex officio members and a normal maximum of five other members. In addition to such other subcommittees or search committees as the executive committee may consider appropriate, the following committees shall be appointed.

   (i)   *Committee on organisation and procedure*: to advise on all aspects of organisational development, including procedures, membership policy and any other matter referred to it by the executive committee.

   (ii) *Committee on the congress programme*: to advise on the structure of the programme and on all areas associated with the triennial world congress.

   (iii) *Committee on research and training*: to advise on all aspects of the operation of research committees and on inter-congress activities.

   (iv) *Committee on awards*: to advise on all aspects of IPSA awards and to evaluate candidates for these, including (1) Stein Rokkan fellowships, (2) the Karl Deutsch award, (3) the Francesco Kjellberg award and (4) any other awards for which provision might be made.

   (v)   *Committee on the status of women and diversity of participation (committee on participation)*: to advise and take initiatives on all matters affecting the status of women in IPSA activities and programmes;

and to build a broader base of participation by women scholars, younger scholars, and all scholars from countries and nationalities underrepresented for whatever reasons.

8. Editors of IPSA publications, including the editors of the *International political science abstracts*, the *International political science review* and the IPSA book series, shall be appointed by the executive committee for three-year periods on the nomination of the president, following consideration of the advice of a search committee if appropriate.

Members of the editorial boards of IPSA publications shall be appointed by the editors following consultation with the president and the secretary general, the appointments to take effect once the executive committee has been informed.

9. At a meeting one year before the congress, the executive committee shall nominate a candidate or candidates for election as president of IPSA. The nomination procedure shall be as follows:

    (i) Any nominee must be proposed in writing by a member of the executive committee; the proposal must be seconded by another member of the executive committee; and there must be evidence that the nominee is prepared to stand.

    (ii) The president may call for nominations in advance of the meeting at which the nomination is to be made, and the president shall judge and report to the executive committee on the validity of nominations.

    (iii) In the event of there being more than one candidate, a secret ballot shall be held during the executive committee meeting. The candidate winning a majority of the votes cast shall be nominated. Should no candidate obtain a majority, the procedure shall be determined by the president subject to the agreement of the executive committee.

    (iv) The executive committee may decide by motion to nominate an additional candidate or candidates. Voting on any such motion shall be by secret ballot.

10. At its first meeting of the congress year and at its immediately pre-congress meeting, the executive committee shall ratify the president's nominees for membership of the IPSA council under clause 11B of the IPSA constitution. The nomination procedure shall be as follows:

    (i) In the case of representatives of research committees, the president nominates the chairs of 12 groups at the spring meeting; these are selected in rotation, following established sequence, from groups which have been recognised for at least three years.

(ii) In the case of other members, the president nominates as early as possible, but no later than the pre-congress meeting, taking account of regional and gender considerations.

IV. Responsibilities

11. As well as carrying out such other responsibilities as may be given to it by the constitution or by the council, the executive committee shall:
    (i)   consider periodic reports of the secretary general on the affairs of the association
    (ii)   approve the audited accounts for the previous financial year
    (iii) adopt the budget for the current or following financial year
    (iv)   consider and take appropriate action in respect of the reports of subcommittees of the executive committee and of the editors of the association's publications
    (v)   approve periodically new subscription rates for individual and associate members
    (vi)   take such measures as are necessary with respect to the organisation of the world congress, inter-congress activities and other activities compatible with IPSA's objectives.

11. Subject to such procedures as it may establish, the executive committee delegates to the secretary general the right to admit individual and associate members of the association.

V. Interpretation

13. The meaning of these rules shall be determined by the president, subject to appeal to the executive committee, whose decision shall be final.

4.5 MEMBERSHIP

(Adopted by the executive committee at meeting no. 78, Krakow, 25-26 April 1999)

I. Eligibility

1. Individual membership of IPSA is open to persons suitably qualified by their professional activity or general interest in political science. Persons employed as teachers or researchers in political science and related disciplines are eligible, and the executive committee may extend eligibility to other categories. Individual members of IPSA pay an annual or triennial subscription fee, fixed from time to time by the IPSA executive committee.

2. Associate membership of IPSA is open to international or national associations, organisations, societies or institutions pursuing objectives compatible with those of IPSA in related fields of activity. Associate

members of IPSA pay an annual subscription fee, fixed from time to time by the IPSA executive committee.

3. Collective membership of IPSA is open to national and regional associations recognised by the executive committee as being representative of political science in their respective countries or regions. Collective members of IPSA pay an annual subscription fee based on a table of payments approved by the IPSA council.

II. Admission procedures

4. Admission to individual and associate membership is available on application to the IPSA secretariat. Admission to collective membership is based on application to the IPSA executive committee, which refers the application to its committee on organisation and procedure. Any application for collective membership should be directed to the IPSA secretariat, and must include the following documents:
   (i)   the constitution of the association as a legal entity
   (ii) the list of members of the association and a statement indicating that they represent the majority of political scientists in the country or region
   (iii) information about the activities of the association, including academic meetings and publications
   (iv) a statement of the financial resources of the association
   (v)   an outline of the future academic plans of the association
   (vi) a list of members of the executive committee together with their institutional affiliations.

5. There shall normally be only one collective member from a country but if, in any country, two or more eligible groups are candidates for collective membership the executive committee may, at its discretion, seek the establishment of a joint committee to which collective membership may be granted, or it may admit one or more of the groups as collective members.

6. Regional associations will normally be admitted to collective membership only in cases where there are no national associations within the region which are collective members of IPSA, but the executive committee may make exceptions to this.

III. Rights of members

7. Individual, associate and collective members of IPSA are entitled to free subscriptions to the *International political science review* and to *Participation* and to other information circulated by the secretariat, and are entitled to subscriptions to the *International political science abstracts* and to the CD-rom edition of congress papers at reduced rates. Individual

members of IPSA are entitled to register at reduced rates for IPSA world congresses and to serve on the officer boards of research committees. Persons affiliated to collective members of IPSA are entitled to membership of IPSA's research committees.

8. Individual members of IPSA may be invited by the president to serve on the IPSA council. Associate members of IPSA may be invited to attend council meetings as observers. Collective members of IPSA are entitled to representation on the IPSA council at a level determined by the executive committee. All new collective members shall initially be accorded one seat on the council. A request for increase in representation shall be considered, on request, after two consecutive world congresses. Any such request should be received by the IPSA secretariat at least two years in advance of the council meeting at which it is desired to bring it into effect. It will be considered by the IPSA executive committee, which refers the application to its committee on organisation and procedure. The application must include information on the following points:

(i) current number of members in the national or regional political science association

(ii) current number of political science departments in the country or region

(iii) current subscriptions to IPSA publications

(iv) organisation of IPSA congresses, roundtables and other activities in the preceding ten years

(v) number of participants in a the last three IPSA world congresses

(vi) active participation in the activities of IPSA research committees over the past ten years

(vii) other services provided in the field of publications and/or research carried out on behalf of IPSA.

9. The IPSA executive committee may also make provision for reducing the number of council seats allocated to a collective member.

IV. Termination of membership

10. Individual and associate membership of IPSA shall terminate automatically on cessation of payment of subscriptions. A collective member of IPSA shall be classified as inactive if its subscription falls more than two years in arrears.

4.6 ROLE OF IPSA SECRETARY GENERAL

(Approved by the executive committee at meeting no. 78, Krakow, 25-26 April 1999)

I. General responsibilities

1. Under the authority of the executive committee and in cooperation with the president, the secretary general is responsible for the development and organisation of the association, its meetings and finances, as well as for overseeing the day-to-day activities of the IPSA secretariat, including the hiring and supervision of staff.
2. In conjunction with the president, he or she shall seek the attainment of the association's objectives, including the spread of information about the development of political science and the fostering of international scholarly networks among political scientists.
3. The secretary general is ex officio member of all IPSA committees. He or she serves as secretary to the executive committee and council and is responsible for their minutes.

II. Specific responsibilities

4. The specific administrative tasks of the secretary general shall include the following:
   (i)   in collaboration with the president, to devise and propose plans and programmes for consideration by the council and the executive committee;
   (ii)   to prepare annual budgets for consideration and approval by the executive committee;
   (iii) to submit annual financial reports and audited accounts to the executive committee and triennial financial reports to the council;
   (iv)   to prepare regular reports on the activities of the association for consideration by the executive committee, and a triennial report for consideration by the council;
   (v)   to assure financial planning and seek to improve the base of funding of the association;
   (vi)   to serve committees as appropriate, including all subcommittees of the executive committee;
   (vii) to oversee the organisation of triennial congresses and other meetings organised by the executive committee;
   (viii) to develop and service the individual, associate and collective membership;
   (ix)   to maintain communication and contacts with research committees;
   (x)   to ensure the regular publication of the association's newsletter;

(xi) to promote and oversee the development of the association's publications;

(xii) to maintain and archive the association's documents and records;

(xiii) to employ and supervise the association's secretarial personnel, including the administrator.

4.7 ORGANISATION OF IPSA CONGRESSES

(Approved by the executive committee at meeting no. 78, Krakow, 25-26 April 1999)

I. General

1. IPSA shall organise a world congress every three years. The executive committee shall determine the dates and venue on the basis of an application to host the congress by a national or regional association that is a collective member of IPSA, or by another body recognised by IPSA as an appropriate host organisation.

   The procedure for proposing and assessing applications to host an IPSA congress is outlined in annex 1.

II. Organisational responsibilities

2. The academic programme of the congress shall be coordinated by a programme committee under a programme chair nominated by the president and ratified by the executive committee. Each congress shall have a theme proposed by the president in collaboration with the programme chair and the programme committee. The programme committee shall determine the general structure of the congress so that it reflects the theme and possible subthemes of the programme. A congress shall normally consist of sessions of the following types:

   (i)   sessions related to the main theme organised by the programme chair and the programme committee

   (ii) sessions organised by research committees

   (iii) sessions organised by individual political scientists and approved by the programme chair and the programme committee

   (iv) sessions of other types, including a small number of plenary sessions, normally organised by the president and programme chair in association with the local organising committee.

   The responsibilities of the programme committee are outlined in annex 2.

3. The physical organisation of the congress shall be carried out by a local organising committee designated by the national association in the host country or by such other body as may be designated by the executive committee. The local organising committee shall ensure:

(i)   that adequate information on travel and accommodation, and an accommodation reservation service, are available;

(ii) that adequate space is available for (a) the congress sessions, (b) such business meetings as may appropriately take place, (c) ancillary services, including book displays and a papers room and (d) such other services as are needed, and that access to these is open to all participants, including those with physical disabilities;

(iii) that an adequate funding structure is in place to ensure the efficient functioning of the congress;

(iv) that an appropriate social programme is on offer;

(v)   that adequate arrangements are in place for registration and for the provision of information about various aspects of the congress.

The responsibilities of the local organising committee are outlined in annex 3.

4. The IPSA secretary general shall ensure that IPSA procedures are followed and that there is free communication between the different agencies involved in congress organisation. He or she shall also ensure that IPSA members are informed of all aspects of the planning of the congress. More specifically, he or she shall:

(i)   publish in *Participation* a call for the organisation of special sessions within the general programme theme, and for the submission of paper proposals for all open sessions;

(ii) publish the preliminary congress programme as a special issue of *Participation*;

(iii) circulate such additional information as is necessary to IPSA members;

(iv) advertise and promote the congress as widely as possible with a view to extending participation and membership.

The responsibilities of the IPSA secretary general are outlined in annex 4.

III. *Participation*

5. Participation shall be open to all IPSA members and to others approved by the programme committee. The principal categories of participation shall be as follows:

(i)   chairs or convenors of sessions

(ii) paper givers

(iii) discussants

(iv) authors of supplementary papers not presented orally.

Guidelines for participation are outlined in annex 5.

IV. Awards and financial assistance

6. The executive committee (on the recommendation of its subcommittees or of the local organising committee) may make provision for specific grants or awards. These may include:
    (i)   IPSA travel grants, drawn from IPSA's resources
    (ii)   special grants, drawn from monies raised by the local organising committee
    (iii) Stein Rokkan fellowships, offered to young scholars
    (iv)   the Karl Deutsch award, offered to a distinguished scholar
    (v)   the Francesco Kjellberg award for the best paper by a new scholar.
    Provisions governing these awards are outlined in annex 6.

Annex 1. Applications to host an IPSA congress

I. General

1. The IPSA executive committee shall from time to time consider applications from national or regional political science associations that are collective members of IPSA to host IPSA congresses.

II. Content of application

2. Applications to host an IPSA congress should normally be made at least five years before the intended date of the congress, and must identify clearly the person or institution undertaking to organise the congress.

3. The application should provide information on the following:
    (i)   the proposed dates
    (ii)   the proposed location (city, and venue within the city)
    (iii) the estimated number of meeting rooms and other areas of different sizes available for plenary sessions, panels and business meetings, and to cover administrative and organisational needs (to include space for IPSA, local organisers, registration, display and social areas); and information on access to all congress venues for persons with physical disabilities
    (iv)   the proposed nature of overnight accommodation, and an estimate of the number of rooms available at different cost levels
    (v)   if relevant, information on transport between the centres of accommodation and the place of meeting, and its cost for participants
    (vi)   the distance between the congress location and a well-served international or other airport, and any other relevant travel information, including information on probable costs of transportation
    (vii) the availability of a local academic and other infrastructure capable of being mobilised to provide adequate organisational support for the congress
    (viii) an estimate of the probable amount of funding that could be raised by the local organisers to cover organisational costs, with an indication of the main sources
    (ix)   the name and coordinates of the contact person with IPSA pending the establishment of a local organising committee

(x) any other information relevant to the offer to host the IPSA world congress.

4. The application should indicate a commitment to establish a local organising committee that would organise the facilities and services outlined in annex 3 (Responsibilities of the local organising committee) and to abide by the rules for the organisation of IPSA congresses.

5. The application should indicate that the host body would undertake financial responsibility for the event. It is understood that registration fees accrue to IPSA, the host body retaining 25% of this income. The host body is also expected to do its utmost to raise funds for travel.

III. Assessment of applications

6. The IPSA executive committee shall respond as quickly as practicable to any application to host a congress, and shall normally make a decision at least four years before the proposed date for the congress.

7. The IPSA executive committee may also consider applications to host a world congress from bodies other than national or regional associations that are collective members of IPSA. In such cases, the application must conform to rules 2-5 above.

Annex 2: Responsibilities of the programme committee

I. Congress theme

1. The IPSA president, in collaboration with the programme chair, proposes a congress theme for approval and elaboration by the programme committee.

II. Congress structure

2. The programme shall consist of at least four parts, in addition to plenary sessions, and the programme committee, on the proposal of the programme chair, shall determine the approximate number of panels to be included in each part and oversee their organisation:
   (i) sessions and plenary sessions under the main theme, organised by convenors, in collaboration with co-convenors as appropriate, appointed by the programme committee and the programme chair;
   (ii) sessions organised by IPSA research committees proposed by the chairs of committees to the programme chair, who shall be responsible for informing and proposing decisions, whenever pertinent, to the programme or executive committees; each research committee shall normally organise two sessions;
   (iii) special sessions organised by individual political scientists and approved by the programme chair and the programme committee;
   (iv) supplementary sessions and sessions of other types, organised by the programme chair in association with the local organising committee and the programme committee; these may include sessions on the "state of the discipline", on global regions or on other topics.

III. Responsibilities of programme chair

3. The programme chair shall have the following responsibilities:
   (i)   he or she shall be in charge of coordinating and distributing all relevant information, as well as making proposals to the programme committee and the executive committee pertaining to the intellectual organisation of the congress
   (ii) in consultation with the programme committee, he or she shall make decisions, or when pertinent propose them to the executive committee, about any issue arising in the process of organising sessions, including the replacement of convenors who for any reason are not performing their duties
   (iii) he or she shall be responsible for gathering, inducing and processing proposals for the third part of the programme, special sessions

4. The programme chair shall ensure that participation in the congress programme (as convenors, chairs, papergivers and discussants) is as open as possible by issuing calls for panels and calls for papers at appropriate times.

5. The programme chair shall ensure that women, younger scholars and scholars from disadvantaged regions are adequately represented in the congress programme.

6. The programme chair shall prepare an initial version of the congress programme (including a list of sessions and coordinates of convenors) for publication in *Participation* and a revised version (including papergivers and titles of their papers) for transmission to the local organising committee.

Annex 3: Responsibilities of the local organising committee

I. General

1. The host national association shall appoint a local organising committee, whose chair shall accept responsibility for the coordination of all local arrangements and for reporting to the IPSA executive committee. In exceptional cases, the IPSA executive committee may make special arrangements for the appointment of a local organising committee. The local organising committee shall:
   (i)   provide a basic organisational plan to the IPSA executive committee for its approval as early as possible;
   (ii) undertake organisational and financial responsibility for all aspects of the physical management of the congress;
   (iii) ensure that the IPSA secretariat, president, executive and programme chair are kept fully informed of all aspects of congress planning.

2. The local organising committee shall, in consultation with the programme chair, arrange the programme for the period of the world congress, and shall ensure that this includes the following components:
   (i)   the scheduling of all academic meetings (plenary sessions and panels);
   (ii) the scheduling of all business meetings;
   (iii) a reception for all participants following the opening ceremony;

(iv) dinner for the IPSA executive and, if possible, the IPSA council;

(v) an optional programme of tours for congress participants and their partners;

(vi) such other events as appear appropriate and feasible.

II. *Finance and personnel*

3. The local organising committee shall ensure that adequate financial support is available. This shall come from the following sources:

(i) 25% of the income from congress registration

(ii) other funds from national and other sources, or support in kind (receptions sponsored by national and local governments, foundations, research institutes, universities, etc.)

(iii) a special travel support grant from the national UNESCO High Commission for third world delegates, for which the local organising committee shall apply

(iv) extra funding for travel grants from other sources.

4. The local organising committee shall hire such staff as are necessary to carry out the efficient organisation of the world congress. These shall normally include:

(i) a full-time congress administrator, for at least one year prior to the congress

(ii) one or more people, or an agency, to handle accommodation reservation for at least six months before the congress

(iii) one person to handle hotel registration difficulties

(iv) an information officer to answer all general inquiries

(v) three or four persons with appropriate linguistic skills to handle registration

(vi) additional personnel to assist at the IPSA desk should this be requested

(vii) two persons for paper room

(viii) one or two persons for the book display.

(ix) some security personnel in the registration area

(x) "floaters" to relieve duty personnel for coffee breaks and meals, and to help out if an area becomes particularly congested

(xi) simultaneous translators for the opening session.

III. *Pre-congress planning*

5. The local organising committee shall ensure that adequate space is provided and that access is available to it by persons with physical disabilities, as follows

(i) such space as is necessary for the efficient operation of the local organising committee, for at least one year in advance of the world congress and one month after this

(ii) a range of public access areas, including

(1) a large registration area with enough space for several lines (two or three for pre-registrants and two or three for those registering on site)

(2) an IPSA information booth

(3) a booth for general and tourist information

(4) a large message board for posting messages

(5) a message board reserved for organisational announcements

(4) a social area nearby, with food and drink facilities, water fountains, wash rooms and telephones

(5) a large, appropriately furnished enclosed space for paper room sales

(6) a large, appropriately furnished enclosed space for book display

(7) a post office/mail room for outgoing mail with supplies for wrapping parcels and postal rate information

(8) an "incoming mail" desk near the message board; this "mail" will consist mainly of papers being left for other members of a panel

(9) a lost and found plus coat and baggage checking service

(iii) rooms for academic sessions: one large amphitheatre (capacity of 1,000-1,500) for the opening ceremony; one large amphitheatre for plenaries throughout the congress; 6-8 small lecture halls (80-125); 10 classrooms (25-50); 6 seminar rooms

(iv) rooms for business meetings: one council meeting room (100); one executive and committee meeting room (30), 20 rooms for business meetings of research committees

(i) appropriately furnished offices for

(1) the IPSA president, including a meeting area

(2) the IPSA secretary general, including a meeting area

(3) the IPSA administrator, with appropriate secretarial, reproduction and communications equipment, telephone and two desks

(4) other IPSA executive members or session convenors (several offices on an ad-hoc basis)

(5) if necessary, an assistant to check travel grantees' identification and to hand out the money in strict confidence.

6. The local organising committee shall undertake the following practical arrangements regarding travel and accommodation before the congress:

(i) inform the local tourist, convention, municipal and police authorities about the congress

(ii) ensure that visa application procedures, where applicable, will operate smoothly

(iii) approach national airlines for special reductions for congress participants

(iv) make arrangements with the host university to reserve a sufficient number of rooms in university residences for congress participants

(v) make arrangements with hotels (which should be as close to the congress site as possible) for special lower rates; and ensure that the hotel will continue to honour special rates for all late registrants.

7. The local organising committee shall prepare and mail the following items:

(i) a congress registration form (approximately nine months before the congress date; to be mailed to all individual and collective members, and persons on the preliminary congress programme)

(ii) a hotel registration form and outline of the social programme, including pre- and post-congress tours, to accompany this

(iii) a paper abstract form (to all designated paper givers)

(iv) a registration confirmation form and local information (to all who have preregistered)

(v) a copy of the preliminary programme (to all who have preregistered).

8. The local organising committee shall make the following arrangements immediately before the congress

(i) prepare and print the book of abstracts in the same format as the *International Political Science Abstracts*

(ii) prepare and print the final congress programme

(iii) set up a bank account for the congress with signing authority held by IPSA secretary-general/administrator and congress chairperson/congress administrator

(iv) prepare kits for delegates with programme, book of abstracts, invitations to: opening ceremony, research institutes, embassy receptions (where applicable), etc.; name badge, information sheet, list of restaurants, etc.

IV. Congress administration

9. The local organising committee shall ensure that the following services are available during the congress

(i) clear signposting of all events

(ii) general information in several languages, as appropriate

(iii) simultaneous translation for the opening ceremony and closing sessions, and appropriate supporting physical arrangements

(iv) banking and foreign exchange facilities, and information on these

(v) adequate communications, word processing and reproduction equipment for congress participants

(vi) audio-visual equipment as needed

(vii) transportation (shuttle service) between hotels and congress site, if applicable

(viii) hotel accommodation for executive, programme chair, IPSA secretariat and IPSA editors

(ix) per diems for executive, programme chair and editors.

10. The local organising committee shall make appropriate arrangements during congress registration for the following:

(i) receipt of congress registration fees from all participants

(ii) disbursement of travel grants (including deduction of registration fees from these, where appropriate)

(iii) recording all financial transactions

(iv) informing the IPSA secretariat of any newly recruited members.

Annex 4: Responsibilities of the IPSA secretary general

I. Publicity

1. The IPSA secretary general shall ensure that all IPSA members are kept informed of developments in relation to congress organisation by publishing in *Participation* as soon as appropriate:

(i) the announcement regarding the date and venue of the congress

(ii)   the elaboration of the congress theme

(iii) calls for panels and papers

(iv) the preliminary programme

(v)   rules for participation in IPSA congresses

(vi) information about travel grants, Rokkan awards and the Kjellberg prize.

2. The IPSA secretary general shall ensure that information about the world congress is also disseminated as widely as possible throughout the profession by means of its web page, by other electronic means as appropriate, and by circulating to all collective members (national and regional political science associations) and editors of newsletters of research committees:

(i)   the announcement regarding the date and venue of the congress

(ii)   the elaboration of the congress theme

(iii) calls for panels and papers

(iv) information about travel grants, Rokkan awards and the Kjellberg award.

3. The secretary general shall use the occasion of the world congress to publicise IPSA and to maximise the recruitment of individual members of IPSA.

II. Communication of information

4. The secretary general shall ensure that those involved in the planning of IPSA congresses (including the programme committee and the local organising committee) are fully informed of procedures, and that these procedures are observed.

5. The secretary general shall ensure unimpeded communication with the programme chair and with the local organising committee, and shall encourage close contact between the programme chair and the local organising committee.

6. The secretary general shall ensure that information on IPSA's membership and on its research committees is available as necessary to the local organisers and to the programme committee.

III. Administration

7. The secretary general shall prepare and administer a programme of travel grants, and shall seek funding to support this.

8. The secretary general shall take such other steps as are appropriate to ensure the success of the world congress.

Annex 5: Guidelines for participation in IPSA world congresses

I. General

1. Participation in IPSA world congresses shall be open to IPSA members, to members of national and regional associations affiliated to IPSA and to other persons approved by the programme committee.

2. Those participating may do so as convenors, co-convenors, session chairs, paper-givers, discussants, supplementary paper givers or simply as persons attending the congress.

II. Organisation of sessions

3. Sessions in all parts of the programme shall be of such length as the programme committee may decide. Each session shall normally include no more than four papergivers, two discussants and one chair. If more than four papergivers are to be listed for any given session, any after the first four shall be listed in the printed programme as "supplementary paper" participants; if convenors fail to specify which papergivers are to be considered in this category, the programme chair reserves the right to choose.

4. Convenors are responsible for organising one or more sessions, and are appointed as follows:
   (i) convenors of sessions related to the main theme: by the programme committee;
   (ii) convenors of sessions organised by research committees: by the respective committees;
   (iii) convenors of special sessions: by the programme committee on the basis of applications from IPSA members and others;
   (iv) convenors of sessions of other types: by the programme committee.

   A co-convenor may be appointed where deemed necessary, subject to the agreement of the programme chair.

   Applications to convene sessions under headings (ii) and (iii) must reach the programme chair as early as possible, and no later than 1 December of the pre-congress year.

III. Duties of convenors, co-convenors and chairs

5. The duties of convenors are as follows:
   (i) to prepare proposals for their sessions and to undertake all necessary organisational initiatives to implement them
   (ii) to consult with the co-convenor (if there is one) on all aspects of the organisation of sessions
   (iii) to take responsibility for all correspondence and other contacts with participants, the programme chair and the IPSA secretariat
   (iv) to designate a chair for any session that is not being chaired by the convenor
   (v) to strive to obtain a balanced representation on the programme of each session in terms of gender, region, and age and career stage, and other criteria arising from the plurality embodied in IPSA and the discipline
   (vi) to ensure that there are adequate opportunities for participation by unsolicited paper givers, by not finalising session programmes prematurely
   (vii) to consider additional paper proposals from the programme chair when these fall within the thematic scope of a particular session
   (viii) to designate "supplementary paper" participants, if more high quality papers are offered than can be accommodated in a session; these may be listed in the official programme and may be moved to the main programme if other members of the panel have withdrawn

(ix) to forward the programme for their sessions to the programme chair as early as possible, but no later than 1 February of the congress year (this should include: (1) session titles, (2) paper titles, and (3) names, addresses and telephone, fax and email coordinates of chairs, papergivers and discussants and anyone else named in the programme)

(x) to circulate all participants in their sessions with (1) a list with names and addresses of papergivers and discussants and (2) a copy of guidelines for participation in IPSA congresses

(xi) to inform the programme chair promptly of developments and problems in their sessions and to defer to a decision of the programme chair in the case of any problem or dispute that the convenor cannot resolve

(xii) to make recommendations as to the award of travel grants

(xiii) to provide a report on the sessions to the programme chair after the congress

(xiv) to designate the name of a candidate for the Francesco Kjellberg award for the best paper by a new scholar

(xv) to take such other steps as are necessary to ensure the success of their sessions.

6. The duties of co-convenors are as follows:
   (i) to consider and advise on the proposals submitted by convenors
   (ii) to assist convenors in such other ways as are needed.

7. The duties of session chairs are as follows:
   (i) to apply the normal rules of good chairmanship, subject to the time allotted to each session by the programme committee
   (ii) to make every effort to maximise the opportunity for discussion
   (iii) to restrict each papergiver to a maximum of 15 minutes for oral presentation;
   (iv) to restrict to no more than 30 minutes the period devoted to discussants and the responses of papergivers;
   (v) to allow at least one hour for general discussion from the floor;
   (vi) to follow judicious practices in eliciting comments and questions from those attending the session; and
   (vii) to prevent lengthy and irrelevant interventions.

IV. Duties of papergivers and discussants

8. The duties of papergivers are as follows:
   (i) to prepare a written paper, in English or French, of no more than 25 typewritten pages, single-spaced on A4 (or 210 x 297mm) paper or equivalent size.
   (ii) to submit to the programme chair a 200-word abstract of the paper in English or French, no later than 1 April of the congress year
   (iii) to circulate copies of the paper, no later than 1 July of the congress year to:
   - the session convenor(s)
   - all listed participants in the relevant session
   - the IPSA secretariat
   - the co-chairs of the local organising committee

(iv) to deliver at least 50 copies of the paper to the local organising committee for the world congress paper room

(v) to present the paper orally, normally for no more than fifteen minutes, at the congress.

9. The duties of discussants are as follows:

(i) to present a short review of the paper or papers that the discussant has been invited to consider

(ii) to restrict this review to no more than five minutes per paper.

10. The duties of supplementary paper givers are as follows:

(i) to prepare a paper to the specifications described in 8 above

(ii) to make copies of this paper available in the congress paper room

(iii) to present this paper orally at the appropriate session, on the invitation of the session convenor or chair, should a vacancy arise.

V. General guidelines for participants

11. All registered participants at the world congress are eligible to attend all meetings that form part of the congress programme, including sessions on the main theme, sessions organised by research committees and sessions of other types.

12. All participants whose names are included in the congress programme must conform to the following rules:

(i) All of those whose names are to be listed on the programme must preregister by 1 June of the congress year

(ii) All paper givers must in addition have submitted an abstract by 1 April of the congress year if their names are to be included in the congress programme and their abstracts in the book of abstracts

13. To permit maximum participation in the world congress, it is necessary to limit the number of appearances of any single individual as follows:

(i) No individual may make more than **one** appearance on the programme in each of the following categories:

- chair of a session
- papergiver
- discussant.

(ii) A person may, in other words, chair a session, present a paper and serve as discussant; the person may not chair two sessions or act as papergiver or discussant in two sessions.

(iii) In calculating such appearances, the entire programme (including the main theme sessions, research committee sessions and special sessions) will be taken into consideration. The programme chair may waive this rule for special workshops and for supplementary and regional sessions.

Annex 6: IPSA awards

I. Types of award

1. With a view to enhancing the quality and diversity of participation in its world congress, IPSA has instituted a series of awards in the following categories:

(i)   Karl Deutsch award
(ii) Stein Rokkan fellowships
(iii) Francesco Kjellberg award
(iv) IPSA travel grants
(v)   special travel grants.

II. *Deutsch award*

2. The purpose of the Karl Deutsch award is to honour a prominent scholar engaged in the cross-disciplinary research of which Karl Deutsch was a master. The recipient presents the Karl Deutsch lecture or leads a special session at the world congress. The award is made on the recommendation of the committee on awards. It is supported by the Karl Deutsch fund.

III. *Rokkan award*

3. The purpose of the Stein Rokkan fellowships is to assist a small number of graduate students in attending the world congress by covering their basic travel and accommodation costs. The recipients receive financial assistance towards travel and subsistence costs. The awards are made on the recommendation of the committee on awards. They are supported by the Stein Rokkan fund.

4. Applicants for the award are expected to submit:
   (i)   a curriculum vitae
   (ii) a statement of the nature of the research project and an indication as to how it could benefit from participation in the congress
   (iii) a letter of reference from an academic familiar with the applicant's work certifying his or her academic status and evaluating his or her suitability for the award
   (iv) a representative sample of written work (whose length should not be greater than a scientific journal article)
   (v)   a statement indicating financial need in respect of the costs of attending the congress.

5. The following are the criteria for the award:
   (i)   each candidate must be registered in a degree granting programme
   (ii) normally candidates must be at the doctoral level but in exceptional cases where qualifications and money allow students at master's level may be considered
   (iii) candidates must demonstrate that their academic institutions and professors have bestowed high academic honour and esteem on them
   (iv) candidates' written work will be assessed by the committee on awards.

III. *Kjellberg award*

6. The purpose of the Francesco Kjellberg award is to encourage scholars who are new to the discipline. The recipient is offered complimentary three-year membership of IPSA and travel costs to the following world congress. The award is made on the recommendation of the committee on awards on the basis of nominations by convenors and chairs at the world congress, and is based on

normal criteria of academic excellence. It is supported by IPSA's own resources.

7. Nominations for the award must be made by convenors or panel chairs and must include the following:
   (i) a letter of recommendation from the chair or convenor indicating that the candidate fulfils the criteria and is worthy of an award
   (ii) the curriculum vitae of the author
   (iii) four copies of the congress paper.

8. The following are the criteria for the award:
   (i) candidates must be new scholars, not more than five years after completion of a PhD, or at the beginning of an equivalent active academic career, at the time of presenting the paper
   (ii) the paper must be original, unpublished and presented personally at the congress
   (iii) the paper must be outstanding, and worthy of publication in a leading political science journal.

IV. IPSA travel grants

9. The purpose of IPSA travel grants is to facilitate attendance at the world congress by making financial assistance available for travel to the congress to persons who would not otherwise be able to afford this. The recipients are required to be listed on the programme of the world congress. The awards are made on the recommendation of the travel grants subcommittee of the programme committee. They are supported by IPSA from its own resources and from funds raised from other sources.

10. Applicants for travel grants are expected to submit:
    (i) a completed application form
    (ii) a curriculum vitae
    (iii) a letter of reference from the convenor or chair of the session at which the candidate is participating indicating his or her academic suitability and financial need for the award
    (iv) an optional supporting statement.

11. The following criteria are taken into account by the travel grants committee in considering applications for awards (the first three are most heavily weighted):
    (i) status on programme (e.g. convenor/chair, papergiver, discussant)
    (ii) economic circumstances of applicant's country
    (iii) geographical region
    (iv) receipt of travel grants to earlier world congresses
    (v) sex (with advantage to women)
    (vi) age (with advantage to younger scholars)
    (vii) membership of IPSA

V. Special travel grants

12. The purpose of special travel grants is to facilitate attendance at the world congress by making financial assistance available to persons who would not oth-

erwise be able to afford attendance at the congress. The awards are made by
the local organising committee from funds raised from various sources.

13. Application procedures and criteria for assessing applications are the same as
for IPSA travel grants.

VI. General provisions

14. Applicants for Rokkan fellowships may also apply for special travel grants
and, if eligible, for IPSA travel grants, but may be awarded only one of these.
Applicants for IPSA travel grants are also considered automatically for special
travel grants, which are allocated at a later stage than IPSA grants.

15. The implementation of IPSA's award scheme is based on criteria approved by
the relevant IPSA committees.

4.8 RESEARCH COMMITTEES

*(Initially adopted by the IPSA executive committee at its meeting no. 42 in Zurich
in 1981; since amended several times; text approved by the executive committee at
meeting no. 78, Krakow, 25-26 April 1999)*

I. Definition

1. The IPSA executive committee shall, in accordance with article 5(e) of
the IPSA constitution, make provision for the establishment and monitoring of research committees to conduct and propagate the results of
research within the various subfields of political science.

2. Research committees are groups of scholars conducting research into a
particular problem or in a particular area of political science approved
by the committee on research and training and the IPSA executive
committee as part of a broad research framework within the discipline
of political science.

II. Objectives

3. Research committees should:
   (i)   develop research in political science, especially work based on in-
         ternational cooperation;
   (ii) organise and maintain personal contacts among political scientists
         with common interests;
   (iii) disseminate information and publish scholarly research; and
   (iv) provide a framework for cooperation between individuals and or-
         ganisations concerned with teaching and research in political and
         other social sciences.

III. Membership

4. Membership of research committees is open to political scientists who
are members of national associations affiliated to IPSA, and to individual members of IPSA.

5. Research committees should be as representative as possible of the different approaches in their special fields, and of the countries and regions of political scientists who conduct research in these fields. They should also make appropriate provision for the inclusion of women, young scholars (including doctoral students) and other disadvantaged groups.
6. Research committees may require their members to pay a small fee to assist in defraying running costs, subject to any maximum fee that may be prescribed by the IPSA executive committee on the recommendation of the committee on research and training.
7. Research committees are required to ensure that their activities are adequately publicised by forwarding to the IPSA secretariat material for publication in *Participation* on a regular basis. They are required to make a prompt and positive response to persons applying for membership. In the event of an application for membership not being accepted, any eligible person may forward an appeal to the committee on research and training.

IV. Organisation

8. The affairs of each research committee shall be directed by an elected board consisting of no fewer than seven and no more than twelve members. The board shall be elected every three years and shall include at least two new members at each election. No officer of a research committee may remain on as an officer in any capacity for more than six years. If possible, board members should represent different countries and approaches in their fields of interest.
9. The board shall have a chair assisted, if necessary, by a vice-chair and a secretary. The chair shall be the primary contact point for IPSA and shall be regarded as the convenor of the research committee, unless the board designates another officer as convenor.
10. No-one may be a board member of more than one research committee. All board members must be individual members of IPSA.

V. Activities

11. Research committees are entitled and expected to organise two sessions at the IPSA world congress.
12. Between congresses research committees should organise meetings, conduct research and publish its results, and circulate news and information about their activities. All research committees are expected to organise at least one academic meeting between congresses, and are required to organise at least one such meeting during any two consecutive inter-congress periods.

13. In the event of a charge being made on participants at any academic meeting organised by a research committee, this shall be set at such a level as to ensure that participation at the meeting is not discouraged, subject to any maximum fee that may be prescribed by the IPSA executive committee on the recommendation of the committee on research and training.

VI. Recognition of research committees

14. The committee on research and training may recommend the recognition of a new research committee on the basis of a request signed by at least 15 political scientists from at least seven different countries and two continents; the signatories must include both men and women.
15. Any application for the formation of a research committee must be accompanied by a statement outlining:
    (i)   the subject of the proposed committee;
    (ii)   the main analytical perspectives and empirical fields to be considered;
    (iii) a list of prospective members; and
    (iv)   a plan of activities and goals, and particularly future meetings and conferences, publications and newsletters.

VII. Review of research committees

16. Research committees are recognised on a probationary basis for an initial three-year period. Their organisation and activities shall subsequently be reviewed every six years by the committee on research and training.
17. Research committees should make every endeavour to keep the IPSA secretariat informed of their activities. In particular, each research committee is required:
    (i)   to provide a report within six weeks of the world congress; this must include a summary of activities during the previous three years, including a list of meetings held, and papers presented, publications and newsletters issued; and
    (ii)   to provide an updated list of the names and full coordinates of office holders and board members after each election of a new board.
18. The committee on research and training may recommend the continuation of a research committee for a further six-year period if in its view it satisfies the following conditions:
    (i)   the organisational requirements in rules 8-10;
    (ii)   the academic requirements in rules 11-13;
    (iii) the reporting requirements in rule 17; and

(iv) such other requirement as the committee may impose to satisfy itself of the bona fide activity of the research committee.

19. The committee on research and training may at any time recommend to the executive committee withdrawal of recognition of a research committee that is in breach of the rules.

VIII. *Committee on research and training*

20. The committee on research and training shall consist of members appointed by the IPSA executive committee.

21. The duties of the committee are:

(i) to consider proposals for new research committees, and to recommend whether or not they should be accepted;

(ii) to review the activities of existing research committees on a six-yearly basis, and to recommend whether or not they should be continued;

(iii) to monitor the scope and activities of research committees as a whole, to encourage their work, and to recommend ways in which its quality might be improved;

(iv) to encourage the systematic development of research on a planned basis by identifying gaps and areas of overlap in the overall pattern of research committees; and

(v) to report its recommendations and conclusions to the IPSA executive committee and, where appropriate, to the IPSA council.

IX. *Interpretation*

22. The committee on research and training shall rule on any ambiguities in these rules, subject to a right of appeal to the IPSA executive committee.

4.9 ACADEMIC ACTIVITIES BETWEEN IPSA CONGRESSES

(Approved by the IPSA executive committee at meeting no. 73, Rio de Janeiro, 6-8 March 1997)

I. *General*

1. The IPSA executive committee may sanction the organisation of roundtable meetings, symposia and workshops/seminars between congresses on the basis of invitations from local organisers or on the initiative of members of the executive committee.

2. The responsibilities of the local sponsoring institution or individual are as follows:

(i) a named individual or body must be prepared to accept responsibility for all aspects of local organisation, including academic ones;

(ii) an appropriate academic theme should be adopted, subject to approval by the IPSA executive committee or of IPSA officers designated by them;

(iii) the speakers and the target audience must include international participation, with at least one half of the participants coming from foreign countries and, normally, some scholars from each of the world's regions; efforts should also be made to ensure that a gender balance is maintained and that there is appropriate representation of younger scholars;

(iv) some opportunity for developing a knowledge of the host country or region should be provided for foreign participants in the form of lectures, tours, excursions, receptions or other such activities;

(v)   in order to increase the visibility of IPSA, it is recommended that the education and/or research authorities of the host country be invited to observe the meeting;

(vi) the local host must normally be prepared to offer to cover all local expenses for foreign visitors, including hotel, meals and excursions; arrangements should be made for meeting and seeing off foreign participants; and an effort should also be made to raise money to support the travel of foreign speakers who do not have financial support from any other source;

(vii) arrangements for the publication of the proceedings and their dissemination by internet should also be considered, and the IPSA book series and the *International political science review* should be seen as potential outlets.

3. The IPSA secretariat will publicise the meeting in the IPSA newsletter, *Participation*, and will also publish brief summaries of the proceedings after the event.

4. Meetings of the IPSA executive committee may be held in conjunction with roundtable meetings, symposia or workshops/seminars sanctioned by the executive committee. In such cases, executive committee members who have competence in the topic of the academic meeting will be invited to assist by presenting a paper. Others may be invited to act as discussants or to chair sessions.

II. Roundtable meetings

5. A roundtable meeting consists of a small group of researchers, preferably numbering not more than 30 participants plus a maximum of 20 observers, held between IPSA congresses and lasting normally for two days.

6. The objectives of roundtable meetings are:

(i)   to permit researchers in specific sub-disciplinary areas to transmit and compare the results of their current research;

(ii) to focus attention on frontier areas of research or neglected topics; and

(iii) to develop new areas of political science and interdisciplinary topics.

7. All participants are expected to present papers or act as discussants, and should ideally do both. Abstracts of approximately 300 words should be made available to the organisers at least one month in advance of the meeting, and an effort should be made to precirculate papers by airmail.

III. *Symposia*

8. An IPSA symposium is a meeting at which selected speakers present a specialist theme to a non-specialist audience; this audience may be relatively large, and will normally be defined by reference to a particular geographical region or continent, and the symposium will typically last for three or four days.

9. The objectives of IPSA symposia are:

(i)   to internationalise approaches to the study of politics;

(ii) to provide scholars of one country or region with insights into the theories, conceptualisations, methodologies, data and findings used elsewhere; and

(iii) to contribute to the development of the discipline in the region or continent in which the symposium is being held.

10. Symposia will normally take place in non-congress years and will normally circulate between continents.

11. A workshop/seminar consists of a set of lectures or courses with a substantial training function that allows adequate time for group discussion and the presentation of research projects.

IV. *Workshops / seminars*

12. The objectives of IPSA workshops/seminars are:

(i)   to contribute towards the development of advanced skills related to the discipline;

(ii) to encourage familiarity with recent developments in the discipline; and

(iii) to promote the infrastructural development of the discipline in other ways.

13. Workshops/seminars will normally be organised to cater for the needs of regions where the discipline is less developed.

5 / RESEARCH COMMITTEES

5.1 GENERAL INFORMATION

Introduction
IPSA currently recognises 46 research committees. Each is cross-national in membership, and its affairs are managed, subject to general IPSA guidelines, by an executive board consisting of IPSA members (see section 4.8 for the current regulations). Each research committee is required to organise at least one roundtable meeting between congresses; research committees are entitled to organise two panels at IPSA's triennial congress.

IPSA monitors the activities of these bodies through its committee on research and training (formerly commission on research committees and study groups), whose membership for 1997-2000 is as follows:

Ursula Vogel (chair)
Renato Boschi
Gideon Doron
L Adele Jinadu
Max Kaase
Paula D McClain
Gunnar Sjöblom

The following is a list of all currently recognised research committees.

Research committees
1. Conceptual and terminological analysis
2. Political elites
3. European unification
4. Public bureaucracies in developing societies
5. Comparative studies on local government and politics
6. Political sociology
7. Women, politics and developing nations
8. Legislative specialists
9. Comparative judicial studies
11. Science and politics
12. Biology and politics
13. Democratisation in comparative perspective
14. Politics and ethnicity

15. Political geography
16. Socio-political pluralism
17. Globalisation and governance
18. Asian and Pacific studies
19. Sex roles and politics
20. Political finance and political corruption
21. Political socialisation and education
22. Political communication
24. Armed forces and society
25. Comparative health policy
26. Human rights
27. Structure and organisation of government
28. Comparative federation and federalism
29. Psycho-politics
31. Political philosophy
32. Public policy analysis
33. Comparative study of the discipline of political science
34. Comparative representation and electoral system
35. Technology and development
36. Political power
37. Rethinking in political development
38. Politics and business
39. The welfare state and developing societies
40. New world orders?
41. Geopolitics
42. System integration of divided nations
43. Religion and politics
44. Military rule and democratisation in the Third World
45. International data development
46. Politics of global environmental change
47. Local-global relations
48. Administrative culture
49. Socialism, capitalism and democracy

How to join
Membership of research committees is open to all individual members of
IPSA and to all members of national associations affiliated to IPSA as collective members. The former may ask to be put in touch with particular
research committees by so indicating on their IPSA membership form.
Others may join by contacting the chairs of the groups in question at the
addresses listed below. Further information on membership and on the

activities of particular committees and groups may also be obtained from these contact persons.

Further information
General information on the work of research committees and study groups may be obtained from the chair of the IPSA committee on research and training below:
Dr Ursula Vogel
Department of Government
University of Manchester
Manchester M13 9PL
tel: +44-161-275 4906; fax: +44-161-275 4925
email: msrgsuv@fsl.ec.man.ac.uk
General information may also be obtained from the IPSA secretariat (Secretary General: John Coakley; Administrator: Margaret Brindley) at the address below:
International Political Science Association
Department of Politics
University College Dublin
Belfield, Dublin 4, Ireland
tel: +353-1 706 8182; fax: +353-1 706 1171
email:ipsa@ucd.ie

5.2 DIRECTORY OF RESEARCH COMMITTEES

The following pages list the research committees that are recognised by IPSA and describe their activities.

RC1: Conceptual and terminological analysis / L'analyse terminologique et les concepts
Background: recognised as research committee in 1976; also recognised as a research committee of the International Sociological Association; known as COCTA.
Objectives: focuses on the meaning of social science terms with a key role in political science and sociological theories. It is oriented towards both the formal and material mode of speech; the group welcomes linguistic approaches and conceptual analysis. It has looked at the theoretical connotations of social science terms and the mapping of the denotation of concepts by means of the construction of indices.
Activities: COCTA creates opportunities for theoretical and empirical discourse within the International Political Science Association and the International Sociological Association. Regular activities include conferences.
Publications: newsletter.

No of members: current membership unreported.
Membership fee: USD15.00 for three years
Contact: committee chair
Professor Fred Riggs
Department of Political Science
University of Hawaii
24244 Maile Way
Honolulu, Hawaii 96822, USA
tel: +1-808-956 8123
fax: +1-808-956 6877
email: fredr@hawaii.edu

RC2: Political elites / Les élites politiques
Background: recognised as research committee in 1972.
Objectives: facilitates the research plans and scholarly communication of political scientists whose studies focus on the recruitment and performance of elites in political life; it seeks to undertake the gathering and interpretation of empirical evidence through a variety of research strategies and conceptual approaches. The committee gives priority to comparative analysis.
Activities: four work groups as follows:
• Higher civil servants (Fred Riggs)
• Political leadership in Central and Eastern Europe (Wlodzimierz Wesolowski)
• Elites and classes (Jan Pakulski)
• Parliamentary elites (Dieter Herzog).
Regular activities include conferences.
Publications: Elites, Crises and the Origins of Regimes (1998)
No of members: 65.
Membership fee: no membership fee is charged.
Contact: committee chair:
Professor Mattei Dogan
Centre National de la Recherche
72 Boulevard Arago
75013 Paris
France
tel: +33-1-4535 8052
fax +333-1-4707 1222

RC3: European unification / L'unification européenne
Background: recognised as research committee in 1972.

Objectives: focuses on the political study of the process of European integration. This research committee brings together academics and European Union experts.

Activities: research on the institutions and political evolution of the European Union.

Publications: Karlheinz Neunreither and Antje Wiener, eds: *European Integration After Amsterdam: Institutional Dynamics and Prospects for Democracy* (Oxford University Press, 2000); research volumes on "Globalisation and regional integration" and "Democracy beyond the nation state", both in relation to European integration will follow.

No of members: 128.

Membership fee: free for IPSA members.

Contact: committee chair:

Professor Karlheinz Neunreither
1 bei der Aarnescht
L-6969 Luxembourg
tel/fax: +352-341 394
email: KhNeunreither@compuserve.com

RC4: *Public bureaucracies in developing societies / Les bureaucraties publiques dans les sociétés en voie de développement*

Background: recognised as study group in 1983; granted research committee status in 1993.

Objectives: investigates issues and problems relating to the organisation and function of public bureaucracies in developing societies. It focuses on the comparative study of the role of bureaucracies in the formulation and implementation of public policies, and their interactions with other political institutions, NGOs, non-state sector and functionaries. Among specific policy areas investigated are the problems faced by developing societies in their quest for modernisation and development. Also studies bureaucracies' interaction with other socio-economic forces, the citizen and the civil society, and its involvement in broader environmental concerns for human development and quality of life. The role of bureaucracies in the changing context of globalisation; and liberalisation and restructuring of economies and the shifts in the conceptual paradigms of public administration, public management and administrative sciences are other areas of research study and concern for the research committee.

Activities: conferences and group discussions on topical issues.

Publications: book publication; newsletter.

No of members: 81

Membership fee: USD20.00 for three years.

Contact: committee chair:

Professor RB Jain
102 SFS, DDA Mukherji Apartments
East of Mukherji Nagar
Delhi 110009
India
tel: +91-11-765 2403
fax: +91-11-765 4794
email: rbjain@ndf.vsnl.net.in

RC5: Comparative studies on local government and politics / Etudes comparées de l'administration et de la politique municipales
Background: recognised as research committee in 1972.
Objectives: examines three themes, namely: "classical" issues of political science research on local politics and governance, such as local power structure, local democracy and local governance; the transformation of local politics and government in Eastern Europe; and the role of local government in development countries.
Activities: conferences; roundtables.
Publications: newsletter.
No of members: 105.
Membership fee: USD20.00 for four years.
Contact: committee chair:
Professor Harald Baldersheim
Department of Political Science
University of Oslo
Box 1097 Blindern
N-0317 Oslo
Norway
tel: +47-22-85 7189
email: harald.baldersheim@stv.uio.no
web: www.statsuitenskap.uio.no/ipsa/ipsarc05

RC6: Political sociology / Sociologie politique
Background: recognised as research committee in 1970; also recognised as a research committee of the International Sociological Association.
Objectives: brings together political scientists and sociologists in this highly diverse, empirically based field of study; promotes the dynamic interdisciplinary exchange of scholars and ideas lies at the core of the CPS and determines its policies. The committee aims to establish a community of like-minded scholars, to facilitate communication and the dissemination of scientific research, and to increase the theoretical and practical significance of the field.

Activities: study groups for the exchange of specialised knowledge; conferences.
Publications: newsletter.
No of members: 165.
Membership fee: USD15.00 for three years.
Contact: committee chair:
  Professor Kay Lawson
  Department of Political Science
  San Francisco State University
  1600 Holloway Ave
  San Francisco, CA 94132
  USA
  tel: +1-510-848 1245
  fax: +1-519-883 9624
  email: klawson@sfsu.edu

RC7: *Women, politics and developing nations / Femmes, politiques et les pays en voie de développement*

Background: recognised as study group in 1988; granted research committee status in 1992.
Objectives: focuses on the process of development, issues of gender-inequality, political regimes, the inter-play of micro-political processes, representation, decision making, the allocation of resources, democratisation and the removal of iniquitous relationships at all levels. The committee has, to date, paid particular attention to the issues of women, debt and structural adjustment, women and the environment, women in the democratisation process and debt and structural adjustment: impact on women; ethnic conflict and women's human rights. The committee is currently undertaking a special study on women's leadership in economic institutions.
Activities: conferences, workshops, roundtables.
Publications: book publication.
No of members: 85.
Membership fee: USD 10.00 for three years.
Contact: committee chair:
  Professor Pam Rajput
  Department of Political Science
  Arts Block IV
  Punjab University
  Chandigarh 160014
  India
  tel: +91-172-541819

RC8: Legislative specialists / Les spécialistes du pouvoir législatif
Background: recognised as research committee in 1971.
Objectives: promotes the study of the comparative forms and effects of legislative institutions, processes and politics; and of national, cross-national, and sub-national aspects of legislatures.
Activities: conferences.
Publications: book publications, *RCLS International Membership Directory and Research Register*; newsletter.
No of members: 180.
Membership fee: USD30.00 for three years.
Contact: committee chair:
    Professor Lawrence Longley
    Department of Government
    Lawrence University
    Appleton, WI 54912
    USA
    tel: +1-920-832 6673
    fax: +1-920-832 6944
    email: powerldl@aol.com

RC9: Comparative judicial systems / Systèmes juridiques comparées
Background: recognised as research committee in 1973.
Objectives: aims to promote the comparative study of judicial processes. This entails analyses of the various components of these processes: the legal profession, the judiciary, courts (as institutions), legal doctrines, legal cultures; and how these components relate to other political institutions and political systems such as executives, legislatures, political parties, constitutions, federalism, political culture. The ultimate aim is to enhance knowledge of the common and disparate factors among the judicial/political systems of the countries of the world.
Activities: conferences.
Publications: book, journal and paper publication; newsletter.
No of membership: 250.
Membership fee: USD10.00 for two years.
Contact: committee chair:
    Professor F L Morton
    Department of Political Science
    University of Calgary
    2500 University Drive NW
    Calgary
    Alberta T2N 1N4
    Canada

tel: +1-403-220 6514
fax: +1-403-282 4773
email: morton@ucalgary.ca

RC11: *Science et politique / Science and politics*

Formation: reconnu comme comité de recherche, 1975.
Objectives: ravaille sur les relations entre science et politique. Il étudie comment la politique (et le politique) influencent le déroulement de la science, dans ses thèmes, ses problématiques, ses méthodes, ses retombées économiques et sociales. A l'inverse, il s'efforce de montrer aussi comment la science par ses avancées, modifie le comportements, les enjeux et les stratégies des acteurs politiques. L'étude des politiques de la science reste un point focal où il est possible d'observer assez bien ces interactions.
Activités: les travaux du comité se deploient dans une perspective descriptive, comparative et explicative, mais ils ambitionnent aussi la construction performative de modes d'action nouveaux dans le domaine où s'entrecroisent politique, science et société. Les activités régulières comprend aussi des tables rondes et publication des travaux des tables rondes.
Adhésion: 40.
Appelations: l'adhésion pour les trois années est gratuit.
Responsable: pour devenir membre, s'addresser au président:
   Dr Réjean Landry
   Département de science politique
   Université Laval
   Québec
   Canada T2N 7P4
   tel: +1-403-220 6514
   fax: +1-418-656 7861
   email: Rejean.Landry@pol.ulaval.ca

RC12: *Biology and politics / Biologie et politique*

Background: recognised as research committee in 1975.
Objectives: explores the linkage between biology and politics. Practically, this translates into a variety of research foci: policy issues emerging from the life sciences (bioethics, health policy, sex preselection); evolutionary bases of human political phenomena; physiological bases of political thinking and behaviour; development of research methods to assay the linkage between biology and politics.
Activities: regular activities include conferences; publications; communication via e-mail distribution lists; on-line discussion group, www home page.

Publications: newsletter; currently working on production of seventh volume in RC12 book series on biology and politics, published by JAI Press.
No of members: 151.
Membership fee: no membership fee is charged.
Contact: committee chair:
　Professor Albert Somit
　School of Law
　Southern Illinois University
　Lesar Law Building
　Carbondale, IL 62901,
　USA
　tel: +1-618-536 7711
　fax: +1-618-453 8769
　web: www.personal.psu.edu/faculty/s/a/sap12
　steven_peterson_6

RC13: Democratisation in comparative perspective / Démocratisation dans une perspective comparée

Background: recognised as study group in 1989; granted research committee status in 1994.
Objectives: deals with the basic conditions of democracy, but also the more specific aspects of the recent "wave", in a systematic comparative manner. The present focus is on the historical and cultural particularities of this process in the major regions of the world (ie Africa, Latin America, Asia and Eastern Europe, thus far). Further work will concentrate on the theoretical implications of these processes and the risks and chances for a further consolidation and deepening of democracy in all parts of the world.
Activities: conferences.
Publications: book publication; newsletter.
No of members: 180.
Membership fee: USD15.00 for three years.
Contact: committee chair:
　Professor Dirk Berg-Schlosser
　Institute of Political Science
　Philipps-University Marburg
　D-35032 Marburg
　Germany
　tel: +49-6421-282 43 97
　fax: +49-6421-282 89 91
　email: bergschl@mailer.uni-marburg.de

RC14: Politics and ethnicity / Les ethnies et la politique

Background: recognised as research committee in 1976.

Objectives: focuses on the politics of ethnicity construed very broadly both in terms of methodology and orientation, ranging from broadly historical and deeply descriptive to more theoretical and empirically rigorous approaches. It touches upon such related themes as nationalism and nation-building; the formation and mobilisation of collective identities; cultural pluralism; irredentism; separatism; and the search for autonomy. It also touches upon questions of race, religion, language, immigration and citizenship, concerns that are reflected in the titles of committee colloquia which deal with specific topics but may include both country-specific case studies as well as comparative analyses.

Activities: regular activities include conferences.

Publications: book, journal and paper publication; newsletter; associated with the journal *Nationalism and Ethnic Politics*.

No of members: 258.

Membership fee: USD15.00 for three years.

Contact: committee chair:

> Professor William Safran
> Department of Political Science
> Campus Box 333
> University of Colorado
> Boulder, CO 80309
> USA
> tel: +1-303-492 7064
> fax: +1-303-492 0978
> email: safran@colorado.edu

RC15: Political geography / Géographie politique

Background: recognised as research committee in 1978.

Objectives: concentrates on the effect of spatial constraints on political systems and inversely the impact of political systems on space. Particular themes of recent focus include capital cities, electoral geography, ethnicity and regionalism, freedom and boundaries, the pattern of international and internal migrations.

Activities: the committee brings together political scientists, geographers, and colleagues from related disciplines to participate in seminars and roundtables.

No of members: 70.

Membership fee: no membership fee is charged.

Contact: either the political science or geography co-chair:

Political science

Professor Jean Laponce
University of British Columbia
Department of Political Science
C472-1866 Main Mall
Vancouver, BC V6T 1Z1
Canada
tel: +1-604-822 2832
fax: +1-604-822 5540
email: jlaponce@interchange.ubc.ca
Geography
Professor Paul Claval
29 rue Soisy
95600 Eaubone
France
tel: +33-1-3959 8383
fax: +33-1-4432 1438

RC16: *Socio-political pluralism / Pluralisme socio-politique*

Background: recognised as research committee in 1976.

Objectives: focuses the study of democratic processes, with special emphasis on the pluralistic potential of ex-socialist countries with regime changes in Central and Eastern Europe having strengthened the East-West focus. Topics include conceptual and theoretical definitions of pluralism, at specific points in time and through history; structures for the articulation of interests and values, such as group and party systems; and pluralism within given institutions, such as the armed forces and firms, as well as in religious organisations and ethnic communities.

Activities: the committee usually meets once a year. According to present rules, membership is conditional on the presentation of a paper at one such meeting. It is also possible to join the committee as a member-at-large, and new members willing to take an active part in the committee's activities are welcomed.

Publications: P. Claeys et al (eds), *Lobbying Pluralism and European Integration*, (Brussels: European Interuniversity Press, 1998). *Revue Internationale de Politique Comparée*, 4/1997.

No of members: 30.

Membership fee: membership fee is currently under review to comply with current IPSA rules.

Contact: committee chair:
Professor Luigi Graziano
University of Turin
Department of Social Sciences

Via S Ottavio 20
I-10124 Torino, Italy
tel: +39-11-670 2606
fax: +39-11-670 2612

RC17: Globalisation and governance / Globalisation et le gouvernance
Background: recognised as research committee (The emerging international
economic order) in 1978 and changed to "Globalisation and governance"
in 1998.
Objectives: focuses on the impacts of regionalism and globalisation on different levels of governance — domestic and international. The committee is
currently examining globalisation as a factor forcing a restructuring of societies, interests, coalitions, party behaviour, state structures and roles at
various levels of political and economic activity — local, provincial, sub-
national regions, transnational regional clusters, nation states, international
regions, multilateral and plurilateral regimes; globalisation as a contributor
to the growth of agency among private and public actors and to changes in
bargaining position among them in policy networks linking them within
policy domains.
Activities: conferences.
Publications: publication of papers.
No of members: 25.
Membership fee: no membership fee is charged.
Contact: committee co-convenor:
    Professor Robert S Walters
    Department of Political Science
    University of Pittsburgh
    4L01 Forbes Quad
    Pittsburgh, PA 15260, USA
    tel: +1-412-648 7265
    fax: +1-412-648 7277
    email: rsw2@pitt.edu

RC18: Asian and Pacific studies / Études politiques sur l'Asie et le Paci-
fique
Background: recognised as research committee in 1979.
Objectives: advances the development of Asian and Pacific studies and
promotion of the study of political science in Asian and Pacific countries.
The work of this committee focuses on the following areas the modernisation of Asian countries, including the economic and political development
of the countries in the Asian and Pacific basin; regional security, including

the rise and decline of alliance systems in Asia; and the impact of national integration and world peace.

Activities: conferences.

No of members: unreported.

Membership fee: no membership fee is charged.

Contact: committee chair:
> Professor Teh-Kuang Chang
> Political Science Department
> Ball State University
> Muncie, IN 47306
> USA
> tel: +1-317-285-8787
> fax: +1-317-285-4411

RC19: Sex roles and politics / Les sexes et la politique

Background: recognised as research committee in 1979.

Objectives: addresses a broad array of issues involving gender and politics, major themes of focus to date including political participation of women; women and public policy in comparative perspective; women in public administration; women and politics in third world countries; women, religion and politics; the role of legislation and the status of women; women and the transition to democracy; strategies for the empowerment of women; feminist theory; women and nationalism; eco-feminism; and the global women's movement and international relations.

Activities: conferences.

Publications: book and paper publication; newsletter; e-mail distribution list and www home page planned.

No of members: 200.

Membership fee: no membership fee (but committee suggests USD5.00 donation).

Contact: committee secretary:
> Professor Janine Mossuz-Lavau
> Centre d'etude de la vie politique française
> 54 boulevard Raspail
> 75006 Paris
> France
> tel: +33-1-4954 2296
> fax: +33-1-4954 2025
> email: mossuz-lavau@msh-paris.fr

RC20: Political finance and political corruption / L'argent et la corruption politique

Background: recognised as research committee in 1979.

Objectives: studies the role of money in the political process and in social interaction with public authorities, including all aspects of campaign and party financing in political systems around the world, transnational payments aiming at the proliferation of democratic government as well as corruption in all its manifestations in individual and governmental behaviour. Members of the research committee cooperate in developing concepts for the analysis of political finance and corruption in politics and administration as well as interactions between them. The committee aims to advance cross-national research and to encourage comparative analysis. Current emphasis on expansion of the committee's field of research is targeting the Latin American region.

Activities: conferences.

Publications: paper depositories (information from which are currently being incorporated into on-line archive containing manuscripts, working papers, bibliographies, datasets and other kinds of material); production of "guidelines on the financing of political parties" NGOs; journal contributions; book publication.

No of members: 600.

Membership fee: USD45.00 for three years

Contact: committee chair:
    Professor Karl-Heinz Nassmacher
    Institute of Comparative Politics
    Carl von Ossietzky University
    PO Box 2503
    D-26131 Oldenburg
    Germany
    tel: +49-441-504 1480
    fax: +49-441-504 0842
    http://www2.colgate.edu/departments/polisci/ipsa

RC21: Political socialisation and education / Socialisation et education politique

Background: recognised as research committee in 1979.

Objectives: comprises a professional network which brings together political scientists (and political psychologists or political educationalists) from all over the world. It aims to advance the study of political socialisation and education by encouraging research, especially cross national studies; to disseminate relevant information at international meetings, workshops and conferences; to publish scholarly research; and to provide a framework for co-operation between individuals and organisations concerned with teaching and research on political socialisation and political education, and citizenship rights and responsibilities.

Activities: conferences.

Publications: book publication; supporting institution of *Politics, Groups and the Individual: International Journal of Political Socialisation and Political Psychology;* newsletter.

No of membership: 150.

Membership fee: USD10 per annum or USD25.00 for three years (prospective members also have the option of paying USD35.00/USD95.00 for one or three year membership, respectively, to include *Politics, Groups and the Individual,* or USD95.00 for three years including a three year subscription to *Politics, Groups and the Individual.*

Contact: committee chair:

Dr Daniel B German
Department of Political Science/Criminal Justice
Appalachian State University
Boone, NC 29608
USA
email: germandb@appstate.edu

RC22: Political communication / La communication politique

Background: recognised as research committee in 1984.

Objectives: encourages scientific analysis and discussion of the political aspects of communication within states (in a comparative framework) and across national boundaries and develops means of facilitating interaction among scholars who are conducting research on related issues and topics. Members are concerned with a diverse set of research interests including the international structure of communication, political theories of communication, the relationship between the public and private broadcasting sectors, cross-national comparative studies, the political impact of the media, the impact of technology and technological change on politics, values and cognition, and models of diplomatic communication.

Activities: international roundtables and smaller panels at other professional meetings such as the International Studies Association, the American Political Science Association, the International Association of Mass Communication Research, and the American and World Association for Public Opinion Research. Organisation of separate workshop on some specific topics (August 1999: "Political communication towards the third millennium").

Publications: publications; newsletter.

No of members: 230.

Membership fee: no membership fee, donation of USD10.00 suggested.
Contact: committee chair:
Professor Philippe J Maarek
41 rue du Colisee
75008 Paris
France
tel: +33-1-4225 8582
fax: +33-1-4359 5703
email: maarek@univ-paris12.fr
http://www.wz-berlin.de/ipsa-rc22

RC24: Armed forces and society / La société et les forces armées
Background: recognised as research committee in 1986.
Objectives: promotes study and research on the armed forces and society. This involves developing an international and cross cultural understanding of military systems, their impact on political systems, and the relationships between peace, war and military systems. It includes the social structure of the armed forces, with particular attention to their political impact; civil-military relations focusing on the nature and character of political systems, organisational structure of the armed forces, and the political consequences arising from the dynamics between the military and civilian systems; and military experience and traditions including the nature and character of military professionalism, professional education, and the military socialisation process.
Activities: conferences.
Publications: publications; newsletter.
No of members: 260.
Membership fee: USD10.00 per annum.
Contact: committee chair:
Professor Daniel Zirker
Dean of Arts and Science
Montana State University
Billings, MT 59101-0298
USA
tel: +1-406-657 2177
fax: +1-406-657 2187
email: dzirker@msubillings.edu

RC25: Comparative health policy / Politique comparative en matière de santé
Background: recognised as study group in 1984; granted research committee status in 1997.

Objectives: takes stock of comparative analyses of health policy studies, and reviews the state of the art in contemporary approaches, methodologies and substantive findings. It addresses options and instruments in health policy including modes of financing, privatisation, corporatist and non-corporatist decision-making, policy networks, self-help, and health promotion. It seeks to compare commonalties over time, place and substance as well as to contrast non-governmental and governmental experiences in organising, financing, regulating and delivering health care services in the ambulatory and the hospital care sector. It also analyses health policy and sustainable development seeking to explore the rewards of investments in human capital and democratic participation in pubic policies for health care.

Activities: conferences.

Publications: book publication—included in which was the 1997 publication of *Health policy reform: national variations and globalisation* in the IPSA book series, published by Macmillan, London.

No of members: 70.

Membership fee: USD10.00 for one year.

Contact: committee chair:
Professor Christa Altenstetter
Program in Political Science
Graduate School/The City University of New York (CUNY)
365 Fifth Avenue
New York, NY 10016-4309
USA
tel: +1-212-817 8670
fax: +1-212-817 1636
email: caltenstetter@gc.cuny.edu

RC26: Human rights/Les droits de la personne

Background: recognised as study group in 1980; granted research committee status in 1987.

Objectives: focuses on the development of internationally recognised human rights; since its inception it has being pursuing the following research themes, among others the foundations of human rights in political tension between the universal nature of human rights and cultural relativism; the nature of human rights as a political concept; the relationship between democracy, development and human rights; the causes of human rights violations; the place of human rights in foreign policy-making; and the role of international governmental and non-governmental organisations.

Activities: conferences.

Publications: journal articles, other.

No of members: 172.
Membership fee: no membership fee is charged.
Contact: committee chair:
   Professor Michael Freeman
   Department of Government
   University of Essex
   Wivenhoe Park
   Colchester CO4 3SQ
   UK
   tel: +44-1206-87 3333
   fax: +44-1206-873598
   email: freema@essex.ac.uk

RC27: Structure and organisation of government / La structure et l'organisation du gouvernement
Background: recognised as study group in 1984; granted research committee status in 1987.
Objectives: seeks to advance the comparative study of executive politics; this includes chief executives and cabinets, the permanent bureaucracy and appointed officials, and the relations between them. SOG is also interested in the development, adoption and implementation of policies, and in the co-ordination and control of decision making.
Activities: conferences.
Publications: quarterly journal, *Governance: An International Journal of Policy and Administration*, which addresses the scientific community and practitioners in most parts of the world; book publication; newsletter; website which includes information on upcoming meetings, the journal and the committee's executive.
No of members: 230.
Membership fee: USD15.00 per annum, USD40.00 for three years
Contact: committee co-chair:
   Professor Joel D Aberbach
   Director, Center for American Politics and Public Policy
   4250 Public Policy Building, Box 951484
   UCLA
   Los Angeles, CA 90095-1484
   USA
   tel: +1-310-206 3109
   email: aberbach@polisci.ucla.edu

RC28: Comparative federalism and federation / La fédération et le fédéralisme: analyse comparative
Background: recognised as study group in 1984; granted research committee status in 1987.
Objectives: promotes the pursuit of knowledge and research on the concept of federalism and the "federal idea", including the decentralisation of the delivery of public services, fiscal relationships, ethnic and cultural diversity, and the structure and functioning of federal and federative institutions.
Activities: exploration of intricate relationships within complex states; conferences.
Publications: book publication; close cooperation with editorial board of journal, *Publius*; planned directory of members and their qualifications which it is proposed will be circulated widely to governments and government agencies which may be interested in employing the expertise of research committee members; newsletter.
No of members: 51.
Membership fee: USD45.00 for three years
Contact: committee chair:
    Professor C Lloyd Brown-John
    Department of Political Science
    University of Windsor
    401 Sunset Avenue
    Windsor, Ontario N9B 3P4
    Canada
    tel: +1-519-253 4232
    fax: +1-519-973 7094
    email: lbj@uwindsor.ca

RC29: Psycho-politics / Psychologie politique
Background: recognised as study group in 1981; granted research committee status in 1987.
Objectives: promotes the use of psychology in understanding political phenomena. A variety of perspectives are encouraged, including those found in psychoanalytic psychology, personality theory and social psychology. The committee aims to keep people informed in various parts of the world on the kind of research that is being done in countries and regions other than their own. Members study governmental institutions and international relations, though the emphasis is on political behaviour.
Activities: conferences.
Publications: newsletter planned.
No of members: 50.

Membership fee: no membership fee is charged.
Contact: committee chair:
Professor Betty Glad
Department of Government and International Affairs
University of South Carolina
Columbia, SC 29208
USA
tel: +1-803-777 4544
fax: +1-803-777 8125
email: glad@gwm.sc.edu

RC31: Political philosophy / La philosophie politique

Background: recognised as study group in 1983; granted research committee status in 1988.
Objectives: promotes research and study in political philosophy. Examples of the subject area considered are conferences held by the research committee on "Markets and democracy" and on "Beyond nationalism; sovereignty, governance and compliance".
Activities: conferences.
Publications: contributions to *The International Review of Sociology* composed of committee members' papers; individual paper and book publication; online newsletter via RC31 online distribution list.
No of members: 175.
Membership fee: USD10.00 per annum
Contact: committee secretary-treasurer:
Professor Percy B Lehning
Political Theory and Public Policy
Faculty of Social Sciences
Erasmus University
PO Box 1738
3000 DR Rotterdam
Netherlands
tel: +31-10-408 2133
fax: +31-10-452 7842
email: lehning@fsw.eur.nl

RC32: Public policy analysis / Analyse des politiques publiques

Background: recognised as study group in 1982; granted research committee status in 1988.
Objectives: promotes the analysis of public policy, defined by Dye as "finding out what governments do, why they do it, and what difference does it make". The work of the group has the following foci: public policy

analysis as a field of political science; the role of policy analysis in government decision-making; the context and scope of policy research; policy research and governmental policy: the relationship between the policy analyst and policy maker, and the institutional consequences of policy choices. *Activities:* collaboration and networking; periodic conference and workshop meetings, information exchange. Members' interests comprise the major approaches to the study of public policy: quantitative, theoretical-historical, and applied.
Publications: newsletter, www (www.spea.indiana.edu/IPSA-RC32/).
No of members: 172.
Membership fee: no membership fee is charged.
Contact: committee chair:
    Professor Lois R Wise
    Faculty of Policy & Administration
    School of Public and Environmental Affairs
    Indiana University
    Bloomington, IN 47405-2100
    USA
    tel: +1-812-855 4944
    fax: +1-812-855 7802
    email: wisel@indiana.edu

RC33: The study of political science as a discipline / L'étude de science politique comme discipline
Background: recognised as study group in 1982; granted research committee status in 1989.
Objectives: promotes theoretical and research studies on the historiography and development of the discipline, either on its own or in conjunction with other IPSA research committees. The committee's approach is a comparative and eclectic one; it is intended to include the theoretical concerns of philosophers of social science, sociological and anthropological views of disciplinary origins and evolution, historical and institutional studies.
Activities: inter-congress workshops and conferences, its major current project, organised in conjunction with other research committees and the IPSA congress programme, involves the establishment of special panels at the Quebec congress to examine various topics on "Development in political science at the year 2000".
Publications: paper and book publication; Internet listserv; bibliographies and reviews of recent works on political science as a discipline; newsletter.
No of members: 60.
Membership fee: USD10.00 per annum or USD25.00 for the inter-entire inter-congress period, 2000–2003.

Contact: committee chair:
Professor Michael B Stein
Department of Political Science
McMaster University
Hamilton, Ontario
Canada L8S 4M4
tel: +1-905-525 9140 ext 23704
fax: +1-905-527 3071
email: steinm@mcmaster.ca

RC34: Comparative representation and electoral systems / La représenta-
tion comparatif et les systèmes électoraux
Background: recognised as study group in 1986; granted research committee status in 1989.
Objectives: focuses on the broad topics of electoral systems and representation. Elections are often viewed as the hallmark of democracy, and the
electoral system and the kind or representation that results from it are at
the heart of this process. Yet electoral systems come in many different
forms, varying in frequency, the office at stake, proportionality of representation, ballot form and so on. Moreover, the rise of many new democracies, along with major changes in the election systems of existing democracies (such as Italy, Japan and New Zealand), have made it very difficult for
anyone to maintain a degree of familiarity with electoral systems world-
wide.
Activities: informing research committee members of new developments
and new research related to those developments; teaching participants in
new democracies about the design and operation of electoral systems; conferences.
Publications: book publication; *ESRC International Membership Directory and*
Research Register; newsletter; the committee also maintains a website de-
tailing its ongoing activities.
No of members: 130.
Membership fee: USD20.00 for three years.
Contact: committee chair:
Professor John Fuh-sheng Hsieh
Department of Government & International Studies
University of South Carolina
Columbia, SC 29208
USA
tel: +1-803-777 5322
fax: +1-803-777 0568
email: hsieh@sc.edu

web site: www.sinica.edu.tw/~ljw/esrc.html

RC35: Technology and development / La technologie et le développement
Background: recognised as study group in 1981; granted research committee status in 1990.
Objectives: examines the complex relationship between technology and development in the context of the political and institutional process, using a comparative framework. Its specific objectives are to identify broad political, administrative and policy strategies related to technology transfer and environmentally sound sustainable development; to analyse policy options for dealing with global, transboundary, and domestic issues relating to technological changes and environmental challenges; to examine the ethical, cultural, legal, political, institutional, administrative, scientific and technological frameworks which underlie and shape the human dimension of global change; to foster a global network of political scientists and others to engage in research in the dynamics of human interactions with science and technology; and to provide a comparative perspective to such issues as sustainable development, managing the environment, technology transfer, global environmental facility, role of international aid agencies; impact of globalisation, and international conventions / agreements.
Activities: conferences, workshops, seminars.
Publications: paper and book publication; projects completed under research grants (eg grant to study industrial and commercial waste in Kanpur city, India).
No of members: 44.
Membership fee: no membership fee is charged.
Contact: committee chair:
    Professor OP Dwivedi
    Department of Political Science
    University of Guelph
    Guelph, Ontario N1G 2W1
    Canada
    tel: +1-519-824 4120 ext 8937
    fax: +1-519-827 9561
    email: odwivedi@uoguelph.ca

RC36: Political power / Le pouvoir politique
Background: recognised as study group in 1983; granted research committee status in 1991.
Objectives: focuses on five dimensions of political power: conceptual analysis, political power structures (the constitution of power), power in configurations / policy networks, forms and resources of power, and measur-

ing power. The impact of globalisation and internationalisation of political, economic and administrative phenomena for the nature of power is increasingly seen as a key research issue. Members represent many analytical perspectives and research traditions. While case study design is often employed, comparative research design is also an important element of the committee's research application.

Activities: conferences.

Publications: newsletter; journal contributions; conference proceedings publications and book publication by individual members.

No of members: 91.

Membership fee: no membership fee is charged.

Contact: committee chair:

  Professor Henri J M Goverde
  School of Public Affairs
  Department of Public Administration
  University of Nijmegen
  PO Box 9108
  6500 HK Nijmegen
  The Netherlands
  tel: +31-24-361 5870
  fax: +31-24-361 2379
  email: h.goverde@bw.kun.nl

RC37: Rethinking political development / Repenser le développement politique

Background: recognised as study group in 1983; granted research committee status in 1991.

Objectives: ranges from "rethinking political development" to implications of various national development experiences for theory construction. Instead of depending solely on universal validity claiming theoretical models, the committee looks to the growing knowledge of the complexities and actualities of historical legacies, cultures, visions of leaders, and internal diversity of different societies. While concentrating on political development, the research committee takes a multi-regional, multi-disciplinary approach to the general problems of development. The successes and failures of development are noted as an empirical backdrop to the analysis of the evolution of the concept of development, its strengths and weaknesses and the interaction of other forms of development with the political arena. Specific questions asked pertain to the concepts of "good governance", "social capital", and "civil society" and how they impact the notions of development.

Activities: conferences, symposia, student orientations.

Publications: publications; newsletter, *Rethinking Political Development.*
No of members: 150.
Membership fee: no membership fee is charged.
Contact: committee chair:
  Professor Brij B Khare
  FERP Professor
  Department of Political Science
  California State University
  San Bernardino, CA 92407
  USA
  tel: +1-909-880 5537
  fax: +1-909-880 7018
  email: bkhare@csusb.edu

RC38: Politics and business / Vie politique et entreprises

Background: recognised as study group in 1985; granted research committee status in 1991.
Objectives: encourages collaboration among scholars throughout the globe who are active in researching the interface between politics and business, in order to develop, promote and advance theoretical, comparative and empirical understanding of the study field.
Activities: conferences.
Publications: paper and book publication, newsletter '*Polibus*', journal, *Politics and Business*; discussion paper series; internet discussion list; web page; membership database; association with the Standing Group on European Level Interest Representation of the ECPR; subcommittees including Australasian, Canadian, American and Spanish-speaking chapters; paper and on-line newsletter.
No of members: 316 members in 37 countries.
Membership application: no membership fee.
Contact: committee chair:
  Professor Justin Greenwood
  Faculty of Management
  School of Public Administration and Law
  The Robert Gordon University
  Garthdee Road
  Aberdeen AB10 7QE
  UK
  tel: +44-1224-263 406
  fax: +44-1224-263 434
  email: j.greenwood@rgu.ac.uk
  http://www.rgu.ac.uk/schools/pal/resgroup/polibus2.htm.

RC39: Welfare states and developing societies / L'état providence et les pays en voie de développement

Background: recognised as study group in 1992 and research committee 1999.

Objectives: aims to promote research and discussion and scholarly interaction on specific welfare states on the one hand and comparative welfare states in a comprehensive framework on the other. It seeks to focus on developments in the sphere of theory and practice pertaining to social welfare policies. An important dimension of such probes is to see how far the experiences of matured welfare states can be useful for developing societies. It undertakes conceptual analyses of the welfare state phenomenon, welcomes both theoretical and empirical discourse and gathers interpretation of empirical data through the latest research modes and strategies and philosophical approaches. Specific areas of research include: comparative welfare states; welfare policy analyses; particular welfare states; crises in welfare states: political, social, and economic; future perspectives on welfare states.

Activities: conferences, seminars, colloquia, workshops.

Publications: newsletter; proposed directory of scholars specialising in welfare state studies.

No of members: 50.

Membership fee: a membership fee is proposed of USD10 from the year 2000.

Contact: group chair/convenor:
> Professor Madan M Sankhdher
> Department of Political Science
> University of Delhi
> 89 Vaishali
> Pitampura
> Delhi 110034
> India
> tel: +91-11-743 8528
> fax: +91-11 744 1284
> email: sankh@hotmail.com

RC40: New world orders? / Ordres nouveaux mondiaux?

Background: recognised as study group in 1994 and research committee in 1999.

Objectives: focuses on some neglected, interrelated areas of international relations/international political economy such as globalisations, regionalisms and internationalisation; encourages alternative, critical and radical approaches which are interdisciplinary and historical by a new generation

of scholars especially from the South. Factors analysed include civil societies, technologies, flexibilisation/feminisation, new coalitions, new security
issues and peace building, etc.

Activities: conferences, workshops/panels often organised with other compatible organisations/institutions.

Publications: newsletter; Ashgate Publishing Series on "The International
Political Economy of New regionalisms"; special issue of *Third World Quarterly* (20 (5), October 1999) on "New Regionalisms in the New Millennium"; and forthcoming special issue of *International Insights* in 2001 on
"Globalizations/Regionalisms/Development",

No of members: 50.

Membership fee: no membership fee is charged.

Contact: group chair:
Professor Timothy M Shaw
Centre for Foreign Policy Studies
Dalhousie University
Halifax, NS B3H 4H6
Canada
tel: +1-902-494 6630
fax: +1-902-494 3825
email: tim.shaw@dal.ca
http://www.dal.ca/~centre

RC41: Geopolitics / La géopolitique

Background: recognised as study group in 1995 and research committee
1999.

Objectives: promotes the study of geopolitics, a concept that today includes
those variables important for a country's foreign policy options, and which
cannot be changed by governmental policy in a short period of time. These
variables include, among others, a country's positioning in the international and regional systems, its relationship to the processes of globalisation, and its relative power resources along different dimensions (economic, political, military, cultural etc.). The research programme includes
case studies concerning the reciprocal relationship between geopolitical
influences and foreign policy behaviour, and contributions to theorising on
the broader relationship between geopolitics and political behaviour.

Activities: informal exchanges of papers and writings; panels at world congresses.

No of members: 50.

Membership fee: no membership fee is charged.

Contact: group chair:
Professor Robert J Lieber

Department of Government
Georgetown University
Washington, DC 20057-1034
USA
tel: +1-202-687 5920
fax: +1-202-338 1406
email: lieberr@georgetown.edu

RC42:   System integration of divided nations / Unification des nations partagées
Background: recognised as study group in 1996 and research committee in 1999.
Objectives: analyses national divisions and unification processes, an increasingly inseparable aspect of world politics as we understand it with a view to enhancing our understanding of the political dynamics of divided nations; exploring the ways and means of fostering system integration of divided nations; enriching our understanding of unification process from a comparative perspective; recasting the political reality of divided nations into a larger picture of national (or ethnic) integration and disintegration and to look into theoretical, empirical, and policy implications; and providing open fora for mutual interaction and communication among scholars of divided nations, as well as to serve as an effective vehicle to form a viable epistemic community.
Membership fee: not given.
Contact: group chair:
    Professor Hakjoon Kim
    Chairman, Board of Trustees
    Dankook University
    Office #206 Dankook Building
    Nonhyun-dong 97
    Kangnam-ku
    Seoul
    Korea
    tel: +82-2-3442 5350
    fax: +82-2-512 7240

RC43: Religion and politics / Religion et politique
Background: recognised as study group in 1986 and research committee in 1999.
Objectives: focuses on the topic of religions confronted with new or neoliberal economic policies, which are generally questioned by the different religions (Christian, Islam, Asian, particularly Indian). Utopias and messi-

anisms, religious as well as political, compared; and modes of access to authority in religious and political organisations have also been areas of ongoing recent study. The group's general goals target comparative study of religious and political organisations and the study of the intrinsic relationship between religions and political bodies.
Activities: conferences.
Publications: books, papers.
No of members: 40.
Membership fee: USD5 is charged at the world congress.
Contact: group chair:
  Professor Jean-Yves Calvez
  Department of Public Ethics
  35 bis rue de Sèvres
  75006 Paris
  France
  tel and fax: +33-1-4439 7518

RC44: *Military rule and democratisation in the third world / Gouvernement militaire et démocratisation dans le tiers monde*
Background: recognised as study group in 1988 and research committee in 1999.
Objectives: examines the processes, content and consequences of military interventions in the political systems of third world countries. Military interventions have been a characteristic feature of these countries over the last 30 years or so. In the mid 1980s there was general public revulsion against the culture of military rule, particularly in Latin America. All these developments created an intellectual sphere which necessitated research in order to examine these processes of democratisation and their consequences. The political economy of military regimes, crisis in civil military relations and the role of military in nascent democracies have also been incorporated as areas of research.
Activities: conferences.
Publications: books; newsletter.
No of members: 51.
Membership fee: USD10.00 per annum (optional).
Contact: group convenor:
  Dr Asha Gupta
  BQ-2, Shalimar Bagh
  Ring Road
  Delhi-110 052, India
  tel: +91-11-747 0575
  fax: +91-11-77 4104

RC45: *Quantitative international politics / La politique international: études quantitatives*

Background: recognised as study group in 1989 and research committee in 1999.

Objectives: explores theoretical and methodological aspects of interstate interaction and comparative politics. This committee seeks to advance the state of data-based knowledge, to enhance the distribution and use of existing datasets and to set up an international framework for improving the global dissemination of quantitative research in international and comparative politics.

Activities: designing, conducting and evaluating research using quantitative international and comparative data; conferences.

Publications: publications; newsletter.

No of members: 40.

Membership fee: no membership fee is charged.

Contact: group co-chair:

Professor Daniel S Geller
Department of Political Science
Deupree Hall 309
University of Mississippi
University, MS 38677
USA
tel: +1-662-915 7401
fax: +1-662-915 7808
email: psgeller@olemiss.edu

Professor Nils Petter Gleditsch
International Peace Research Institute
Fuglehauggata 11
N-0260 Oslo
Norway
tel: +1-47-22 54 7700
fax: +1-47-22 54 7701
email: npg@prio.no

RC46: *Global environmental change / Changement global de l'environnement*

Background: recognised as study group in 1992 and research committee in 1999.

Objectives: facilitates the exchange of ideas among political scientists and stimulates co-operative effort on global environmental change. Three major areas of research are covered: on inputs into the political system (public opinion, the study of mediating agents, and the study of how scientific findings influence policy decisions); outputs (how governments respond to environmental change, as shaped by the institutional context, and the values, beliefs, skills and interests which decision makers bring to a problem) and outcomes: the implementation of public policy, the impact on society and the impact of policy-induced change on the environment.

Activities: inventory of political science research directly relevant to the IHDP; conferences.

Membership fee: no membership fee is charged.

Contact: group chair:
Professor Matthijs Hisschemoller
Institute for Environmental Studies
Free University
De Boelelaan 1115
1081 HV Amsterdam
The Netherlands
tel: +31-20 444 9523
fax: +31-20 444 9553
email: matthijs.hisschemoller@vu.ivm.nl

RC47: Local-global relations / Relations globales-locales

Background: recognised as study group in 1995 and research committee in 1999.
Objectives: focuses on the emergence and shifts of new and old "localisms", neighbourhoods, local communities, ethnic and language identities, affinity groups, economic and political associations and their networks that create regions and impact on the incipient world system.
The theoretical context in which this group operates includes spatial and temporal relations, the development of increased complexity or integrated diversity that transcends traditional boundaries, the logics of regionalism, including those of political integration as well as classical concepts from territorial human organisation.
Activities: preparation of data sets; conferences.
No of members: current membership figure not given.
Membership fee: no membership fee is charged.
Contact: group chair:
Professor Henry Teune
Political Science Department
University of Pennsylvania
Stiteler Hall
Philadelphia, PA 19104-6215
USA
tel: +1-215-898 4209
fax: +1-215-573 2073
email: hteune@mail.sas.upenn.edu

RC48: Administrative culture / Culture administrative

Background: recognised as study group in 1995 and research committee in 1999.
Objectives: aims to evolve a new conceptual and analytical tool for the evaluation of the performance of an administrative system. It explores pos-

sibilities of making "administrative culture" as one of the evaluative criteria for purposes of evolving a conceptual framework for comparing administrative systems. It studies behavioural patterns, value structures and belief-systems of administrators and the impact of these variables in modifying and influencing administrative performance.

Activities: classification of administrative systems; seminars, conferences and research projects to study. Administrative cultures of different continents.

Publications: book publication; newsletter, journal *Administrative behaviour and administrative culture* (twice yearly).

No of members: 47.

Membership fee: USD10.00, no membership fee charged to members from South America, Africa (except South Africa), and Asia (except Japan and Israel).

Contact: group chair:
Professor R D Sharma
Institute of Policy Research & Analysis
Summer Resort
near Luxmi, Narayan Temple
Sanjauli - Shimla-171006
India
tel/fax: +99-177-241 245

RC49: Socialism, capitalism and democracy / Socialisme, capitalisme et démocratie

Background: recognised as study group in 1995 and research committee in 1999.

Objectives: aims to provide a forum for discussion and collective work among political scientists, with various subject matter specialisations, who are interested in critical discussion of theories which regard the capitalist system as an environment fundamentally hostile to democratic politics and which advocate the replacement of production to the fulfilment of human needs. Its interests include theoretical and conceptual discussion of possible democratic alternatives to capitalist economic systems; the analysis of existing political institutions and practices in capitalist systems, particularly with regard to their relation to the economic structure; study of political strategies to ameliorate basic social problems such as racism, sexism, poverty, environmental degradation, and war; and the political study of reform and revolutionary movements.

Activities: conferences.

Publications: publications; newsletter; the group also maintains online information on the chair's web page.

No of members: 69, plus an additional 120 affiliated individuals.
Membership fee: no membership fee is charged.
Contact: group chair:
  Professor John C Berg
  Department of Government
  Suffolk University
  Boston, MA 02114-4280
  USA
  tel: +1-617-573 8126
  fax: +1-617-367 4623
  email: jberg@world.std.com
  web: www.cas.suffolk.edu/berg/jberg.html

6 / NATIONAL POLITICAL SCIENCE ASSOCIATIONS

6.1 GENERAL INFORMATION

Since IPSA's foundation in 1949, national political science associations have constituted its core. Its founder members were, indeed, national associations: the American, Canadian, French and Indian political science associations.

Collective membership by national associations dominated IPSA in its earliest years. Thus, four more national associations joined in 1950 (Israel, Poland, Sweden and the United Kingdom), another four in 1951 (Austria, Belgium, Greece and Mexico), and six in 1952 (Brazil, Finland, Germany, Italy, Japan and Yugoslavia). By the end of the 1950s a further ten national associations had joined: Australia and the Netherlands (1954), Ceylon, Cuba and the Soviet Union (1955), Egypt and Norway (1956), Lebanon and Spain (1958), and Switzerland (1959).

Of course, not all of these associations survived as IPSA members (some, indeed, disappeared completely). Those associations whose membership was discontinued were nevertheless fewer in number than newly affiliating associations, with the result that IPSA's collective membership has been expanding steadily. By the end of 1999, 42 associations were collective members.

In terms of fees payable to IPSA, collective members are divided into a number of categories based on a measure of their relative wealth and capacity to pay (beginning in 1998, this has been based on the size of their relative contribution to the UNESCO budget and the number of members in the national association). Each collective member is represented on IPSA's central governing organ, the council, by one, two or three members. The council lays down broad policy guidelines for the association and elects the executive committee, which is charged with responsibility for the conduct of the affairs of IPSA between congresses.

The following is a list of all associations that are currently affiliated to IPSA as collective members, together with the number of representatives to which they are entitled on the IPSA council. The listing is by order of the country or region in question (associations in italics are inactive members).

African Association of Political Science	(2)
Argentine Association of Political Analysis-SAAP	(2)
Australasian Political Studies Association	(2)
Austrian Political Science Association	(1)
Association belge de science politique	(1)
Flemish Political Science Association	*(1)*
Brazilian Political Science Association	(2)
Bulgarian Political Science Association	*(1)*
Canadian Political Science Association	(3)
Croatian Political Science Association	(1)
Chilean Political Science Associations	(1)
Czech Political Science Association	(1)
Danish Association of Political Science	(1)
Finnish Political Science Association	(2)
Association française de science politique	(3)
German Political Science Association	(3)
Hellenic Political Science Association	(1)
Hungarian Political Science Association	(1)
Indian Political Science Association	*(3)*
Political Studies Association of Ireland	(1)
Israel Political Science Association	(2)
Italian Political Science Association	(2)
Japanese Political Science Association	(3)
Korean Political Science Association	(2)
Korean Association of Social Science	*(1)*
Lithuanian Political Science Association	(1)
Dutch Political Science Association	(2)
Norwegian Political Science Association	(2)
Polish Association of Political Science	(3)
Romanian Association of Political Science	(1)
Russian Association of Political Science	(3)
Slovak Political Science Association	(1)
Slovenian Political Science Association	(1)
South African Political Studies Association	(1)
Spanish Association of Political and Administrative Science	(1)
Swedish Political Science Association	(2)
Swiss Political Science Association	(2)
Chinese Association of Political Science (Taipei)	(1)
Turkish Political Science Association	(1)
Political Studies Association of the UK	(3)
American Political Science Association	(3)
Union Political Science Association of Yugoslavia	(1)

6.2 DIRECTORY OF NATIONAL ASSOCIATIONS

The following pages contain general information and contact details in respect of those national associations for which we have been able to obtain them. It should be noted that in the case of certain associations information has been carried over without correction year after year, and the details may now be out of date.

African Association of Political Science
Founded: 1973; affiliated to IPSA 1974.
Members: 1,360.
Publications: journal, newsletter, books:
* *African journal of political science* (AJPS)
* AAPS Occasional paper series
* AAPS newsletter
Biennial meeting: 19-22 June 2001 in Yaounde, Cameroon.
Other activities: public fora on current political issues, research networks, conferences
President: Professor Rwekaza Mukandala
Deputy President: Professor Ibrahim Nasr el Din
Administrative Secretary: Professor Kwame A Ninsin
Address: African Association of Political Science
    AAPS House
    19 Boodle Avenue, Eastlea
    PO Box MP111, Mount Pleasant
    Harare, Zimbabwe
    tel: +263-4-73-9 023/024/025
    fax: +263-4-73 0403
    email: aaps1@samara.co.zw

Argentine Association of Political Analysis — SAAP
Founded: 1983; an earlier association, founded in 1957, affiliated to IPSA in 1961.
Members: 490.
Publications: bulletin (2 issues per year):
* *Boletin SAAP*
Biennial meeting: 2001.
Other activities: interim meetings.
President: Professor Eugenio Kvarternik
General Secretary: Professor Ricardo Falcon
Treasurer: Professor Torcuato Sozio
Address: Argentine Association of Political Analysis
    Fundacion Simon Rodrigues

Castex 3217 Piso 1
C 1425 CDC - Buenos Aires, Argentina
tel: +54-11-4802 4538
fax: +54-11-4806 6019
email: saap@arnet.com.ar
http://usuarios.arnet.com.ar/saap

Australasian Political Studies Association
Founded: 1952 as the Australian Political Studies Association (changed to "Australasian" in 1966); affiliated to IPSA in 1954.
Members: 425.
Publications: a journal, directory and number of books:
• *Australian Journal of Political Science*
• Directory of Australian Political Scientists 1993/94
• Essay Writing and Style Guide
• Australian Theses in Political Science to 1990
President: Professor Andrew Parkin
Vice-president: Professor Stephanie Lawson
Secretary: Dr Tod Moore
Address: Australasian Political Studies Association
    Department of Political Science
    University of Melbourne
    Parkville, Victoria 3052, Australia
    email: tmoore2@metz.une.edu.au

Austrian Political Science Science Association
Founded: 1970; an earlier association affiliated to IPSA in 1951.
Members: 482.
Biennial meeting: 13 October 2000.
Publications: newsletter, review and journal:
• AUPSA newsletter (Rundbrief)
• Austrian journal of political scence (*Österreichische Zeitschrift für Politikwissenschaft*)
Chair: Professor Dr Ferdinand Karlhofer
General Secretary: Dr Peter Biegelbauer
Address: Austrian Political Science Association
    ÖGPW, Stumpergasse 56
    A-1060 Vienna, Austria
    tel: +43-1-59 991 166
    fax: +43-1-59 991 171
    email: hafner@ihs.ac.at
    http://www.oegpw.at/oegpw

Flemish Political Science Association
Founded: 1979, when the Belgian Institute of Political Science divided; the Belgian Institute had been founded in 1951 and had been an IPSA member since the same year.
Members: 450.
Publications: journal:
• *Res Publica*
President: Professor Helmut Gaus
Secretary: Mr P Janssens
Treasurer: Professor Y vanden Berghe
Address: Flemish Political Science Association
    Flemish Political Science Association
    Politologisch Instituut
    Adolf Baeyensstraat 192
    9040 Gent
    Belgium

Association Belge de Science Politique — Communauté Française de Belgique
Founded: 1996, replaced the Institut de Science politique which was founded in 1979, when the Belgian Institute of Political Science divided; the Institute had been founded in 1951 and had been an IPSA member since the same year.
Members: 150.
Annual meeting: Next meeting will be held in 2002.
Other activities: political scientists database; working groups; electronic mailing list ("information relay").
Chair: Professor Bérengère Marques-Pereira
Vice chair: Dr Marco Martiniello
Treasurer: Professor Benoît Rihoux
Secretary: Oliver Paye
Address: Association Belge de Science Politique — Communauté française
    de Belgique
    CP 124, Avenue F Roosevelt, 50
    B-1050 Bruxelles
    Belgium
    tel: +32-2-650 3383
    fax: +32-2-650 3521
    email: absp@ulb.ac.be or absp@spri.ucl.ac.be
    http://www.ulb.ac.be/soco/sciencespo/absp or
    www.absp.spri.ucl.ac.be

Brazilian Political Science Association
Founded: affiliated to IPSA 1952.
President: Lourdes Sola
Directors: Helgio Trindade, Marcus Andre Melo, Mario Brockmann
   Machado, Renato Boschi, Sonia Draibe
Executive Secretary: Renato Lessa
Assistant Secretary: Fabiano Guilherme M. Santos
Address: Associacao Brasileira de Ciencia Politica, ABCP
   Rua da Matriz 82, Botafogo 22260-100
   Rio de Janeiro RJ, Brazil
   tel: +55-21-537 8020
   fax: +55-21-286 7146
   email: rlessa@omega.lncc.br

Bulgarian Political Science Association
Founded: 1973; an earlier association had affiliated to IPSA in 1968.
Members: 72.
Publications: journal:
• Political Studies
President: Professor G Karasimeonov
Secretary: Professor Tanya Burudjieva
Address: Bulgarian Political Science Association
   Department of Political Science
   Sofia University, Sofia
   Bul Tsarigradsko Shosse 125, blok 4
   Bulgaria
   tel: +359-2-7115 1227
   fax: +359-2-70 5394

Canadian Political Science Association
Founded: 1913, as an multidisciplinary association; founder member of
IPSA in 1949; reconstituted 1968 as a purely political science association.
Members: 1,200.
Publications: journal, newsletter and books:
• *Canadian Journal of Political Science*
• Bulletin
• Directory of Political Scientists in Canada
Annual meeting: 29 July-1 August 2000.
Other activities: prizes (book, thesis).
President: Professor Thomas Pocklington
President–Elect: Professor Donald Savoie
Past–President: Professor Jane Jensen

Secretary-Treasurer: Dr Leslie Seidle
Executive Secretary: Michelle Hopkins
Address: Canadian Political Science Association/ Association canadienne de
    science politique
    204-260 rue Dalhousie Street, Ottawa
    Ontario, Canada K1N 7EA
    tel: +1-613-562 1202
    fax: +1-613-241 0019
    email: cpsa@csse.ca
    http://www.uottawa.ca/associations/cpsa-acsp

Chilean Political Science Association
President: Alfredo Joignant Rondón
Vice-president: Ampara Menèndez-Carrión
Secretary General and Treasurer: Tomàs Chuaqui
Address: Chilean Political Science Association
    Maria Guerrero 940, Providencia
    Santiago 664 0372, Chile
    tel: +56-2- 235 6664
    fax: +56-2-264 2500
    email: tchuaqui@puc.cl

Chinese Association of Political Science
Founded: reconstituted in 1980.
Members: 1,025.
President: Jiang Liu
Secretary General: Zhang Zhi-Rong
Address: Chinese Association of Political Science
    Chinese Academy of Social Sciences
    15 Shatan Beijie
    Beijing 100720, China

Croatian Political Science Association
Founded: 1966; affiliated to IPSA 1992.
Members: 100.
Publications: planning to start newsletter, journal:
• *Politicka misao* (Political Thought)
Annual meeting: October 2001.
Other activities: conferences, public lectures, book promotions.
President: Dr Edravko Petak
Secretary: Dr Goran Cular
Address: Croatian Political Science Association
    Lepušieva 6, HR 10000 Zagreb, Croatia

tel: +385-1-455 8022
fax: +385-1-465 5316
email: zdravko.petak@fpzg.hr, goran.cular@frzg.hr

Czech Political Science Association
Founded: 1964; the Czechoslovak association has been affiliated to IPSA since 1964.
Members: 200.
Publications: conference papers, review:
• *Politologická Revue*
Other actvities: conferences and monthly public discussions.
President: Professor Jan Škaloud
Vice President: Dr Aleš Gerloch
Secretary: Dr Vladimír Prorok
Address: Czech Political Science Association
    Katedra politologie, University of Economics
    Nam. W Churchilla 4
    130 67 Praha 3, Czech Republic
    tel: +42-2-2409 5204
    fax: +42-2-2422 0657
    email: skaloud@vse.cz

Danish Association of Political Science
Founded: 1960; affiliated to IPSA 1961.
Members: 350.
Publications: newsletter.
Other activities: "brush-up" seminars.
Annual meeting: October 2001.
President: Professor Jacob Torfing
Secretary: Dr Roger Buch Jensen
Address: Danish Association of Political Science
    att: Jacob Torfing
    Department of Social Sciences, Roskilde University
    PO Box 260, DK-4000 Roskilde, Denmark
    tel: +45-46-742 185
    fax: +45-46-743 080
    email: jtor@ruc.dk

Finnish Political Science Association
Founded: 1935; affiliated to IPSA 1952.
Members: 550.
Publications: review:
• *Politikka*

Annual meeting: 11-12 January 2001, Helsinki.
Other activities: seminars.
President: Professor Jukka Paastela
Secretary: Mr Timo Moilanen
Address: Finnish Political Science Association
   Department of Political Science
   PO Box 54, University of Helsinki
   FIN-00014 Helsinki, Finland
   tel: +358-9-191 8856
   fax: +358-9-191 8832
   email: Timo.Moilanen@Helsinki.FI
   http://www.helsinki.fi/jarj/vty

Association française de science politique
Founded: 1949; founder member of IPSA in that year.
Members: 1,030.
Publications: review:
• *Revue française de science politique*
Triennial meeting: 2002.
Other activities: working groups, meetings.
President: Professor Jean Leca
Secretary General: Professor Pierre Muller
Treasurer: Professor Jean-Luc Domenach
Address: Association française de science politique
   54 Boulevard Raspail
   75006 Paris, France
   tel: +33-1-4954 2136
   fax: +33-1-4954 2161
   email: afsp@msh-paris.fr

German Political Science Association
Founded: 1951; affiliated to IPSA 1952.
Members: 1,300.
Publications: journal:
• *Politische Vierteljahresschrift* (PVS)
Annual meeting: 2003.
President: Professor Dr Christine Landfried
Secretary General: Felix W Wurm, Dipl Soz Wiss, MA
Address: German Political Science Association
   Deutsche Vereinigung für Politische Wissenschaft (DVPW)
   c/o Universitaet Osnabrueck
   FB 1 – Sozialwissenschaften

D-49069 Osnabruek, Germany
tel: +49-541-969 6264
fax: +49-541-969 6266
email: dvpw@uos.de
http:/www.dvpw.de

Hellenic Political Science Association
Founded: 1957; and earlier association affiliated to IPSA in 1951.
Members: 265.
Publications: review and books:
- Greek Political Science Review (biannual)
- Elections and Parties in the 1980s
- Social and Political Forces in Greece
- The 1981 Elections
- Society and politics: Facets of the Third Hellenic Republic, 1976-1994
- Prefectual Self-government. Prospects and Perspectives
- The Dictatorship of 1967-1974. Political Practice – Ideological Discourse Resistance

Other activities: lectures, seminars, conferences, workshops.
Annual meeting: June 2001.
President: Dimitris Charalambis
Vice-president: Elias Nikolakopoulos
Address: Hellenic Political Science Association
    19 Omirou St, 10672 Athens, Greece
    tel/fax: +30-1-361 4298
    email: hpsagr@cc.uoa.gr

Hungarian Political Science Association
Founded: 1982; an earlier association affiliated to IPSA in 1968.
Members: 468.
Publications: journal:
- Politikatudomanyi Szemle

Other activities: István Bibó prize, regional cooperation of central European associations.
President: Dr Bayer József
Secretary General: Dr Navracsics Tibor
Address: Hungarian Political Science Association
    1014 Budapest, Országház u 30
    BoxL H-1399 Budapest Pf 694/115, Hungary
    tel: +36-1-224 6724
    fax: +36-1-224 6727
    email: mptt@mtapti.pu

Indian Political Science Association

Founded: 1935; founder member of IPSA in 1949.
Members: 1,600.
Publications: journal and newsletter:
* *Indian Journal of Political Science*

Other activities: seminars and workshops.
President: Professor Hoshiar Singh
General Secretary and Treasurer: Professor GK Prasad
Address: Indian Political Science Association
    Department of Politics and Public Administration
    University of Madras, Chennai - 600005, India
    tel: +91-44-536 2244
    email: gkp@md3.vsnl.net.in

Political Studies Association of Ireland

Founded: 1982; affiliated to IPSA 1994.
Members: 247.
Publications: bulletin, journal and several books:
* PSAI Bulletin
* *Irish Political Studies* (yearbook)
* *How Ireland voted, 1987* [1989, 1992, 1997, etc]
* *Politics in the Republic of Ireland*
* Political Science in Ireland

Annual meeting: 13-15 October 2000, Cork
Other activities: conferences, seminars, meetings.
President: Dr Yvonne Galligan
Vice-president: Dr Paul Mitchell
Secretary: Dr Gary Murphy
Treasurer: Dr Emmet O'Connor
Address: Political Studies Association of Ireland
    DCU Business School, Dublin City University
    Dublin 9, Ireland
    tel: +353-1-704 5265
    fax: +353-1-704 5446
    email: Gary.Murphy@dcu.ie
    http://www.kerna.ie/psai/

Israel Political Science Association

Founded: affiliated to IPSA 1950.
Members: 250.
Publications:
* *State Government and International Relations*

Other activities: study groups, professional meetings.
President: Professor Gideon Doron
Address: Israel Political Science Association
Department of Political Science, Tel Aviv University
PO Box 39040, Tel Aviv 69978, Israel

Italian Political Science Association
Founded: 1975; an earlier association affiliated to IPSA in 1952.
Annual meeting: not given.
Members: 220.
President: Professor Giorgio Freddi
Secretary General: Dr Giliberto Capano
Address: Italian Political Science Association
Dipartmento di Organizzazione e Sistema Politico
Strada Maggiore 45, 40125 Bologna, Italia
tel: +39-543-45 0221
fax: +39-543-45 0219
email: gcapano@spfo.unibo.it

Japanese Political Science Association
Founded: 1948; affiliated to IPSA 1952.
Members: 1,278.
Publications: annual:
• *'Nenpo Seijigaku'* The Annual of the JPSA
Other activities: promotion, exchange and communication of information among members and with foreign political science associations.
President: Professor Takeshi Sasaki
Secretary General: Professor Yasuo Baba
Address: Japanese Political Science Association
The University of Tokyo, Faculty of Law
Hongo 7-3-1, Bunkyo-ku
Tokyo 113, Japan
tel: +81-3-3812 2111
fax: +81-3-3816 7375

Korean Political Science Association
Founded: 1953; affiliated to IPSA 1967.
Members: 2000.
Publications: a review and a newsletter:
• *The Korean Political Science Review*
• KPSA newsletter
Annual meeting: first week in December (Thursday-Saturday).

Other activities: conferences and seminars on contemporary issues ten times yearly.
President: Professor Hak Joon Kim (president, University of Inchon)
President-Elect: Professor Young Rae Kim
Address: The Korean Political Science Association
Sajo B/D, 1001, Deachi-Dong
Kangnam-Gu, Seoul, 135-280, Korea
tel: +82-2-3452 9555
fax: +82-2-3452 9557
email: kpsa@chollian.net

Korean Association of Social Scientists
Founded: 1979, affiliated to IPSA 1994.
Members: 1,465.
Publications: newsletter; aids publication of journals and books by member institutes.
Other activities: member of Federation of World Future Studies (WFSF) and of the International Federation of Social Science Organisations (IFSSO).
Secretary-General: Professor Kim Myong-u
Address: Korean Association of Social Scientists
PO Box 128, Pyongyang, DPR of Korea
tel: +85-02-381 4160
fax: +85-02-381 4512

Lithuanian Political Science Association
Founded: 1991, affiliated to IPSA 1994.
Members: 86.
Publications: journals:
* *Politologija*
* Newsletter of LPSA
Annual meeting: 23 November 2001.
President: Dr Gediminas Vitkus
Secretary General: Dr Algimantas Jankauskas
Address: Lithuanian Political Science Association
Institute of International Relations and Political Science
Didlaukio 47-205, Vilnius LT-2057, Lithuania
tel: +370-2-700 089
fax: +370-2-700 779
email: tspmi@tspmi.vu.lt
web page: www.lpasoc.lt

Mexican Political Science Association
President: Enrique Gonzalez Pedrero

Secretary General: Roberto Solcedo Aquino
Address: Mexican Political Science Association
  Lomas Quebradas 145-3, San Jeronimo Lidice
  10200-Magdalena Contreras, Mexico, DF, Mexico

Dutch Political Science Association
*Founded:*1966; an earlier association, founded in 1950; affiliated to IPSA in 1954.
Members: 350.
Publications: journal:
- *Acta politica*
Annual meeting: 14-15 June 2001.
Chair: Professor RH Lieshout
Secretary: Dr Bob Reinalda
Address: Nederlandse Kring voor Wetenschap de Politick — Dutch Political Science Association
  School voor Bestuurswetenschappen
  Katholieke Universiteit Nijmegen, PO Box 9108
  6500 HK Nijmegen, The Netherlands
  tel: +31-24-361 3075
  fax: +31-24-361 2379
  nkwp@politicologie.nl
  http://www.politicologie.nl

Nepalese Political Science Association
President: Professor Tribhuwan Nath Jaiswal
Vice-president: Dr Sharada Bahadur Singh
Geneneral secretary: Dr Pushpa Bhusal
Address: PO Box 6419
  Kathmandu, Nepal
  tel: +977-412 994

New Zealand Political Studies Asssociation
Founded: 1974.
Publications: journal and newsletter:
- *Political Science*
Annual meeting: not given.
Chair: Nigel Roberts
Secretary: Patrick Moloney
Address: New Zealand Political Studies Association
  Department of Politics, Victoria University
  Private Bag, Wellington, New Zealand
  tel: +64-4-471 5351

fax: +64-4-96 5414

Nigerian Political Science Association
President: Claud Ake
Address: Nigerian Political Science Association
c/o School of Political Sciences
University of Port Harcourt
PMB 53232A Port Harcourt
Nigeria

Norwegian Political Science Association
Founded: affiliated to IPSA 1956.
Members: 500.
Annual meeting: 10 May 2001.
Publications: journal and newsletter:
*   *Norsk statsvetenskapelig tidsskrift*
*   News from the NPSA
President: Professor Ann Lise Fimreite
Treasurer: Mr Roar Kristiansen
Address: Norwegian Political Science Association
Department of Comparative Politics
University of Bergen
Christiesgate 15
N-0313 Bergen
Norway
tel: +47-55-582 235
fax: +47-55-589 425
email: anne.fimreite@nsd.uib.no
www.los.uib.no/nsf

Pakistan Political Science Association
Founded: 1950.
Members: 300.
Publications: journal:
*   *Pakistan Political Science Review*
President: Arshad Syed Karim
Secretary: Iqbal Qureshi
Address: Pakistan Political Science Association
Department of Political Science, University of Karachi
Karachi, Pakistan

Philippine Political Science Association
Publications: journal:

- *Philippine Political Science Journal*
President: Carmencita T Aguilar
Secretary: Olivia C Caoili
Address: Philippine Political Science Association
c/o Philippine Social Science Center
UP, PO Box 205, Diliman, Quezon City 3004, Philippines

Polish Association of Political Science
Founded: affiliated to IPSA 1950.
Members: 200.
Publications: books:
- Polish Yearbook of Political Science
- Culture, Sociology and Politics
President: Professor Marian Edward Halizak
Address: Polish Association of Political Science
Polna 18/20, 00-625 Warsaw, Poland
tel: +48-22-25 5221
fax: +48-22-25 2146

Romanian Association of Political Science
Founded: 1968; affiliated to IPSA 1968.
Members: 188.
Publications: in preparation.
President: Professor Ovidiu Trasnea
Address: Romanian Association of Political Science
Academia Romana, Calea Victoriei 125-71 102
Bucuresti, Romania
tel: +40-1-610 2328
fax: +40-1-312 2535

Russian Political Science Association
Founded: 1960 as the Soviet Political Science Association; reconstituted 1991 as the Russian Political Science Association; an association has been affiliated to IPSA since 1955.
Members: 300.
President: Academician Professor Anatoly Dmitriev
First Vice President: Professor William Smirnov
Address: Russian Political Science Asociation
Russian Academy of Science, Znamenka str. 10
Moscow 119841, Russia
tel: +7-095-291 8789
fax: +7-095-291 8754

Slovak Political Science Association
Founded: 1990, affiliated to IPSA 1994.
Members: 150.
Annual meeting: October 2000.
Publications: journal, occasional papers and books:
• Slovakia: Problems of democratic consolidation
• Slovakia 1998-1999. A global report on the state of Society
• Success of failure? Ten years after
• Slovakia 1998-1999. A global report on the state of society
• The 1998 parliamentary elections and elections and democratic rebirth in Slovakia
Other activities: meetings, seminars, conferences, panel discussions, workshops, joint research projects with other institutions.
Chairperson: Dr Dagmar Horna
Secretary General: Dr Grigoriy Meseznikov
Address: Slovak Political Science Association
    Department of Political Science, Comenius University
    Gondova 2, 818 01 Bratislava, Slovak Republic
    fax: +421-7-52923640
    email: Dagmar.Horna@fphil.uniba.sk

Slovenian Political Science Association
Founded: 1968, affiliated to IPSA 1992.
Members: 220.
Publications: journal, proceedings of SLOPSA annual conferences from 1989 on, in Sovene with English summaries; publications of other conference proceedings; books:
• Civil society, political society, democracy
• Conflicts and consensus: pluralism and neocorporativism in new and old democracies at the region
• Consolidation of democracy in Central Europe
Annual meeting: First weekend in June 2001, Hotel Metropol, Portorose.
Other activities: scientific conferences, discussions on recent publications, sponsoring political research, bilateral, regional and other international cooperation.
Secretary General: Miro Hacek
Address: Slovensko politolosko drustvo
    Slovenian Political Science Asociation, Faculty of Social Sciences
    Kardeljeva ploscad 5, 1000 Ljubljana, Slovenia
    tel: +386-1-580 5175
    fax: +386-1-580 5101
    email: miro.hacek@uni-lj.si; drago.zajc@uni-lj.si

South African Political Studies Association
Founded: 1973, affiliated to IPSA 1995.
Members: 186.
Publications: journal:
• *Politikon*
Other activities: research colloquium and conference in annual rotation.
President: Professor Albert Venter
Secretary-General: Mr Anthoni van Nieuwkerk
Address: South African Political Studies Association
   PO Box 1041, 1710 Florida, South Africa
   tel: +27-11-717 3927
   fax: +27-11-717 3695
   email vannieuwkerk.a@pdm.wits.ac.za
   http://www.h-net.msu.edu/~sapsa

Spanish Association of Political and Administrative Science
*Founded:*1993; an earlier association affiliated to IPSA in 1958.
Members: 253.
Publications::
• Libro de Programa y resúmenes del I Congreso (II Congreso and III Congresso)
• *Revista Español de Ciencia Política y de la Administración*
• Memoria del Area de Ciencia Política y de la Administración, Universidad del País Vasco
• Conferencia de apertura II Congreso: Democracy and Administration: the varieties of administrative reform (B Guy Peters).
President: Professor Julián Santamaría Ossorio
Vice-presidents: Professor Josep M Vallés
   Professor Francisco J Llera
Secretary General: Professor María Teresa Gallego
Executive Secretary: Professor Esther de Campo
Address: Spanish Association of Political and Administrative Science
   Alfonso XII, 18-5, 28014 Madrid, Spain
   tel: +34-1-523 2741
   fax: +34-1-523 2741
   email: aecpa@iesam.csic.es

Swedish Political Science Association
Founded: 1970, affiliated to IPSA 1950.
Members: 264.
Publications: quarterly newsletter.
President: Associate Professor Sverker Gustavsson

Secretary: Dr Mikael Axberg
Address: Swedish Political Science Association
   Department of Government, Uppsala University
   Box 514, S-751 20 Uppsala, Sweden
   tel: +46-18-471 3437
   fax: +46-18-471 3409
   email: spsa@statsvet.uu.se

Swiss Political Science Association
Founded: 1950; affiliated to IPSA 1959.
Members: 1,000.
Publications: newsletter, journal, yearbook, books:
* *Revue Suisse de Science Politique*
* *Année Politique Suisse*
* *Handbook of the Swiss Political System,* Vol 1, Foundations, 1983; Vol 2, Structures and Processes, 1984; Vol 3, Federalism, 1986; Vol 4, Policy Areas, 1993..

Other activities: working groups, contributes to varous research programmes funded by the Swiss National Research Fund.
President: Professor Peter Knoepfel
Address: Swiss Political Science Association
   IDHEAP, Route de la Maladière, 21,
   1022 Chavannes-près-Renens, Switzerland
   tel: +41-21-694 0600
   fax: +41-21-694 0609
   email: peter.knoepfel@idheap.unil.ch

Chinese Association of Political Science (Taipei)
Founded: 1932; affiliated to IPSA 1989.
Members: 350.
Publications: bi-annual review:
* *Chinese Political Science Review*

Other activities: conference twice yearly, meeting on comtemporary issues six times yearly.
President: Professor Song Shi Yuan
Secretary General: Professor John Fuh-sheng Hsieh
Address: Chinese Association of Political Science (Taipei)
   PO Box 1-52, Mucha, Taipei, Taiwan
   tel/fax: +886-2-8661 1453
   email: jhsieh@cc.nccu.edu.tw

Political Science Association of Thailand
President: Professor Amara Raksasataya

Address: Political Science Association of Thailand
The National Institute of Development Administration
Bangkapi, Bangkok 10240, Thailand

Turkish Political Science Association
Founded: affiliated to IPSA 1964.
Members: 120.
President: Professor Ergun Özbudun
Address: Turkish Political Science Association
Ahmet Rasim Sokak 27, Cankaya — Ankara, Turkey
tel: +90-312-438 6744
fax: +90-312-440 9106

Political Studies Association of the UK
Founded: 1950; affiliated to IPSA 1950.
Members: 1,200.
Publications: newsletter, journals:
• *Political studies*
• *British journal of politics and international relations*
• *Politics*
• PSA News
• PSA Directory
• PSA media register
• PSA survey of the profession
Annual meeting: not given.
Other activities: conferences, monitoring government policy in higher education, administration of book prize, dissertation prize, teaching prize.
Chair: Professor RAW Rhodes
Honorary secretary: Dr Paul Carmichael
Address: Political Studies Association of the UK
Department of Politics
University of Newcastle
Newcastle-upon-Tyne
NE1 7RU, UK
tel: +44-191-222 8823
fax: +44-191-222 5069
email: R.A.W.Rhodes@newcastle.ac.uk
http://www.lgu.ac.uk/psa/psa.html

American Political Science Association
Founded: 1903.
Members: 13,300 individuals, 2,700 institutions.
Publications: newsletter, journals, directories, syllabi, numerous books:

- *PS: Political Science and Politics*
- *American Political Science Review*
- Personnel Services newsletter

Annual meeting: 30 August – 2 September 2001, San Francisco.

Other activities: standing committees, award committees, sections organised around common scholarly and professional interests, departmental services programme.

President: Professor Robert Jervis
President-Elect: Professor Robert Putnam
Secretary: Professor Judith Stiehm
Treasurer: Professor James Stimson
Executive Director: Dr Catherine E Rudder
Address: American Political Science Association
    1527 New Hampshire Ave NW
    Washington DC 20036, USA
    tel: +1-202-483 2512
    fax: +1-202-483 2657
    email: apsa@apsanet.org
    http://www.apsanet.org

Association of Political Science of Uzbekistan

President: Professor Kadir Z Alimov
Address: Association of Political Science of Uzbekistan
    Lahuty Str 6, f 27, Tashkent, Uzbekistan 700015
    tel: +7-3712-56 6795
    fax: +7-3712-41 5453

Venezuelan Political Science Association

Founded: 1974
Address: Venezuelan Political Science Association
    Avds 7 No 81.11, apartado 3611, Maracaibo 4001-A, Venezuela

Yugoslav Political Science Association

affiliated to IPSA 1954
President: Professor Vucina Vasovic
Address: Yugoslav Political Science Association
    Proletarskih Brigade, 74, 11000 Beograd, Yugoslavia
    tel/fax: +381 11 471 911

7 / POLITICAL SCIENCE DEPARTMENTS

7.1 OVERVIEW

This chapter provides a listing of political science departments worldwide. The data have been compiled from a wide range of sources, and are necessarily variable in quality from one part of the world to another. The reality is that North America is already very well served by APSA's outstanding guide, *Graduate faculty and programs in political science* (various years; see www.apsanet.org). For Europe, the ECPR's *Handbook of West European political science* (1995) and *Handbook of Central and East European political science* (1994) are invaluable, and there is an on-line listing of ECPR member institutions (see www.essex.ac.uk/ecpr/member/ecprmemb.htm). For other parts of the world we have had to rely on personal contacts, and the variable quality of the outcome (in terms of the inclusion of institutions that might be excluded were more information available, the omission of institutions that should rightly be listed, and simple inaccuracies in coordinates) is obvious in the list below.

Furthermore, our own inclusion criteria have varied. Because of the very high quality of information that is readily available in respect of the United States, there is a case for altogether omitting US universities. This would appear peculiar in a global listing, so we have compromised: we have confined this listing only to departments that offer a doctoral programme (we thus include only 131 US departments, omitting 192 others that form part of the APSA list). There is a case for a similar selection in respect of Europe, but the information available to us did not permit us to introduce a filter of this kind. It must be stressed, then, that the listing below excludes (either deliberately or otherwise) a number of important political science departments, while including others on which we have little qualitative information.

Notwithstanding the poor quality of our data, it is instructive to make some general remarks about the nature of the institutions covered. The formal name can sometimes be revealing, but we must stress that "political science" carries many different meanings around the world. Table 7.1 reports the formal name of the subject in the various departments.

Table 7.1: Formal name of discipline in institutions teaching political science

Continent	political science	political science and other	other	total
Africa	74	11	8	93
America, North	164	10	4	178
America, South	38	30	18	86
Asia	227	70	32	329
Europe, C and E	32	8	2	42
Europe, West	178	40	60	278
Oceania	25	1	1	27
Total	738	170	125	1,033
(excluding US institutions)	160	20	12	192

Note: "political science" includes related words such as "politics" and "government"; "political science and other" refers to a range of subject combinations that include political science.

Most department names (750) incorporate the expression "political science" in the singular or the plural, either as their formal English name or through translation that could yield no other result. A much smaller number (76) describe themselves as departments of "politics"; others use the designation "government" (23), "political studies" (18), "politology" (3, though the number of departments bearing a name of this kind but translating it as "political science" is probably much greater), or "political sociology" (2).

In terms of their status, the institutions were typically departments (633 in all); others were described as "area", "division" or "programme" (35), as institutes or centres (30), or, in a large number of cases, as faculties, schools or colleges (290). The remaining 45 institutions fell into other categories or were unclassifiable.

7.2 ASSOCIATE MEMBERS OF IPSA

Many of the institutions included in the listing below have a special relationship with IPSA — they are associate members of the association. Like IPSA's other categories of membership, associate members are concentrated heavily in Europe and North America. The institutions themselves are listed here; further details on many of them will be found in section 7.3.

1. Africa
South Africa, 1
University of South Africa
Total: 1

2. Ameria, North
Canada, 11
Carleton University
Department of Foreign Affairs
McMaster University
Queen's University
Simon Fraser University
Societé Québecoise de Science Politique
Université Laval
University of British Columbia
University of Calgary
University of Toronto
York University
Jamaica, 1
University of West Indies
USA, 14
Alma College
Central Washington University
Harvard University
Iowa State University
Northwestern University
Southwest Texas State University
Stanford University
Tulane University
University of Bridgeport
University of California
University of Missouri
US Army War College
Utah State University
Yale University
Total: 26

3. Asia
India, 1
University of Bombay
Israel, 1
Bar-Ilan University
Japan, 1
Keio University
Korea, 1
Sejong Institute

Malaysia, 1
Utara Malaysia University
Taiwan, 1
National Chung Hsing University
Thailand, 2
Chulalongkorn University
Thammasat University
Total: 8

5. Europe
Belgium, 1
Centre de Recherche, Brussels
Czech Republic, 1
Czech Academy of Sciences
Finland, 3
Åbo Akademi
University of Tampere
University of Turku
France, 4
Fondation nationale de science politique, Paris
IEP de Bordeaux
Université de Grenoble
Université de Lyon 2
Germany, 9
Friedrich-Ebert-Stiftung
Institut für Politische Wissenschaft, Köln
Konrad-Adenauer-Stiftung e.V.
Universität Hamburg
Universität Heidelberg
Universität Kiel
Universität Köln
Universität Münster
Universität Mannheim
Iceland, 1
University of Iceland
Italy, 1
Biblioteca Solari
Lithuania, 1
Klaipeda University Library
Netherlands, 1
University of Leiden
Norway, 7
Institute for Social Research
Lillehammer College

LOS Centre
Norwegian Institute of Human
Rights
Norwegian School of Management
University of Oslo
University of Trondheim
Sweden, 2
Institute for Democracy & Electoral
Assistance
University of Umeå
Switzerland, 4
Institute Universitaire, Geneva
Université de Genève
Université de Lausanne
Zentralbibliothek Zurich
United Kingdom, 7

British Library
Institute of Development Studies,
Sussex
London School of Economics
University College of Wales
University of Manchester
University of Southampton
University of Strathclyde
Total: 42
6. Oceania
Australia, 1
National Library of Australia
Total: 1
Grand Total: 78

7.3 DIRECTORY OF DEPARTMENTS

In the listing that follows, we have tried to include, in the case of each institution, the name and coordinates, including telephone, fax, email and web addresses where available. Unfortunately, it quickly became clear that even establishing names was problematic: our sources of information sometimes conflicted, or were vague.

In some cases, what is described as a department of political science may in reality function under a different name. Postal addresses are sometimes incomplete. Telephone and fax numbers are in some cases those of central university administrations. By contrast, email addresses are sometimes those of individuals — perhaps those who are currently acting as department heads. We have attempted in all cases to provide generic information (i.e. relating precisely to the political science area), but where this proved impossible we felt that partial information was better than none. Web addresses reported here need to be interpreted carefully; because of their length and complexity, many of them have been broken at an inappropriate point by our typesetting programme.

Algeria

Institute of Political Science
University of Algiers, 2 rue Did-
douche Mourad, Algiers, Algeria
Institute of Social Sciences
Université de Annaba, BP 12 El
Hadjar, Annaba, Algeria
Institute of Social Sciences
Université de Constantine, Route
d'Ain El Bey, Constantine, Algeria

Benin

*Faculté des Sciences Juridiques,
Economiques et Politiques*
Université Nationale du Benin, BP
526, Cotonou, Benin
tel: +229-360 074, fax: +229-300 028
email: rntia@bj.refer.org
http://www.refer.fr/benin_ct/edu
/univ-be/univ-be.htm

Botswana

*Department of Political and Admin-
istrative Studies*
University of Botswna, P Bag 00705,
Gaborone, Botswana
http://www.ub.bw

Burkina Faso

Faculty of Law and Political Sciences
University of Ougadougou, BP
7021, Ouagadougou 03, Burkina
Faso
tel: +226-307 065, fax: +226-307 242
email:
kourita.sandwidi@bf.refer.org
http://www.refer.fr/faso_ct/edu/s
up/univ/acceuil.htm

Burundi

Département des Sciences Politiques
Université du Burundi, BP 5161,
Bujumbura, Burundi

Cameroon

Département de Science Politique
Université du Buea, PO Box 63,
Buea, South West Province, Camer-
oon
tel: +237-322 134, fax: +237-322 272
*Faculté des Sciences Juridiques et
Politiques*
Université du Ngaoundere, BP 454,
Ngaoundere, Cameroon
tel: +237-251 245, fax: +237-252 573
*Faculté des Sciences Juridiques et
Politiques*
Université de Douala, BP 4982,
Douala, Cameroon
tel: +237-425 369, fax: +237-420 050
http://www.uninet.cm/ed_sup/Ex
ternal/universities/douala/frame.
html
*Faculté des Sciences Juridiques et
Politiques*
Université de Dschang, BP 66,
Dschang, Cameroon
tel: +237-451 267, fax: +237-451 202
http://www.uninet.cm/ed_sup/Ex
ternal/universities/dschang/frame
.html
*Faculté des Sciences Juridiques et
Politiques*
Université de Yaounde II, BP 7759,
Yaounde, Cameroon
tel: +237-200 334, fax: +237-222 983
http://www.uninet.cm/ed_sup/Ex
ternal/universities/soa/frame.html

Congo (Democratic Republic)

*Faculty of Social, Administrative,
and Political Sciences*
University of Kisangani, BP 2012,
Kisangani, Haut Zaire, Congo
tel: +242-12-211 335
*Faculty of Social, Political and Ad-
ministrative Sciences*
University of Lubumbashi, BP 1825,
Lubumbashi, Shaba, Congo
tel: +242-225 403, fax: +242-32-676
8099

Egypt

Department of Political Science
Alexandria University, 22 El-Geish
Avenue, El-Shatby, Alexandria,
Egypt
email: msherbiny@igsrnet.net
http://www.igsrnet.net

Department of Political Science
Ain Shams University, Kasr-El-
Zaafaran, Abbsiya, Cairo, Egypt
email: postmaster@shams.eun.eg
http://www.frcu.eun.eg/www/un
iversities/html/shams.html

Department of Political Science
American University in Cairo, PO
Box 2511, Cairo, Egypt
tel: +20-2-954 2964, fax: +20-2-355
7565
email: webley@aucegypt.edu
http://auc-inf.org/www/main.
html

Department of Political Science
Assiut University, Assiut, Egypt
email: sup@aun.eun.eg
http://www.aun.eun.eg/

Department of Political Science
Cairo University, Orman, Giza,
Cairo, Egypt
tel: +20-2-572 9584, fax: +20-2-62
8884
http://www.cairo.eun.eg/

Department of Political Science
Menia University, Menia, Egypt
http://www.frcu.eun.eg/www/un
iversities/html/minia.html

Department of Political Science
Menoufia University, Shebeen El-
Kome, Egypt
email: shebin@frcu.eun.eg
http://www.frcu.eun.eg/www/un
iversities/html/menof.html

Department of Political Science
Tanta University, Tanta Elgeish
Street, Tanta, Egypt
email: mnaby@dec1.tanta.eun.eg
http://dec1.tanta.eun.eg/

Eritrea

Department of Political Science
University of Eritrea, POB 1220,
Asmara, Eritrea
http://www.newafrica.com/educat
ion/institutions/eritrea.htm

Ethiopia

*Department of Political Science and
International Relations*
University of Addis Ababa, PO Box
1176, Addis Ababa, Ethiopia
tel: +251-1-550 844, fax: +251-1-550
655
http://www.abyssiniacybergatewa
y.net/ethiopia/aau/departments.ht
ml

Ghana

Department of Political Science
University of Cape Coast, PO Cape
Coast, Ghana
http://www.ghana.com/gh/ucc/

Department of Political Science
University of Ghana, PO Box 25,
Legon, Legon, Ghana
tel: +233-21-501 967, fax: +233-21-
502 701
http://www.ug.edu.gh/

*Department of Social, Political and
Historical Studies*
University of Development Studies,
Tamale, Box 24, Navorongo, Upper
East Region, Ghana
email: UDS@ug.gn.apc.org
http://acs.brockport.edu/~rocanse
y/ghana/uds.htm

Kenya

Department of Political Science
Moi University, POB 3900, Eldoret,
Kenya

Department of Government
University of Nairobi, PO Box
30197, Naoirobi, Kenya

Lesotho

Department of Political and Administrative Studies
National University of Lesotho, PO
Roma 180, Roma, Lesotho

Liberia

Department of Political Science
University of Liberia, College of Social Sciences and Humanities, Monrovia, Liberia

Libya

Department of Political Science
The Open University, Tripoli, Libya

Malawi

Department of Political and Administrative Studies
University of Malawi, Box 280,
Zomba, Malawi
email: university.office@unima.wn.
apc.org
http://members.tripod.com/~unim
al/

Morocco

Faculty of Law, Economics, Social Studies and Political Science
Université Hassan II, BP 9167,
Casablanca, Morocco
tel: +212-2-273 737, fax: +212-2-275
160
http://www.refer.fr/miroirs/maro
c_ct/edu/casa/casa.htm

Department of Political Science
Mohammed I University Oujda, BP
524, Oujda 6000, Morocco
tel: +212-6-744 785, fax: +212-6-744
779
email: recteur@univ-oujda.ac.ma

Department of Political Science
Mohammed V Agdal University
Rabat, BP 554, 3 rue Michlifen, Agdal, Rabat-Chellah, Morocco
tel: +212-7-671 318, fax: +212-7-671
401

Mozambique

Department of Political Science and Public Administration
Eduardo Mondhlane University,
Maputo, Mozambique

Namibia

Department of Political Science and Administrative Studies
University of Namibia, Box 13301,
Windhoek, Namibia
email: adupisani@unam.na
http://www.unam.na/

Niger

Faculté des Sciences Economiques et Juridiques
Université de Niamey, BP 237,
Niamey, Niger

Nigeria

Department of Political Science
Delta State University, PMB 1,
Abraka, Delta State, Nigeria

Department of Political Science
University of Abuja, PMB 117,
Abuja, Federal Capital Territory,
Nigeria

Department of Political Science
Ondo State University, PMB 5363,
Ado-Ekiti, Ekiti State, Nigeria

Department of Political Science
Ogun State University, PMB 2002,
Ago-Iwoye, Ogun State, Nigeria

Department of Political Science
Mnamdi Azikiwe University, PMB
5025, Awka, Anambra State, Nigeria
tel: +234-46-550 018, fax: +234-46-
550 018

Department of Political Science
University of Uyo, PMB 1017, Uyo,
Akwa Iborn State, Nigeria
tel: +234-85-202 696, fax: +234-85-
202 694
email: vc@uniuyo.edu.ng

Department of Political Science
University of Benin, PMB 1154, Benin, Edo State, Nigeria

Department of Political Science
University of Calabar, Calabar, Cross Rivers State, Nigeria

Department of Political Science
University of Ibadan, Ibadan, Nigeria
tel: +234-22-810 1188, fax: +234-22-810 2921

Department of Political Science
Obafemi Awolowo University, Ile-Ife, Oshun State, Nigeria

Department of Political Science
University of Ilorin, Ilorin, Kwara State, Nigeria

Department of Political Science
University of Jos, Jos, Jos Plateau State, Nigeria

Department of Political Science
Bayero University, PMB 3011, Kano, Nigeria
tel: +234-64-666 023, fax: +234-64-665 904

Department of Political Science
Lagos State University, PMB 1087 Apapa, Lagos, Lagos State, Nigeria

Department of Political Science
University of Maiduguri, PMB 1069, Maiduguri, Bornu State, Nigeria

Department of Political Science
Benue State University, PMB 102119, Makurdi, Benue State, Nigeria

Department of Political Science
University of Nigeria, Nsukka, Enugu State, Nigeria

Department of Political Science
University of Port Harcourt, Port Harcourt, Rivers State, Nigeria

Department of Political Science
Ahmadu Bello University, Samaru-Zaria, Kaduna State, Nigeria

Department of Political Science
Usmanu Dan Fodiyo University, PMB 2346, Sokoto, Sokoto State, Nigeria

Department of Political Science
Abia State University, PMB 2000, Uturu, Abia State, Nigeria

Senegal

Faculté des Sciences Juridiques et Politiques
Université Cheik Anta Diop, BP 5005, Dakar-Fann, Senegal
tel: +221-250 530, fax: +221-252 883
email: info@ucad.sn
http://www.ucad.sn/

Sierra Leone

Department of Political Science
University of Sierra Leone, Fourah Bay College, Freetown, Sierra Leone
tel: +232-22-223 258

South Africa

Department of Political Science and Public Administration
Fort Hare University, P Bag X1314, Alice 5700, South Africa

Department of Political Science
University of the Western Cape, P Bag X17, Bellville 7535, South Africa

Department of Political Science
University of Orange Free State, PO Box 339, Bloemfontein 9300, South Africa
tel: +27-51-401 9111, fax: +27-51-401 2117
email: aag@rs.uovs.ac.za

Department of Philosophy and Political Science
University of Durban-Westville, Private Bag X54001, Durban 4000, South Africa
tel: +27-31-204 4111, fax: +27-31-204 4340
email: mwallis@pixie.udw.ac
http://www.udw.ac.za/UDW/homepages/pubad.html/

Department of Politics
University of Natal-Durban, King George V Avenue, Durban 4001, South Africa

Department of Political Science
Potchefstroom University, PB x6001, Potchefstroom 2520, South Africa
http://www.puk.ac.za

Department of Political Science
Rand Afrikaans University, PO Box 524, Auckland Park 2006, South Africa
http://www.rand.ac.za

Department of Political Science
Rhodes University, PO Box 94, Grahamstown 6140, South Africa

Department of Political Science
University of Zululand, Box 1001, Kwadlangezwa, South Africa

Department of Political Science
University of Stellenbosch, Private Bag X1, Matieland 7602, South Africa
tel: +27-21-808 9111, fax: +27-21-808 3800
email: mts@maties.sun.ac.za
http://www.sun.ac.za

Department of Political Science
University of the North-West, P Bag X 2046, Mmabatho 2735, South Africa

Department of Political Studies
University of Natal, Faculty of Human Sciences, University of Natal, Pietermaritzburg, South Africa
tel: +27-33-260528
email: uzodiken@Politics.unp.ac.za
http://www.hs.unp.ac.za/politics/

Department of Political Science
University of North-Qwaqwa Campus, P Bag X13, Phuthadgjaba, South Africa

Department of Political Science
University of Port Elizabeth, Box 1600, Port Elizabeth 6000, South Africa

Department of Political Science
University of Pretoria, Lynnwood Road, Hillcrest, Pretoria 0002, South Africa
tel: +27-12-420 4111, fax: +27-12-342 2712
email: ddmarais@ccnet.up.ac.za
http://www.up.ac.za

Department of Political Science
University of South Africa, PO Box 392, Preller St Extension, Muckelneuk Ridge, Pretoria, Gauterg, 0003, South Africa
tel: +27-12-429 3111, fax: +27-12-429 3221
email: msimact@alpha.unisa.ac.za
http://www.unisa.ac.za

Department of Political Science
Vista University, P Bag X634, Pretoria 0001, South Africa

Department of Politics
University of Cape Town, Rondebosch 7700, South Africa

Department of Political Science
University of the North, P Bag X1106, Sovenga 0727, South Africa
tel: +27-152-267 8911, fax: +27-152-267 0142

Department of Political Science
University of Transkei, P Bag X1, Umata 5100, South Africa

Department of Political Science
Univeristy of Venda, P Bag X5050, Thohoyandou Venda 0950, South Africa

Department of Political Studies
University of Witwatersrand, P Bag X3, Wits 2050 Witwatersrand, South Africa
tel: +27-11-717 4363, fax: +27-11-403 7482
email: 064hab@muse.wits.ac.za
http://www.wits.ac.za/fac/arts/politics/index.htm

Sudan

Faculty of Economic and Social Studies
University of Juba, PO Box 82, Juba, Sudan
tel: +249-11-451 351, fax: +249-11-451 351

Department of Political Science
University of Khartoum, PO Box 321, Khartoum 12702, Sudan
tel: +249-11-780 056, fax: +249-11-776 338
http://www.columbia.edu/~tm146/Khar/UofK.html

Swaziland

Department of Political Science
University of Swaziland, Box 4, Kwaluseni, Swaziland
email: uniswapgs@uniswa.sz
http://www.uniswa.sz

Tanzania

Department of Political Science and Public Administration
University of Dar es Salaam, PO Box 35051, Dar es Salaam, Tanzania
http://www.uib.no/udsm

Tunisia

Faculty of Law, Economics and Political Science
University of the Centre, Sousse, BP 526, 43 Avenue Mohamed Karoui, 4002 Sousse, Tunisia
tel: +216-3-234 011, fax: +216-3-234 013

Faculty of Law and Political Science
University of Law, Economics and Management (Tunis III), 29 Rue Asdrubal, 1002 Tunis, Tunisia
tel: +216-1-787 502, fax: +216-1-788 768

Uganda

Department of Political Science and Public Administration
Makerere University, PO Box 7062, Kampala, Uganda
tel: +256-41-532 752, fax: +256-41-533 640
http://www.muk.ac.ug/faculty/social~1/index.html

Department of Political Science
Islamic University in Uganda, PO Box 2555, Mbale, Uganda
tel: +256-41-533 417, fax: +256-41-254 576

Zambia

Department of Development Studies
University of Zambia, PO Box 32379, Lusaka, Zambia

Zimbabwe

Department of Political and Administrative Studies
University of Zimbabwe, PO Box MP167, Mt Pleasant, Harare, Zimbabwe

AMERICA, NORTH

Canada

Department of Political Science
St Francis Xavier University, Antigonish, Antigonish, Nova Scotia B2G 2W5, Canada
tel: +1-902-867 5085, fax: +1-902-867 3243
email: jbickert@stfx.ca
http://www.stfx.ca/academic/political-science/

Department of Political Science
Simon Fraser University, Burnaby, Burnaby, British Columbia V5A 1S6, Canada
tel: +1-604-291 4293, fax: +1-604-291 4786
email: mcbridea@sfu.ca
http://www.sfu.ca/politics

Department of Political Science
University of Calgary, Room 756,
Social Science Tower, Calgary, Alberta T2N 1N4, Canada
tel: +1-403-220 5920, fax: +1-403-282
4773
email: rkeith@ucalgary.ca
http://www.uca;gary.ca/UofC/fac
ulties/SS/POLI

Department of Political Studies
University of Prince Edward Island,
Charlottestown, Prince Edward Island C1A 4P3, Canada
tel: +1-902-566 0331, fax: +1-902-566
0512
email: bartmann@upei.ca
http://www.upei.ca/~regoff/poly_
1.html

Department of Political Science
University of Alberta, Edmonton,
Edmonton, Alberta T6G 2H4, Canada
tel: +1-780-492 3555, fax: +1-708-492
2586
email: sharon.moroshan@ualberta.
ca
http://www.arts.ualberta.ca/~polis
ci/index.html

Department of Political Science
St Thomas University, Fredericton,
Fredericton, New Brunswick E3B
5G3, Canada
tel: +1-506-452 0642 or 7700, fax: +1-
506-450 9615
email: pmalcolm@stthomasu.ca
http://www.stthomasu.ca/academi
cs/depts/poliscin.htm

Department of Political Science
University of New Brunswick, 219
Tilley Hall, College Hill, PO Box
4400, Fredericton, New Brunswick
E3B 5A3, Canada
tel: +1-506-453 4826, fax: +1-506-453
4755
email: polisci@unb.ca
http://www.unb.ca/departs/arts/
Poli

Department of Political Science
University of Guelph, Guelph, Ontario N1G 2W1, Canada
tel: +1-519-824 4120 ext 2184, fax:
+1-519-837 9561
email: mancuso@uoguelph.ca
http://polisci.uoguelph.ca/

Department of Political Science
Dalhousie University, 6299 South
Street, Halifax, Nova Scotia B3H
4H6, Canada
tel: +1-902-494 2396, fax: +1-902-494
3825
email: david.cameron@dal.ca
http://www.dal.ca/~poliwww/pol
iwww.html

*Political and Canadian Studies De-
partment*
Mount Saint Vincent University, 166
Bedford Highway, Halifax, Nova
Scotia B3M 2J6, Canada
tel: +1-902-457 6196, fax: +1-902-457
6455
email: michael.macmillan@msvu.ca
http://www.msvu.ca/calendar/pol
s.htm

Department of Political Science
Saint Mary's University, Halifax,
Halifax, Nova Scotia B3H 3C3, Canada
tel: +1-902-420 5836, fax: +1-902-420
5181
email: tarsenea@shark.stmarys.ca
http://www.stmarys.ca/academic/
arts/politic.htm

Department of Political Science
McMaster University, 1280 Main
Street West, Hamilton, Ontario L8S
4M4, Canada
tel: +1-905-525 9140 ext 24741, fax:
+1-905-527 3071
email: stubbsr@mcmaster.ca
http://socserv2.socsi.mcmaster.ca/
~polisci/

*Department of Philosophy, History
and Politics*
University College of the Cariboo,
900 College Drive, Box 3010, Kam-
loops, British Columbia V2C 5N3,

Canada
tel: +1-705-675 1151 ext 4320, fax:
+1-250-371 5510
email: bbaugh@cariboo.bc.ca
http://www.cariboo.ca/ae/php/h
ome.htm

Department of Political Science
Queen's University, Kingston, Ontario K7L 3N6, Canada
tel: +1-613-533 6230, fax: +1-613-533 6848
email: scp2@qsilver.queensu.ca
http://qsliver.queensu.ca/politics/

Department of Politics and Economics
Royal Military College of Canada,
PO Box 17000 Stn Forces, Kingston,
Ontario K7K 7B4, Canada
tel: +1-613-541 6000 ext 6423, fax:
+1-613-541 6733
email: sokolsky-J@rmc.ca
http://www.rmc.ca/academic/arts/rmcpolecon.html

Department of Political Studies
Bishop's University, Lennoxville,
Quebec J1M 1Z7, Canada
tel: +1-819-822 9600 ext 2635, fax:
+1-819-822 9661
email: astritch@ubishops.ca
http://www.ubishops.ca/ccc/div/soc/pol

Department of Political Science
University of Lethbridge, 4401 University Drive, Lethbridge, Alberta
T1K 3M4, Canada
tel: +1-403-329 2580, fax: +1-403-382 7148
email: mccormick@uleth.ca
http://home.uleth.ca/pol/

Department of Political Science
University of Western Ontario,
London, Ontario N6A 5C2, Canada
tel: +1-519-661 3266, fax: +1-519-661 3904
email: young@julian.uwo.ca
http://yoda.sscl.uwo.ca/polysci

Département de Science Politique
Université de Moncton, Moncton,
Nouveau Brunswick E1A 3E9, Canada

ada
tel: +1-506-858 4380, fax: +1-506-858 4508
email: helmyg@umoncton.ca
http://www.umoncton.ca/scpol

Department of Political Science
McGill University, 855 Sherbrooke
Street West, Montréal, Quèbec H3A
2T7, Canada
tel: +1-514-398 4800, fax: +1-514-398 1770
email: meadwell@leacock.1an.mcgill.ca
http://www.arts.mcgill.ca/programs/polisci/

Department of Political Science
Université Concordia, 1455 de Maisonneuve Blvd West, Montréal,
Quèbec H3G 1M, Canada
tel: +1-514-848 2105, fax: +1-514-848 4072
email: reetact@vax2.concordia.ca
http://132.205.57.9/politicalsc/

Département de Science Politique
Université du Montréal, 3150 rue
Jean-Brillant, local C-4012, CP 6128,
Montréal, Quèbec H3C 3J7, Canada
tel: +1-514-343 6578, fax: +1-514-343 2360
email: ducateng@ere.umontreal.ca
http://www.fas.umontreal.ca/POL

Département de Science Politique
Université du Quèbec a Montréal,
1255, rue Saint-Denis, Local A-3045,
CP 8888, Montréal, Quèbec H3C
3P8, Canada
tel: +1-514-987 4141, fax: +1-514-987 4749
email: dept.sc.politiques@uqam.ca
http://www.repertoire.uquam.ca/?detail_U5664

Department of Political Science
York University, 4700 Keele Street,
North York, Ontario M3J 1P3, Canada
tel: +1-416-736 5265, fax: +1-416-736 5686
email: snewman@yorku.ca
http://www.yorku.ca/dept/polisci

Department of Political Science
Carleton University, 1125 Colonel
By Drive, Ottawa, Ontario K1S 5B6,
Canada
tel: +1-613-520 2777, fax: +1-613-520
4064
email: glen_williams@carleton.ca
http://www.carelton.ca/polisci/

Département de Science Politique
University of Ottawa, 75 Laurier
Avenue East, Ottawa, Ontario K1N
6N5, Canada
tel: +1-613-562 5754, fax: +1-613-562
5106
email: dmoggach@uottowa.ca
http://www.uottowa.ca/academic
/socsci/politi/

Political Science Programme
University of Northern British Columbia, 3333 University Way, Prince
George, British Columbia V2N 4Z9,
Canada
tel: +1-604-960 6668, fax: +1-604-960
5544
email: michalos@unbc.ca
http://quarles.unbc.edu/politics/h
ome.html

Département de Science Politique
Université Laval, Local 3457, Pavillon Charles De Koninck, Quèbec,
Quèbec G1K 7P4, Canada
tel: +1-418-656 2407, fax: +1-418-656
7861
email: guy.laforest@pol.ulaval.ca
http://www.ulaval.ca/sg/annuaire
s/dep/pol.htm

Department of Political Science
University of Regina, Regina, Saskatchewan S4S 0A2, Canada
tel: +1-306-585 4206, fax: +1-306-585
4815
email: phillip.hansen@uregina.ca
http://www.uregina.ca/arts/psci

Department of Political Studies
Mount Allison University, 144 Main
Street, Sackville New Brunswick
E4L 1A7, Canada
tel: +1-506-364 2326, fax: +1-506-364
2625

email: mjtucker@mta.ca
http://www.mta.ca/faculty/socsci
/polisci/index.htm

Department of Politics
Brock University, Taro Hall, TA 468,
St Catherines, Ontario L2S 3A1,
Canada
tel: +1-905-688 550 ext 3476, fax: +1-
905-988 9388
email: nbaxterm@spartan.ac.brocku
.ca
http://www.brocku.ca/politics

Department of Political Science
Memorial University of Newfoundland, St John's, Newfoundland A1B 3X9, Canada
tel: +1-709-737 8179, fax: +1-709-737
4000
email: gunther@morgan.ucs.mun.ca
http://www.mun.ca/posc/

Department of Political Science
Laurentian University, Sudbury,
Ontario P3E 2C6, Canada
tel: +1-705-675 1151 ext 320, fax: +1-
705-675 4852
email: crabier@nickel.laurentian.ca
http://www.laurentian.ca/www/p
olisci/eIndex.html

Department of Political Science
Lakehead University, 955 Oliver
Road, Thunder Bay, Ontario P7B
5E1, Canada
tel: +1-807-343 8477, fax: +1-807-343
7831
email: doug.west@lakeheadu.ca
http://www.lakeheadu.ca/~regww
w/politics.html

Department of Political Science
University of Toronto, 100 St
George Street, Room 3019, Toronto,
Ontario M5S 1A1, Canada
tel: +1-416-978 3343, fax: +1-416-978
5566
email: rvipond@chass.utoronto.ca
http://www.library.utoronto.ca/w
ww/arts_and_science/page_pol

Department of Political Science
University of British Columbia,
C472-1866 Main Mall, Vancouver,

British Columbia V6T 1Z1, Canada
tel: +1-604-822 2717, fax: +1-604-822
5540
email: rkcarty@unixg.bc.ca
http://www.arts.ubc.ca/polisci/po
lisci.htm

Department of Political Science
University of Victoria, PO Box 3050,
Victoria, British Columbia V8W 3P5,
Canada
tel: +1-604-721 7486, fax: +1-604-721
7485
email: jtully@uvic.ca
http://www.cous.uvic.ca/poli/

Department of Political Science
University of Waterloo, 200 University Avenue West, Waterloo, Ontario N2L 3G1, Canada
tel: +1-519-888 4567 ext 3396, fax:
+1-519-746 5622
email: akapur@watarts.uwaterloo.ca
http://arts.uwaterloo.ca/PSCI/poli
sci.html

Department of Political Science
Wilfrid Laurier University, 75 University Avenue West, Waterloo,
Ontario N2L 3C5, Canada
tel: +1-519-884 1970 ext 3374, fax:
+1-519-746 3655
email: btanguay@wlu.ca
http://www.wlu.ca/~wwwpolsc/

Department of History, Philosophy and Political Science
University of Windsor, 410 Sunset
Avenue, Windsor, Ontario N9B 3P4,
Canada
tel: +1-519-253 4232 ext 2347, fax:
+1-519-973 7094
email: allard@delta.uwindsor.ca
http://www.uwindsor.ca/political.
science/

Department of Political Studies
University of Manitoba, 531 Fletcher
Argue, Winnipeg, Manitoba R3T
5V5, Canada
tel: +1-204-474 9521, fax: +1-204-474
7585
email: wfw_neville@umanitoba.ca

http://www.umanitoba.ca/facultie
s/arts/political_studies

Department of Political Science
University of Winnipeg, 6L07-515
Portage Avenue, Winnipeg, Manitoba R3B 2E9, Canada
tel: +1-204-786 9340, fax: +1-204-774
4134
email: claudia.wright@uwinnipeg.
ca
http://www.uwinnipeg.ca/academ
ic/as/polsci

Department of Political Science
Acadia University, 323 Beveridge
Arts Centre, Wolfvilee Nova Scotia,
BOP 1X0, Canada
tel: +1-902-585 1506, fax: +1-902-585
1070
email: malcolm.grieve@acadiau.ca
http://aca.acadiau.ca/polisci

Department of Political Studies
Trent University, Champlain College, 1600 Westbank Drive, Peterborough, Ontario K9J 7B8, Canada
tel: +1-705-748 1430, fax: +1-705-748
1047
email: dtorgerson@trentu.ca
http://ivory.trentu.ca/www/politi
cs/flash_index.html

Department of Political Studies
University of Saskatchewan, Saskatoon, Saskatchewan S7N 5A5,
Canada
tel: +1-306-966 5200, fax: +1-306-966
5250
email: smithd@sask.usask.ca
http://www.usask.ca/politic/

Department of Politics and School of Public Administration
Ryerson Polytechnic University, 350
Victoria Street, A712, Toronto, Ontario M5B 2K3, Canada
tel: +1-406-979 5057, fax: +1-416-979
5289
email: ccassidy@acs.ryerson.ca
http://www.ryerson.ca/dept/politi
cs.html

Department of Political Science
University of Victoria, PO Box 3050,
Victoria, British Columbia V8W 3P5,
Canada
tel: +1-604-721 7486, fax: +1-604-721
7485
email: jtully@uvic.ca
http://www.cous.uvic.ca/poli

USA

Department of Political Science
State University of New York, 1400
Washington Ave, Albany, NY
12222, USA
tel: +1-716-645 2251, fax: +1-716-645
2166
email: fczagare@acsu.buffalo.edu
http://wings.buffalo.edu/soc-
sci/pol-sci/Polsci.html

Department of Political Science
University of New Mexico, Albuquerque, NM 87131, USA
tel: +1-805-277-2821, fax: +1-805-277
5104
email: nmitchell@unm.edu
http://polisci.unm.edu/default.htm

Department of Political Science
University of Massachusetts,
Amherst, MA 01003-7520, USA
tel: +1-508-999 8369, fax: +1-508-999
8819
email: 1porto@umassd.edu
http://www.umassd.edu/GladYou
Asked/GYAPoliSci.html

Department of Political Science
University of Michigan, 5601 Haven
Hall, Ann Arbor, MI 48109-1045,
USA
tel: +1-734-764 6312, fax: +1-734-764
3522
email: polisci@umich.edu
http://polisci.lsa.umich.edu

Department of Political Science
University of Georgia, 390 Millstone
Circle, Athens, GA 30602, USA
tel: +1-706-542 2057, fax: +1-706-542
4421
email: polisci@arches.uga.edu
http://www.uga.edu/~pol-sci/

Department of Political Science
Clark-Atlanta University, Atlanta,
GA 30314, USA
tel: +1-404-880 8718, fax: +1-404-880
8717
email: hgibrill@cau.edu
http://www.cau.edu

Department of Political Science
Emory University, 327 Tarbutton
Hall, 1555 Pierce Drive, Atlanta, GA
30322, USA
tel: +1-404-727 6572, fax: +1-404-727
4586
email: polisci@emory.edu
http://www.emory.edu/POLS/ind
ex.html

Department of Political Science
Georgia State University, Atlanta,
GA 30303, USA
tel: +1-404-651 3152, fax: +1-404-651
1431
email: wwwpol@panther.gsu.edu
http://www.gsu.edu/~wwwpol/in
dex.html

Department of Political Science
Auburn University, 7080 Haley
Center, Auburn, AL 36849-5208,
USA
tel: +1-334-844 5370, fax: +1-334-844
5348
email: bernsra@mail.auburn.edu
http://www.auburn.edu/academic
/liberal_arts/poli_sci

Department of Government
University of Texas, Burdine Hall
536, Austin, TX 78712, USA
tel: +1-512-471 1061, fax: +1-512-471
5121
email: fishkin@mail.utexas.edu
http://www.la.utexas.edu/depts/g
ov/

Department of Political Science
Johns Hopkins University, Baltimore, MD 21218, USA
tel: +1-410-516 7540, fax: +1-410-516
5515
email: political.science@jhu.edu
http://www.jhu.edu/~polysci/

Department of Political Science
Louisiana State University, Baton
Rouge, LA 70803-5433, USA
tel: +1-225-388 2142, fax: +1-225-388
2540
email: poeubk@lsu.edu
http://www.artsci.lsu.edu/poli/

Department of Political Science
University of California-Berkeley,
1337 Martin Luther King Jr Way,
Berkeley, CA 94720-1950, USA
tel: +1-510-642 6323, fax: +1-510-642-
9515
email: rprice@socrates.berkeley.edu
http://www.polisci.berkeley.edu/p
olisci

Department of Political Science
State University of New York,
Binghamton, NY 13902-6000, USA
tel: +1-607-777 2252, fax: +1-607-777
2675
email: canders@binghamton.edu
http://www.binghamton.edu/pols
ci/

*Center for Public Administration and
Policy*
Virginia Polytechnical Institute and
State University, 104 Draper Road,
Mail Stop 0520, Blacksburg, VA
24062, USA
tel: +1-540-231 6571, fax: +1-540-231
6078
email: twluke@vt.edu
http://www.majbill.vt.edu/polisci
/index.html

Department of Political Science
Indiana University, Bloomington,
IN 47405, USA
tel: +1-812-855 6308, fax: +1-812-855
2027
email: iupolsci@indiana.edu
http://www.indiana.edu/~iupolsci

Department of Political Science
Boston University, 232 Bay State
Road, Boston, MA 02215, USA
tel: +1-617-353 2540, fax: +1-617-353-
5508
http://www.bu.edu/POLISCI

Department of Political Science
University of Colorado-Boulder,
Boulder, CO 80309-0333, USA
tel: +1-303-492 7871, fax: +1-303-492
0978
email: Jana.Murphy@colorado.edu
http://socsci.colorado.edu/POLSCI

Department of Political Science
Fordham University, Bronx, NY
10458, USA
tel: +1-718-817 3950, fax: +1-718-817
3972
email:
fleisher@murray.fordham.edu
http://www.fordham.edu/gsas/po
sc/posc.html

Department of Political Science
State University of New York, 520
Park Hall, Buffalo, NY 14260, USA
tel: +1-716-645 2251, fax: +1-716-645
2166
email: mclellan@acsu.buffalo.edu
http://wings.buffalo.edu/soc-
sci/pol-sci/

Department of Government
Harvard University, Cambridge,
MA 02138, USA
tel: +1-617-495 2148, fax: +1-617-495
0438
email: sbaker@latte.harvard.edu
http://www.gov.harvard.edu

Department of Political Science
Massachusetts Institute of Technology, Cambridge, MA 02139, USA
tel: +1-617-253 5262, fax: +1-617-258
6164
http://web.mit.edu/afs/athena.mit
.edu/org/p/polisci/www

Department of Political Science
Southern Illinois University,
Carbondale, IL 62901, USA
tel: +1-618-536 2371, fax: +1-618-453
3163
email: udesai@siu.edu
http://www.siu.edu/departments/
cola/polysci/

Department of Political Science
University of North Carolina,
Chapel Hill, NC 27599-3265, USA

tel: +1-919-962 3041, fax: +1-919-962 0432
email: psweb@unc.edu
http://www.unc.edu/depts/polisci

Department of Government and Foreign Affairs
University of Virginia, Charlottesville, VA 22903, USA
tel: +1-804-924 6990, fax: +1-804-924 3359
email: rf@virginia.edu
http://minerva.acc.Virginia.EDU:80/govtfa/

Department of Political Science
Boston College, Chestnut Hill, MA 02167, USA
tel: +1-617-552 4160
email: sandra.macdonald@bc.edu
http://infoeagle.bc.edu/bc_org/avp/cas/polsc/

Department of Political Science
Loyola University of Chicago, 6525 North Sheridan Road, Chicago, IL 60626, USA
tel: +1-773-508 3047, fax: +1-773-508 3131
http://www.luc.edu/depts/polisci

Department of Political Science
University of Chicago, 5828 South University Avenue, Chicago, IL 60637, USA
tel: +1-773-702 3042, fax: +1-773-702 1889
email: ka-anderson@uchicago.edu
http://www.spc.uchicago.edu/depts/polsci

Harris Graduate School of Public Policy Studies
University of Chicago, 1155 East 60th Street, Chicago, IL 60637, USA
tel: +1-773-702 8401, fax: +1-773-702 0926
email: r-michael@uchicago.edu
http://www.harrisschool.uchicago.edu/

Department of Political Science
University of Illinois, 1007 W Harrison Street, Chicago, IL 60607-7137, USA

tel: +1-312-996 3105, fax: +1-312-413 0440
email: mlane@uic.edu
http://www.uic.edu/depts/pols/

Department of Political Science
University of Cincinnati, Cincinatti, OH 45221-0375, USA
tel: +1-513-556 3300, fax: +1-513-556 2314
email: James.Stevens@uc.edu
http://ucaswww.mcm.uc.edu/polisci/polisci.html

School of Politics and Economics
Claremont Graduate University, 170 East 10th Street, Claremont, CA 91711-61663, USA, fax: +1-909-621-8545
email: David.Enriquez@cgu.edu
http://www.cgu.edu/spe

Department of Political Science
Case Western Reserve University, Mather House, Cleveland, OH 44106-7109, USA
tel: +1-216-368 2424, fax: +1-216-368 4681
email: sxs22@po.cwru.edu
http://www.cwru.edu/artsci/posc/posc.html/

Department of Government and Politics
University of Maryland, College Park, MD 20742-8221, USA
tel: +1-301-314 4156, fax: +1-301-314 9690
email: cabell@gvpt.umd.edu
http://www.bsos.umd.edu/gvpt/

School of Public Affairs
University of Maryland, 2101 Van Munching Hall, College Park, MD 20742, USA
tel: +1-301-405 6330, fax: +1-301-405 8107
email: sschwab@deans.umd.edu
http://www.puaf.umd.edu

Department of Political Science
Texas A&M University, College Station, TX 77843, USA
tel: +1-409-845 2511, fax: +1-409-847 8924

email: information@polisci.tamu.edu
http://www-polisci.tamu.edu

Department of Political Science
University of Missouri-Columbia,
Columbia, MO 65211, USA
tel: +1-573-882 2843, fax: +1-573-884 5131
email: gomal@missouri.edu
http://www.missouri.edu/~polsw ww/

Department of Government and International Studies
University of South Carolina, Columbia, SC 29208, USA
tel: +1-803-777 3109, fax: +1-803-777 8255
email: Starr-harvey@sc.edu
http://www.cla.sc.edu/GINT/

Department of Political Science
Ohio State University, Columbus, OH 43210-1373, USA
tel: +1-614-292 2880, fax: +1-614-292 1146
email: Beck.9@osu.edu
http://psweb.sts.ohio-state.edu

Graduate School of International Studies
University of Miami, PO Box 248123, Coral Gables, FL 33124-3010, USA
tel: +1-305-284 4303, fax: +1-305-284 2507
http://www.miami.edu/internatio nal-studies/

Department of Political Science
University of California-Davis, Davis, CA 95616-8682, USA
tel: +1-530-752 0966, fax: +1-530-752 8666
email: mnincic@ucdavis.edu
http://ps.ucdavis.edu

Department of Political Science
Northern Illinois University, Dekalb, IL 60115, USA
tel: +1-815-753 7040, fax: +1-815-753 6302
email: dkempton@niu.edu

http://www.niu.edu/acad/polisci /pols.html
Department of Political Science
University of North Texas, PO Box 5338, Denton, TX 76203-5338, USA
tel: +1-940-565 2276, fax: +1-940-565 4818
email: jbooks@facstaff.cas.unt.edu
http://www.psci.unt.edu/

Department of Political Science
University of Denver, Denver, CO 80208, USA
tel: +1-970-871 2743, fax: +1-970-871 2045
email: jehill@du.edu
http://www.du.edu/plsc/

Department of Political Science
Wayne State University, 2040 Faculty Administration Building, Detroit, MI 48202, USA
tel: +1-313-577 2630, fax: +1-313-933 3435
email: ab6166@wayne.edu
http://www.cla.wayne.edu/polisci

Department of Political Science
Duke University, Box 90204, Durham, NC 27708-0204, USA
tel: +1-919-660 4300, fax: +1-919-660-4330-
email: dcross@duke.edu
http://www.poli.duke.edu

Department of Political Science
University of Oregon, PO Box 11233, Eugene, OR 97403-1284, USA
tel: +1-541-346 4864, fax: +1-541-346 4860
email: polisci@oregon.uoregon.edu
http://darkwing.uoregon.edu/~pol isci/

Department of Political Science
Northwestern University, Scott Hall, 601 University Place, Evanston, IL 60208, USA
tel: +1-847-491 7450, fax: +1-847-491 8985
email: political-science@norhtwestern.edu
http://www.polisci.nwu.edu/

Department of Public and Interna-

tional Affairs
George Mason University, 4400 University Drive, Fairfax, VA 22030-4444, USA
tel: +1-703-993 1400, fax: +1-703-993 1399
email: mhanson1@gmu.edu
http://www.gmu.edu/department s/pia/

Department of Political Science
Northern Arizona University, PO Box 15036, Flagstaff, AZ 86011, USA
tel: +1-520-523 1515, fax: +1-520-523 6654
email: Fred.Solop@nau.edu
http://www.nau.edu/~srl/

Department of Political Science
Colorado State University, Fort Collins, CO 80523, USA
tel: +1-970-491 5156, fax: +1-970-491 2490
http://www.colostate.edu/Depts/PoliSci/

Department of Political Science
University of Hawaii, 2424 Maile Way, Porteus 640, Honolulu, HI 96822, USA
tel: +1-808-956 8357, fax: +1-808-956 6877
email: polisci@hawaii.edu
http://www2.soc.hawaii.edu/pols

Department of Political Science
Rice University, PO Box 1892, Houston, TX 77251, USA
tel: +1-713-348 4842, fax: +1-713-348 5273
email: poli@rice.edu
http://www.ruf.rice.edu/~poli/

Department of Political Science
University of Houston, 4800 Calhoun, Houston, TX 77204-3474, USA
tel: +1-713-743 3590, fax: +1-713-743 3972
http://crystal.polsci.uh.edu/uhdps

Department of Political Science
University of Iowa, Iowa City, IA 52242-1409, USA
tel: +1-319-335 2358, fax: +1-319-335 3400

email: polisci@uiowa.edu
http://www.uiowa.edu/~polisci

Department of Politics and Society
University of California-Irvine, Irvine, CA 92717, USA
tel: +1-949-824 5439, fax: +1-949-854-5180-
email: deaston@uci.edu
http://aris.ss.uci.edu/pol/pol.html

Department of Politics
University of Dallas, 1848 East Northgate Drive, Irving, TX 75062, USA
tel: +1-972-721 5023, fax: +1-972-721 4007
email: poldept@acad.udallas.edu
http://www.udallas.edu/politics

Department of Government
Cornell University, McGraw Hall, Ithaca, NY 14853, USA
tel: +1-607-255 3594, fax: +1-607-255 4530
email: cu_govt@cornell.edu
http://falcon.arts.cornell.edu/Govt

Department of Political Science
Western Michigan University, 3302 Friedmann Hall, Kalamazoo, MI 49008, USA
tel: +1-616-387 5680, fax: +1-616-387 3999
email: David.Houghton@wmich.edu
http://www.wmich.edu/politics/

Department of Political Science
Kent State University, Kent, OH 44242, USA
tel: +1-330-672 2060, fax: +1-330-672-3362
email: emccoy1@kent.edu
http://www.kent.edu/polisci/

Department of Political Science
University of Tennessee, Knoxville, TN 37996-0410, USA
tel: +1-423-974 2261, fax: +1-423-974 7037
email: pfreelan@utk.edu
http://web.utk.edu/~polisci

Department of Political Science
University of California-San Diego,
9500 Gilman Drive, La Jolla, CA
92093, USA
tel: +1-858-534 3548, fax: +1-858-534
7130
email: polisci@weber.ucsd.edu
http://dssadmin.ucsd.edu/PoliSci

Department of Political Science
Michigan State University, 303 S
Kedzie Hall, Lansing, MI 49924-
1032, USA
tel: +1-517-335 6590, fax: +1-517-432
1091
email: weinber8@pilot.msu.edu
http://www.ssu.msu.edu/~pls/

Division of Government
University of Kansas, 504 Blake
Hall, Lawrence, KY 66045, USA
tel: +1-913-864 3523, fax: +1-913-864
5700
email: s-
maynardmoody@ukans.edu
http://raven.cc.ukans.edu/~kups/

Department of Political Science
University of Kentucky, Lexington,
KY 40506-0027, USA
tel: +1-606-257 7029, fax: +1-606-257
7034
email: baclay01@pop.uky.edu
http://www.uky.edu/ArtsSciences
/PoliSci/

Department of Political Science
University of Nebraska, Lincoln, NE
68588-0828, USA
tel: +1-402-472 2543, fax: +1-402-472
8192
email: jcomer@unlserve.unl.edu
http://www.unl.edu/polisci/home

Department of Political Science
University of California, 405 Hil-
gard Avenue, Los Angeles, CA
90024-1472, USA
tel: +1-310-825 4331, fax: +1-310-825
0175
email: tkang@polisci.ucla.edu
http://www.polisci.ucla.edu/

Department of Political Science
University of Southern California,
University Park, Los Angeles, CA
90089-0044, USA
tel: +1-213-740 6998, fax: +1-213-740
8893
email: posc@usc.edu
http://www.usc.edu/dept/polsci

School of International Relations
University of Southern California,
Los Angeles, CA 90089-0043, USA
tel: +1-213-740 2136, fax: +1-213-742
0281
email: sppd@usc.edu
http://www.usc.edu/dept/puad

Department of Political Science
Texas Tech University, Lubbock, TX
79409-1015, USA
tel: +1-806-742 3121, fax: +1-806-742
0850
email: p.h.marshall@ttu.edu
http://www.ttu.edu/~polisci

Department of Political Science
University of Wisconsin, 110 North
Hall, 1050 Bascon Mall, Madison,
WI 53706, USA
tel: +1-608-263 2414, fax: +1-608-265
2663
email: weeks@polisci.wisc.edu
http://www.polisci.wisc.edu

*Fletcher School of Law and Diplo-
macy*
Tufts University, Medford, MA
02155, USA
tel: +1-617-627 3700, fax: +1-617-628-
5508
email: mknokey@infonet.tufts.edu
http://fletcher.tufts.edu

Department of Political Science
University of Wisconsin-
Milwaukee, Milwaukee, WI 53201,
USA
tel: +1-414-229 4221, fax: +1-414-229
5021
email: emmi@uwm.edu
http://www.uwm.edu/Dept/Polsc
i/

Department of Political Science
University of Minnesota, 267 19th
Avenue South, Minneapolis, MN
55455, USA
tel: +1-612-626 7599, fax: +1-612 624
4144
email: office@polisci.umn.edu
http://www.polisci.umn.edu

Department of Political Science
Mississippi State University, PO Box
PC, Mississippi State, MS 39762-
6003, USA
tel: +1-601-325 2711, fax: +1-601-325
2716
http://www.msstate.edu/Dept/Pol
iticalScience/

*Department of Political Science and
Public Administration*
Auburn University-Montgomery,
Montgomery, AL 36117-3596, USA
tel: +1-334-244 3698, fax: +1-334-244
3826
email: russ@strudel.aum.edu
http://sciences.aum.edu/popa/

Department of Political Science
West Virginia University, PO Box
6317, Morgantown, WV 26506, USA
tel: +1-304-293 3811, fax: +1-304-293
8644
http://www.as.wvu.edu/polsci/

Department of Political Science
University of Idaho, Moscow, ID
83843, USA
tel: +1-208-885 6328, fax: +1-208-885
5102
email: polsci@uidaho.edu
http://www.ls.uidaho.edu/PolS/

Department of Political Science
Vanderbilt University, Box 1817,
Station B, Nashville, TN 37235, USA
tel: +1-423-322 6222, fax: +1-423-343
6003
email: james.l.ray@vanderbilt.edu
http://www.vanderbilt.edu/psci/p
scimain.htm

Department of Political Science
Rutgers University, Hickman Hall,
Douglass Campus, New Brunswick,
NJ 08903, USA

tel: +1-201-932 9261, fax: +1-201-932
7170
http://www.rci.rutgers.edu/~polsc
i/

Department of Political Science
Yale University, 3532 Yale Station,
New Haven, CT 06520-3532, USA
tel: +1-203-432 5230, fax: +1-203-432
6196
http://cis.yale.edu/gradsch/grad/
3d5.html

Department of Political Science
Tulane University, New Orleans,
LA 70118-5698, USA
tel: +1-504-865 5166, fax: +1-504-862
8745
email: langston@tulane.edu
http://www.Tulane.edu/~polisci/
PoliDept.html

Department of Political Science
University of New Orleans, Lake-
front, New Orleans, LA 70148, USA
tel: +1-504-280 6383, fax: +1-504-280
3838
email: chadley@uno.edu
http://www.uno.edu/~poli/

*Graduate Program in Political Sci-
ence*
City University of New York, 33
West 42nd Street, New York, NY
10036, USA
tel: +1-212-817 8670, fax: +1-212-642
1980
http://www.gc.cuny.edu/Directori
es/Programs/index.htm

Department of Political Science
Columbia University, 420 West
118th Street, New York, NY 10027,
USA
tel: +1-212-222 3636, fax: +1-212-222
0598
email: kea6@columbia.edu
http://www.columbia.edu/cu/poli
sci/

Department of Political Science
New School for Social Research, 65
Fifth Avenue, New York, NY 10003,
USA
tel: +1-212-229 5747, fax: +1-212-807

1669
email: Shealy@newschool.edu
http://www.newschool.edu/gf/po
lsci/index.htm

Department of Politics
New York University, 715 Broadway, New York, NY 10003, USA
tel: +1-212-998 8500, fax: +1-212-995 4184
http://www.nyu.edu/cas/dept/po li.htm/

Graduate School of Public Administration
Rutgers University, 360 Dr Martin Luther King Blvd, Newark, NJ 07102, USA
tel: +1-973-353 5093, fax: +1-973-353 5907
email: gaild@andromeda.rutgers.edu
http://rutgers-newark.rutgers.edu/pubadmin/default.

Department of Political Science and International Relations
University of Delaware, Newark, DE 19716-2574, USA
tel: +1-201-831 2355, fax: +1-201-831 4452
email: mwh@udel.edu
http://www.udel.edu/poscir/

Department of Political Science and Geography
Old Dominion University, Norfolk, VA 23529-0086, USA
tel: +1-757-683 3841, fax: +1-757-683 4763
email: LAllen@odu.edu
http://web.odu.edu/al/artsandlett ers/polisci/

Department of Political Science
University of Oklahoma, 455 W Lindsey, Room 205, Norman, OK 73019-2001, USA
tel: +1-405-325 2061, fax: +1-405-325 0718
email: mfrance@ou.edu
http://www.ou.edu/cas/psc/

Department of Government and International Studies
University of Notre Dame, Notre Dame, IN 46556, USA
tel: +1-219-631 9017, fax: +1-219-631 4405
email: govt.govtgrad.1@nd.edu
http://www.nd.edu:80/~governme

Department of Public Administration
University of Nebraska-Omaha, 60th and Dodge Streets, Omaha, NE 86182-0276, USA
tel: +1-402-554 2624, fax: +1-402-554 4860
email: plsc001@unomaha.edu
http://www.unomaha.edu/~himbe rger/pahome.html

Department of Political Science
Miami University, Oxford, OH 45056, USA
tel: +1-513-529 2010, fax: +1-513-529 1709
email: paganoma@muohio.edu
http://www.muohio.edu/graduate school/

Division of Social Sciences
California Institute of Technology, Pasadena, CA 91125, USA
tel: +1-818-395 4065, fax: +1-818-405 9841
email: sgd@hss.caltech.edu
http://www.caltech.edu/caltech/H andSS.html

Department of Political Science
Temple University, Philadelphia, PA 19122, USA
tel: +1-215-204 1469, fax: +1-215-204 3770
email: polsci@blue.temple.edu
http://www.temple.edu/polsci/

Department of Political Science
University of Pennsylvania, 217 Stiteler Hall, Philadelphia, PA 19104-6215, USA
tel: +1-215-898 7641, fax: +1-215-573 2073
email: pkozak@sas.upenn.edu
http://www.ssc.upenn.edu/polysci

H John Heinz III School of Public Policy and Management
Carnegie Mellon University, Pittsburgh, PA 15213, US
tel: +1-412-268 3840, fax: +1-412-268 7036
http://info.heinz.cmu.edu/

Graduate School of Public and International Affairs
University of Pittsburgh, 3J34 Forbes Quandrange, Pittsburgh, PA 15260, USA
tel: +1-412-648 7640, fax: +1-412-648 7641
email: gspia+@pitt.edu
http://www.gspia.pitt.edu/

Department of Political Science
University of Pittsburgh, 4L01 Forbes Quadrangle, Pittsburgh, PA 15260, USA
tel: +1-412-648 7250, fax: +1-412-648 7277
email: polisci+@pitt.edu
http://www.pitt/edu/~polisci/

Department of Political Science
Idaho State University, Campus Box 8073, Pocatello, ID 83209, USA
tel: +1-208-236 2211, fax: +1-208-236 4610
email: hardcher@isu.edu
http://www.isu.edu/departments/polsci/

Department of Politics
Princeton University, Princeton, NJ 08544-1012, USA
tel: +1-609-258 4760, fax: +1-609-258 4772
email: janehale@princeton.edu
http://www.princeton.edu/~politics

Woodrow Wilson School of Public and International Affairs
Princeton University, Robertson Hall, Room 416A, Princeton, NJ 08544-1013, USA
tel: +1-609-258 4800, fax: +1-609-258 1418
email: mrothsch@princeton.edu
http://www.wws.princeton.edu/

Department of Political Science
Brown University, Providence, RI 02912, USA
tel: +1-401-863 2825, fax: +1-401-863 7018
email: ida_cirillo@brown.edu
http://www.brown.edu/Departments/Political_Science

Department of Political Science
Washington State University, Pullman, WA 99164-4880, USA
tel: +1-509-335 2544, fax: +1-509-335 7990
http://www.wsu.edu/~libarst/

Department of Political Science
University of Nevada-Reno, Reno, NV 89557, USA
tel: +1-775-784 4601, fax: +1-775-784 1473
email: psdept@scs.unr.edu
http://www.unr.edu/artsci/polisci

Department of Political Science
University of California-Riverside, Riverside, CA 92521, USA
tel: +1-909-787 5540, fax: +1-909-787 3933
email: lichbach@wizard.ucr.edu
http://wizard.ucr.edu/polisci/

Department of Political Science
University of Rochester, Rochester, NY 14627-0146, USA
tel: +1-716-275 4291, fax: +1-706-271 1616
email: kyct@troi.cc.rochester.edu
http://www.rochester.edu/College/PSC/

Department of Political Science
University of Utah, 252 Orson Spencer Hall, Salt Lake City, UT 84112, USA
tel: +1-801-581 7031, fax: +1-801-585 6492
email: jaime.kimball@poli-sci.utah.edu
http://www.poli-sci.utah.edu/

Department of Political Science
University of California-Santa Barbara, Santa Barbara, CA 93016-9420, USA

tel: +1-805-893 3740, fax: +1-805-893 3309
email: bonnevil@sscf.ucsb.edu
http://www.polsci.ucab.edu/

Department of Political Science
University of Washington, 111 Gowen Hall, DO-30, Seattle, WA 98195, USA
tel: +1-206-543 2700, fax: +1-206-685 2146
http://depts.washington.edu/polisci/

Department of Political Science
University of Missouri-St Louis, 8001 Natural Bridge Road, St Louis, MO 63121, USA
tel: +1-314-516 5521, fax: +1-314-516 5268
http://www.umsl.edu/~polisci

Department of Political Science
Washington University-St Louis, One Brokings Drive, St Louis, MO 63130-4899, USA
tel: +1-314-935 5822, fax: +1-314-935 5856
email: polisci@artsci.wustl.edu
http://www.artsci.wustl.edu/~polisci/

Department of Public Policy Studies
Saint Louis University, 221 North Grand Blvd, St Louis , MO 63103, USA
tel: +1-314-977 3934, fax: +1-314-977 3943
email: domahimr@slu.edu
http://www.slu.edu/colleges/cops/pps/

Department of Political Science
Stanford University, Stanford , CA 94305-2044, USA
tel: +1-650-723 1806, fax: +1-650-723 1808
email: weingast@leland.stanford.edu
http://www.stanford.edu/group/polisci/

Department of Political Science
State University of New York, Stony Brook, NY 11794-4392, USA

tel: +1-631-632 7632, fax: +1-631-632 4116
email: maryann.bell@sunysb.edu
http://www.sunysb.edu/polsci/

Department of Political Science
University of Connecticut, 341 Mansfield Road, Storrs, CT 06269-1024, USA
tel: +1-860-486 2440, fax: +1-860-486 2347
email: rourke@uconnvm.uconn.edu
http://vm.uconn.edu/~wwwpolsc

Department of Political Science
Syracuse University, Syracuse, NY 13210, USA
tel: +1-315-443 2416, fax: +1-315-443 9082
email: psc_ul@maxwell.syr.edu
http://www.maxwell.syr.edu/psc

Department of Political Science
Florida State University, Tallahassee, FL 32306-2049, USA
tel: +1-904-644 5727, fax: +1-904-644 1367
http://www.fsu.edu/~spap/

Department of Political Science
Arizona State University, Tempe, AZ 85287, USA
tel: +1-480-965 7667, fax: +1-480-965 3929
email: polisci@asu.edu
http://www.asu.edu/clas/polisci

Department of Political Science
University of Arizona, Tucson, Tucson, AZ 85721, USA
tel: +1-520-621 5051, fax: +1-520-621 5051
email: prhyner@u.arizona.edu
http://w3.arizona.edu/~polisci/

Department of Political Science
University of Alabama, Box 870213, Tuscaloosa, AL 35487, USA
tel: +1-256-890 6192, fax: +1-256-890 6949
http://www.uah.edu/colleges/liberal/ps/

Department of Political Science
University of Mississippi, Deupree Hall 309, University, MS 38677, USA

tel: +1-662-915 7401, fax: +1-662-915 7808
email: ahorn@olemiss.edu
http://www.olemiss.edu/depts/political_science/

Department of Political Science
Pennsylvania State University, University Park, PA 16802, USA
tel: +1-814-898 8290, fax: +1-814-898 6032
http://pserie.psu.edu/hss/polsc/plscindx.htm

Department of Political Science
University of Illinois, Urbana-Champaign, 391 Lincoln Hall, 702 South Wright Street, Urbana, IL 61801-3696, USA
tel: +1-217-333 3881, fax: +1-217-244 5712
email: nardulli@uiuc.edu
http://www.pol.uiuc.edu

Department of Politics
Brandeis University, Waltham, MA 02254, USA
tel: +1-781-736 2750, fax: +1-781-736 2777
email: polisci@brandeis.edu
http://www.brandeis.edu/departments/politics/

Department of Politics
Catholic University of America, Washington, DC 20064, USA
tel: +1-202-319 5128, fax: +1-202-319 6289
email: foley@cua.edu
http://arts-sciences.cua.edu/pol/

Department of Political Science
George Washington University, 2201 G Street NW, Washington, DC 20052, USA
tel: +1-202-994 6290, fax: +1-202-994 7743
http://www.gwu.edu/~psc/

Department of Government
Georgetown University, 681 Intercultural Center, Washington, DC 20057, USA
tel: +1-202-687 6130, fax: +1-202-387 5858

http://www.georgetown.edu/departments/government

Department of Political Science
Howard University, Washington, DC 20059, USA
tel: +1-202-806 6720, fax: +1-202-265 3527
email: athornton@fac.howard.edu
http://www.howard.edu/polisci/

School of Advanced International Studies
Johns Hopkins University, 1740 Massachussetts Avenue NW, Washington, DC 20036, USA
tel: +1-202-663 5630, fax: +1-202-663 7788
email: admission@mail.jhuwash.jhu.edu
http://www.sais-jhu.edu/

AMERICA, SOUTH

Argentina

Department of Political Science
Catholic University of Argentina, Edifico 'Santo Tomas Moro', Avenida Alicia Moreau de Justo 1400, 1107 Buenos Aires, Argentina
tel: +54-1-349 0249, fax: +54-1-349 0230
email: webuca@uca.edu.ar
http://www.uca.edu.ar

Political Science Programme
CEMA Instituto Universitario, Av. Córdoba 374, 1054 Buenos Aires, Argentina
tel: +54-11-4314 2269, fax: +54-11-4315 1054
email: info@cema.edu.ar
http://www.cema.edu.ar/supcp.

Institute of Political Sciences
Institute of Higher University Studies - 'Patricios Bank Foundation', Avenida Callao 312, 1022 Buenos Aires, Argentina
tel: +54-1-412 9180, fax: +54-1-801 0178
email: jonun@criba.edu.ar

Faculty of Political and Social Sciences
National University of San Juan,
Avenida del Linertador 1800, 1646
San Fernando (Buenos Aires), Argentina
tel: +54-6-421 4613, fax: +54-6-421 4586
http://www.unsj.edu.ar

School of Political Science
Palermo University, Mario Bravo 1302, 1175 Buenos Aires, Argentina
tel: +54-1-963 8624, fax: +54-1-963 1560
email: postmaster@unpalb.edu.ar
http://www.palermo.edu.ar

Department of Political Science
Universidad Del Salvador, Viamonte 1856, 1056 Buenos Aires, Argentina
tel: +54-1-322 31260, fax: +54-1-322 31260
email: uds.rect@salvador.edu.ar
http://www.salvador.edu.ar

Department of Political Science
University of Belgrano, Zabala 1837, 1426 Buenos Aires, Argentina
tel: +54-1-788 5400, fax: +54-1-788 8840
email: porto@ub.edu.ar
http://www.ub.edu.ar

Department of Political Science
University of Social Studies Buenos Aires, Avenida Corrientes 1723, 1042 Buenos Aires, Argentina
tel: +54-1-375 4601, fax: +54-1-375 4600

Faculty of Political Science and International Relations
Catholica University of Cordoba, Obispo Trejo 323, 500 Cordoba, Argentina
tel: +54-5-123 5331, fax: +54-5-123 1937

Faculty of Political Science
Universidad Nacional de Cuyo, Mendoza, Argentina
http://www.uncu.edu.ar/politic/

Faculty of Political Science and International Relations
Universitad Nacional de Rosario, Cordoba 1814, 200 Rosario (Santa Fe), Argentina
tel: +54-4-125 7146, fax: +54-4-1259454
email: postmaster@fcpolit.unr.edu.ar
http://www.unr.edu.ar/facultades/fcpolit.htm

Faculty of Law and Political Sciences
Catholic University of Santiago del Estero, Campus Universitario, Casilla de Correo 285, 4200 Santiago del Estero, Argentina
tel: +54-8-5213820, fax: +54-8-521 9754

Bolivia

Faculty of Law and Political Sciences
University of San Simon
Cochabama, Casilla Postal 992, Calle Sucre, Trinidad, Beni, Bolivia
tel: +591-4-62 1590, fax: +591-4-62 0236

Faculty of Law and Political Science
University of San Andres-La Paz, Casilla Postal 6042, Avenida Villazon 1995, La Paz (Murillo), Bolivia
tel: +591-2-35 9490, fax: +591-2-39 2232
email: webmaster@umsanet.edu.bo
http://www.umsanet.edu.bo

Faculty of Law and Political and Social Sciences
Technical University of Oruro-Oruro, Avenida 6 de Octubre, Casilla Postal 49, Oruro, Bolivia
tel: +591-52-50 100, fax: +591-52-42 215
email: dicyt@utonet.bo

Faculty of Law, Political and Social Sciences
University of San Francisco Xavier-Sucre, Casilla Postal 212, Junin esq. Estudiantes 692, Sucre Chuquisaca, Bolivia
tel: +591-64-53 245, fax: +591-64-62 205

email: gonzales@mara.scr.entelnet.
bo

Brazil

Instituto de Pesquisas Socias
Fundacao Jaoquim Nabuco, Rua
Dois Irmaos, 92, Apipucos PE
52071-440, Brazil
tel: +55-81-441 5537
email: clovati@fundaj.gov.br

Political science
Universidad de Brasilia, Caxia
Postal 15299, Campus Universitario
Darcy Ribeiro, Asa Norte 70910-900,
Brazil
tel: +55-61-348 2022, fax: +55-61-272
0003
email: unb@guarany.cpd.unb.br
http://www.unb.br

Museu Paraense Emilio Goeldi
Universidade Federal do Para, Av
Perimetral, 1901, Guama, Belem PA
66077-505, Brazil
tel: +55-91-249 4857, fax: +55-91-226
1615

Mestrado em Cienca Politica
UFMG, Av Antonio Carlos, 6627,
Pamphula, Belo Horizonte, MG
31270-900, Brazil
tel: +55-31-499 5030, fax: +55-31-499
5060
email: avritzer@fafich.ufmg.br

Department of Political Science
State University of Campinas, Cidade Universitaria Zefferino Vaz,
13081-900 Campinas (Sao Paolo),
Brazil
tel: +55-19-239 3000, fax: +55-19-239
4683
email: jmartins@ifi.unicamp.br
http://www.unicamp.br

*Prog de Politica Cientifica e Tec-
nologica*
Universidade Estadual de Campinas,
Cidade Universitaria Zefferino Vaz,
Instituto de Geociencias, Campinas
SP 13083-970, Brazil
tel: +55-19-788 4555, fax: +55-19-289

1562
email: furtado@ige.unicamp.br

Nucleo de Estudos de pol. Publicas
Universidade de Campinas, Av Albert Einstein, 1300-Distrito Campinas, Campinas, SP 13081-970, Brazil
tel: +55-19-289 3143, fax: +55-19-289
4519
email: pbar@nepp.unicamp.br

*Faculty of Political Sciences and
Economics*
Universidad de Cruz Alta, Andrade
Neves 308, 98025-810 Cruz Alta (Rio
Grande do Sul), Brazil
tel: +55-55-322 8400, fax: +55-55-322
8000
email: webmas-
ter@main.unicruz.tche-br
http://www.unicruz.tche.br

Political science
Universidade do Santa Catarina,
Caixa Postal 476, Campus Universitario 'Trinidade', 88040-900 Flori-
anopolis, Brazil
tel: +55-48-331 9320, fax: +55-48-234
4069
email: gabinete@reitoria.ufsc.br
http://www.ufsc.br

Mestrado em Ciencias Socias
Universidade Federal do Rio
Grande do Norte, Campus Universitario, BR 101, Laoa Nova, Natal
RN 59072-970, Brazil
tel: +55-84-215 3556
email: ppgcs@cchla.ufrn.br

*Institute of Sociology and Political
Science*
Universidad Federal do Pelotas,
Caixa Postal 354, Campus Universitario, 96010-900 Pelotas, Brazil
tel: +55-53-275 7000, fax: +55-53-275
9023
http://www.ufpel.br

*Centro de mestrado em cienca poli-
tica*
Universidade Federal de Pernambuco, Av Academico Helio Ramos
S/N, Recife PE 50740-530, Brazil
tel: +55-11-271 8283

Faculty of Political Science and Economics
Candido Mendes University, Praca XV de Novembro 101, Centro, 20010 Rio de Janeiro, Brazil
tel: +55-21-222 6201

Centro Pesq doc Historia
Fundacao Getulio Vargas, Prais do Botafogo 190-12 Andar, Botafogo, RJ 22253-900, Brazil
tel: +55-201-536 9421
email: bomeny@fgv.br

Prog de Pos Grad em Cienca Politica
Instituo de Pesq do Rio de Janeiro, Rua da Matriz, 82, Botafogo RJ 22260-100, Brazil
tel: +55-21-537 8020, fax: +55-21-286 7146
email: mjasmin@iuperj.br

Instituto de Relacoes Internacionais
Pontificia Universidade Catolica do Rio de Janeiro, Rua Marques de Sao Vicente, 225, Gavea, RJ 22453-900, Brazil
tel: +55-21-529 9494, fax: +55-21-274 1296
email: iripuc@rdc.puc-rio.br

Instituto de Filosofia e Ciencias Humanas
Universidade Federal do Rio de Janeiro, Campus Marcana, Pavilhao Joao Lyra Filo 9 andar, 9 andar, Blocos B & F, Rio De Janeiro, Brazil
tel: +55-21-587 7678
email: ifch@uerj.br
http://www.uerj.br

School of Political Science
Pontifical Catholic University of Rio Grande do Sul, Caixa Postal 1429, Avenida Ipiranga 6681, Partenon 90619-900, Porto Alegre, Brazil
tel: +55-51-339 1020, fax: +55-51-339 1564
email: gabreit@tauros.pucrs.br
http://www.pucrs.br

Centro de mestrado em cienca politica
Universidade Federal Fluminense, Campus Gragoata Blocco 'O', Salas,

Sao Domingos, RJ 24210-350, Brazil
tel: +55-21-620 5194, fax: +55-21-719 8012
email: ppgacp@web4u.com.br

CEDOPE
Universidade do Vale do Rio dos Sinos, Avenida Unisinos, 950 CP 275, Sao Laopoldo RS 96022-000, Brazil
tel: +55-51-590 1611, fax: +55-51-592 9292
email: cedope@netu.unisinos.tche.br

Political science
IDESP, Rua Desembargador Guimaraes, 21, Aqua Branca, SP 05002-050, Brazil
tel: +55-11-864 7500, fax: +55-11-263 1605

Mestrado em Cienca Politica
UNICAMP, IFCH-CX Postal 6110, Cidade Universitaria, Cidade Universitaria, Campinas SP 13083-970, Brazil
tel: +55-19-788 1609
email: rachel@turing.unicamp.br

Philosophy, Letters and Human Sciences
Universidad de Sao Paulo, Caixa Postal 3751, Rua de Reitoria, Cidade Universitaria, SP CEP 05508-900, Brazil
tel: +55-11-818 4645
email: extensao_fflch@recad.usp.br
http://www.fflch.usp.br/bem-vindo

Centro de Estudos rurais e urbanos
Universidade de Sao Paolo, Av Prof Luciano Gualberto, Cidade Universitaria, Sao Paulo 05508-900, Brazil
tel: +55-11-210 9416
email: cea@edu.usp.br

Chile

Faculty of Political Science
Catholic University of Chile, Avda Bernardo O'Higgins, 340 Offici-D, Santiago, Chile
tel: +56-2-222 4516, fax: +56-2-222 5515

email: nalsina@lascar.puc.cl
http://www.puc.cl

School of Political Science
Central University Santiago, Toesca,
1783 Santiago, Chile
tel: +56-2-699 5151, fax: +56-2-672
7322
email: jsepulve@montt.ucentral.cl
http://www.ucentral.cl

Instituto de Cienca Politica
Universidad de Chile, Av B
O'Higgins 1058, Santiago, Chile
tel: +56-2-671 5651/671 7725, fax:
+56-2-695 3915
email: icpuch@uchile.cl
http://www.cien-politica.uchile.cl

Department of Political Science
University Academy of Christian
Humanism Santiago, Alonso Ovalle
1475, Santiago, Chile
tel: +56-2-695 4831, fax: +56-2-695
4824

Department of Political Science
University of the Republic Santiago,
Agustinas 1831, Santiago, Chile
tel: +56-2-697 0562, fax: +56-2-671
8457

Colombia

Faculty of Political Science
Colegio Mayor de Nuestra Senora
del Rosario, Calle 14 No 6-25, Santafe de Bogota, Colombia
tel: +57-1-282 0088, fax: +57-1-281
8583
email: mlom-
bana@claustro.urosario.edu.co
http://www.urosario.edu.co

*Department of Political and Admin-
istrative Sciences*
College of Public Administration
'ESAP' Bogota, Diagonal 40 No
46A-37, Santafe de Bogota, Colombia
tel: +57-1-269 9147, fax: +57-1-222
4356

Faculty of Law and Political Science
Universidad La Gran Colombia,
Apartado aereo 7909, Carrera 6 No
13-40, Santafe de Bogota, Colombia
tel: +57-1-343 8047, fax: +57-1-282
8386

*Faculty of Political and Social Sci-
ences*
Universidad Nacional de Colombia,
Apartado 14490, Ciudad Universitaria, Santafe de Bogota, Colombia
tel: +57-1-316 5000, fax: +57-1-221
9891
email: ori@bacata.usc.unal.edu.co
http://www.usc.unal.edu.co

Faculty of Law and Political Science
University Santo Tomas Bogota,
Carrera 13, 51-16, Santafe de Bogota
2, Colombia
tel: +57-1-211 0085, fax: +57-1-211
6368
email: rector@usta.edu.co
http://www.usta.edu.co

Costa Rica

Department of Political Science
Universidad Nacional, Apartado 86,
Heredia, Costa Rica
tel: +506-261 0101, fax: +506-237
7032
http://www.una.ac.cr

Department of Political Sciences
Universidad Costa Rica, Ciudad
Universitaria Rodrigo Facio, San
Jose 2060, Costa Rica
tel: +506-253 5353, fax: +506-234
0452
email: ucrector@cariari.ucr.ac.cr
http://cariari.ucr.ac.cr

Dominican Republic

Faculty of Law and Political Science
Central University of the East, San
Pedro de Macoris, Avenida Circunvalacion, San Pedro de Macoris,
Dominican Republic
tel: +1809-529-3562, fax: +1809-529-
5146

Faculty of Law and Political Science
Autonomous University of Santo
Domingo, Avenida Alma Mater, Ciudad Universitaria, Ciudad Universitaria, Santa Domingo, Dominican
Republic
tel: +1809-533-1104, fax: +1809-553-
1106

Faculty of Law and Political Science
Santo Domingo Catholic University,
c/Santo Domingo 3, La Julia, Santo
Domingo, Dominican Republic
tel: +1809-544-2812, fax: +1809-540-
2351

Ecuador

*Faculty of Law and Political and
Social Sciences*
Catholic University of Cuenca, Calle
Bolivar y Benigo Malo 9-49, Apartado de Correos 19A, Cuenca, Ecuador
tel: +593-7-842 606, fax: +593-7-838
011

*Faculty of Law, Social and Political
Sciences*
Civil University 'Eloy Alfaro' de
Manabi, Via San Mateo, Casilla
2732, Manta, Manabi, Ecuador
tel: +593-4-620 288, fax: +593-4-623
009

*Faculty of Law, Social and Political
Sciences*
Central University of Ecuador
Quito, Avenida America y Alfredo
Perez Guerrero, Apartado 166,
Quito, Ecuador
tel: +593-2-524 714

El Salvador

Faculty of Political Science
New University San Salvador, Calle
Arce y 23 Avenida Sur No 1243, San
Salvador, El Salvador
tel: +503-221-2288, fax: +503-221-
2729

Guatemala

Faculty of Political Science
University Rafael Landivar Guatemala, Vista Hermosa 111, Zona 16,
Guatemala
tel: +502-2-364 0162, fax: +502-2-364
0464

Mexico

*College of Political Science and Pub-
lic Administration*
Autonomous University of Campeche, Ciudad Universitaria, 24030
Campeche, Mexico
tel: +52-98-165 243, fax: +52-98-165
243
http://www.uacam.mx

*School of Political and Social Sci-
ences*
University of Colima, Avenida Universidad 333, 28000 Colima, Mexico
tel: +52-33-128 510, fax: +52-33-143
006
http://www.ucol.mx

*Department of Political and Social
Sciences*
Iberian-American University Mexico, Temistocles 33, 11560 Colonia
Polanco, Mexico
tel: +52-5-280 4868, fax: +52-5-281
1838
http://www.uia.mx/default.html

*Faculty of Political and Social Sci-
ences*
National Autonomous University of
Mexico, Ciudad Universitaria, 04150
Coyoacan, Mexico
tel: +52-5-622 1280, fax: +52-5-616
0035
email: fbarnes@servidor.unam.mx
http://serpiente.dgsca.unam.mx

Department of Political Science
Autonomous University of Nuevo
Leon, Ciudad Universitaria, 6400
Monterrey, Mexico
tel: +52-83-522-885, fax: +52-83-767
757
http://www.dsi.uanl.mx

Faculty of Political Science
Autonomous University of Queretaro, Centro Universitario, Cerro de
las Campanas, 76010 Queretaro,
Mexico
tel: +52-42-163 242, fax: +52-42-164
917
email: webmas-
ter@sunserver.uaq.mx
http://www.uaq.mx

*Department of Political Science and
Public Administration*
Autonomous University of the
North East, Saltillo, Monoclova
1561, Col Republica, 25280 Saltillo,
Mexico
tel: +52-84-164 677, fax: +52-84-163
153

Department of Political Science
Autonomous University of Tlaxcala,
9 Avenida Universidad 1, 90000
Tlaxcala, Mexico
tel: +52-91-246 21167, fax: +52-91-
246 21167
email: rectoria@garza.uatx.mx
http://www.uatx.mx

Department of Political Science
Universidad Torreon, Blvd Revolu-
cion 590 Ote, Torreon, Mexico
tel: +52-17-122 379, fax: +52-17-167-
488
http://www.sal.uadec.mx

Panama

*Department of Law and Political
Science*
Santa Maria La Antigua University
Panama, Apartado 6-1696, Estafeta
El Dorado, Panama 6, Panama
tel: +507-361-868, fax: +507-361-022
http://www.usma.ac.pa

Faculty of Law and Political Science
University of Panama, Ciudad Universitaria, Dr Octavio Mendez
Pereira, El Cangrejo-Estafeta Universitaria, Panam 3, Panama
tel: +507-223-0654, fax: +507-264-
3733

email: info@up.ac.pa
http://www.up.ac.pa

Paraguay

Department of Political Science
Catholic University, Asuncion,
Independencia Nacional y Comu-
neros, Casilla 1718, Asuncion, Paraguay
tel: +595-21-441 044, fax: +595-21-
445 245

Peru

Faculty of Law and Political Sciences
Catholic University of Santa Maria,
CP 1350, Samuel Velarde 320, Uma-
collo, Arequipa, Peru
tel: +51-54-251 112, fax: +51-54-252
542
email: lcarpio@ucsm.edu.pe

Faculty of Law and Political Science
'Los Andes' Private University,
Huancayo, Jr Puno 551-561, Huancayo, Junin, Peru
tel: +51-64-234 480, fax: +51-64-223
848

Faculty of Law and Political Science
University of Huanuco, Jr Hermilio
Valdizan 871, Jiron Constitucion
650, Huanuco, Peru
tel: +51-64-513 154, fax: +51-64-513
154

Faculty of Law and Political Science
National University 'La Libertad'
Trujillo, Independencia 431, Oficina
216, Casilla 315, Trujillo, La Libertad, Peru
tel: +51-44-243 721, fax: +51-44-256
629

Department of Political Science
Inca Private University 'Garcilaso
de la Vega', Lince, Avenida Arequipa 1841, Lince, Lima, Peru
tel: +51-1-711 421

Faculty of Law and Political Science
National University of San Marcos,
Lima, Avenida Republica de Chile

295, Lima, Peru
tel: +51-1-431 4629

Faculty of Law and Political Science
University of Lima, Avenida Javier
Prado Este s/n, Monterrico, Lima
33, Peru
tel: +51-1-437 6767, fax: +51-1-437
8066
email: duii@ulima.edu.pe
http://www.ulima.edu.pe

*Department of Social and Political
Sciences*
University of the Pacific, Lima,
Avenida Salaverry 2020, Apartado
4683, Jesus Maria, Lima 11, Peru
tel: +51-1-472 9635, fax: +51-1-470
6121
email: up@up.edu.pe
http://www.up.edu.pe

Faculty of Law and Political Science
Women's University of the Sacred
Heart, Lima, Avenida Los Frutales
s/n, Monterrico, Lima, Peru
tel: +51-14-364 641, fax: +51-14-436
3247
email: postmaster@unife.edu.pe

Faculty of Law and Political Science
National University 'Federico Vil-
larreal', San Miguel, Calle Carlos
Gonzales 285, San Miguel, Lima,
Peru
tel: +51-1-464 1301, fax: +51-1-464
4370

Uruguay

Instituto de Cienca Politica
Universidad de la Republica, Emilio
Frugoni 1385, 2o Piso, Montevideo,
Uruguay
tel: +598-2-409 8168/1652, fax: +598-
2 480 303
http://www.rau.edu.uy

Venezuela

Faculty of Political Sciences and Law
Central University of Venezuela Caracas, Ciudad Universitaria, Los
Chaguaramas, Caracas 1051, Venezuela

tel: +58-2-605 40 50, fax: +58-2-605
47 97
http://www.ucv.edu.ve

Faculty of Law and Political Sciences
University of the Andes, Merida,
Avenida 3, Plaza Bolvar, Entre cal-
les 23 y 24, Edificio del Rectorado,
Merida, Venezuela
tel: +58-74-40 1111
http://www.ula.ve

Faculty of Law and Political Sciences
Catholic University of Tachira,
Apartado 366, San Cristobal (
Estado Tachira), Venezuela
tel: +58-76-442 080, fax: +58-76-446
183

ASIA

Afghanistan

Faculty of Law and Political Science
Kabul University, Aliabad, Kabul,
Afghanistan
tel: +93-873-40341

Armenia

Faculty of Political Sciences
American University of Armenia,
Marshal Bagramian St 40, 375019
Yerevan, Armenia
tel: +374-2-270 309, fax: +374-2-151
048
email: auacs@aua.arminco.com

Azerbaijan

Department of Political Science
University of Hazar, Ul Mehseti,
Baku 370096, Azerbaijan
tel: +994-12-21 79 27, fax: +994-12-98
93 79
email: khazar@azeri.com

Faculty of Political Science
Western University of Baku, Ul Isti-
glalliyat 27, Baku 370001, Azerbaijan
tel: +994-12-92 74 18, fax: +994-12-92

67 01
email: rektorat@western.baku.az

Bangladesh

Department of Political Science
University of Chittagong, Chittagong, Chittagong, Bangladesh
tel: +880-31-682031-39, 714923, fax: +880-31-726310

Department of Government and Politics
Jahangirnagar University, Savar, Dhaka, Bangladesh

Department of Political Science
University of Dhaka, Dhaka 1000, Bangladesh
tel: +880-2-9661 92059 ext 4460, fax: +880-2-8615583
email: duregstr@bangla.net

Department of Political Science and Public Adninistation
Islamic University, Kushtia, Bangladesh
tel: +880-71-53029, fax: +880-71-54400

Department of Political Science
University of Rajshahi, PO Rajshahi University, Rajshahi 6025, Bangladesh
tel: +80-721-750041, fax: +880-721-750064

Department of Political Science and Public Administration
Shahjalal University of Science and Technology, Slyhet, Bangladesh
tel: +880-821-713491, fax: +880-821-715257

Brunei

Department of Political Science
University of Brunei Darussalam, Jalan Tungku Link, Gadong BE 1410, Negara Brunei Darussalam, Brunei

China

Institute of Political Science
Beijing Normal University, 19 Xinjiekouwai Street, Beijing 100875, China
tel: +86-10-622 07960, fax: +86-10-620 0567

College of International Relations
Peking University, Zhongguancun, Haidan District, Beijing 100871, China
http://www.pku.edu.cn

Department of Political Science and Public Administration
Peking University, Loudouqiao, Haidian District, Beijing 100871, China
tel: +86-10-255 4002, fax: +86-10-256 4095

Institute of Public Administration and Political Science
People's University of China, 175 Haidian Road, Haidian District, Beijing 100872, China
tel: +86-10-625 11301, fax: +86-10-625 15332
email: rmdxwsc@public.btd.net.cn

Department of Political Science
Jilin University, 79 Jeifang Road, Changchun, Jilin Province 130023, China
tel: +86-431-431 3907, fax: +86-431-43 16776
http://www.jlu.edu.cn

Department of Political Science
Guangxi Normal University, Guilin, Guangxi 541004, China
tel: +86-77-344-2982, fax: +86-77-344 2383

Department of Politics
Zhongshan University, 135 Xingang West Road, Guangzhou 510275, China
http://www.zsu.edu.cn

Department of Political Science
Hangzhou University, 34 Tien Mu Shan Road, Hangzhou, Zheijang Province 310028, China

tel: +86-571-807 1224, fax: +86-571-807 0107
http://www.hzuniv.edu.cn

Department of Political Science
Zhejiang University, 20 Yugu Road, Hangzhou, Zhejinag Province 310027, China
tel: +86-571-517 2244, fax: +86-571-795 1358
email: ipo-qjz@sun.zju@edu.cn
http://www.zju.edu.cn

Department of Political Science
Shanxi Normal University, Linfen, Shanxi Province 041004, China

Department of Political Science
Nanjing University, 22 Hankou Road, Nanjing, Jiangsu Province 210093, China
tel: +86-25-330 2728, fax: +86-25-663 7551
www.math.latech.edu/nanda

Department of Politics
East China Normal University, Zhongshang North Road, Shanghai 200433, China
http://www.ecnu.edu.cn

Department of International Politics
Fudan University, 220 Handan Road, Shanghai 200433, China
http://www.fdu.edu.cn

Department of Political Science
Liaoning University, Zhongshan West Road, Huanggu District, Shenyang 110036, China

Department of Political Science
Shanxi University, 36 Wucheng Road, Taiyuan, Shanxi Province 300006, China
tel: +86-351-707 4960, fax: +86-351 704 0981
email: zhj@shanxi.ihep.ac.cn
http://www.sxu.edu.cn

Department of Political Science
Nankai University, 94 Weijin Road, Tianjin, Tientsin 300071, China
tel: +86-22-235 08229, fax: +86-22-235 02990
http://www.nankai.edu.cn

Department of Political Science
Central China Normal University, 100 Luoyu Avenue, Wuhan, Hubei Privince 430070, China
tel: +86-27-871 85601, fax: +86-27-871 86070

Department of Political Science
Central South University of Finance and Economics, 114 Wuluo Road Wuhan, 430064 Hubei Province, China
tel: +86-27-888-75042, fax: +86-27-888 71730

Department of Political Sciences
Wuhan University, Luojiashan, Wuhan District, Wuhan, Hubei Province 430072, China
tel: +86-27-888 12712, fax: +86-27-878 12661
http://www.whu.edu.cn

Department of Political Science
Zhengzhou University, 75 Daxue Road, Zhengzhou, Hanan Province 420052, China
tel: +86-371-797 3682, fax: +86-371-797 3895
http://www.zzu.edu.cn

China:Hong Kong

Faculty of Political and Social Sciences
Lingnan College, Tuen Mun, Hong Kong, China:Hong Kong
tel: +852-2-616 8888, fax: +852-2-463-8383
email: registry@ln.edu.hk
http://www.ln.edu.hk

India

Department of Political Science
MDS University of Ajmer, Ajmer, Rajasthan 305001, India

Department of Political Science
Aligarh Muslim University, Aligarh, UP 202002, India
tel: +91-571-700 994/700087
http://www.olemiss.edu/rikhan

Department of Political Science
University of Allahabad, Allahabad,
UP 211002, India
tel: +91-532-545020, fax: +91-532-
424021

Department of Political Science
Guru Nanak Dev University, Amritsar 143005, India
tel: +91-183-258811/258822
email: hssoch@gndu.ernet.in

Department of Political Science
Sri Krishna Devaraya University,
PO Sri Venkateswarapuram, Anan-
tapur, AP 515003, India
tel: +91-85-545 5231, fax: +91-85-545
5244

Department of Political Science
Annamalai University, PO An-
namalainagar, South Arcot Dist,
Tamil Nadu 608002, India
tel: +91-41-443 8283/8214

*Department of Political Science and
Public Administration*
BR Ambedkar Marathwada University, Aurangabad, 431004 Maharashtra, India
tel: +91-240-331069/331007, fax:
+91-240-334291

Department of Political Science
University of Lucknow, Badshah
Bagh, Lucknow, UP 226007, India
tel: +91-522-330065/385592

Department of Political Science
Banasthali University, PO Banasthali Vidyapeeth, Rajasthan 304002,
India
tel: +91-14-382 8373/8340, fax: +91-
14 382 8365
email: ds@bv.ernet.in

Department of Political Science
Bangalore University, Jnana Bhar-
thi, Bangalore, Karnataka 560056,
India
tel: +91-80-321 3172, fax: +91-80-338
9295
email: bang@sirnetb.ernet.in

*Department of Politics and Admini-
stration Unit*
Institute for Social and Economic
Change, Bangalore 560072, India

Department of Political Science
Berhampur University, Berhampur,
Dist Ganjam, Dist Ganjam, Orissa
760007, India
tel: +91-680-282233/200460, fax:
+91-680-282227

Department of Political Science
Bhagalpur University, Bhagalpur,
Bihar 812007, India
tel: +91-641-422600/401240, fax:
+91-641-422576

Department of Political Science
Barkatullah Vishav Vidyala,
Hoshangabad Road, Bhopal MP
462026, India
tel: +91-755-587236/585854, fax:
+91-755-581835

Department of Political Science
Utkal University, PO Vani Vihar,
Bhuwaneswar, Bhuwaneshwar,
751004 Orissa, India
tel: +91-674-481 850/354

Department of Political Science
Guru Ghasidas University, P O
Koni, Bilaspur, Bilaspur, Madhya
Pradesh 495009, India
tel: +91-775-240784/242786, fax:
+91-775-240785

Department of Political Science
Magadh University, Bodh Gaya, Bihar 844234, India
tel: +91-631-400995/420714, fax:
+91-631-420717

Department of Politics and Civics
University of Bombay, Vidyavihar,
Kalina Campus, Fort Bombay
400032, India

*Department of International Rela-
tions*
Jadavpur University, Calcutta
700032, W Bengal, India
tel: +91-33-473 5508, fax: +91-33-473
6236
email: anb@jufs.ernet.in

Department of Political Science
Rabindra Bharati University, Dwar-
kanath Tagore Lane, Calcutta
700007, India
tel: +91-33-556 8019, fax: +91-33-556
8079

Department of Political Science
University of Calcutta, 87 College
Street, Calcutta 700073, W Bengal,
India
tel: +91-33-241 3288, fax: +91-33-241
3222
email: registrar@evcc.ernet.in

Department of Political Science
Manipur University, Canchipur,
Imphal Manipur 795003, India
tel: +91-385-220529, fax: +91-385-
221429

Department of Political Science
Panjab University, Sector 14,
Chandigarh 160014, India
tel: +91-17-254 1945, fax: +91-17-254
1022
email: pulib@puchd.ren.nic.in

Department of Political Science
University of Delhi, Delhi 110007,
India
tel: +91-11-725011, fax: +91-11-
725049
http://www.du.ac.in

Department of Political Science
Dibrugarh University, PO Di-
brugarh University, Assam 786004,
India

*Department of Political Science and
Development Administration*
Gandhigram Rural Institute
(Deemed University), Gandhigram,
Dindigul District, India
tel: +91-451-452371, fax: +91-451-
452323
email: Gricc@md3.vsnl.net.in

Department of Political Science
Siddhu Kanhu University, Santal
Pargana, Drumka, Bihar 814101, India
tel: +91-643-423 006, fax: +91-643-
422 415

Department of Political Science
Gauhati University, PO Gopinath
Bardoloi Nagar, Guwahati, Assam
781014, India
tel: +91-361-570412, fax: +91-361-
570133

Department of Political Science
Goa University, PO Santa Cruz, Tal-
eigao Plateau, Goa 403002, India
tel: +91-83-222 1377, fax: +91-83-222
4184
email: vc@univgoa.ernet.in

Department of Political Science
University of Gorakhpur, Gorakhpur, UP 273009, India

*Department of Political Science and
Public Administration*
Doctor Harisingh Gour University,
Gour Nagar, Sagar MP 470003, India
tel: +91-758-223796, fax: +91-758-
223236

Department of Political Science
Sardar Patel University, PB No 10,
Vallabh Vidyanagar 388120, Gujarat, India
tel: +91-26-924 6573, fax: +91-26-924
6475
email: root@patel.ernet.in

Department of Political Science
North Gujarat University, PO Box
21, University Road, Patan,
Mehsana Gujarat 384265, India
tel: +91-27-663 0427, fax: +91-27-663
1917

Department of Political Science
Gulbarga University, Gulbarga,
Karnataka 585106, India
tel: +91-84-724 5447, fax: +91-84-724
5632
email: gu@vsnl.com

Department of Political Science
University of Kashmir, Hazaratbal,
Srinagar, J&K State 190006, India
tel: +91-194-423345, fax: +91-194-
421357

Department of Political Science
Dr Babasaheb Ambedkar Open
University, Road No 46, Jubilee
Hills, Hyderabad, India
tel: +91-40-354 4830, fax: +91-40 354
4830
email: aou@aouni.ren.nic.in

Department of Political Science
Osmania University, Hyderabad,
AP 500007, India
tel: +91-40-701 8048, fax: +91-40-701
9020
email: vcou@staff.osmania.ac.in

Department of Political Science
University of Hyderabad, PO Central University, Hyderabad AP
500046, India
tel: +91-40-301 0170, fax: +91-40-301
1090
http://www.uphyd.ernet.in

Department of Political Science
Arunachal University, Rono Hills,
Doimukh, Itanagar, AP 791111, India
tel: +91-36-277 252, fax: +91-36-277
317
http://www.uphyd.ernet.in

Department of Political Science
University of Rajasthan, Jaipur, Rajasthan 302004, India
tel: +91-141-516 470

Department of Political Science
Jamia Milia Islamia University,
Jamia Nagar, New Delhi 110025,
India
tel: +91-11-684 4650, fax: +91-11-682
2153
email: cit@jmi.ernet.in

Department of Political Science
University of Jammu, New Campus,
Jammu Tawi, J&K State 180004, India
tel: +91-191-435 368, fax: +91-191-
450 014

Department of Political Science
Bundelkhand University, Jhansi, UP
284001, India

Department of Political Science
Jia Narain Vyas University, Jodhpur, Rajasthan 342001, India
tel: +91-291-432 947

International Studies School
Pondicherry University, Kalapet,
Pondicherry 605104, India
tel: +91-413-655 175
email: vtpatil@pondiuni.ren.nic.in

Department of Political Science
University of Kalyani, PO Kaliani,
Dist Nadia 741235, W Bengal, India
tel: +91-316-282 8690
email: postmaster@klyuniv.uunet.in

Department of Political Science
LN Mithila University, Kameshwar
Nagar, Darbhanga, Bihar 846004,
India
tel: +91-62-722 2463, fax: +91-62-722
2598

Department of Political Science
Kota Open University, Rawatbhata
Road, Akelgarh, Kota, Rajasthan
324010, India
tel: +91-74-442 1254, fax: +91-74-442
6451
email: root@kou.raj.nic.in

Department of Political Science
Kurukshetra University, Kurukshetra, Haryana 132119, India
tel: +91-174-420 417, fax: +91-174-
420 277
email: vc@kuk.ernet.in

*Department of Political Science and
Public Administration*
University of Madras, Centenary
Building, Chepauk, Madras 600 005,
India
tel: +91-44-536 1074, fax: +91-44-536
7654
email: vcoffice@univmad.ernet.in

Department of Political Science
Mangalore University, Mangala
Gangotri, Gangotri, 574199 Karnataka, India
tel: +91-824-742 139, fax: +91-824-
742 367
email: vc@mnglr.ernet.in

Department of Political Science
Indira Gandhi National Open University, IGNOU Campus, Maidan Garhi, ND 110068, India
tel: +91-11-686 2707, fax: +91-11-686 5933
email: ignou@giasdl01.vsnl.net.in

Department of Political Science
Chaudhary Charan Singh University (Meerut University), Meerut, UP 250001, India

Department of Political Science
University of Bihar, Muzzafarpur, Bihar 842001, India

Department of Political Science
University of Mysore, BP No 406, Mysore, Karnataka 570005, India
tel: +91-821-564 666, fax: +91-821-521 263
email: uomeb@guasbg01.vsnl.net.in

Department of Political Science
Nagarujana University, Nagarjuna Nagar, Dist Guntur, AP 522510, India
tel: +91-86-329 3238, fax: +91-86-329 3378
email: nagavc@ind3.vsnl.net.in

Department of Political Science and Public Administration
Nagpur University, Nagpur, 440001 Maharashtra, India
tel: +91-712-523 045, fax: +91-712-523 841

Department of Political Science
Kumaon University, Nainital, UP 263001, India

Department of Political Science
Gujarat University, Navrangpura, Ahmedabad 380 009, India
tel: +91-79-644 0341, fax: +91-79-644 1664

Centre for International Politics
Jawaharlal Nehru University, Mehrauli Road, New Delhi 110067, India
tel: +91-11-616 2016, fax: +91-11-616 8234
email: adatta@juniv.ernet.in

Department of Political Science
Madurai Kamaraj University, Palkalai Nagar, Madurai, Tamil Nadu 625021, India
tel: +91-452-859 166, fax: +91-452-585 449
email: vcmku@vsnl.com

Department of Political Sciences
Punjabi University, Patiala, 147002 Punjab, India
tel: +91-175-282 418, fax: +91-175 283 073
email: jsa@pbi.ernet.in

Department of Political Science
Patna University, Patna, Bihar 800005, India
tel: +91-612-670 352, fax: +91-612-670 877
email: rksebipu@bih.nic.in

Department of Political Science
University of Pune, Pune, Maharashtra 411007, India
tel: +91-20-565 3868, fax: +91-20-565 3899
email: puvc@unipune.ernet.in

Department of Political Science
Shri Jagannath Sanskrit University, Shri Vihar, Puri, Orissa 752002, India

Department of Political Science
Ravishankar Shukla University, Raipur, Madhya Pradesh 4920100, India

Department of Political Science
University of Burdwan, PO Rajbati, Dist Burdwan 713014, W Bengal, India
tel: +91-342-62900, fax: +91-342-64452
email: vcdkbasu@dte.vsnl.net.in

Department of Political Science
Saurashtra University, Kalavad Road, Rajkot 360005, Gujarat, India

Department of Political Science
Ranchi University, Ranchi, Bihar 834001, India
tel: +91-651-206 177

Department of Political Science
Awadesh Pratap Singh University,
Rewa, Madhaya Pradesh 486003,
India
tel: +91-776-251 519
email: uni@asprewa.mp.nic.in

Department of Political Science
Maharishi Dayanand University,
Rohtak, Haryana 124001, India
tel: +91-12-627 3427
email: vc@mdui.ernet.in

Department of Political Science and
Public Administration
Sambalpur University, Jyoti Vihar
Burla, Sambalpur, Orissa 768017,
India
tel: +91-66-343-0158

Department of Political Science
Vishva Bharati University, PO
Shantiniketan, Dist Birbhum, 731235
WB, India

Department of Political Science
North Eastern Hill University, Shillong, Meghalaya 793001, India
tel: +91-364-250 101

Department of Political Science
Himachal Pradesh University,
Summer Hills, Shimla, HP 171005,
India
tel: +91-177-231 363

Department of Political Science
Assam University, PO Box 63, Silchar, Assam 788001, India
tel: +91-38-427 0801, fax: +91-38-427 0802

Department of Political Science
Andhra Pradesh Open University,
6-3-645 Somajiguda, Hyderabad
500482, India

Department of Political Science
HN Bahuguna Garhwal University,
Srinagar, Dist Garhwal, UP 246174,
India
tel: +91-138-852 167
email: vc@hnbgugrw.ren.nic.in

Department of Public Administration
South Gujarat University, PO Box
49, Udhana Magdalla Road, Surat

395007, India
tel: +91-261-227 942
email: sgsurat@guj.nic.in

Department of Political Science
University of Kerala, University PO,
Thiruvananthapuram 695034, Kerala, India
tel: +91-471-306 634
email: keralauniversity@vsnl.com

Department of Political Science
Sri Venkateshwara University,
Tirupati, Dist Chittoor, 517502
Andhra, India
tel: +91-857-427 727
email: vc@svuni.ren.nic.in

Department of Political Science
Mohan Lal Sukhadia University,
Udaipur, Rajasthan 313001, India
tel: +91-29-441 3597
email: vc@misu.ernet.in

Department of Political Science
Vikram University, Ujjain, 456010
MP, India
tel: +91-734-552 070

Department of Political Science
Banaras Hindu University, Varanasi, UP 221005, India
tel: +91-54-231 6938
email: vcbhu@banaras.ernet.in

Faculty of Social Sciences and Political Science
Mahatma Gandhi Kashi Vidyapith,
Varanasi, Uttar Pradesh 221002, India
tel: +91-54-235 8160, fax: +91-54-235 0268

Department of Political Science
Jiwaji University, Vidya Vihar,
Gwalior, MP 474011, India

Department of Political Science
Shivaji University, Vidyanagar,
Kohlapur 416004, Maharashtra, India
tel: +91-231-692 122

Department of Political Science
Kakatiya University, Warangal, AP
506009, India
tel: +91-871-239 966, fax: +91-871-

239 600
email: kakatiya@ap.nic.in

Indonesia

Faculty of Social and Political Sciences
Pattimura University, Jalan lr M
Putuhenan, Kotak Pos 95, Kampus
Unpatti Poka-Ambon, Ambon, Indonesia
tel: +62-911-69520, fax: +62-911-69560

College of Social and Political Sciences
University of Lampung, Jalan Prof
Dr Sumantri, Brojonegoro, Bandar
Lampung, Indonesia
tel: +62-721-702 673, fax: +62-721-702 767

Faculty of Social and Political Sciences
Padjadjaran University, Jalan Dipati
Ukur 35, Bandung 40132, Indonesia
tel: +62-22-250 3271, fax: +62-22-250 1977

Faculty of Social and Political Sciences
17 August 1945 University Banyuwangi, Jalan Adi Sucipto 26,
Banyuwangi, East Java, Indonesia
tel: +62-333-23235

Faculty of Social and Political Sciences
University of Bengkulu, Jalan Raya
Kandang, Limun, Bengkulu 38371,
Indonesia
tel: +62-736-22105, fax: +62-736-22105
email: rectorat@bengkulu.wasantara.net.id

Centre of Social and Political Sciences Research
Mahendradatta University, Jalan
Ken Arok 5, Denpasar, Indonesia
tel: +62-361-34827

Faculty of Social and Political Sciences
17 August 1945 University, Jalan
Sunter Permai, Rayai, Jakarta Utara
14350, Indonesia
tel: +62-21-687 301, fax: +62-21-687 301

Faculty of Social and Political Sciences
Dr R Mustopo University, Jalan
Hanglekir 1/8, Blok H, Kebayoran
Baru, Jakarta, Indonesia
tel: +62-21-770 269

Faculty of Social and Political Sciences
Ibn Khaldun University Jakarta,
Jalan Pemuda I Kav 97, Rawamangun, Jakarta 133220, Indonesia
tel: +62-21-472 2059, fax: +62-21-470 2564

Faculty of Political and Social Sciences
Jayabaya University, Jalan A Yani,
By-pass, Jakarta, Indonesia
tel: +62-21-470 0871, fax: +62-21-470 0872

Faculty of Social and Political Sciences
Muhammadiyah University of Jakarta, Jalan KH Ahmad Dahlan
Cirendeu Ciputat, Jakarta Selatan,
Indonesia
tel: +62-740-1894, fax: +62-740-0756
email: umjcom@rad.net.id
http://www.still.co.id/umj/index.
htm

Faculty of Political Science
National University Jakarta, Jalan
Sawo Manila, Pejaten, Pasar
Minggu, Jakarta 12510, Indonesia
tel: +62-21-780 6700, fax: +62-21-780 2718

Faculty of Political and Social Sciences
University of Inonesia Jakarta, Jalan
Salemba Raya 4, Jakarta Pusat
10430, Indonesia
tel: +62-21-727 0020, fax: +62-21-727 0017

email: rektor@makara.cso.ui.ac.id
http://www.ui.ac.id

Faculty of Social and Political Sciences
Airlangga University, Jalan Airlangga 4-6, Surabaya 60286, East Java, Indonesia
tel: +62-31-53 41348
email: bapsi@unair.ac.id

Faculty of Social and Political Sciences
Islamic University 'Sheikh Yusuf', Babakan, Tangerang, Jawa Barat, Indonesia
tel: +62-22-340

Faculty of Social and Political Sciences
Parahyangan Catholic University, Jalan Ciumbuleuit 94, Bandung 40141, Jawa Barat, Indonesia
tel: +62-22-232 655, fax: +62-22-231 110
email: suke@gw.unpar.ac.idcqw-panme.itb.ac.id

Faculty of Social and Political Sciences
Muhammadiyah University of Jember, Jalan Karimata 43, Kotak Pos 104, Jember 68121, East Java, Indonesia
tel: +62-21-640

Faculty of Social and Political Sciences
University of Jember, Jalan Kalimantan III/24, Kampus Bumi Tegal, Jember East, Indonesia
tel: +62-331-87422, fax: +62-331-87422

Faculty of Social and Political Sciences
Darul'ulum University of Jombang, Jalan Merdeka 29A, Jombang, East Java, Indonesia
tel: +62-321-81517, fax: +62-321-81631

Faculty of Social and Political Sciences
Tidar University of Magelang, Jalan Kapten Suparman 39, Magelang, Indonesia
tel: +62-293-62438

Faculty of Political and Social Sciences
Merdeka University Malang, Jalan Terusan Raya Dieng 62-64, Malang 65146, Indonesia
tel: +62-341-28395, fax: +62-641-64994

Faculty of Social and Political Sciences
Muhammadiyah University of Malang, Jalan Bandung 1, Malang 65113, Indonesia
tel: +62-341-51253, fax: +62-341-82060

Faculty of Social and Political Sciences
Sam Ratulangi University, Kampus Unsrat, Bahu, 95115 Manado, North Sulawes, Indonesia
tel: +62-431-63586, fax: +62-431-64386

Faculty of Social and Political Sciences
Darma Agung University, Jalan Bantam 21, Medan, North Sumatra 20153, Indonesia
tel: +61-535-631, fax: +62-61-549-562

Faculty of Social and Political Sciences
Islamic University of North Sumatra, Jalan Sisingamangaraja, Teladan, Medan 20217, Indonesia
tel: +62-61-24382

Faculty of Social and Political Sciences
University of North Sumatra, Jalan Dr T Mansyur 9, Kampus USU, Medan 20155, Indonesia
tel: +62-61-814 210, fax: +62-61-811 633

Faculty of Social and Political Sciences
University of Sriwijaya, Jalan Srijaya Negara, Palembang 30319, Indonesia
tel: +62-711-358 688, fax: +62-711-

580 644
http://www.viol.com/polyunsri

Faculty of Social and Political Sciences
University of Tanjug Pura, Jalan A
Yani, Pontianak 78122, Kalimantan
Barat, Indonesia
tel: +62-581-39636, fax: +62-581-
39630

Faculty of Social and Political Sciences
General Soedirman University, PO
Box 15, Kampus Unsoed, Pur-
wokerto 53122, Central Java, Indonesia
tel: +62-281-38337

Faculty of Social and Political Sciences
Islamic University of Riau, Jalan
Kaharuddin, Perhentian Marpoyan
113, Pekanbaru, Riau, Indonesia
tel: +62-761-72126, fax: +62-761-
33664
email: tdahril@uir.ac.id

Faculty of Social and Political Sciences
Mulawarman University, Jalan
Kampus Gunung Kelua 5, Sama-
rinda, PO Box 68, Indonesia
tel: +62-541-41118, fax: +62-541-
32870

Faculty of Social and Political Sciences
17 August 1945 University Semer-
ang, Jalan Seteran Dalam 9, Semer-
ang 50134, Indonesia
tel: +62-24-318 202

Faculty of Social and Political Sciences
Wijayakusuma University of Surabaya, Jalan Dukukh Kupang XXV,
54 Surabaya, Surabaya 60225, Indonesia
tel: +62-31-567 7577, fax: +62-31-567
9791

Faculty of Social and Political Sciences
Sebelas Maret University, Jalan lr
Soetami 36A, Kentingan, Surakarta

57125, Indonesia
tel: +62-271-42283, fax: +62-271-
46655
email: due-uns@indo.net.id

Faculty of Political Sciences
Tadulako University, Kampus Bumi
Bahari, Tadulako, Palu 94118, Indonesia
tel: +62-451-22355, fax: +62-451-
22844

Faculty of Social and Political Sciences
The Indonesian Open Learning
University Pondok Cabe, Jalan Cabe
Raya, Pondok Cabe, Ciputat, Tangerang 15418, Indonesia
tel: +62-21-749 0941, fax: +62-21-749
0147

Faculty of Social and Political Sciences
Hasanuddin University, Jalan Per-
entis Kemerdekaan, Kampus Ta-
malanera, Ujung, Indonesia
tel: +62-411-510 102, fax: +62-411-
510 088
email: unhas@unhas.ac.id
http://www.unhas.ac.id

Faculty of Social and Political Sciences
Atma Jaya Yogyakarta University,
Jalan Babarsari 44, Yogyakarta 5281,
Indonesia
tel: +62-274-56 411, fax: +62-274-565
258
email: uajy@uajy.org
http://www.ua.jy.org

Faculty of Social and Political Sciences
Gadjah Mada University, Bulaksu-
mur, Yogyakarta 55281, Indonesia
tel: +62-274-562 011, fax: +62-274-
569 223

Iran

Department of Political Science
University of Isfahan, Hezar Jarib,
Darvazeh Shiraz, Esfahan 81744,
Iran
tel: +98-31-683 090, fax: +98-31-687

396
email: uis@math.ui.ac.ir
http://www.ui.ac.ir
Faculty of Economics and Political Science
Shahid Beheshti University, PO Box 19395/4716, Evin Square, Tehran 19834, Iran
tel: +98-21-21411

Faculty of Law and Political Sciences
University of Tehran, Enghelab Sqaure, Tehran 4174, Iran
tel: +8-21-640 6111, fax: +98-21-640 9348

Iraq

College of Law and Political Science
University of Baghdad, Jadyriya, Baghdad, Iraq
tel: +964-1-776 7819, fax: +964-1-776 3952

Israel

Faculty of Humanities and Social Sciences
Ben Gurion University of the Negev, PO Box 653, Beer-Sheva 84105, Israel
tel: +972-7-646 1111, fax: +972-7-623 7682
email: ascsec@bgumail.bgu.il
http://www.bgu.ac.il

Department of Political Science
University of Haifa, Mount Carmel, Haifa 31905, Israel
tel: +972-4-824 0111, fax: +972-4-834 2101
email: mrect36@haifauvm.bitnet
http://www.haifa.ac.il

Department of Political Science
Hebrew University of Jerusalem, Mount Scopus, Jerusalem 91905, Israel
http://www.huji.ac.il/unew/subbar2m.html

Department of Political Science
Bar-Ilan University, Ramat Gan 52100, Israel

tel: +972-3-531 8121, fax: +972-3-535 4918
email: biuspoke@mail.ac.il
http://www.biu.ac.il

Department of Sociology and Political Science
Open University of Israel, PO Box 39328, 16 Klausner St, Tel-Aviv 61392, Israel
tel: +972-3-646 0460, fax: +972-3-646 0582
email: elissa@oumail.openu.ac.il
http://www.openu.ac.il

Department of Political Science
Tel Aviv University, PO Box 39040, Ramat-Aviv 69978, Israel
tel: +972-3-640 8111, fax: +972-3-640 7174
email: lanir@post.tau.ac.il
http://www.tau.ac.il

Japan

School of Law
Nagoya University, Furo-cho, Chikusa-ku, Nagoya-shi, Aichi 464-8601, Japan
tel: +81-52-789 4901, fax: +81-52-789 4900
http://www.nomolog.nagoya-u.ac.jp/index.en.html

Faculty of Law
Nanzan University, 18 Yamazato-cho, Showa-ku, Nagoya-shi, Aichi 466-8673, Japan
tel: +81-52-832 3111, fax: +81-52-833 6985
email: webmaster@ic.nanzan-u.ac.jp
http://ww.ic.nanzan-u.ac.jp/index-eng.html

Faculty of Law and Political Science
Rissho University, 4-2-16 Osaki, Koriyama-shi, Fukushima 963, Japan
tel: +81-24-932 8931, fax: +81-24-9337372

Department of Political Science and Economics
University of Tsukuba, 1-1-1 Tennodai, Tsukuba-shi, Ibaraki 305, Japan

tel: +81-29-853 2111, fax: +81-29-853 6019
http://www.sec.tsukuba.ac.jp

Faculty of Law and Political Science
Doshisha University, Imadegawa-dori, Karasuma-Higashiiru, Kamigyo-ku, Kamigyo-ku, Kyoto-shi, Japan
tel: +81-75-251 3260, fax: +81-75-251 3075
http://doshisha.ac.jp

Faculty of Law
Kyoto University, Sakyo-ku, Kyoto-shi, Kyoto 606-8501, Japan
tel: +81-75-753 3102, fax: +81-75-753 3290
http://www.law.kyoto-u.ac.jp/l-English.htm

Faculty of Law
Ritsumeikan University, 56-1 Tohjin-Kitamachi, Kita-ku, Kyoto-shi, Kyoto 603-77, Japan
tel: +81-75-465 8175
http://www.ritsumei.ac.jp/kic/ja/htdocs/ehtdocs/eindex.html

Faculty of Law
Kyushu University, 6-19-1 Hakozai, Higashi-ku, Fukuoka-shi, Fukouka 812-8581, Japan
tel: +81-92-642 2439
http://www.kyushu-u.ac.jp/english/index-e.htm

Faculty of Law
Tohoku University, 2-1-1 Katahira, Aoba-ku, Sendai-shi, Miyagi 980-8577, Japan
tel: +81-22-217 6175, fax: +81-22-217 6249
http://www.tohoku.ac.jp/index-e.html

Department of Law and Political Science
Okayama University, 3-1-1 Tsushimanaka, Okayama-shi, Okayama 700-0082, Japan
tel: +81-86-252 1111, fax: +81-86-254 6104
http://www.okayama-u.ac.jp/index-e.html

Department of Law and Political Science
University of the Ryukyu, 1 Senbaru, Nishihara-cho, Nakagami-gun, Okinawa 903-01, Japan
tel: +81-98-895 2221, fax: +81-98-895 6096
http://www.ie.u-ryukyu.ac.jp

Faculty of Law
Osaka University, 1-6 Machikane-yama, Toyonaka-shi, Osaka 560-0043, Japan
tel: +81-6-6850 5142, fax: +81-6-6879 7039
email: kokusai@user.center.osaka-u.ac.jp
http://www.law.osaka-u.ac.jp/

School of International Politics, Economics and Business
Aoyama Gakuin University, 4-4-25 Shibuya, Shibuya-ku, Tokyo 150-8366, Japan
tel: +81-3-3409 8111
http://www.siped.aoyama.ac.jp/index-e.html

Faculty of Law and Political Science
Chuo University, 742-1 Higashi-Nakano, Tokyo 192-03, Japan
tel: +81-42-674 2211, fax: +81-42-674 2214
email: intlcent@tamajs.chuo-u.ac.jp
http://www.chuo-u.ac.jp

Faculty of Law and Political Science
Daito Bunka University, 1-9-1 Takashimadaira, Itabashi-ku, Tokyo 175, Japan
tel: +81-3-5399 7323, fax: +81-3-5399 7823
email: dbuinter@ic.daito.ac.jp

Faculty of Law and Political Sciences
Gakushuin University, 1-5-1 Mejiro, Tokushima-ku, Tokyo 171, Japan
tel: +81-3-3986 0221, fax: +81-3-3986 1005

Faculty of Law
Hitosubashi University, 2-1 Naka, Kunitachi-shi, Tokyo 186-8601, Japan
tel: +81-42-580 8000

http://www.hit-
u.ac.jp/foreigner/index.htm
Faculty of Law and Political Science
Hosei University, 2-17-1 Fujimi,
Chiyoda-ku, Tokyo 102, Japan
tel: +81-3-3264 9315, fax: +81-3-3238
9873
email: ic@fujimi.hosei.ac.jp
http://www.ic.hosei.ac.jp
*Division of Social Sciences, The Col-
lege of Liberal Arts*
International Christian University,
3-10-2 Osawa, Mitaka, Tokyo 181-
8585, Japan
tel: +81-42-233 3131, fax: +81-42-233
3355
email: president-office@icu.ac.jp
http://www.icu.ac.jp
Faculty of Law and Political Science
Keio University, 2-15-45 Mita, Minato-ku, Tokyo 108, Japan
tel: +81-3-3453 4511, fax: +81-3-3769
2047
http://www.keio.ac.jp
*Faculty of Political Science and Eco-
nomics*
Kokushikan University, 4-28-1 Setagaya, Setagaya-ku, Tokyo 154, Japan
tel: +81-3-5481-3206, fax: +81-3-5481
3210
Faculty of Law and Political Science
Meiji Gakuin University, 1-2-37 Shi-
rokane-dai, Minato-ku, Tokyo 108-
8636, Japan
tel: +81-3-5421 5111, fax: +81-3-5421
5458
email: ci-
cet@mguad.meijigakuin.ac.jp
http://www.meijigakuin.ac.jp
*School of Political Science and Eco-
nomics*
Meiji University, 1-1 Kanda Suru-
gadai, Chiyoda-ku, Tokyo 101, Japan
tel: +81-3-3296 4545, fax: +81-3-3296
4360
http://www.meiji.ac.jp

Department of Political Science
Nihon University, 2-3-1 Misaki-cho,
Chiyoda-ku, Tokyo 102, Japan
tel: +81-3-5275 8116, fax: +81-3-5275
8315
http://ftp.nc.nihon-u.ac.jp
College of Law and Politics
Rikkyo University, 3-34-1 Nishi-
Ikebukuro, Tomashima-ku, Tokyo
171-8501, Japan
tel: +81-3-3985 2202
http://law.rikkyo.ac.jp/
*Graduate School of Law and Politi-
cal Science*
Seikei University, 3-3-1 Kichijoji-
Kitamachi, Musashino-shi, Tokyo
180, Japan
tel: +81-42-237 3531, fax: +81-42-237
3883
*Institute of Law and Political Sci-
ence*
Senshu University, 3-8-1 Kanda-
Jimbo-cho, Chiyoda-ku, Tokyo 101,
Japan
tel: +81-3-3265 6211, fax: +81-3-3265
3649
Faculty of Law
Sophia (Jochi) University, 7-1 Koi-
cho, Chiyoda-ku, Tokyo 102-8554,
Japan
tel: +81-3-3238 3179, fax: +81-3-3238-
3539
http://www.sophia.ac.jp/home.nsf
/E/home?OpenDocument/
*Faculty of Political Science and Eco-
nomics*
Takushoku University, 3-4-14 Kohi-
nata, Bunkyo-ku, Tokyo 112, Japan
tel: +81-3-3947 2261, fax: +81-3-3947
5333
http://www.takushoku-
u.ac.jp/welcome-e.html
Faculty of Law and Political Science
Tokyo Metropolitan University, 1-1
Minami-Ohsawa, Tokyo 192-03, Japan
tel: +81-42-677 1111, fax: +81-42-677
2009

Faculty of Law and Political Science
University of Tokyo, 7-3-1 Hongo,
Tokyo 113, Japan
tel: +81-3-381 2211, fax: +81-3-568
44957
email: mkobaya@adm.u-tokyo.ac.jp
http://www.u-tokyo.ac.jp

College of Arts and Sciences
University of Tokyo, 3-8-1 Komaba,
Meguro-ku, Tokyo 153-8902, Japan
tel: +81-3-5454 6049
email: www-admin@www.c.u-
tokyo.ac.jp
http://www.c.u-tokyo.ac.jp/

*School of Political Science and Eco-
nomics*
Waseda University, 1-6-1 Nishi-
Waseda, Shinjuku-ku, Tokyo 169-
8050, Japan
tel: +81-3-3203 4141, fax: +81-3-3208
1032
email: intl-ac@mn.waseda.ac.jp
http://www.waseda.ac.jp

Jordan

Department of Political Science
Applied Science University, Shafa
Badran District, 11931 Amman, Jordan
tel: +962-6-523 7181, fax: +962-6-523
2899

Department of Political Science
Al Al-Bayt University, Mafraq PO
Box 772, Jubaiha, Jordan
tel: +962-6-432 858, fax: +962-6-846
721
http://petra.nic.gov.jo/aabu

Department of Political Science
University of Jordan, Jubaiha, Amman, Jordan
tel: +962-6-535 5000, fax: +962-6-535-
5533
email: admin@ju.edu.jo
http://www.ju.edu.jo

Department of Political Science
Mu'tah University, PO Box 7,
Mu'tah, Al-Karak, Jordan
tel: +962-6-461 7860, fax: +962-6-465
4061

email: dahiyat@mutah.edu.jo
http://www.mutah.edu.jo

Korea, Republic of

Department of Political Science
Cheju National University, 1 Ara 1-
dong, Cheju 690-756, Republic of
Korea
tel: +82-64-754 2950, fax: +82-64-725
2073
email: cnu@cheju.ac.kr
http://www.cheju.ac.kr

*Division of Political Science and
Public Administration*
Gyeongsang National University,
900, Gazoa-dong, Chinju 600-701,
Republic of Korea
tel: +82-591-751 6051, fax: +82-591-
754 6395
email: ir6051@nongae.gsnu.ac.kr
http://www.gsnu.ac.kr

*Department of Political Science and
Diplomacy*
Won Kwang University, 344-2
Shinyong-dong, Iricsan, Chollabu-
kdo 570-749, Republic of Korea
tel: +82-653-850 6581, fax: +82-653-
850 7307
http://www.wongwang.ac.kr

*Department of Political Science and
Diplomacy*
Chongbuk National University, 664-
14, 1-ka, Dukjin-dong, Dukjin-ku,
Chonju, Chongbuk 561-756, Republic of Korea
tel: +82-652-270 2934, fax: +82-652-
270 2935
email: pol@moak.chongbuk.ac.kr
http://www.social.chonbuk.ac.kr

Department of Political Science
Chongju University, 36 Naedok-
dong, Sang-dang-ku, Chongju-shi
360-764, Republic of Korea
tel: +82-431-229 8248, fax: +82-431-
229 8248
http://www.chongju.ac.kr

Department of Political Science
Mokpo National University, 61, To-
rim-ri, Chongye-mion, Maum-gum,

Chonnam 534-729, Republic of Korea
tel: +82-636-450 2260, fax: +82-636-450 6469
http://www.mokpo.ac.kr

Department of Political Science and International Relations
Chungbuk National University, 48 Kaesin-dong, Hongduk-gu, Jungwon-gun, Chungbuk 383-870, Republic of Korea
tel: +82-431-261 2204, fax: +82-431-271 1713

Department of Political Science
Inchon National University of Education, 177, Donghwa-dong, Namgu, Kyeyang-Ku, Inchon 403-753, Republic of Korea
tel: +82-32-770 8340, fax: +82-32-770 8301
email: khshin@gyeyang.inchon-e.ac.kr
http://www.inchon-e.ac.kr

Department of Political Science and Diplomacy
Inha University, 253 Yonghyon-dong, Nam-gu, Inchon 402-751, Republic of Korea
tel: +82-32-860 9760, fax: +82-32-860 9760
email: hongdp@dragon.inha.ac.kr
http://www.inha.ac.kr

Department of Political Science
Hallym University, 1, Oakchung-dong, Chun-chon, Kangwon 200-702, Republic of Korea
tel: +82-361-240 1350, fax: +82-361-256 3424
http://www.hallym.ac.kr

Department of Political Science
Kangwon National University, 192-1, Hoejan-dong, Chun-chon, Kangwon 200-701, Republic of Korea
tel: +82-361-255 6840, fax: +82-361-250 6840
http://www.kwangwon.ac.kr

Department of Political Science
Chonnam National University, 300 Yongbong-dong, Puk-gu, Kwangiu

500-757, Republic of Korea
tel: +82-62-530 2620, fax: +82-62-530 2639
email: cnup@chonnam.ac.kr
http://www.chonnam.ac.kr

Department of Political Science
Chosun University, Seosuk-dong, Kwangju 501-759, Republic of Korea
tel: +82-62-230 6709
http://www.chosun.ac.kr

Department of Political Science and Diplomacy
Honam University, 59-1 Seobong-dong, Kwangsan-ku, Kwangju 506-090, Republic of Korea
tel: +82-62-940 5227, fax: +82-62-940 5116
email: kssuh@honam.honam.ac.kr
http://www.honam.ac.kr

Department of Political Science
Catholic University of Taegu, 330 Kumrak I-ri, Hayang-up, Kyongsan-shi, Kyoungbuk 712-702, Republic of Korea
tel: +82-53-850 3328, fax: +82-53-850 3302
email: webmaster@cuth.categu.ac.kr
http://www.categu.ac.kr

Department of Political Science and Diplomacy
Yeungnam University, 214-1 Daedong, Kyongsan, Kyoungbuk 712-749, Republic of Korea
tel: +82-53-810 2640, fax: +82-53-814 3270
http://www.yeungnam.ac.kr

Department of Political Science and Diplomacy
Inje University, 607, Adbang-dong, Kimhae, Kyoungnam 621-749, Republic of Korea
tel: +82-525-320 3441, fax: +82-525-321 8343
http://www.inje.ac.kr

Department of Political Science and Diplomacy
Ajou University, 5-San, Wonchun-don, Paldal-gu, Soowon, Kyungki 442-749, Republic of Korea

tel: +82-331-219 2736, fax: +82-331-219 1618
http://www.ajou.ac.kr

College of Political Science
Chung-ang University, 40-1 nae-ri, Daeduk-Myun, Ansung-Kun, Kyungki-Do 456-756, Republic of Korea
tel: +82-2-820 6122, fax: +82-2-813 8069
email: djung@cau.ac.kr
http://www.cau.ac.kr

International Relations
Changwon National University, 9 Sarim-dong, Changwon, Kyungnam 641-773, Republic of Korea
tel: +82-551-279 7320, fax: +82-551-279 7159
http://www.chanwon.ac.kr

Department of Political Science and Diplomacy
Kyungnam University, 449 Wolyong-dong, Habpo-gu, Masan 631-701, Republic of Korea
tel: +82-551-249 2532, fax: +82-551-249 2989
http://www.kyungnam.ac.ke

Department of International Relations
Pusan University of International Relations, 55-1, Wowam-dong, Nam-gu, Pusan 780-738, Republic of Korea
tel: +82-51-640 3030, fax: +82-51-645 4525
http://www.pufu.ac.kr

Department of Political Science
Dong Eui University, 24 Kaya-dong, Pusanjin-gu, Pusan 614-014, Republic of Korea
tel: +82-51-890 1387, fax: +82-51-890 1359
email: mskoo@hyomin.dongeui.ac.kr
http://www.dongeui.ac.kr

Department of Political Science
Dong-a University Pusan, 840 Hadan 2-dong, Saha-gu, Saha-gu, Pusan 604-714, Republic of Korea

tel: +82-51-240 2705, fax: +82-51-241 1959
http://www.donga.ac.kr

Department of Political Science
Kyungsung University, Taeyon-dong, Nam-gu, Pusan 608-736, Republic of Korea
tel: +82-51-622 5331, fax: +82-51-628 1170
http://sarang.kyungsung.ac.kr

Department of Political Science and Diplomacy
Pusan National University, 30 Changjeon-dong, Keumjong-ku, Keumjong-ku, Pusan 607-035, Republic of Korea
tel: +82-51-510 1558, fax: +82-51-582 8508
email: academic@hyowon.pusan.ac.kr
http://www.pusan.ac.kr

Department of Political Science and Diplomacy
Chuang University, 221, Huksuk-dong, Dongjak-gu, Seoul 156-756, Republic of Korea
tel: +82-2-820 5473, fax: +82-2-820 5473
http://www.cau.ac.kr

Department of Political Science and Diplomacy
Dankook University Seoul, 8 Han-nam-dong, Youngsan-gu, Seoul 140-714, Republic of Korea
tel: +82-2-709 2474, fax: +82-2-709 2474
http://www.dankook.ac.kr

Department of Political Science
Dongguk University, 26, 3-ga Pil-dong, Chung-gu, Seoul 100-715, Republic of Korea
tel: +82-2-2260 3240, fax: +82-2-2260 3513
email: userid@dgu4680.dongguk.ac.kr
http://www.dongguk.ac.kr

Department of Political Science and Diplomacy
Ewha Women's University, 11-1, Daehyun-dong, Sudaemoon-gu, Seoul 120-750, Republic of Korea
tel: +82-2-3277 2760, fax: +82-2-3277 2826
http://www.ewha.ac.kr

Department of Political Science and Diplomacy
Hangkook University of Foreign Studies Seoul, 270 Imun-dong, Dongdaemun-gu, Seoul 130-791, Republic of Korea
tel: +82-2-961 4224, fax: +82-2-961 4224
http://www.hufs.ac.kr

Department of Political Science and Diplomacy
Hanyang University, 17-San, Hang-dang-dong, Sungdong-gu, Seoul 133-791, Republic of Korea
tel: +82-2-2290 0820, fax: +82-2-2281 4554
http://www.hanyang.ac.kr

Department of Political Science
Konkuk University, 93-1, Mojin-dong, Kwangjin-gu, Seoul 143-701, Republic of Korea
tel: +82-2-450 3554, fax: +82-2-450 3551
http://www.konkuk.ac.kr

Department of Political Science
Kookmin University, 861-1, Jun-grung-dong, Sungbuk, Seoul 136-702, Republic of Korea
tel: +82-2-910 4450, fax: +82-2-910 4429
http://www.kookmin.ac.kr

Department of Political Science and Diplomacy
Korea University Seoul, 1, 5-ka, Anam-dong, Sungbuk-gu, Seoul 136-701, Republic of Korea
tel: +82-2-3290 2180, fax: +82-2-3290 2180
email: sknam@kuccx.korea.ac.kr
http://www.korea.ac.kr

Department of Law and Political Science
Kwangwoon University Seoul, 447-1 Wolgye-dong, Nowon-gu, Seoul 139-701, Republic of Korea
tel: +82-2-910 5114, fax: +82-2-917 6417
http://www.kwangwoon.ac.kr

Department of Political Science
Kyunghee University Seoul, 1 Hoegi-dong, Dongdaemoon-gu, Seoul 130-701, Republic of Korea
tel: +82-2-961 0623, fax: +82-2-961 0622
http://www.kyunghee.ac.kr

Department of Political Science
Seoul National University, San 56-1, Shinnim-dong, Kwanak-gu, Seoul 151-742, Republic of Korea
tel: +82-2-880 6330, fax: +82-2-885 5272
http://www.snu.ac.kr

Department of Political Science
Sogang University, Shinsu-dong, Mapo-ku, Seoul 121-742, Republic of Korea
tel: +82-2-705 8387, fax: +82-2-705 8176
http://www.sogang.ac.kr

Department of Political Science and International Relations
Sookmyung Women's University, 53-12 Chungpa-dong 2 ka, Yongsan-gu, Seoul 140-742, Republic of Korea
tel: +82-2-710 9488, fax: +82-2-710 9648
http://www.sookmyung.ac.kr

Department of Political Science and Diplomacy
Soong Sil University Seoul, 1-1, Sangdo 5 Dong, Dongjak-ku, Seoul 156-743, Republic of Korea
tel: +82-2-820 0520, fax: +82-2-822 3486
email: mgkim@saint.soongsil.ac.kr
http://www.soongsil.ac.kr

Department of Political Science and Diplomacy
Sungkyunkwan University Seoul, 53, 3-ga, Myungryun-dong,, Chun-

gro-gu, Seoul 110-745, Republic of Korea
tel: +82-2-760 0379, fax: +82-2-760 0379
http://www.skku.ac.kr

Department of Political Science and Diplomacy
Sungshin Women's University
Seoul, 249-1, 3-ga, Dongsun-dong, Sungbuk-gu, Seoul 136-742, Republic of Korea
tel: +82-2-920 7127, fax: +82-2-953 2035
http://www.sungshin.ac.kr

Department of International Relations
University of Seoul, 90, Cheong-dong, Tongdaemun-gu, Seoul 130-743, Republic of Korea
tel: +82-2-2210 2558, fax: +82-2-2214 2550
http://www.uos.ac.kr

Department of Political Science and Diplomacy
Yonsei University, 134, Shinchon-dong, Shudaemoon-gu, Seoul 120-749, Republic of Korea
tel: +82-2-361 2940, fax: +82-2-393 7642
http://www.yonsei.ac.kr

Department of Political Science
Kyungpook National University, 1370 Sankyok-dong, Puk-gu, Taegu 702-701, Republic of Korea
tel: +82-53-950 5206, fax: +82-53-950 6206
email: yhwkim@kyungpook.ac.kr
http://www.knu.ac.kr

Department of Political Science and Diplomacy
Chungnam National University, Gung-dong, Yusung-gu, Taejon 305-764, Republic of Korea
tel: +82-42-821 5851, fax: +82-42-823 6348
http://www.chungnam.ac.kr

Politics, Communication and International Studies
Hannam University, 133, Ojung-dong, Deaduk-gu, Taejon 306-791, Republic of Korea
tel: +82-42-629 7650, fax: +82-42-629 7650
http://www.hannam.ac.kr

Department of Political Science
Paichai University, 439-6, Doma 2-dong, Shu-gu, Taejon 302-735, Republic of Korea
tel: +82-42-520 5566, fax: +82-42-520 5661
http://www.paichai.ac.kr

Politics and Diplomacy Major
Taejon University, 96-3, Youngwun-dong, Dong-gu, Taejon 300-716, Republic of Korea
tel: +82-42-280 2274, fax: +82-42-283 7171
http://www.taejon.ac.kr

Department of Political Science and Diplomacy
Ulsan University, 29-san, Moogu-dong, Nam-gu, Ulsan 680-749, Republic of Korea
tel: +82-52-259 2445, fax: +82-52-277 1720
http://www.uou.ac.kr

Department of Political Science and Diplomacy
Myongji University, 38-2 San Nam-dong, Yongin, Kyunggi-do 449-728, Republic of Korea
tel: +82-2-300 1535, fax: +82-2-300 1535
http://www.myongji.ac.kr

Kyrgystan

Department of Political Science
Biskek Humanities University, Manas Avenue 27, 720044 Biskek, Kyrgystan
tel: +996-33-1254 1405, fax: +996-33-1254 1405
email: rectorat@bgupub.freenet.bishbek.su

Lebanon

Department of Political Science
Haigazian University College, Rue
du Mexique, BP 1748, Beirut, Lebanon
tel: +961-1-442 433, fax: +961-1-581
240

*Faculty of Law, Political Science and
Administration*
Lebanese University Beirut, Place
du Musée, Beirut, Lebanon
tel: +961-1-386 817
http://www.kleudge.com/ul/defa
ult.htm

Faculty of Law and Political Sciences
St Joseph University Beirut, Rue de
Damas, 175208 Beirut, Lebanon
tel: +961-1-426 456, fax: +961-1-423
369
email: rectorat@usj.edu.lb
http://www.usj.edu.lb

Malaysia

Department of Political Science
International Islamic University
Malaysia (IIUM), Jalan Gombak
53100, Kuala Lumpur, Malaysia
tel: +60-3-20564870, fax: +60-3-
20565140
http://www.iiu.edu.my

Faculty of Political Science
University of Science Malaysia,
Minden 11800, Minden 11800,
Penang, Malaysia
tel: +60-4-6577888 ext 3369, fax: +60-
4-6570918
email: soc@usm.my
http://www.usm.my

Department of Political Science
University Kebangsaan Malaysia
(UKM), 43600 Bangi, Selangor Darul
Ehsen, Malaysia
tel: +60-3-8293646, fax: +60-3
8252836
email: dfskk@pkrisc.cc.ukm.my
http://www.ukm.my

*Politics & Development Program,
Department of Social and Develop-*
ment Studies
University Putra Malaysia, 43400
UPM Serdang, Selangor Darul Ehsen, Malaysia
tel: +60-3-9486101 ext 1733, fax: +60-
3 9435385
email: zahid@ecol.upm.edu.my
http://www.upm.edu.my

Nepal

Department of Political Science
Tribhuvan University Kathmandu,
Kirtipur, Kathmandu, Nepal
tel: +977-1-330 433, fax: +977-1-331
964
email: vc-office@npl.healthnet.org

Pakistan

Department of Political Science
University of Baluchistan, Saraib
Road, Quetta, Baluchistan, Pakistan
tel: +92-81-921 1243

*Department of International Rela-
tions*
Qaid-i-Azam University, PO Box
1090, Islamabad, Pakistan
tel: +92-51-829 391

Department of Political Science
University of Sindh, Jamshoro,
Sindh, Pakistan

Department of Political Science
University of Karachi, University
Road, Karachi 75270, Sindh, Pakistan
tel: +92-21-479 011

Department of Political Science
Punjab University, New Campus,
Lahore, Pakistan
tel: +92-42-586 3982, fax: +92-42-583
8263
email: polidep@brain.net.pk

Department of Political Science
Peshawar University, Peshawar,
NW Frontier Province, Pakistan
tel: +92-91-921 6751

Palestine

Department of Political Science
An-Najah National University, PO
Box 7, Omar Ibn El Kattab (West
Bank), Palestine
tel: +972-9-381 113, fax: +972-9-387
982
email: president@anajah.edu
http://www.najah.edu

Philippines

Department of Political Science
Baguio Central University, 18 Bonifacio Street, Baguio City, Philippines
tel: +63-74-442 4949

Department of Political Science
Araullo University, Bitas, Ca-
banatuan City 3100, Philippines
tel: +63-44-463 2212, fax: +63-44-463
0952
email: au@mozcom.com

Department of Political Science
University of San Carlos, P del Rosario Street, Cebu City 6000, Philippines
tel: +63-32-54341, fax: +63-32-54341
email: cnms@usc.edu.ph
http://www.usc.edu.ph

Department of Political Science
Notre Dame University, Notre
Dame Avenue, Cotabato City 9600,
Philippines
tel: +63-64-421 4312, fax: +63-64-421
4312
email: ndu@galileo.fapenet.prg
http://www.ndu.pafenet.org

Department of Political Science
Foundation University, Dr E Me-
ciano Road, Dumaguete City 6200,
Negros Oriental, Philippines
tel: +63-35-225 0618, fax: +63-35-225
0620

Department of Political Science
Silliman University, Hibbard Avenue, Dumaguete City 6200, Negros
Oriental, Philippines
tel: +63-35-225 4532, fax: +63-35-225

4768
email: succfred@durian.usc.edu.ph

Department of Political Science
Mindanao State University, Andres
Bonifacio Avenue, Iligan City 9200,
Philippines
tel: +63-2-214 050, fax: +63-2-214 056
email: msuiit@cc1.msuiit.edu.ph
http://www.msuiit.edu.ph

Department of Political Science
Central Philippine University, Jara,
Iloilo City 5000, Philippines
tel: +63-33-73470, fax: +63-33-73470
http://www.users.iloilo.net/fneil/c
pu/cpu.html

Department of Political Science
University of Saint Anthony, San
Miguel, Iriga City 4431, Philippines
tel: +63-4-032 401

Department of Political Science
Northwestern University of the
Philippines, Brgy, Bengcap, Airport
Avenue, Laoag City 2900, Philip-
pines
tel: +63-7-720 322, fax: +63-7-720 333

Department of Political Science
Aquinas University, Penaranda,
Rawis, Legazpi City 4500, Philippines
tel: +63-52-482 0543, fax: +63-52-482
0540

Department of Political Science
Adamson University, 900 San
Marcelino Street, Ermita, Manila
1000, Philippines
tel: +63-2-502 011

Department of Political Science
Arellano University, 2600 Legarda,
Sampaloc, Manila, Philippines
tel: +63-2-734 7371

Department of Political Science
Centro Escolar University, 9
Mendiola Street, San Miguel, Manila, Philippines
tel: +63-2-735 5991, fax: +63-2-735
5991
email: ceul@galileo.fapenet.org

Department of Political Science
De La Salle University, 2401 Taft
Avenue, PO Box 3819, Manila 1004,
Philippines
tel: +63-2-523 4281, fax: +63-2-536
1403
email: opbag@dlsu.edu.ph
http://www.dlsu.edu.ph

Department of Political Science
National University, 551 MF Jhoc-
son Street, Sampaloc, Manila, Philippines
tel: +63-2-749 8221, fax: +63-2-749
8210

Department of Political Science
Philippine Christian University,
1648 Taft Avenue & Corner Pedro
Gil, PO Box 907, Manila, Philippines
tel: +63-2-524 6671, fax: +63-2-526
5110
email: phchruni@mnl.sequel.net
http://www.sequel.net/phchruni

Department of Political Science
Univeristy of Santo Tomas, Espana
Street, Sampaloc, Manila 2806,
Philippines
tel: +63-2-731 3101, fax: +63-2-732
7486

Department of Political Sciences
University of the East-Manila, 2219
CM Recto Avenue, Manila 1008,
Philippines
tel: +63-2-735 6973, fax: +63-2-735
6972
email: ue1@mozcom.com
http://www.ue.edu.ph

Department of Political Science
Misamis University, Mabini and
Bonifacio Streets, Ozamiz City,
Philippines
tel: +63-65-20367, fax: +63-65-20054

Department of Political Science
New Era University, St Joseph
Street, Milton Hills, Diliman, Quezon City, Philippines
tel: +63-9-214 221, fax: +63-9-290 013

Department of Political Sciences
Western Mindanao State University,
Normal Road, Baliwasan, Zambo-

anga City, Philippines
tel: +63-62-991 1771

Department of Political Science
Ateneo de Manila University,
Loyola Heights, Quezon City 1108,
Philippines
tel: +63-2-426 6001
http://www.admu.edu.ph/loyolas
chools/departments/political%20sc
ience/polisci.htm

Singapore

Department of Political Science
National University of Singapore, 10
Kent Ridge Crescent, Singapore
0511,
tel: +65-874 3970, fax: +65-7796815-
email: polsec@nus.edu.sg
http://www.fas.nus.edu.sg./pd/

Sri Lanka

*Department of History and Political
Science*
University of Colombo, "College
House", 94 Cumaratunga Muni-
dasa, Mawatha, Colombo-3, Sri
Lanka
tel: +94-1-500433, fax: +94-1 583810
email: postmast@arts.cmb.ac.lk
http://www.cmb.ac.lk

Department of Political Science
University of Peradinya, University
Park, Peradinya, Sri Lanka
tel: +94-8-388345, fax: +94--8 388345
email: dean@arts.pdn.ac.lk
http://www.pdn.ca.lk/arts

Syria

Faculty of Political Science
Higher Institute of Political Sciences,
Al-Tall, Damascus, Syria
tel: +963-11-591 1740, fax: +963-11-
591 1526

Taiwan

Department of Political Science
National Chung-Cheng University,
160, San Hsing, Ming Hsiung, Chia

Yi 62117, Taiwan
tel: +886-5-272 0411 ext 5571, fax:
+886-5-272 1195
email: polsci@ccunix.ccu.edu.tw

Department of Political Science
National Open University, 172
Chung Cheng Road, Lu chow, Tapei
County 24702, Taiwan
tel: +886-2-2282 9355, fax: +886-2-
2283 1721

Department of Political Science
Tunghai University, 181 Taichung
Harbor Road, Sec 3, Taichung
40704, Taiwan
tel: +886-4-359 0121, fax: +886-4-359
0256
email: politic@mail.thu.edu.tw
http://mail.thu.edu.tw/~politic/en
glish.htm

Department of Political Science
Chinese Culture University, 55 Hua-
gan Road, Yang Ming Shan, Taipei
111, Taiwan
tel: +886-2-2861 0511 ext 280 281
email: yfyang@cuu016.pccu.edu.tw
http://www.pccu.edu.tw/dept/ula
ps

Department of Political Science
National Cheng-chi University, 64
Chih-nan Road, Sec 2, Wenshan,
Taipei 116, Taiwan
tel: +886-2-2938 7056-7, fax: +886-2-
2937 9611
email: politics@nccu.edu.tw
http://cyberpolitics.nccu.edu.tw

Department of Political Science
National Taiwan University, 21
Hsu-chou Road, Sec. 4, Taipei
10764, Taiwan
tel: +886-2-2391 8756, fax: +886-2-
2341 2806
email: politics@ms.cc.edu.tw
http://politics.law.ntu.edu.tw

Department of Political Science
Soochow University, 70 Lin-Hsi
Road, Shih Lin, Taipei 11102, Taiwan
tel: +886-2-2881 9471 ext 6254-3, fax:
+886-2-2882 2437

email: politics@mail.scu.edu.tw
http://www.scu.edu.tw/politics/

Thailand

Faculty of Political Science
Chulalongkorn Univeristy, Phyathai
Road, Bangkok 10330, Thailand
tel: +66-2-215 0871, fax: +66-2-215
3600
http://www.chula.edu

*Department of Political Science, Fac-
ulty of Social Sciences*
Kasetsart University, 50 Phaholyo-
thin Road, Bankhen, Bangkok
10900, Thailand
tel: +66-2-579 0113, fax: +66-2-579
6555
email: fro@nontri.ku.ac.th
http://www.ku.ac.th

Faculty of Political Science
Ramkhamhaeng University,
Ramkhamhaeng Road, Huamark
Bangkapi, Bangkok 10240, Thailand
tel: +66-2-318 0903, fax: +66-2-318
0917

Faculty of Political Science
Thammasat University, 2 Prachan
Road, Tha Prachan, Bangkok 10200,
Thailand
tel: +66-2-221 6111, fax: +66-2-224
8099
http://alpha.tu.ac.th

*Department of Political Science, Fac-
ulty of Social Sciences*
Chiang Mai University, Huay Kaew
Road, Changwat Chiang Mai 50200,
Thailand
tel: +66-53-221 699, fax: +66-53-217
143
email:
opxxo004@cmu.chiangmai.ac.th
http://www.chiangmai.ac.th

School of Political Science
Sukhothai Thammathirat Open
University, 9/9 Moo 9, Tambon
Bangpood, Changwatana Road,
Pakkred, Nonthaburi 11120, Thai-
land
tel: +66-2-503 2121, fax: +66-2-503

3607
email: vpdev@samsorn.stou.ac.th
http://www.stou.ac.th

Faculty of Management Sciences
Prince of Songkhla University, PO
Box 102, Hat Yai, Songkhla 90110,
Thailand
tel: +66-74-211 030, fax: +66-74-212
828
email: ssthor@ratree.psu.ac.th
http://www.psu.ac.th

Turkey

Faculty of Political Science
Ankara University, Tandogan Me-
dyani, 06100 Ankara, Turkey
tel: +90-312-212 6040, fax: +90-312-
223 6370
email: hot-line@ankara.edu.tr
http://www.ankara.edu.tr

Department of Political Science and
Public Administration
Bilkent Üniversitesi, 06533 Ankara,
Turkey
tel: +90-4-2664040, fax: +90-4
2664960
email: heper@trbilun.bitnet

Department of International Rela-
tions
Bilkent Üniversitesi, 06533 Ankara,
Turkey
tel: +90-312-266 4040 or 4195, fax:
+90-312-266 49 60
email: muge@bilkent.edu.tr

Department of Political Science and
Public Administration
Middle East Technical University
(Orta Gogu Teknik Üniversitesi),
Ismet Inonu Bul, 06531 Ankara,
Turkey
tel: +90-312-2101242, fax: +90-312-
2101107
email: cakir@trmetu

Department of Political Science and
International Relations
University of the Bosophorus (Bo-
gaziçi Üniversitesi), 80815 Bebek
Istanbul, Turkey
tel: +90-263-15 00, fax: +90-265-63 57

Faculty of Economics, Administra-
tive and Social Sciences
Bilkent Üniversitesi, 06533 Bilkent-
Ankara, Turkey
tel: +90-312-266 41 37, fax: +90-312-
266 49 60

Department of International Rela-
tions
University of Bursa, Faculty of
Business Administration and Economics, Görükle Campus, Bursa,
Turkey
tel: +90-24-42 80 13, fax: +90-24-42
80 88

Institute of Turkish Studies
Marmara Üniversitesi, Göztepe
Kampüsü, 81040 Fikirtepe, Istanbul,
Turkey
tel: +90-216-346 65 82, fax: +90-216-
336 95 91

School of Law
Hokkaido Univeristy, Kita-9 Nishi-
7, Kita-ku, Sapporo-shi, Hokkaido
060-0809
tel: +81-11-706 3119, fax: +81-11-706
4948
email: shomu@juris.hokudai.ac.jp
http://www.juris.hokudai.ac.jp/

EUROPE, EAST

Bulgaria

Department of Political Science
University of Sofia, Biel Tsarigradsko Shosse 125, Blok 4, Sofia 1113,
Bulgaria
tel: +35-9-271151, fax: +35-9-2463589

Croatia

Faculty of Political Science
University of Zagreb, Lepusiceva 6,
Zagreb, Croatia
tel: +385-1-4558022, fax: +385-1-41
22 83

Czech Republic

Department of Constitutional Law

and Political Science
Masaryk University, Brno, Veveri
70, 602 00 Brno, Czech Republic
tel: +420-54-155 9271, fax: +420-54-
121 2162
email: pfiala@fss.muni.cz

Department of Political Studies
University Paleckeho, Krizkovskeho
12, 771 80 Olomouc, Czech Republic
tel: +420-68-56 3301, fax: +420-68-
522 5148
email: fialav@risc.upol.cz

*Department of Political and Re-
gional Studies*
Slezska Univerzita, Berucovo nam
13, 746 01 Opava, Czech Republic
tel: +420-65-321 9020, fax: +420-65-
321 9020
email: koul0ksv@axpsu.fpf.slu.cz

*Department of Social and Political
Sciences*
Zapadoceska Univerzita, Sedlack-
ova 31, 301 11 Plzen, Czech Republic
tel: +420-19-22 6704, fax: +420-19-22
2465
email: Kuna@Pythia.zcu.cz

Department of Political Science
Charles University, Prague, Celetna
13, 110 00 Praha 1, Czech Republic

Department of Political Science
Prague University of Economics,
Nam W Churchilla 4, 130 67 Praha,
Czech Republic

Department of Political Science
Karlova Univerzita, Celetna 20, 110
00 Praha 1, Czech Republic
tel: +420-2-421 2500, fax: +420-2-481
0987
email: hnizdo@s.fsv.cuni.cz

Department of Political Studies
Univerzita JE Purkyne, Ceske
mladeze 8, 400 21 Usti nad Labem,
Czech Republic
tel: +420-47-521 4417, fax: +420-47-
521 2053

Estonia

Department of Political Science
Tartu University, Ulikooli 18, EE-
2400 Tartu, Estonia
tel: +372-3435110, fax: +372-3475880

Hungary

Department of Political Science
Budapest University of Economics,
Fovam ter 8, H-1093 Budapest,
Hungary
tel: +36-1-118 8049, fax: +36-1-117
6714
http://www.bkae.hu

Department of Political Science
Eotvos Lorand University, Egyetem
ter 1-3, H-1053 Budapest, Hungary
tel: +36-1-267 0820
http://www.elte.hu

Department of Political Science
Kossuth Lajos University, Egyetem
ter 1, H-3052 Debrecen, Hungary
http://www.lib.klte.hu/

*Department of Sociology and Politi-
cal Science*
University of Miskolc, Egyetemva-
ros, H-3515 Miskolc, Hungary
http://www.uni-
miskolc.hu/~bolcsweb/indexeng

Department of Political Science
Jozsef Attila University, Szeged,
Petofi sugarut 34, H-6722 Szeged,
Hungary
tel: +36-6-232 1611
http://www.jate.u-szeged.hu

Latvia

Department of Political Science
University of Latvia, Rainis Boulevard 19, LV-1098, Riga, Latvia
tel: +371-2-217338, fax: +371-9-
340156

Lithuania

Institute of International Relations and Political Science
Vilnius University, 47-205 Didlaukio Street, 2057 Vilnius, Lithuania
tel: +370-2-701883, fax: +370-2-223563

Moldova

Faculty of Political Science
Moldova State University, Strada A Mateevici 60, 2009 Chisnau, Moldova
tel: +373-2-240 041, fax: +373-2-240 655
email: stahi@cinf.usm.md
http://www.usm.md

Poland

Department of International Relations
University of Gdansk, Wosia Budzisza 4, 81-712 Sopot, Poland
tel: +48-5-851 2400, fax: +48-5-857 0675

Institute of Political Science
Jagiellonian University, Jablonowskich 5, 31-114 Krakow, Poland

Institute of Political Science
Catholic University of Lublin, Al Raclawickie 14, 20-950 Lublin, Poland
tel: +48-8130432, fax: +48-8130433

Institute of Political Sciences and Journalism
University of Silesia, ul Bankowa 11, 40-007 Katowice, Poland
tel: +48-3-258 0415

Institute of Political Science and Journalism
Adam Mickiewicz University, ul Szamarzewskiego 89A, 60-568 Poznan, Poland
tel: +48-6-147 0041, fax: +48-6-147 1555

Department of International Relations
University of Maria Curie-Sklodowska, Plac Litewski 3, 20-282 Lublin, Poland
tel: +48-8126845, fax: +48-5-857 0675

Institute of Philosophy and Political Science
University of Szczecin, ul Tarczynskiego 1, 70-387 Szczecin, Poland
tel: +48-91-330821, fax: +48-5-857 0675

Institute of Political Science
University of Warsaw, Krakowskie Przedmiescie 3, 00-047 Warszaw, Poland

Institute of Political Science
University of Wroclaw, ul Pocztowa 9, 53-313 Wroclaw, Poland

Romania

Department of Political Science
National School of Political Studies and Public Administration, B-dul Schitu Magureanu nr 1, Sect 5, Bucuresti, Romania

Department of Philosophy, Politology and Sociology
University of Craiova, Alexandru Ioan Cuza 13, cod 1100 Craiova, Judetul DOLJ, Romania
tel: +40-9-411 6574 ext 184

Russia

Department of Political Science
Moscow State University, Lenin Hills, Moscow 117234, Russia

Division of Political Sciences
Saratov State University, ul Astrahanskaja 83, Saratov 410026, Russia
tel: +7-845-224 1696, fax: +7-845-224 0466
http://www.ssu.runnet.ru

Department of Political Science
Baltic 'Ustinov' State Technical University, 1-ja Krasnoarmejskaja, Sank-Peterburg 198005, Russia
tel: +7-812-316 2394, fax: +7-812-316

2409
email: komdep@stu.spb.su

*Department of History and Political
Science*
Tomsk Polytechnic University, pr
Lenina 30, Tomsk 634004, Russia
tel: +7-832-241 5806, fax: +7-832-241
5865
email: tpu@tpu.ru
http://www.tpu.ru

*Department of Sociology and Politi-
cal Science*
Vladimir State Pedagogical University, pr Stroitelej 11, Vladimir
600024, Russia
tel: +7-092-223 6302, fax: +7-092-223
6302
email: rector@peduniver.elecom.ru

Department of Political Science
Far Eastern State University, ul
Suhanova 8, Vladivostok 690600,
Russia
tel: +7-423-226 1280, fax: +7-423-225
7200
email: idp@online.ru

Slovakia

*Department of Comparative Politics
and Theory of Politics*
University of Matej Bel, Kuzmanyho
1, 974 01 Banska Bystrica, Slovakia
tel: +421-88-415 4405, fax: +421-88-
415 2432
email: norikas@bb.sanet.sk

Department of Political Science
Comenius University, Gondova 2,
818 01 Bratislava, Slovakia
tel: +421-7-529 23640, fax: +421-7-
529 23640
email: kpol@fphil.uniba.sk

*Department of Political Science and
European Studies*
University of Konstantin and Me-
tod, Hodzova1, 949 74 Nitra, Slovakia
tel: +421-87-414 947, fax: +421-87-
414 947
email: jkucirek@ff.ukf.sk

Department of Political Science
University of PJ Safarik, Presov,
Ulica 17 novembra 1, 081 78 Presov,
Slovakia
tel: +421-91-773 3231-2, fax: +421-91-
773 1344
email: Kravlova@unipo.sk

Slovenia

Faculty of Social Sciences
University of Ljubljana, PO Box 47,
61009 Ljubljana, Slovenia
tel: +38-6-118 1461, fax: +38-6-134
1522

Yugoslavia

Institute of Political Science
University of Belgrade, Jove Ilica
165, 11000 Belgrade, Yugoslavia
http://www.bg.ac.yu

EUROPE, WEST

Austria

Institut für offentliches Recht
Karl-Franzens Universität Graz,
Universitatsstr 15, A-8010 Graz,
Austria
tel: +43-316-380 ext 3365 or 3380,
fax: +43-316-384093
email: erika.thurner@kfunigraz.ac.at
http://www.kfunigraz.ac.at/

Institut für Politikwissenschaft
Leopold-Franzens Universität Innsbruck, Universitatsstr 15, A-6020
Innsbruck, Austria
tel: +43-512-507 7051, fax: +43-512-
507 2849
email: ellen.palli@uibk.ac.at
http://www.uibk.ac.at/c/c4/c402/

Institut für Politikwissenschaft
Universität Innsbruck, Christoph
Probst Platz, A-6020 Innsbruck,
Austria
tel: +43-512-507 7051, fax: +43-512-
507 2849
email: ellen.palli@uibk.ac.at
http://info.uibk.ac.at/c/c4/c402

Institut für Politikwissenschaft
Universität Salzburg, Rudolfskai 42,
A-5020 Salzburg, Austria
tel: +43-662-8044 6600, fax: +43-662-
8044 413
email: franz.kok@sbg.ac.at
http://www.sbg.ac.at/pol/welcom
e.htm

Institut für Politikwissenschaft
Universität Wien, Währingerstr 28,
A-1090 Wien, Austria
tel: +43-1-4277 or 47705, fax: +43-1-
310 4277/9477
email:
claudia.millmann@univie.ac.at
http://www.univie.ac.at/politikwis
senschaft/

*Institut für Staats- und Politikwis-
senschaft*
Universität Wien, Hohenstaufen-
gasse 9, A-1010 Wien, Austria
tel: +43-1-4277 38301, fax: +43-1-
4277 9383
email: Politikwissenschaft-
Sowi@univie.ac.at
http://www.univie.ac.at/Politikwis
senschaft-Sowi/

Belgium

*Faculteit Politieke en Sociale Weten-
schappen,*
Universitaire Faculteiten Sint-
Ignatius te Antwerpen, Prinsstraat
13, B-2000 Antwerpen, Belgium
tel: +32-3-220 4111, fax: +32-3-220
4325
email:
fps.dierickx.G@alpha.ufsia.ac.be
http://www.ufsia.ac.be/FPSW/

*Departament Politieke en Sociale
Wetenschappen*
Universitaire Instelling Antwerpen,
UIA, Universiteitsplein 1, B-2610
Antwerpen (Wilrijk), Belgium
tel: +32-3-820 2851, fax: +32-3-820
2882
email: meulmns@uia.ua.ac.be
http://www.uia.ac.be

*Faculty of Political and Social Sci-

ences*
Katholieke Universiteit Brussel,
Vrijehiedslaan 17, B-1080 Brussels,
Belgium
tel: +32-2-412 4211, fax: +32-2-412
4200
email: fpsw@kubrussel.ac.be
http://www.kubrussel.ac.be/psw/

Centrum voor Politicologie
Vrije Universiteit Brussel, Pleinlaan
2, B-1050 Brussels, Belgium
tel: +32-2-629 2040
email: kris.deschouwer@vub.ac.be
http://www.vub.ac.be

*Faculté des Sciences Economiques,
Sociales et Politiques*
Facultes Universitaires Saint Louis,
Bld du Jardin Botanique 43, B-1000
Bruxelles, Belgium
tel: +32-2-211 7811, fax: +32-2-211
7997
email: kerchove@fusl.ac.be
http://webmaster@fusl.ac.be

Institut de Sociologie
Université Libre de Bruxelles, CP
124, 44 Avenue Jeanne, B-1050
Bruxelles, Belgium
tel: +32-2-650 42 79, fax: +32-2-650
49 56
email: cerap@ulb.ac.be

Section of Political Science
Université Libre de Bruxelles, Soco
CP135, 50 Av FD Roosevelt, B-1050
Bruxelles, Belgium
tel: +32-2-650 3263, fax: +32-2-650
3521
email: mtelo@ulb.ac.be
http://www.ulb.ac.be/iee/

*Centre de Recherches et
d'Informations Socio-Politiques
(CRISP)*
Rue du Congrès 35, B-1000 Brussels,
Belgium
tel: +32-2-218 32 26, fax: +32-2-219
79 34
email: crisp@cfwb.be

Departament of Political Science
Universiteit Gent, Universiteitstraat
8, B-9000 Gent, Belgium

tel: +32-9-264 6870, fax: +32-9-264 6991
email: helmut.gaus@rug.ac.be
http://www.psw.rug.ac.be

Departiment Politieke Wetenschappen
Katholieke Universiteit Leuven, E
Van Evenstraat 2B, B-3000 Leuven,
Belgium
tel: +32-16-32 32 50, fax: +32-16-32 30 88
email: magda.verboomen@soc. kuleuven. ac.be
http://www.kuleuven.ac.be/facde p/social/pol

Sciences Politiques--Administration Publique
Universite de Liege, 7 Bld du Recto-rant Bat B31, B-4000 Liege, Belgium
tel: +32-4-366 3035, fax: +32-4-366 4557
email: jleroy@ulg.ac.be
http://www.ulg.ac.be/facdroit/scp c

Départment des Sciences Politiques et Sociales
Universite Catholique de Louvain, 1/7 Place de Montesquieu, B-1348 Louvain-la-Neuve, Belgium
tel: +32-10-47 42 77, fax: +32-10-47 27 36
email: frognier@spri.ucl.ac.be
http://www.pols.ucl.ac.be/pols/

Faculté des Sciences Politiques
Facultes Universitaires Catholiques, Mons, 151 Chaussée de Binche, B-7000 Mons, Belgium
tel: +32-65-323252, fax: +32-65-323363
email: pietrzyk@message.fucam.ac.be
http://www.message.fucam.ac.be

Cyprus

Department of Social and Political Sciences
University of Cyprus, 75 Kallipoleos Avenus, PO Box 537, 1678 Nicosia, Cyprus
tel: +357-2-756 186, fax: +357-2-756 198
email: admin@zeus.cc.ucy.ac.cy
http://www.ucy.ac.cy

Denmark

Departments of Politics, Economics and Public Administration
Aalborg Universitet, Fibigerstraede 1, DK-9220 Aalborg, Denmark
tel: +45-9635-8080, fax: +45-9815-5346
email: institut2@socsci.auc.dk

Department of Political Science
Aarhus Universitet, Universitet-sparken, DK-8000 Aarhus C, Denmark
tel: +45-8942-1133, fax: +45-8613-9839
email: ps@ps.au.dk
http://www.ps.au.dk

Institute of Organisation and Indus-trial Sociology
Copenhagen School Of Economics and Social Science, Blaagaardsgade 23 B, DK-2200 Copenhagen N, Denmark
tel: +45-37-05 55

Institute of Political Science
Copenhagen Universitet, Rosen-borggade 15, DK-1130 Copenhagen K, Denmark
tel: +45-35-32 26 26, fax: +45-35-32 33 99
email: kvik-sk@ifs.ku.dk
http://www.polsci.ku.dk

Department of Political Science
Odense Universitet, Campusvej 55, DK-5230 Odense M, Denmark
tel: +45-661-58600, fax: +45-661-92577
email: politics@busieco.ou.dk
http://www.busieco.ou.dk/e/dept /pol/

Department of Social Sciences
Roskilde Universitetscenter, PO Box 260, DK-4000 Roskilde, Denmark
tel: +45-467-42000, fax: +45-467-43080

email: bgr@ruc.dk
http://www.ssc.ruc.dk

Finland

Department of Political Science
Åbo Akademi, Hus Lindman, Biskopsgatan 15, SF-20500 Åbo, Finland
tel: +358-2-2154 316, fax: +358-2-2154 585
email: marina.hamberg@abo.fi
http://www.abo.fi/fak/esf/lindman/poleng.htm

Department of Political Science
University of Helsinki, PO Box 54, SF-00014 Helsinki, Finland
tel: +358-9-191 8829, fax: +358-9-191 8832
email: pol-sci@helsinki.fi
http://www.valt.helsinki.fi/vol

Department of Social Sciences and Philosophy
University of Jyväskylä, PO Box 35, SF-40351 Jyväskylä, Finland
tel: +358-14-260 2831, fax: +358-14-260 3101
email: pkonen@jyu.fi
http://www.jyu.fi/~yhtfil

Department of Political Science and International Relations
University of Tampere, PO Box 607, SF-33101 Tampere, Finland
tel: +358-3-2156 417, fax: +358-3-2156 552
email: poltutklaitos@uta.fi
http://www.uta.fi/laitokset/politiikka/endex.htm

Department of Political Science
University of Turku, FIN 20014, SF-20500 Turku, Finland
tel: +358-2-333 5390, fax: +358-2-333 5090
email: heikki.paloheimo@utu.fi
http://www.utu.fi/yht/valtio-oppi/

France

Institut d'Etudes Politiques (IEP)
Aix-en-Provence, 25 rue Gaston de Saporta, 13625 Aix-en-Provence, France
tel: +33-4-42 17 01 62, fax: +33-4-42 96 36 99
http://www.iep-aix.fr

Institut d'Etudes Politiques (IEP)
Université de Droit d'Économie et des Sciences Aix Marseille, 25 rue Gaston de Saporta, 13625 Aix-En-Provence Cedex 1, France
tel: +33-4-42 17 01 60, fax: +33-4-42 96 36 99

Centre Universitaire de Recherches Administratives et Politiques Picardie
Université de Picardie, Pôle Universitaire Cathédrale, BP 2716, France
tel: +33-3-22 82 71 48, fax: +33-3-22 82 71 34
email: curapp@u-picardie.fr
http://www.u-picardie.fr/curapp/curapp.htlm

Faculté de Droit et de Science Politique
Université de Clermont I, 41 blvd François Mitterrand, BP54 - 63002 Clermont-Ferrand, France
tel: +33-4-73 43 42 00, fax: +33-4-73 43 42 45
email: aroche@u-clermont1.fr

Centre d'Etudes et de Recherche Politiques (CERPO)
Université de Bourgogne, 4 blvd Gabriel, 21000 Dijon, France
tel: +33-3-80 39 53 24, fax: +33-3-80 39 56 48

Institut d'Etudes Politiques (IEP)
Grenoble, BP45, 38402 Saint Martin d'Hères, France
tel: +33-4-76 82 60 00, fax: +33-4-76 82 60 70
email: schemeil@cidsp.upmf-grenoble.fr

Institut d'Etudes Politiques (CERAT)
Université Pierre Mendès France,
Grenoble II, BP48, 38040 Grenoble
Cedex 9, France
tel: +33-4-76 82 60 24, fax: +33-4-76
82 60 99
email: saez.cerat@iep.upmf-
grenoble.fr
http://www.upmf-
grenoble.fr/cerat/

Law and Political Science
Université de La Rochelle, 45 rue F
de Vaux de Foletier, 17000 La
Rochelle, France
tel: +33-5-46 45 85 20, fax: +33-5-46
45 85 33
email: johanna.simeant@univ-lr.fr
http://www.univ-lr.fr

Institut d'Etudes Politiques (IEP)
Lille, 50 rue Gauthier de Chatillon,
59000 Lille, France
tel: +33-3-20 90 48 40, fax: +33-3-20
90 48 60
email: iep.univ-lille2.fr

*Institut d'Etudes Politiques de Lyon
(CERIEP)*
Université Lumière Lyon II, 1 rue
Raulin, 69365 Lyon Cedex 07,
France
tel: +33-4-37 28 38 57, fax: +33-4-37
28 38 59
email: http://iep.univ-
lyon2.fr/Recherche/Ceriep/ceriep

*Centre Comparatif d'etudes sur les
Politiques et des Espaces Locaux
(CEPEL)*
Université de Montpellier I, 39 rue
de l'Université, 34060 Montpellier
Cedex, France
tel: +33-4-67 61 54 60, fax: +33-4-67
61 54 82
email: cepel@sc.univ-montp1.fr

*Centre Universitaire d'Etudes Poli-
tiques*
Université de Nancy 2, 4 rue de la
Ravinelle, 5400 Nancy, France
tel: +33-3-83 35 62 52, fax: +33-3-83
32 68 64
email: cuep@droit-eco.univ-

nancy2.fr
http://www.univ-nancy2.fr

*Law and Political Sciences,
CRUARAP*
Université de Nantes, BP 8107,
44313 Nantes Cedex 3, France
tel: +33-2-40 14 16 04, fax: +33-2-40
14 16 44
email: cruarap@droit.univ-nantes.fr
http://palissy.humana.univ-
nantes.fr/LABOS/CRUARAP/

Institut d'Etudes Politiques (IEP)
Fondation Nationale des Sciences
Politiques, 27 rue St Guillaume,
75337 Paris Cedex, France
tel: +33-01-45 49 50 50, fax: +33-1-45
49 47 49
email: jeanl.domenach@sciences-
po.fr
http://www.sciences-po.fr

*Institut d'Etudes Economiques et
Sociales*
Institut Catholique de Paris, 21 rue
d'Assas, 75006 Paris, France
tel: +33-1-44 39 52 89, fax: +33-1-45
44 27 14

Département de Science Politique
Université de Paris I (Panthéon-
Sorbonne), 17 rue de la Sorbonne,
75231 Paris Cedex 05, France
tel: +33-1-40 46 27 98, fax: +33-1-40
46 31 65
email: depscpo@univ-paris1.fr
http://www.univ-paris1.fr

*Centre d'Etudes Politiques et Institu-
tionnelles*
Université Paris II, 83 bis, rue Notre-
Dame-des-Champs, 75006 Paris,
France
tel: +33-1-44 41 59 2, fax: +33-1-45 87
04 93

Institut d'Etudes Politiques
Fondation Nationale des Sciences
Politiques, 27 rue Saint Guillaume,
75337 Paris, France
tel: +33-1-45 49 50 50, fax: +33-1-42
22 39 64
email: jeanl.domenach@sciences-

po.fr
http://www.sciences-po.fr

CERI, Faculté de Droit et de Science Politique
Université de Reims Champagne-Ardenne, 57 bis rue Pierre Taittinger, 51100 Reims, France
tel: +33-3-26 05 38 38, fax: +33-3-26 04 20 74
email: jc.nemery@univ-reims.fr
http://www.univ-reims.fr/crdt

Faculté de Droit et Science Politique
Université de Rennes, 9 rue i Macè, 35042 Rennes Cedex, France
tel: +33-2-99 84 39 33, fax: +33-2-99 84 39 02
email: erik.neveu@rennes.iep.fr
http://www.rennes.iep.fr

Institut d'Etudes Politiques (IEP)
Université de Rennes I, 104 blvd de la Duchesse Anne, 35700 Rennes, France
tel: +33-2-99 84 39 39, fax: +33-2-99 84 39 00
email: morabito@rennes.iep.fr
http:/www.rennes.iep.fr

Institut d'Etudes Politiques (IEP)
Université de Strasbourg, 47 avenue de la Foret-Noire, 67000 Strasbourg, France
tel: +33-3-88 41 77 25, fax: +33-3-88 41 77 78
email: renaud.dorandeu@iep.u-strasbg.fr
http//www-iep.u-strasbg.fr

Institut d'Etudes Politiques (IEP)
Université de Bordeaux IV, Domaine Universitaire, 33405 Talence Cedex, France
tel: +33-5-56 84 42 81, fax: +33-5-56 84 43 29
email: cervl@iep.u-bordeaux.fr
http://www.iep.u-bordeaux.fr

Institut d'Etudes Politiques (IEP)
Toulouse, 2 ter rue des Puits Creusés, 3100 Toulouse, France
tel: +33-5-61 11 02 60, fax: +33-5-61 22 94 80

email: iep@univ-tlse1.fr
http://www-uni-tlse1.fr/iep/

Département de Science Politique
Université de Versailles, Saint-Quentin-en-Yveline, 3 rue de la Division Leclerc, 78280 Guyancourt, France
tel: +33-1-30 43 44 50

Centre de Recherches Administratives Politiques et Sociales (CRAPS)
Université de Lille II, 1 place Déliot, BP 169, 59653 Villeneuve d'Ascq Cedex, France
tel: +33-3-20 90 74 51, fax: +33-3-20 90 77 00
email: craps@hp-sc.univ-lille2.fr
http://www.hp-sc.univ-lille2.fr/droit/CRAPS

Germany

Lehrstuhl Politische Wissenschaft
Universität Augsburg, Universitätstr 10, D-86159 Augsburg, Germany
tel: +49-821-598 5591, fax: +49-821-598 5591

Department of Political Science
Otto-Friedrich Universität Bamberg, Postfach 1549, D-96045 Bamberg, Germany
tel: +49-951-863 2640/2605, fax: +49-951-863 2641/2606
email: margit.jones.@sowi.uni-bamberg.de
http://www.uni-bamberg.de/~babpo99/

Zentralinstitut für Sozialwissenschaftliche Forschung
Freie Universität Berlin, Malteserstr 74-100, D-12249 Berlin, Germany
tel: +49-30-7792 202 or 447, fax: +49-30-7759 685
http://www.fu-berlin.de/POLWISS/

Fakultätinstitut Sozialwissenschaften
Humboldt-Universität zu Berlin, Unter den Linden 6, D-10099 Berlin, Germany

tel: +49-30-2093 4219, fax: +49-30
2093 4223
email: eckhard.schroeter@rz.hu-
berlin.de
http//www2.hu-berlin.de/sowi

*Max-Planck-Institut für Bildungsfor-
schung*
Lentzeallee 94, D-14195 Berlin
(Dahlem), Germany
tel: +49-221-2767 0, fax: +49-221-
2767 555
email: mpi@mpi-fg-koeln.mpg.de
http://www.mpi-fg-koeln.mpg.de

*Wissenschaftzentrum für Sozialfor-
schung Berlin*
Reichpietschufer 50, D-10785 Berlin,
Germany
tel: +49-30-254 910, fax: +49-30-254
91 684

*Fakultät für Sozialwissenschaft - Der
Dekan*
Ruhr-Universität Bochum, Gabäude
GC04/47, Postfach 10 21 48, D-
44780 Bochum, Germany
tel: +49-234-700 5172, fax: +49-234-
7094 507
email: uw@pw2.ruhr-uni-
bochum.de
http://www.pw2.ruhr-uni-
bochum.de/index.htm

Zentrum für Socialpolitik
Universität Bremen, Barkhof,
Parkallee 39, D-28209 Bremen,
Germany
tel: +49-421-218 4051, fax: +49-421-
218 4052
email: mgs@zes.uni-bremen.de
http://www.barkhof.uni-
bremen.de

Institut für Politikwissenschaft
Technische Hochschule Darmstadt,
Residenzschloss, D-64283 Darmstadt, Germany
tel: +49-615-116 2045, fax: +49-615-
116 3992
email: sandner@pg.tu-darmstadt.de
http://www.ifs.tu-
darmstadt.de/pg/politik.htm

Fach Politikwissenschaft
Dortmund Universität, Fachbereich
14, Emil Figge Str 50, D-44221
Dortmund, Germany
tel: +49-231-7551, fax: +49-231-755
5452
email: figge8h.5d/d44227ordmund

*Departments of Politics, Sociology,
and Mass Communication Studies*
Technische Universität Dresden,
Akademisches Auslandsamt, D-
01062 Dresden, Germany
tel: +49-351-463 4716/7043, fax: +49-
351-463 7085
email: zimmer-e@rcs.urz.tu-
dresden.de

Department of Political Science
Universität Duisburg Gesam-
thochschule, Fachberiech 1, Lo-
tharstr 65, D-47048 Duisburg, Germany
tel: +49-203-379 2052, fax: +49-203-
379 3840

*Geschichts- und Gesellschaftswissen-
schaftliche Fakultät*
Katholische Universität Eichstätt,
Ostenstr 26, Zimmer 113, D-85071
Eichstätt, Germany
tel: +49-84-212 0497, fax: +49-84-218
9966

*Fachbereich Gesellschaftswissen-
schaften*
Johann Wolfgang Goethe-
Universität Frankfurt, Robert-
Mayer-Str 5, D-60054 Frankfurt-am-
Main, Germany
tel: +49-69-7982252, fax: +49-69-
79828465
http://www.uni-frankfurt.de

Institute for Work & Technology
Wissenschaftszentrum Nordrhein-
Westfalen, Florastr 26-28, D-45879
Gelsenkirchen 1, Germany
tel: +49-209-17070, fax: +49-209-
1707110

Institut für Politikwissenschaft
Fernuniversität Hagen, Feithstr
140/AVZ II, D-58084 Hagen, Germany

tel: +49-2331-987 2160, fax: +49-
2331-987 326
email: Nicole.Mauska@FernUni-
Hagen.de
http://www.fernuni-
hagen.de/polinst/welcome.html

Institut für Politikwissenschaft
Martin-Luther-Universität, Halle-
Wittenberg, Postfach 8, D-06009
Halle, Germany
tel: +49-345-5224 221, fax: +49-345-
5227 145
email: boll@politik.uni-halle.de
http://sparc20.soziologie.uni-
halle.de

Institut für Politikwissenschaft
Universität Hamburg, Allende-Platz
1, D-20146 Hamburg, Germany
tel: +49-40-4123 46 95 or 57, fax:
+49-40-4123 4506

*Department of Social and Economic
History*
Universität Hamburg, Allende-Platz
1, D-20146 Hamburg, Germany
tel: +49-40-4123 4695 or 4657, fax:
+49-40-4123 4506

Institut für Politische Wissenschaft
Universität Hannover, Schneider-
berg 50, D-30167 Hannover, Germany
tel: +49-511-762 4683, fax: +49-511-
762 4199

Institut für Politische Wissenschaft
Ruprecht-Karls-Universität Heidelberg, Marstallstr 6, D-69117 Heidelberg, Germany
tel: +49-6221-542860, fax: +49-6221-
542896
email: frank.pfetsch@urz.uni-
heidelberg.de
http://www.uni-heidelberg.de

Institute for Political Science
Friedrich-Schiller Universität, Carl
Zeiss Str 3, D-07743 Jena, Germany
tel: +49-641-945430, fax: +49-641-
945432
email: s6kldi@rz.uni-jena.de
http://www.uni-
jena.de/svw/powi/

Fachgebiet Politikwissenschaft
Universität Kaiserslautern, Pfaffen-
bergstr 95, D-67663 Kaiserslautern,
Germany
tel: +49-631-205 2013 or 2461, fax:
+49-631-205 3850

*Research Institute for Political Sci-
ence and European Affairs*
Universität zu Köln, Gottfried-
Keller-Str 6,, D-50931 Köln 41, Germany
tel: +49-221-470 2855, fax: +49-221-
470 5101
email: polwi.sek@uni-koeln.de
http://www.uni-koeln.de

*Max-Planck-Institut fuer Gesell-
schaftsforschung*
Lothringer Str 78, D-50677 Köln,
Germany
tel: +49-221-336050, fax: +49-221-
33605 55
email: mpi@mpi-fg-koeln.mpg.
dbp.de

*Fakultät für Verwaltungswissen-
schaft*
Universität Konstanz, Universitätsstr 10, Postfach 55 60, D-78461
Konstanz, Germany
tel: +49-7531-88 2150, fax: +49-7531-
88 2601
email: Volker.Schneider@uni-
konstanz.de
http://www.uni-
konstanz.de/FuF/Verwiss/

Institut für Politikwissenschaft
Universität Leipzig, Augustusplatz
29, D-04109 Leipzig, Germany
tel: +49-341-97 35610, fax: +49-341-
97 35619
email: politsek@rz.uni-leipzig.de
http://www.uni-
leipzig.de/~politik

Department of Social Sciences
Universität Lüneburg, Postfach 24
40, D-21332 Lüneburg, Germany
tel: +49-4131-782501, fax: +49-4131-
78 2507

Institut für Politikwissenschaft Forschungsgruppe Europa
Johannes Gutenberg-Universität
Mainz, Colonel-Kleinmann-Weg 2,
D-55099 Mainz, Germany
tel: +49-6131-393450, fax: +49-6131-392992

Mannheimer Zentrum für Europäische Sozialforschung (MZES)
Mannheim Universität, Postfach, D-68131 Mannheim, Germany
tel: +49-621-292 5287, fax: +49-621 292 5289
email: bkohler@sowi.uni-mannheim.de
http//www.uni-mannheim.de/fakul/sowi/

Institut für Politikwissenschaft
Philipps-Universität Marburg,
Wilhelm-Röpke-Str 6, D-35032 Marburg, Germany
tel: +49-6421-28 4397 or 4384, fax: +49-6421-28 8913
email: bergschl@papin.hrz.uni-

Geschwister-Scholl Institut für Politische Wissenschaft
Ludwig-Maximilians Universität
München, Ludwigstr 10, D-80539
München, Germany
tel: +49-89-2180 3010, fax: +49-89-2180 3069
http://www.lrz-muenchen.de/~intpol/

Institut für Politikwissenschaft
Westfälische-Wilhelms-Universität
Münster, Platz der Weißen Rose, D-48151 Münster, Germany
tel: +49-251-83 9357, fax: +49-251-83 4372

Faculty of Economic and Social Sciences
Universität Potsdam, PO Box 900
327, D-14439 Potsdam, Germany
tel: +49-331-977 4604, fax: +49-331-977 4604
email: hdoering@rz.uni-potsdam.de

Institut für Polikwissenschaft
Universität Regensburg, Universitätsstr 31, D-93053 Regensburg,

Germany
tel: +49-941-943 35 14 or 16, fax: +49-941-943 4992
email: hacker@alf4.ngate.uni-regensburg.de

Institut für Politikwissenschaft
Universität des Saarlandes, Postfach
15 11 50, D-66041 Saarbrücken,
Germany
tel: +49-681-302 2126, fax: +49-681-302 3591
email: ww51jdmk@rz.uni-sb.de

Institut für Politikwissenschaft
Universität Stuttgart, Keplerstr 17,
D-70174 Stuttgart, Germany
tel: +49-711-121 3430, fax: +49-711-121 2333
email: oscar.gabriel@po.pol.uni-stuttgart.de
http://www.uni-stuttgart.de/uniuser/ipw/

Department of Political Science
Universität Trier, Universitätsring
15, D-54286 Trier, Germany
tel: +49-651-201 2128, fax: +49-651-201 3917
email: gellner@pcmail.uni-trier.de

Institut für Politikwissenschaft
Eberhard-Karls-Universität Tübingen, Melanchthonstr 36, D-72074
Tübingen, Germany
tel: +49-7071-29 54 45, fax: +49-7071-29 24 17

Greece

Department of Political Science and Public Administration
National and Capodistrian University of Athens, 19 Omirou Street,
106 72 Athens, Greece
tel: +30-1-368 8913-9, fax: +30-1-368 8920
email: aidmetax@hellasnet.gr
www.uoa.gr/polisci

Institute of Political Sociology (INPOLS)
National Centre of Social Research
(EKKE), Messoghion Av 14-18, 115
27 Athens, Greece

tel: +30-1-7489128, fax: +30-1-74 89801
email: inpos@ekke.gr
http://www.ekke.gr
Institute of International Relations (IRR)
Panteion University of Social and Political Sciences, 3-5 Hill Street, 176 71 Athens, Greece
tel: +30-1-33 12325-7, fax: +30-1-33 13575
email: idis@mbox.ariadne-t.gr
http://www.idis.gr
Department of Political Science and History
Panteion University of Social and Political Sciences, Leoforos Sygrou 136, 176 71 Athens, Greece
tel: +30-1-92 15926, fax: +30-1-92 37876
email: politicsc@panteion.gr
http://www.panteion.gr
Department of Political Science
University of Crete, University Campus, 741 00 Rethymno, Greece
http://www.uch.gr/Department/
Sector of Political Sociology
University of Thessaly, Terma Argonafton, Volos, Greece
tel: +30-4-21 36735, fax: +30-4-21 34355
email: geogouga@uth.gr
http://www.uth.gr

Iceland

Department of Political Science
University of Iceland, Oddi vid Sturlugötu, 101 Reykavík, Iceland
tel: +354-1-569 4502, fax: +354-1-26806

Ireland

Department of Government
University College Cork, Cork, Ireland
tel: +353-21-490 2770, fax: +353-21-491 3321
email: government@ucc.ie
http://www.ucc.ie/acad/govt.html

Department of Politics
University College Dublin, Belfield, Dublin 4, Ireland
tel: +353-1-706 8397, fax: +353-1-706 1171
email: jean.brennan@ucd.ie
Department of Political Science
University of Dublin, Trinity College, Dublin 2, Ireland
tel: +353-1-608 1651, fax: +353-1-677 0546
email: mlaver@vax1.tcd.ie
Department of Political Science and Sociology
University College Galway, Galway, Ireland
tel: +353-91-24411 ext 2355, fax: +353--91 25700
Department of Government and Society
University of Limerick, Limerick, Ireland
tel: +353-61-333644, fax: +353-61-330316
email: browne@ul.ie

Italy

Facoltà di Scienze Politiche
Università del Piemonte Orientale, Cozzo T Borsalino 50, I-15100 Alessandria, Italy
tel: +39-1-31 283 745
email: segrsp.ol.unipmn.it
http://www.sp.ol.unipmn.it
Facoltà di Giurisprudenza di Bari
Università degli Studi di Bari, Piazza Battisti, 1, I-70121 Bari, Italy
Facoltà di Scienze Politiche di Forlì
Università degli Studi di Bologna, Strada Maggiore 45, I-40125 Bologna, Italy
tel: +39-51-2092700, fax: +39-51-234036
email: gualmini@spbo.unibo.it
www.spbo.unibo.it

Facoltà di Scienze Politiche di Cagliari
Università degli Studi di Cagliari, Viale S Ignazio da Laconi 78, I-09123 Cagliari, Italy
tel: +39-70-6753003, fax: +39-70-651680

Facoltà di Giurisprudenza di Camerino
Università degli Studi di Camerino, Via del Bastione, 2, I-62032 Camerino, Italy

Dipartimento di Scienze Economiche Gestionali e Sociali (SEGeS)
Università degli Studi del Molise, Via Cavour 11/A, I-86100 Campobasso, Italy
tel: +39-874-310 187 or 188, fax: +39-874-92895

Facoltà di Scienze Politiche di Catania
Università degli Studi di Catania, Via Vittorio Emanuele 49, I-95131 Catania, Italy
tel: +39-95-7347899, fax: +39-95-7347205
email: attinaf@vm.unict.it
http://www.fscpo.unict.it/vademec/dsp.htm

Facoltà di Scienze Politiche di Cosenza
Università degli Studi della Calabria, Arcavacata di Rende, I-87036 Cosenza, Italy
tel: +39-984-839570, fax: +39-984-839522
email: sociolog@unical.it
http://www.unical.it/dipartimenti/sociolog

Dipartimento di Scienza della Politica e Sociologia Politica (DISPO)
Università degli Studi di Firenze, Via Francesco Valori N 9, I-50129 Firenze, Italy
tel: +39-55-5032411, fax: +39-55-5032426
email: dispo@unifi.it
http://www.dispo.unifi.it

Facoltà di Scienze Politiche di

Salerno
Università degli Studi di Salerno, Via Ponte don Melillo, I-84084 Fisciano (Salerno), Italy
tel: +39-89-962 084 or 085, fax: +39-89-962086
email: dissp@ponza.dia.unisa.it

Facoltà di Scienze Politiche di Genova
Università degli Studi di Genoa, Largo Zecca 8-19, I-16124 Genoa, Italy
tel: +39-10-209 9015, fax: +39-10-209 9027
email: dispos@csb-scpo.unige.it
http://www.csb-scpo.unige.it/dispos/

Facoltà di Scienze Politiche di Milano
Università Cattolica del Sacro Cuore, Largo Gemelli 1, I-62100 Macerata, Italy
tel: +39-2-7234 2295, fax: +39-2-7234 3649
email: oliscipol@mi.umicatt.it
http://umicatt.it

Facoltà di Scienze Politiche di Macerata
Università degli Studi di Macerata, Piazza della Libertà 23, I-62100 Macerata, Italy

Facoltà di Scienze Politiche di Messina
Università degli Studi di Messina, Centro Servizi Generali, Via Tommaso Cannizzaro N 9, I-98123 Messina, Italy
tel: +39-90-29 39 562, fax: +39-90-692859

Facoltà di Scienze Politiche di Milano
Università degli Studi di Milano, Via Conservatorio 7, I-20122 Milan, Italy
tel: +39-2-76074351, fax: +39-2-76015104
email: dipa@sociol.unimi.it
http://www.sociol.unimi.it

Facoltà di Scienze Politiche di Na-

poli
Università degli Studi di Napoli
Largo San Marcellino 70, I-80138
Mapoli, Italy
tel: +39-81-781 0611, fax: +39-81-781
0621
email: dipsocio@unina.it
http://www.unina.it/sociologia

Facoltà di Scienze Politiche di Palermo
Università degli Studi di Palermo,
Via Maqueela 324, I-80100 Napoli,
Italy
tel: +39-91-6110539, fax: +39-91-6112023
email: dpds@ncbox.unipa.it
http://www.unipa.it/dpds

Dipartimento di Sociologia
Università di Napoli, Largo San
Marcellino 10, I-80138 Napoli, Italy
tel: +39-81-55 20053, fax: +39-55-21076

Facoltà di Scienze Politiche di Padova
Università degli Studi di Padova,
Via S Canziano 8, I-35122 Padova,
Italy
tel: +39-49 827 4321, fax: +39-49-657
508
email: dipsoc@ux1.unipd.it

Facoltà di Scienze Politiche di Pavia
Università degli Studi di Pavia,
Strada Nuova 65, I-27100 Pavia, Italy
tel: +39-382-504800, fax: +39-382-26544
email: ferrera@ipv36.unipv.it
http://www.unipv.it/webdsps/ho
mepage.htm

Facoltà di Scienze Politiche di Perugia
Università degli Studi di Perugia,
Via Elce di Sotto, I-06123 Perugia,
Italy
tel: +39-75-5855 405 or 406, fax: +39-75-585 5405

Facoltà di Scienze Politiche di Pisa
Università degli Studi di Pisa, Via
Serafini 3, I-56100 Pisa, Italy

tel: +39-50-501597, fax: +39-50-501597

Facoltà di Scienze Politiche di Roma
Libera Università degli Studi "S Pio
V", Via delle Sette Chiese 139, I-00145 Roma, Italy

Facoltà di Scienze Politiche di Roma
LUISS - Libera Università Internazionale degli Studi Sociali Guido
Carli, Via di Villa Massimo 57, I-00161 Roma, Italy

Facoltà di Scienze Politiche di Roma
LUMSA - Libera Università "Maria
SS Assunta", Via della Traspontina
21, I-00193 Roma, Italy

Facoltà di Scienze Politiche di Roma
Università degli Studi di Roma "La
Sapienza", Piazzale Aldo Moro 5, I-00185 Roma, Italy
tel: +39-6-49910599, fax: +39-6-4451392
email: soclanc@axrma.uniroma1.it
http://www.uniroma1.it

Diparimento di Scienze Politiche
Università di Roma III, Via Corrado
Segre 2, I-00146 Roma, Italy
tel: +39-6-55 17 62 55, fax: +39-6-55
17 62 48
email: dip_poli@uniroma3.it

*Dipartimento di Scienze Politiche e
Sociologia*
European University Institute, Via
dei Roccettini 9, I-50016 San Domenico di Fiesole, Firenze, Italy
tel: +39-55-46851, fax: +39-55-4685201
email: catotti@datacomm.iue.it
http://www.iue.it

Facoltà di Scienze Politiche di Sassari
Università degli Studi di Sassari, Piazza Università 21, I-07100 Sassari,
Italy

*Dipartimento de Scienze Storiche,
Giuridiche, Politiche e Sociali*
Università degli Studi di Siena, Piazza S Francesco 7, I-53100 Siena,
Italy

tel: +39-5-77 298734, fax: +39-5-77 298754
email: bartali@unisi.it
http://www.unisi.it/ateneo/dipart

Facoltà di Scienze Politiche di Teramo
Università degli Studi di Teramo, Viale Crucioli 122, I-64100 Teramo, Italy
tel: +39-8-61 266 514, fax: +39-8-61 266 514
email: prespol@spol.unite.it

Facoltà di Scienze Politiche di Torino
Università degli Studi di Torino, Via Verdi 25, I-10123 Torino, Italy
tel: +39-11-670 3236, fax: +39-11-670 3249
email: mastro@cisi.unito.it
http://www.unito.it

Facoltà di Scienze Politiche di Trieste
Università degli Studi di Trieste, Piazzale Europa 1, I-34127 Trieste, Italy
tel: +39-40-676 3279, fax: +39-40-577867
email: boscoa@sp.univ.trieste.it
http://www.iscmt.univ.trieste.it

Facoltà di Scienze Politiche di Urbino
Università degli Studi di Urbino, Via Bramante 17, I-61029 Urbino, Italy
tel: +39-722-3031, fax: +39-722-2955

Netherlands

Politicologie
Universiteit van Amsterdam, OZ Achterburgwal 237, 1012 DL Amsterdam, Netherlands
tel: +31-20-525 2147, fax: +31-20-525 2086

Department of Political Science and Public Administration
Vrije Universiteit Amsterdam, De Boelelaan 1081-C, 1081 HV Amsterdam, Netherlands
tel: +31-20-444 6805, fax: +31-20-444 6820
email: pjm.pennings@scw.vu.nl

HTTP://polbk.scw.vu.nl/english/index.htm

Department of Public Administration and Public Policy
Universiteit Twente, Postbus 217 Twente, 7500 AE Enschede, Netherlands
tel: +31-53-489 3200, fax: +31-53-489 4734
email: j.j.a.thomassen@bsk.utwente.nl

Departement Politieke Wetenschap
Universiteit Leiden, Postbus 9500, 2300 BA Leiden, Netherlands
tel: +31-71-527 5936/3939, fax: +31-71-527 3815
http://www.fsw.leidenuniv.nl/www/w3_pol/pol.htm

European Institute of Public Administration
PO Box 1229, 6201 BE Maastricht, Netherlands
tel: +31-43-3296 222, fax: +31-43-3296 296
email: eipa@eipa.nl
http://www.eipa.nl

Department of Political Science
Katholieke Universiteit Nijmegen, PO Box 9108, 6500 HK Nijmegen, Netherlands
tel: +31-24-361 2754, fax: +31-24-361 2379
email: E.deJonge@bw.kun.nl
http://www.kun.nl/politic

Faculty of Social and Political Sciences
Erasmus University Rotterdam, PO Box 1738, 3000 DR Rotterdam, Netherlands
tel: +31-10-408 2039, fax: +31-10-452 7061
email: groeneweg@pol.fsw.eur.nl
http://www.eur.nl/fsw/pol

Norway

Department of Administration and Organisation Theory
Universitetet i Bergen, Christiesgate 17, N-5007 Bergen, Norway

tel: +47-5558-8604, fax: +47-5558-9890
email: aorg@aorg.uib.no
http://www.svf.uib.no

Department of Comparative Politics
Universitetet i Bergen, Christiesgate 15, N-5007 Bergen, Norway
tel: +47-555-82175, fax: +47-555-89425
email: Ragnhild.Stolt-Neilsen@isp.uib.no
http://hermes.svl.uib.no/sampol

Department of Social Sciences
Bodø College, N-8002 Bodø, Norway
tel: +47-75-51 72 00, fax: +47-75-51 73 78
email: bsa@isv.hsn.no

Department of Sociology and Political Science
Universitetet i Trondheim, N-7055 Dragvoll, Norway
tel: +47-73-59 17 04, fax: +47-73-59 15 64
email: ola.listhaug@avh. unit.no
www.ntu.no

Department of Political Science
Harstad College, PB 2130 Kanebogen, N-9401 Harstad, Norway
tel: +47-77-07 02 33, fax: +47-77-7 43 05

Department of Economy and Social Sciences
Agder College, Postuttak, N-4604 Kristiansand, Norway
tel: +47-38-7 95 00, fax: +47-38-7 95 01
email: dagj@hia.no
http://www.hia.no

Department of Political Studies
Lillehammer College, Box 1004 Skurva, N-2601 Lillehammer, Norway
tel: +47-61-28 80 00, fax: +47-61-26 07 50
email: beatrice@odh.no

Seksjon for Administrative Fag
Molde College, Britvegen 2, N-6400 Molde, Norway

tel: +47-71-21 40 00, fax: +47-71-21 41 00
email: Turid.Aarseth@himolde.no
http://www.himolde.no

Institutt for Samfunnsforskning (ISF)
Universitetet i Oslo, Munthesgt 31, N-0260 Oslo, Norway
tel: +47-22-55 45 10, fax: +47-22-43 13 85
email: bernt.aardal@isaf.no

Department of Political Science
Universitetet i Oslo, Box 1097 Blindern, N-0317 Oslo, Norway
tel: +47-22-85 51 81, fax: +47-22-85 44 11
http://www.sv.uio.no/stv/eng.ht m

Department of Organisation and Management
Norwegian School of Management, Elias Smiths, VEI 15, PO Box 580, N-1301 Sandvika, Norway
tel: +47-67-57 5 00, fax: +47-67-57 05 70
http://www.bi.no

Department of Political Science
Universitetet i Tromsø, N-9037 Tromsø, Norway
tel: +47-776-44296, fax: +47-776-44905
email: stv@sv.uit.no
http://www.uit.no

Portugal

Centro de Estudios Sociais
Universidade de Coímbra, Praça D Dinis, Apartado 3087, 3000 Coimbra, Portugal
tel: +351-39-26459 or 20354

Instituto de Ciencias Sociais
Universidade Lisboa, Rua Miguel Ludi 18, 1200 Lisboa, Portugal
tel: +351-1-3903141, fax: +351-1-3920615

Department of Political Science
Universidade Lusiade, Rua Junqverira 188, 1300 Lisboa, Portugal
tel: +351-1-361 1500, fax: +351-1-362

2955 / 363 8307
email: mjbfs@lis.ulusiada.pt
http://www.ulusiada.pt/lisboa/

Centro de Estudos de Relações Internacionais e Estratégia (CERIE)
Universidade Dos Açores, Rua da
Mae de Deus, N 58, 9500 Ponta Delgada, S Miguel, Acores, Portugal
tel: +351-96-653388, fax: +351-96-653388

Departamento de Economia & Sociologia
Universidade de Trás-os-Montes e
Alto Douro, POB 202, 5001 Vila
Real, Portugal
tel: +351-59-32 1631 or 2545, fax:
+351-67-61 54 60

Spain

Constitutional Law and Political Science
Universidad Barcelona, Diagonal
684, 08034 Barcelona, Spain
tel: +34-93-402 4408, fax: +34-93-402 4409
email: dccp@riscdz.eco.ub.es

Departament de Ciència Política
Universidad Pompeu Fabra, Rambla
Santa Mónica 32, 08002 Barcelona,
Spain
tel: +34-93-484 9900, fax: +34-93-484 9999

Estudis de Ciènces Politiques i Gestio Publica
Universidad Pompeu Fabra, Ramon
Trias Fargas 25-27, 08005 Barcelona,
Spain
tel: +34-93-54 22357, fax: +34-93-5421654
email: estudis.cpgp@grup.upf.es

Institut de Ciències Politiques i Socials
c/ Mallorca 244, 2º 1ª, 08008 Barcelona, Spain
tel: +34-93-487 1076, fax: +34-93-487 1149

Departament de Ciència Política i de Dret Públic
Universidad Autònoma de Barcelona, Campus Universitari, 08193
Bellaterra (Barcelona), Spain
tel: +34-93-581 1767, fax: +34-93-581 2439
email: d.c.politica@uab.es
http://cpdp.uab.es

Departmento de Sociologia, Ciencia Política y de la Administration
Universidad de Coruna, Campus de
Elvira, 15071 Coruna, Spain
tel: +34-98-116 7000, fax: +34-98-116 7103
email: samigo@udc.es
http://www.udc.es

Departmento de Ciencia Política y de la Administration
Universidad de Granada, C/ Rector
Lopez-Argueta S/N, 18071 Granada, Spain
tel: +34-958-244198, fax: +34-958-588969
email: cpoliti @azahsr.ugr.es

Centro de Estudios Avanzados en Ciencias Sociales
Juan March de Estudios e Investigaciones, c/ Castelló 77, 28006 Madrid, Spain
tel: +34-91-435 4240, fax: +34-91-576 3420
email: webmast@mail.march.es
http://www.march.es

Departamento de Ciencia Política y de la Administración
Universidad Autónoma de Madrid,
Crta Colmenar KM 15, 28049 Madrid, Spain
tel: +34-91-3974380, fax: +34-91-39741661
email: angel.cebollero@uam.es
http://www.uam.es

Ciencia Politica y Sociologia
Universidad Carlos III de Madrid,
28903 Getafe, Spain
tel: +34-91-62 498 09, fax: +34-91-62 495 74

email: udma@polsoc.uc3m.es
http://www.uc3m.es

Departmento de Ciencia Política y de la Administration
Universidad Complutense de Madrid, Campus de Somosaguas, 28023 Madrid, Spain
tel: +34-91-39 426 97, fax: +34-91-39 428 68
email: jso@cps.ucm.es
www.ucm.es/info/cpuno

Departamento de Ciencia Política y de la Administración
Universidad Nacional de Educacion a Distancia, Facultad de Ciencias Políticas y Sociología c/ Obispo Trejo s/n, 28040 Madrid, Spain
tel: +34-91-3987089 / 98, fax: +34-91-3987003
email: paguilar@poli.uned.es
www.uned.es

Facultad de Ciencias Politicas y Sociologia
Universidad Pontifica de Salamanca, Paeso Juan XXIII, 3, 28040 Madrid, Spain
tel: +34-91-533 5200, fax: +34-91-552 5249
email: fra@jis.org

Centro de Estudios Constitucionales
Plaza de la Marina Española 9, 28013 Madrid, Spain
tel: +34-91-547 19 50, fax: +34-91-541 95 74
email: cepc@cepc.es
http://www.cepc.es

Facultad de Ciencias Politicas y Sociologia Leon XIII
Universidad Pontifica de Salamanca, Paseo Juan XXIII, 3, 28040 Madrid, Spain
tel: +34-91-533 5200

Departamento de Cienca Politica
Universidad de Malaga, Facultad de Derecho, Campus Universitario de Teatinos, s/n, 29071 Malaga, Spain
tel: +34-952-13 22 40 / 22 51, fax: +34-952-13 23 38

email: avalencia@uma.es
http://www.uma.es

Area de Ciencia Politica, Facultad de Ciencias Sociales
Universidad de Salamanca, Campus Miguel Unamuno, 37001 Salamanca, Spain
tel: +34-923-294400 ext 1617, fax: +34-923-294637
email: malcanta@gugu.usal.es
http://www.usal.es

Instituto de Estudios de Iberoamerica y Portugal
Universidad de Salamanca, San Pablo 26, 37001 Salamanca, Spain

Ciencias Politicas y Sociales
Universidad de Santiago de Compostela, Campus Universitario Sur, campus Sur, Spain
tel: +34-981-56 31 00, fax: +34-981-59 69 51
email: cppiolla@usc.es

Department of Constitutional Law and Political Science
Universidad La Laguna, Campus de Guajara, 38071 Tenerife, Spain
tel: +34-922-317079, fax: +34-922-253742 / 317427
email: jhdezb@ull.es

Facultad de Ciencias Sociales y de la Informacion
Universidad del País Vasco, Vizacaya, 48940 Lejona, Spain
tel: +34-94-464 7700, fax: +34-94-464 8299
email: francisco_llera@gustat.es
http://www.ehv.es

Sweden

Department of Political Science
Göteborgs Universitet, Sprängkullsgatan 19, S-411 23 Göteborg, Sweden
tel: +46-31-773 1229, fax: +46-31-773 4599
email: Margaretha.Hellgren-Glimje@pol.gu.se
http://www.pol.gu.se/httpsida/pol/

Department of Social Science
Universitet i Linköping, S-581 83
Linköping, Sweden
tel: +46-13-281 000
http://www.liu.se

Department of Political Science
Lunds Universitet, Box 52, S-221 00
Lund, Sweden
tel: +46-46-222 8952, fax: +46-46-222
4006
email: svet@svet.lu.se
http://www.svet.lu.se

Department of Social Sciences, Section of Politics
Örebro Universitet, PO 923, S-701 30
Örebro, Sweden
tel: +46-19-303000, fax: +46-19-303484
email: sam@hoe.se
http://www.hoe.se/english

Department of Political Science
Universitet Stockholm, Universitetsvägen 10 F, S-106 91 Stockholm, Sweden
tel: +46-8-162000, fax: +46-8-152529
www.statsvet.su.se

Department of Social Science
Mid Sweden University, S-851 70
Sundsvall, Sweden
tel: +46-60-148600, fax: +46-60-148783
email: Goran.Bostedt@fof.mh.se

Department of Political Science
Umeå Universitet, S-901 87 Umeå,
Sweden
tel: +46-90-786 50 00, fax: +46-90-786
66 81
email: kjell.lundmark@pol.umu.se
http://www.pol.umu.se

Department of Political Science
Uppsala Universitet, Skytteanum,
Box 514, S-751 20 Uppsala, Sweden
tel: +46-18-471 3413, fax: +46-18-471
3409
http://www.statsvet.uu.se

Department of Political Science,
School of Social Sciences
Högskolan i Växjö, Box 5035, S-351
95 Växjö, Sweden

tel: +46-470-708000, fax: +46-470-84425
email: politologia@svi.hv.se
http://www.hv.se

Switzerland

Institut für Politikwissenschaft
Universität Bern, Unitobler, Lerchenweg 36, CH-3000 Bern 9, Switzerland
tel: +41-31-631 8331, fax: +41-31-631
8590
email:
klaus.armingeon@ipw.unibe.ch
http://www.cx.unibe.ch/ipw/

Département de Science Politique
Université de Genève, 102 Blvd
Carl-Vogt, CH-1211 Geneva 4, Switzerland
tel: +41-22-705 8363, fax: +41-22-705
8364
email: secretariat@politic.unige.ch
http://www.unige.ch/ses/spo

Institut d'Etudes Politiques
Université de Lausanne, BFSH 2,
CH-1015 Lausanne-Dorigny, Switzerland
tel: +41-21-692 31 40, fax: +41-21-692
31 45
email: jbeguin@eliot.unil.ch
http://www-ssp.unil.ch/iepi/

Institut de Science Politique
Université de Neuchâtel, Pierre A
Mazel 7, CH-2000 Neuchâtel, Switzerland
tel: +41-32-718-1230, fax: +41-32-718
1231
email: Ernest.Weibel@seco.unine.ch
http://www.unine.ch/uer/uer_sci_
polit.htm/

Institut für Politikwissenschaft
Hochschule St Gallen, Dufourstr 45,
CH-9000 St Gallen, Switzerland

Forschungsstelle für Politische Wissenschaft
Universität Zürich, Karl Schmid-Str
4, CH-8006 Zürich, Switzerland
tel: +41-1-634 3841, fax: +41-1 634

4925
email: ukloeti@pwi.unizh.ch

UK

School of Public Administration and Law
Robert Gordon University, Garthdee Road, Aberdeen AB10 7QE, UK
tel: +44-1224-263 406, fax: +44-1224-262929
email: J.Greenwood@rgu.ac.uk
http://www.rgu.ac.uk/subj/las

Department of International Politics
University of Wales, Aberstwyth, Penglais, UK
tel: +44-1970-622702, fax: +44-1970-622709
email: myh@aber.ac.uk
http://www.aber.ac.uk/~inpwww

School of Social Sciences
University of Bath, Bath BA2 7AY, UK
tel: +44-1225-826826, fax: +44-1225-826381

Department of Politics
Queen's University of Belfast, Belfast, BT1 7NN, UK
tel: +44-1232-335028, fax: +44-1232-235373
email: g.devlin@qub.ac.uk
http://www.qub.ac.uk/ss/pol/

School of Public Policy, Economics and Law
University of Ulster, Jordanstown, Co Antrim BT37 OQB, Northern Ireland, UK
tel: +44-1232-366346, fax: +44-1232-366847
email: m.trew@ulst.ac.uk
http://www.ulst.ac.uk

Department of Political Science and International Studies
University of Birmingham, Edgbaston, Birmingham B15 2TT, UK
tel: +44-121-414 6278, fax: +44-121-414 3496

Department of Peace Studies
University of Bradford, Bradford, West Yorks BD7 1DP, UK
tel: +44-1274-733466, fax: +44-1274-385240

Department of Politics and Social Policy
University of Lincolnshire and Humberside, Brayford Pool, LN6 7TS, UK
tel: +44-1522-882000, fax: +44-1522-886033
email: hbochel@lincoln.ac.uk
http://www.lincoln.ac.uk

International Relations Subject Group
University of Sussex, School of Social Sciences, Falmer, Brighton, BN1 9QN, UK
tel: +44-1273-606755, fax: +44-1273-678466
email: m.b.nicholson@sussex .ac. uk

Politics Subject Group
University of Sussex, Arts E, Falmer, Brighton, BN1 9QN, UK
tel: +44-1273-678892, fax: +44-1273-673563
email: s.a.stay@sussex.ac.uk
http://www.sussex.ac.uk/units/politics/

Sussex European Institute
University of Sussex, Arts A, Falmer, Brighton, BN1 9QN, UK
tel: +44-1273-678578, fax: +44-1273-678571
email: sei@sussex.ac.uk
http://www.sussex.ac.uk/units/SEI/

Department of Politics
University of Bristol, 10 Priory Road, Bristol BS8, UK
tel: +44-117-928 7898, fax: +44-117-973 2133
email: politics@bris.ac.uk
http://www.bris.ac.uk/depts/politics/

School of Politics
University of the West of England, Coldharbour Lane, Frenchay, Bristol

BS16 1QY, UK
tel: +44-1179-656261, fax: +44-1179-763870

Department of Social and Political Sciences
University of Cambridge, Free School Lane, Cambridge CB2 3RQ, UK
tel: +44-1223-4520, fax: +44-1223-4550
email: sps-admin@lists.cam.ac.uk
http://www.sps.cam.ac.uk

Department of Politics and International Relations
University of Kent, Rutherford College, University of Kent at Canterbury, Canterbury, CT2 7NT, UK
tel: +44-1277-764000, fax: +44-1277-823077
email: J.M.Hudson@ukc.ac.uk
http://www.ukc.ac.uk/

School of European Studies
University of Wales College of Cardiff, PO Box 908, Cardiff CF1 3YQ, UK
tel: +44-1222-874808, fax: +44-1222-874946
email: euros@cardiff.ac.uk
http://www.cf.ac.uk/uwcc/euros

School of Human Studies
University of Teesside, Borough Road, Middlesbrough, Cleveland TS1 3BA, UK
tel: +44-1642-218121, fax: +44-1642-342067
email: j.gibbins.uk.ac.teesside

Department of Politics and International Studies
University of Warwick, Coventry CV4 7AL, UK
tel: +44-1203-523302, fax: +44-1203-524221
email: PORCB@csv.warwick.ac.uk
http://www.warwick.ac.uk/PAIS

Department of Political Science and Social Policy
University of Dundee, Dundee DD1 4HN, UK

tel: +44-1382-223181, fax: +44-1382-344675

Department of Politics
University of Durham, 48 Old Elvet, Durham DH1 3LZ, UK
tel: +44-191-374 2810, fax: +44-191-374 7630
email: j.m.richardson@durham.ac.uk
http://www.dur.ac.uk/~dp10www

Department of International Politics
University College of Wales, Aberystwyth, Dyfed SY23 3DA, UK
tel: +44-1970-622691, fax: +44-1970-622709
email: dyh@aber.ac.uk

Department of Politics
University of Edinburgh, 31 Buccleuch Place, Edinburgh EH8 9JT, UK
tel: +44-131-650 4253, fax: +44-131-650 6512
email: c.d.raab@uk.ac.ed.

Department of Government
University of Essex, Wivenhoe Park, Colchester, Essex CO4 3SQ, UK
tel: +44-1206-873333, fax: +44-1206-873598
email: carole@essex.ac.uk
http://www.essex.ac.uk

Department of Politics
University of Exeter, Amory Building, Rennes Drive, Exeter EX4 4RJ, UK
tel: +44-1392-263178, fax: +44-1392-263305

Centre for European Studies
University of Exeter, Streatham Court, Rennes Drive, Exeter EX4 4RJ, UK
tel: +44-1392-264490, fax: +44-1392-263305

Department of International Relations
University of St Andrews, College Gate, St Andrews, Fife KY16 9AL, UK
tel: +44-1334-62937, fax: +44-1334-62937/8

Department of Social Sciences
Glasgow Caledonian University,
Cowcaddens Road, Glasgow G4
OBA, UK
tel: +44-141-331 3489, fax: +44-141-
331 3439

Department of Politics
University of Glasgow, Adam Smith
Building, Bute Gardens, Glasgow
C12 8RT, UK
tel: +44-141-330 5980, fax: +44-141-
330 5071
email: c.j.berry@socsci.gla.ac.uk
http://www.gla.ac.uk/department
s/politics/

Department of Government
University of Strathclyde, McCance
Building, 16 Richmond Street, Glasgow G1 1XQ, Glasgow G1 1XQ, UK
tel: +44-141-548 2733, fax: +44-141-
552 5677
email: T.T.mackie@strath.ac.uk
http://www.strath.ac.uk/departme
nts/government

*Division of Politics, School of Hu-
manities*
University of Huddersfield,
Queensgate, Huddersfield, HD1
3DH, UK
tel: +44-1484-422288 ext 2290, fax:
+44-1484-472655

*Department of Politics and European
Community Research Unit*
University of Hull, Hull HU6 7RX,
UK
tel: +44-1482-466209, fax: +44-1482-
466208
email: pol-as@hull.ac.uk
http://www.hull.ac.uk/css_web/

*Department of Politics and Interna-
tional Relations*
University of Lancaster, Lancaster
LA1 4YL, UK
tel: +44-1524-65201, fax: +44-1524-
594238
email: d.denver@lancaster.ac.uk

Department of Politics
University of Leeds, Woodhouse
Street, Leeds LS2 9JT, UK

tel: +44-113-233 4382, fax: +44-113-
233 4400
email: r.c.bush@leeds.ac.uk
http://www.leeds.ac.uk/politics

*Department of Public Policy and
Managerial Studies*
De Montfort University, Scraptoft
Campus, Leicester LE7 9SU, UK
tel: +44-1162-577780, fax: +44-1162-
577866
email: ppms@dmu.ac.uk

Department of Politics
University of Leicester, 6 Salisbury
Road, Leicester, LE1 7QR, UK
tel: +44-116-252 3944, fax: +44-116
252 3944
email: cspo@le.ac.uk
http://www.le.ac.uk/scarman

*Department of Social Policy & Poli-
tics*
Goldsmiths College, University of
London, New Cross, London SE14
6NN, UK
tel: +44-207-914 7740 or 7746, fax:
+44-207-919 7743

Department of War Studies
King's College, University of London, Strand, London WC2R 2LS, UK
tel: +44-207-873 2193, fax: +44-207-
873 2026

European Institute
London School of Economics and
Political Science, Houghton Street,,
London WC2A 2AE, UK
tel: +44-171-955 6780, fax: +44-171-
955 7546
email: j.gray@lse.ac.uk
http://www.lse.ac.uk/depts/europ
ean/

Department of Government
London School of Economics and
Political Science, Houghton Street,
London WC2A 2AE, UK
tel: +44-207-955 7204, fax: +44-207-
831 1707

School of History and Politics
Middlesex University, White Hart
Lane, London N17 8HR, UK

tel: +44-208-362 6027, fax: +44-208-362 6027

Department of Political Studies
Queen Mary and Westfield College, University of London, Northampton Square, Mile End Road, London E1 4NS, UK
tel: +44-207-975 5003, fax: +44-207-980 9142

Institute of Commonwealth Studies
University of London, 28 Russell Square, London WC1B 5DS, UK
tel: +44-171-580 5876, fax: +44-171-255 2160
email: r.kochanowska@sas.ac.uk

Department of European Studies
University of Loughborough, Ashby Road, Loughborough LE11 3TU, UK
tel: +44-1509-222991, fax: +44-1509-269395

Department of Politics and Public Policy
University of Luton, Park Square, Luton LU1 3JU, UK
tel: +44-1582-732862, fax: +44-1582-734265
email: john.dickens@luton.ac.uk
http://www.luton.ac.uk

Department of Politics and Philosophy
Manchester Metropolitan University, Cavendish Street, Manchester M15 6BR, UK
tel: +44-161-247 3436, fax: +44-161-247 6312

Department of Government
University of Manchester, Dover Street, Manchester M13 9PL, UK
tel: +44-161-275 4885, fax: +44-161-275 4925
email: marilyn.dunn@man.ac.uk
http://les.man.ac.uk/government/

Academic Centre for Political Studies
42 Cooper House, Boundary Lane, Manchester M15 6DX, UK

Department of Government
Brunel University, Uxbridge, Middlesex UB8 3PH, UK

tel: +44-1895-56461, fax: +44-1895-812595

Social Sciences Faculty
The Open university, Walton Hall, Milton Keynes MK7 6AA, UK
tel: +44-1908-65 4443, fax: +44-1908-65 4488

Department of Politics
University of Newcastle, Newcastle-upon-Tyne NE1 7RU, UK
tel: +44-191-222 6000, fax: +44-191-222 5069
email: t.s.gray@ncl.ac.uk
http://www.ncl.ac.uk

Politics Section, School of Economic and Social Studies
University of East Anglia, University Plain, Norwich, Norfolk NR4 7TJ, UK
tel: +44-1603-456161, fax: +44-1603-250434
email: b.goodwin@uea.ac.uk
http://www.uea.ac.uk

Department of Economics and Politics
Nottingham Trent University, Burton Street, Nottingham NG1 4BU, UK
tel: +44-115-941 8418, fax: +44-115-948 6808
email: lawrence.wilde@ntu.ac.uk
http://www.ntu.ac.uk

Department of International Studies
Nottingham Trent University, Clifton Campus, Nottingham NG11 8NS, UK
tel: +44-115-941 8418, fax: +44-115-948 6672

Department of Politics
University of Nottingham, University Park, Nottingham NG7 2RD, UK
tel: +44-115-951 4862, fax: +44-115-951 4859
email: politics@nottingham.ac.uk
http://www.nottingham.ac.uk/~id zwww

Department of Politics and International Relations
University of Aberdeen, Edward Wright Building, Old Aberdeen AB9 2TY, UK
tel: +44-1224-272716, fax: +44-1224-272181
email: pol039@abdn.ac.uk
http://www.abdn.ac.uk

Centre for European Politics, Economics & Society
University of Oxford, Social Studies Faculty Centre, George Street, Oxford OX1 2RL, UK
tel: +44-1865-278718, fax: +44-1865-278725
email: anita.allam@social-studies.ox.ac.uk

St Anthony's College
University of Oxford, Oxford OX2 6JF, UK
tel: +44-1865-59651 or 274470, fax: +44-1865-274478

Nuffield College
University of Oxford. New Road, Oxford OX1 1NF, UK
tel: +44-1865-278500, fax: +44-1865-278621

Department of Applied Social Studies
University of Paisley, High Street, Paisley PA1 2BE, UK
tel: +44-141-848 3777, fax: +44-141-848 3891
email: TURN-ASØ@PAISLEY.AC.UK

Department of Politics
University of Plymouth, 10 Portland Villas, Drake Circus, Plymouth PL4 8AA, UK
tel: +44-1752-233275, fax: +44-1752-233206
email: crallings@plymouth.ac.uk
http://www.plym.ac.uk

School of Social and Historical Studies
University of Portsmouth, SSHS, Milldam, Burnaby Road, Portsmouth, UK
tel: +44-1705-842173, fax: +44-1705-842174
email: andrew.massey@port.ac.uk

School of Languages and Area Studies
University of Portsmouth, SLAS, Park Building, King Henry Street, Portsmouth PO1 2BU, UK
tel: +44-1705-846033, fax: +44-1705-846340
email: richard.gillespie@port.ac.uk
http://www.hs.port.ac.uk/

Department of European Studies
University of Central Lancashire, Harris Building, Preston PR1 2HE, UK
tel: +44-1722-893920, fax: +44-1772-892919

School of European and International Studies
Reading University, PO BOX 218 Whiteknights, Reading RG6 2AA, UK
tel: +44-118-931 8501, fax: +44-118-975 3833
email: P.A.Hicks@reading.ac.uk
http://www.rdg.ac.uk//acaDepts/

Department of Politics and Contemporary History
University of Salford, Salford M5 4WT, UK
tel: +44-161-295 5000, fax: +44-161 295 5077
email: l.a.harris@pch.salford.ac.uk
http://www.salford.ac.uk

Department of Politics
University of Sheffield, Elmfield, 132 Northumberland Road, Sheffield S10 2TN, UK
tel: +44-114-222 1700, fax: +44-114-273 9769
email: politics@sheffield.ac.uk
www.shef.ac.uk/uni/academic/N-O/pol/

Department of Politics
University of Southampton, Southampton SO17 1BJ, UK
tel: +44-1703-594743, fax: +44-1703-593276

email: jl@socsci.soton.ac.uk
http://www.soton.ac.uk/~polweb/

Department of Politics
University of Keele, Keele, Staffordshire ST5 5BG, UK
tel: +44-1782-583452, fax: +44-1782-
583592
email: pobl9@pol.keele.ac.uk
http://www.keele.ac.uk

Department of Political Studies
University of Stirling, Stirling FK9
4LA, UK
tel: +44-1786-467568, fax: +44-1786-
466266
email: e.d.shaw@stir.ac.uk
http://www.stir.ac.uk/politics/

Department of Political Studies
University of Staffordshire, College
Road, Stoke-on-Trent ST4 2DE, UK
tel: +44-1782-290000, fax: +44-1782-
746553
email: d.s.morrice@staffs.ac.uk
http://www.staffs.ac.uk/welcome.
html

*Department of Social and Political
Science*
Royal Holloway, University of London, Egham, Surrey TW20 OEX, UK
tel: +44-1784-443149, fax: +44-1784-
434375
email: M.Saward@rhbnc.ac.uk
http://www.rhbnc.ac.uk/www/sp
ss.html

*Department of Political Theory and
Government*
University of Wales, Singleton Park,
Swansea SA2 8PP, UK

*School of Languages and European
Studies*
University of Wolverhampton, Stafford Street, Wolverhampton WV1
1SB, UK
tel: +44-1902-322484, fax: +44-1902-
322739
email: ie1925@ccub.wlv.ac.uk

Division of Politics
University of Greenwich, Churchill
House, Wellington Street, Wool-
wich, London SE18 6PF, UK

tel: +44-208-316 8000, fax: +44-208-
316 8805

Department of Politics
University of York, Heslington,
York YO1 5DD, UK
tel: +44-1904-433540 or 433542, fax:
+44-1904-433563

OCEANIA

Australia

*School of Politics and International
Studies*
Flinders University, GPO Box 2100,
Adelaide, SA 5001, Australia
tel: +61-8-8201 2168, fax: +61-8-8201
5111
email: politics@flinders.edu.au
http://www.ssn.flinders.edu.au/Po
litics/

Politics Department
University of Adelaide, Napier
Building, North Terrace, Adelaide,
SA 5005, Australia
tel: +61-8-8303 5699, fax: +61-8-8308
3446
email: chris-
tine.mcelhinney@adelaide.edu.au
http://chomsky.arts.adelaide.edu.a
u/politics/

Political Science Department
University of New England, Armi-
dale, NSW 2351, Australia
tel: +61-2-6773 3333, fax: +61-2-6773
3122
email: bdrew@netz.une.edu.au
http://www.une.edu.au

Department of Politics
University of New England, Armi-
dale, NSW 2351, Australia
email: dwells@metz.une.edu.au

Department of Government
University of Queensland, QLD
4072, Australia
tel: +61-7-3365 2635, fax: +61-7-3365
1388
email: Government@mailbox.uq.

edu.au
http://www.uq.edu.au/govt/

School of Politics
Australian Defence Force Academy,
Canberra, ACT 2600, Australia
tel: +61-2-6268 8845, fax: +61-2-6268 8852
email: s-ramsay@adfa.edu.au
http://www.pol.adfa.oz.au

Department of Political Science
Australian National University,
Canberra, ACT 2600, Australia
tel: +61-2-6249 2659, fax: +61-2-6249 5054
email: Political.Science@anu.edu.au
http://www.anu.edu/polsci/polsci.htm

Department of Political Science
Northern Territory University,
Darwin, Australia
tel: +61-8-8946 6765, fax: +61-8-8946 6955
email: arts.seas@ntu.edu.au
http://www.ntu.edu.au/faculties/arts/sseas/politics.htm

School of Government
University of Tasmania, GPO Box 252-22, Hobart, Tasmania 7001, Australia
tel: +61-3-6226-2329, fax: +61-3-6224 0973
email: Aynsley.Kellow@utas.edu.au
http://www.utas.edu.au/governm ent/

Humanities and Social Sciences
University of Tasmania, GPO Box 252-51, Hobart, Tasmania 7005, Australia
tel: +61-3-6226 2999, fax: +61-3-6226 7862
email: international.office@utas.edu.au
http://www.utas.edu.au/docs/hu msoc/political_science/polsci/

School of Sociology, Politics and Anthropology
La Trobe University, Melbourne, Australia
tel: +61-3-9479 2287, fax: +61-3-9479

1997
email: M.Gurry@latrobe.edu.au
http://www.latrobe.edu.au/www/socpol/

Department of Politics and International Studies
Monash University, Melbourne, Australia
http://www.arts.monash.edu.au/politics/

Political Science Department
Murdoch University, South Street, Murdoch, WA 6150, Australia
tel: +61-8-9360 6000, fax: +61-8-9360 2507
email: davidson@murdoch.edu.au

Discipline of Politics
Curtin University, GPO Box U1987, Perth, WA 6845, Australia
tel: +61-8-9266 7032, fax: +61-8-9266 3166
email: blackd@spectrum.curtin.edu.au
http://www.curtin.edu.au/curtin/det/ssal/Disciplines/#Politics

Department of Political Science
University of Western Australia, Nedlands WA 6907, Perth, WA, Australia
tel: +61-8-9380 2086, fax: +61-8-9380 1060
email: Political.Science@uwa.edu.au
http://www.arts.uwa.edu.au/PoliticsWWW/PoliticsHome.html

Department of Political Science
Macquarie University, North Ryde, NSW 2109, Australia
tel: +61-2-9850 7111, fax: +61-2-9850 7433
email: iso@mcq.edu.au
http://www.mq.edu.au/~philosop/pol.html

School of Political Science
University of New South Wales, Sydney 2052, NSW, Australia
tel: +61-2-9385 2381, fax: +61-2-9385 1555
email: p.hall-ingrey@unsw.edu.au

http://www.arts.unsw.edu.au/poli
ticalscience/

Political Science Department
University of New South Wales,
Chancellery Building Gate 9, Hight
Street, Randwick, Sydney, NSW
2052, Australia
tel: +61-2-9385 1000, fax: +61-2-9385
2000
email: records.admin@unsw.edu.au
http://www.unsw.edu.au

*Department of Government and Pub-
lic Administration*
University of Sydney, NSW 2006,
Australia
tel: +61-2-9351 4074, fax: +61-2-9351
3624
email: patricia@econ.usyd.edu.au
http://www.econ.usyd.edu.au/gov
t/

School of Politics
James Cook University, School of
Humanities, Townsville 4811, Australia
tel: +61-7-4781 4594
email: Hayden.Lesbirel@jcu.edu.au
http://raptor.jcu.edu.au/profiles/st
ructure

Political Science Department
University of Melbourne, Grattan
Street, Parkville, Victoria 3052,
Australia
tel: +61-3-9344 4000, fax: +61-3-9344
5104
email:
j.potter@registrar.unimelb.edu.au
http://www.arts.unimelb.edu.au/
Dept/Politics/home.html

Department of Political Science
University of Melbourne, Victoria
3010, Australia
tel: +61-3-8344 6571, fax: +61-3-834
7906
email:
r.deamicis@politics.unimelb.edu.au
http://www.politics.unimelb.edu.a
u/

New Zealand

Department of Political Studies
University of Auckland, Private Bag
92019, Auckland, New Zealand
tel: +64-9-373 7599 ext 8093, fax:
+64-9-373 7449
email: r.burns@auckland.ac.nz
http://www.arts.auckland.ac.nz/p
ol/

Department of Political Science
University of Canterbury, Private
Bag 4800, Christchurch, New Zealand
tel: +64-3-364 2099, fax: +64-3-364
2007
email: j.dolby@pols.canterbury.ac
.nz
http://www.pols.canterbury.ac.nz

Department of Political Studies
University of Otago, PO Box 56,
Dunedin, New Zealand
tel: +64-3-479 8660, fax: +64-3-479
7174
email: political.studies@otago.ac.nz
http://www.ac.nz/politicalstudies

*Department of Political Science and
Public Policy*
University of Waikato, Private Bag
3105, Hamilton, New Zealand
tel: +64-7-856 2889, fax: +64-7-838
4443
http://www.waikato.ac.nz

*School of Political Science and Inter-
national Relations*
Victoria University of Wellington,
PO Box 600, Wellington, New Zealand
tel: +64-4-463 5351, fax: +64-4-463
5414
email: Nigel.Roberts@vuw.ac.nz
http://www.vuw.ac.nz/pols/

8 / INDIVIDUAL MEMBERS OF IPSA

8.1 OVERVIEW

In chapter 2, we have already reported on the general characteristics of IPSA members on 31 December 1999. The list below extends over a slightly different set of people: it includes all members on 31 December 1999 who consented to the publication of the information detailed here, together with those who joined in the early part of 2000. In all, the listing below comprises 1,064 individual members of IPSA. The are broken down by gender and continent in table 8.1. The mean age of those listed is 51 (for men, 53, with ages ranging from 22 to 98; and for women, 47, ranging from 24 to 84).

In the directory that follows, we have sought to include in the case of each member full postal address, as well as fax number and email address where available. Because of the number of members who requested that their telephone numbers not be included, we have excluded this information in all cases. Members were also given the option of indicating their research interests, using a crude classification system adopted many years ago by IPSA. It will be noted that this will give only a general indication of research interests. Where members have specified that their research focuses on a particular global region or area, this is indicated in square brackets.

Table 8.1: IPSA members, June 2000

Continent	men	women	total
Africa	15	3	18
America, North	292	89	383
America, South	45	13	58
Asia	142	59	206
Europe, C and E	24	9	33
Europe, West	277	62	340
Oceania	19	7	26
Total	814	242	1,064

Note: Data on gender was not supplied in eight cases, and it was not possible to infer this from the member's name.

8.2 DIRECTORY OF IPSA MEMBERS

Aberbach, Joel D – UCLA; *address*: 10453 Colina Way, Los Angeles, CA 90077, USA; *fax*: +1-310-206 7110; *email*: aberbach@polisci.ucla.edu; *research interests*: political executives, public administration, legislatures [USA, industrial democracies]

Abraham, Henry J – University of Virginia; *address*: 906 Fendall Terrace, Charlottesville, VA 22903-1617, USA; *fax*: +1-804-924 3359; *research interests*: political executives, comparative politics, judicial politics [USA, Western Europe]

Abramson, Paul R – Michigan State University-East Lansing; *address*: Department of Political Science, Michigan State University, East Lansing, MI 48824-1032, USA; *fax*: +1-517-432 1091; *email*: abrason@msu.edu; *research interests*: comparative politics, elections and voting behaviour, political parties [Western Europe]

Acevedo, Luz del Alba – University of Puerto Rico; *address*: UPR Station, PO Box 21606, San Juan, 00931-1606, Puerto Rico; *fax*: +1-787-764 3133; *email*: scholar@coqui.net; *research interests*: women and politics, development politics, legislatures [Caribbean, Latin America]

Adler, Glen – University of Witswatersrand; *address*: Department of Sociology, University of Witwatersrand, PO Wits 2050, South Africa; *fax*: +27-11-717 4459; *email*: 029mets@muse.arts.wits.ac.za; *research interests*: comparative politics, area studies, development politics [Africa]

Agbaje, Adigun AB – University of Ibadan; *address*: Department of Political Science, University of Ibadan, PO Box 22344, University PO, Ibadan, Nigeria; *fax*: +234-2-810 4077; *email*: agbaje@mail.skannet. com; *research interests*: comparative politics, development politics [Africa]

Agranoff, Robert – Indiana University; *address*: 5747 W Lost Branch Road, Nashville, IN 47488, USA; *fax*: +1-812-855 5058; *email*: agranoff @indiana.edu; *research interests*: federalism and intergovernmental relations, public administration, public policy [USA, Spain, federal countries]

Ahn, Chung-Si – Seoul National University; *address*: Department of Political Science, College of Social Sciences, Seoul National University, Seoul 151-742, Korea; *fax*: +82-2-887 4375; *email*: csahn@plaza.snu.ac.kr; *research interests*: comparative politics, area studies, political science methods [Asia, Southeast Asia]

Akhtar, Shamim – Guwahati College; *address*: PNGB Road, Santipur West, Guwahati 781009, Dist Kamrup, Assam, India; *fax*: +91-361-561 067; *email*: nezone_combine @hotmail.com; *research interests*: public administration, area studies [India]

Alba, Carlos R – Universidad Autónoma de Madrid; *address*: Alfonso XII-18-5o, 28014 Madrid, Spain; *fax*: +34-91-397 4162; *email*: carlos.alba@uam.es

Albrecht, Steven – Hamburg University; *address*: University of Hamburg, Research Unit of TA, Ohnhorststrasse 18, D-22609 Hamburg, Germany; *fax*: +49-40-4821 6254; *email*: alwold5@aol.com; *research interests*: political executives, political theory and philosophy, public policy [EU, Africa]

Alexander, Herbert E – University of Southern California; *address*: 2900 N Leisure World Boulevard, #311, Silver Spring, MD 20906, USA; *fax*: +1-301-438 3472; [USA and comparative]

Alexe, Janina — Transilvania University; *address*: Str Zorilor Nr 16, bl. B10, sc A, apt 35, Brasov, 2200, Romania; *email*: janinaalexe@yahoo.com; *research interests*: women and politics, comparative politics, pressure groups [Eastern Europe]

Alfred, Taiaiake — University of Victoria; *address*: Indigenous Governance Program, PO Box 1700, STN CSC, Victoria, BC, V8W 2Y2, Canada; *fax*: +1-250-472 4724; *email*: taiaiake@uvic.ca; *research interests*: comparative politics, political theory and philosophy, area studies, indigenous politics

Alger, Chadwick F — Ohio State University; *address*: Mershon Center, Ohio State University, 1501 Neil Avenue, Columbus, OH 43201-2602, USA; *fax*: +1-614-292 2407; *email*: alger.1@osu.edu; *research interests*: international relations, public policy, international law

Alker, Hayward — University of Southern California; *address*: VKC 330, School of International Relations, University of Southern California, Los Angeles, CA 90089-0043, USA; *fax*: +1-213-742 0281; *email*: alker@usc.edu; *research interests*: international relations, political science methods, political theory and philosophy

Allan, Pierre — Université de Genève; *address*: Département de Science Politique, Université de Genève, Uni Mail, 102 Boulevard Carl Vogt, 1211 Genève 4, Switzerland; *fax*: +41-22-705 8364; *email*: pierre.allan @politic.unige.ch; *research interests*: international relations, political science methods, ethics

Altenstetter, Christa — City University of New York; *address*: PhD Program in Political Science, Graduate School-CUNY, 365 Fifth Avenue, New York, NY 10016-4309, USA; *fax*: +1-212-617 1532; *email*: caltestetter@gc.cuny.edu; *research interests*: comparative politics, area

studies, comparative public policy [Western Europe, EU]

Ananiadis, Blanca M — University of La Verne; *address*: 34 P Ioakim Street, 10675 Athens, Greece; *fax*: +30-1-722 0882; *email*: banan@laverne.edu.gr; *research interests*: comparative politics, area studies, international relations [Europe]

Ananiadis, Grigoris — University of the Agean; *address*: 34 P Ioakim Street, 10675 Athens, Greece; *fax*: +30-1-722 0882; *email*: ananiadi@compulink.gr; *research interests*: political theory and philosophy, ideology and discourse analysis [Europe, Balkans]

Anckar, Carsten — Åbo Akademi; *address*: Åbo Akademi, University, Department of Political Science, 20500 Turku, Finland; *fax*: +358-2-2154 585; *email*: carsten.anckar@abo.fi; *research interests*: comparative politics, elections and voting behaviour, political parties [worldwide]

Andreassen, Berd-Anders — University of Oslo, Institute of Human Rights; *address*: Universitetsgt 22-24, 0162 Oslo, Norway; *fax*: +47-22-842 002; *email*: baard.andreassen@nihr.uio.no; *research interests*: human rights, development politics, comparative politics [East and Southern Africa]

Andrew, Caroline — University of Ottawa; *address*: Department of Political Science, University of Ottawa, Ottawa, ON, KIN 6N5, Canada; *fax*: +1-613-562 5106; *email*: candrew@ottawa.ca; *research interests*: local and urban politics, women and politics [Canada]

Arat, Yesim — Bogazici University; *address*: Department of Political Science &, International Relations, Bogazici University, Bebek, 80815 Istanbul, Turkey; *fax*: +90-212-265 1479; *email*: araty@boun.edu.tr; *research interests*: women and politics, area studies, comparative politics

[Turkey, Middle East]
Arat, Zehra F—Purchase College, SUNY; *address*: 220 Midland Avenue, Tuckahoe, NY 10707, USA; *fax*: +1-914-251 6603; *email*: zarat @purchase.edu; *research interests*: comparative politics, international relations, women and politics [new democracies, Muslim societies, Turkey]

Arbos, Xavier—Universitat de Girona; *address*: Departament de Dret Public, Universitat de Girona, Campus de Montilivi, 17071 Girona, Spain; *fax*: +34-972-418 121; *email*: arbos@dret.udg.es; *research interests*: comparative politics, political theory and philosophy, federalism, [North America]

Archenti, Nélida—Universidad de Buenos Aires; *address*: Hipolito Yrigoyen 2569, Piso 2-D, 1090 Buenos Aires, Argentina; *fax*: +54-11-4951 4151; *email*: narchenti @hotmail.com; *research interests*: women and politics, elections and voting behaviour, political theory and philosophy [Argentina]

Arentsen, Maarten J—Centre for Clean Technology and Environmental Policy; *address*: University of Twente CSTM, PO Box 217, NL-7500 AE Enschede, Netherlands; *fax*: +31-53-489 4850; *email*: m.j.arentsen@cstm.utwente.nl; *research interests*: public policy, public administration, political theory and philosophy

Arian, Asher—City University of New York; *address*: PhD Program in Political Science, City University of New York, 365 Fifth Avenue, New York, NY 10016, USA; *fax*: +1-201-692 1360; *email*: crgaa-2@idt.net; *research interests*: elections and voting behaviour, public opinion

Armijo, Leslie Elliott—Reed College; *address*: 3927 Tempest Drive, Lake Osweg, OR 97035, USA; *email*: Leslie.Armijo@mindspring.com; *research interests*: political economy,

comparative politics, international relations [Latin America, South Asia]

Asami, Masae—Shumei University; *address*: #703 Hara-Machida 4-10-19, Machida-shi, Tokyo 194-0013, Japan; *fax*: +81-42-727 2641; *email*: CZE07547@nifty.ne.jp; *research interests*: area studies, public policy [Europe]

Assima, Georges—Université de Lausanne; *address*: 152 Avenue Winston Churchill, B-1180 Bruxelles, Belgium; *research interests*: central government, area studies, international relations [Middle-East, Europe, Africa]

Atienza, Maria Ela—University of the Philippines; *address*: Department of Political Science, University of the Philippines, Diliman, Quezon City 1101, Philippines; *fax*: +63-2-924 4875; *email*: eatienza @kssp.upd. edu.ph; *research interests*: local and urban politics, pressure groups, women and politics [Philippines, Southeast Asia, EU]

Auclair, Celine—Forum of Federations; *address*: Forum of Federations, 325 Dalhousie Street, Suite 700, Ottawa K1N 7G2, Canada; *fax*: +1-613-244 3372; *email*: auclair@ciff.on.ca; *research interests*: public administration, comparative politics, development politics

Aunger, Edmund A—University of Alberta; *address*: Faculté Saint Jean, University of Alberta, Edmonton Alberta, T6C 4G9, Canada; *fax*: +1-780-465 8760; *email*: edmund. aunger@ualberta.ca; *research interests*: comparative politics, area studies [Canada]

Avelino, Hermenegildo Manuel—University Jean Piaget; *address*: PO Box 6741, Luanda, Angola; *email*: Gildo.Avelino@horyzont.com.pl; *research interests*: political parties, comparative politics, development politics [Africa, East Europe]

Ayberk, M Ural—Université de Gen

ève; *address*: 82 route de Florrisant, 1206 Genève, Switzerland; *fax*: +41-22-705 8364; *email*: ayberk@ politic.unige.ch; *research interests*: elections and voting behaviour, comparative politics, international relations [Europe]

Aydelotte-Wodesky, Denise — University of Dayton; *address*: PO Box 1381, Stafford, Virginia, VA 22555, USA; *fax*: +1-540-657 0484; *email*: edenaw@msn.com; *research interests*: international relations, women and politics, international politico-military affairs [Europe, Middle East]

Aznar, Luis — Universidad de Buenos Aires, Universidad de San Andreas; *address*: Hipolito Yrigoyen 2569, Piso 2D, 1090 Buenos Aires, Argentina; *fax*: +54-11-4951 4151; *email*: laznar@udesa.edu.ar; *research interests*: comparative politics, political parties, political theory and philosophy [Latin America]

Bacchi, Carol — University of Adelaide; *address*: Politics Department, University of Adelaide, Adelaide, SA 5005, Australia; *fax*: +61-8-303 3446; *email*: carol.bacchi@adelaide.edu.au; *research interests*: political theory and philosophy, public policy, women and politics

Back, Jong G — Gyeongsang National University; *address*: 900 Gazwadong, Chinju, Republic of Korea; *fax*: +82-591-546 295; *email*: jgback@nongae.gsnu.ac.kr; *research interests*: international relations, comparative politics, area studies [Latin America]

Baker, David — University of Warwick; *address*: Department of Politics & International Studies, University of Warwick, Coventry, CV4 7AL, UK; *email*: poscv@dsredd.csu.warwick.ac.uk; *research interests*: political parties, legislatures, political theory and philosophy [UK, Europe]

Baldersheim, Harald — University of

Oslo; *address*: Department of Political Science, Box 1097 Blindern, 0317 Oslo, Norway; *email*: harald.bal dersheim@stv.io.no; *research interests*: public administration, local and urban politics, regionalism, development politics [Eastern Europe]

Baldwin, David — Columbia University; *address*: Institute of War and Peace Studies, Columbia University, New York, NY 10027, USA; *fax*: +1-212-864 1686; *email*: dab12@co lumbia.edu; *research interests*: international relations

Bale, Tim — Victoria University of Wellington; *address*: School of Political Science & International Relations, Victoria University, Wellington, PO Box 600, Wellington, New Zealand; *fax*: +64-4-463 5414; *email*: tim.bale@vuw.ac.nz; *research interests*: political parties, comparative politics [Europe, New Zealand]

Barber, Benjamin R — Walt Whitman Center; *address*: 1019 River Road, Piscataway, NJ 08854, USA; *fax*: +1-732-932 1922; *email*: bbarber@rci.rutgers.edu; *research interests*: political theory and philosophy, international relations, technology and politics [USA, Europe]

Barber, Charles T — University of Southern Indiana; *address*: Political Science Department, University of Southern Indiana, 8600 University Boulevard, Evansville, IN 47712-3534, USA; *fax*: +1-812-464 1960; *email*: cbarber@usi.edu; *research interests*: international relations, area studies, international organisations [Mediterranean, Middle East]

Barrasso, Graziella — Free University of Brussels; *address*: Rue Commandant Ponthier 17, 1040 Brussels, Belgium; *fax*: +32-2-463 0832; *email*: graziella.barrasso@tetrapak.com; *research interests*: public policy, pressure groups, government-business relations [EU, Canada, CEEC]

Barry, Jim — University of East London; *address*: 9 Thornton House, Cambridge Park, Wanstead, London E11 2PZ, UK; *fax*: +44-181-849 3529; *email*: j.j.barry@uel.ac.uk; *research interests*: women and politics, local and urban politics, public policy

Bashevkin, Sylvia — University of Toronto; *address*: Department of Political Science, University of Toronto, 100 St George Street, Toronto, ON M5S 3G3, Canada; *fax*: +1-416-946 3066; *email*: sbashevk@ chass.utoronto.ca; *research interests*: comparative politics, women and politics, pressure groups [Canada, USA, UK]

Bashkirova, Elena — ROMIR Group (Russian Public, Opinion and Market Research, Inst.); *address*: Novaya Basmannaya St 10, Entrance 6, Floor 600, Office 600, Moscow 107078, Russia; *fax*: +7-095-883 9280; *email*: romir@msk.tsi.ru; *research interests*: political parties, international relations, elections, political consultancy [Russia, CIS, Eastern Europe]

Batson, Mary — Fachhochschule Fulda; *address*: Wilhelm-Liebknecht-Str 18, D-35396 Giessen, Germany; *email*: mbatson@lycosmail.com; *research interests*: international relations, comparative politics, women and politics

Bau, Tzong-Ho — National Taiwan University; *address*: 21 Hsu Chow Road, Taipei, Taiwan; *fax*: +886-2-341 2806; *email*: politics@ms.cc.ntu. edu.tw; *research interests*: international relations, comparative politics, political science methods [USA, China]

Baum, Michael — UMass-Dartmouth; *address*: Department of Political Science, UMass-Dartmouth, 285 Old Westport Road, Dartmouth, MA 02747, USA; *fax*: +1-508-999 8819; *email*: mbaum@umassd.edu; *research interests*: comparative politics, elections and voting behaviour, area

studies [Southern Europe]

Bayes, Jane H — California State University at Northridge; *address*: Political Science Department, California State University, Northridge, CA 91330, USA; *fax*: +1-310-459 7151; *email*: jbayes@csun.edu; *research interests*: comparative politics, women and politics, development politics [USA]

Beach, Walter E — Helen Dwight Reid Educational Foundation; *address*: 5719 Chevy Chase Parkway NW, Washington, DC 20015, USA; *fax*: +1-202-296 5149; *email*: wbeach7421 @aol.com; *research interests*: legislatures, public policy, international relations

Becker, Uwe — Vrije Universiteit; *address*: Buiksloterdijk 162, 1025 WB Amsterdam, Netherlands; *fax*: +31-20-525 2086; *email*: becker@pscw. uva.nl; *research interests*: comparative politics, political theory and philosophy, public policy [Europe]

Beer, Francis A — University of Colorado; *address*: Political Science Department, Campus Box 333, University of Colorado, Boulder, CO 80309, USA; *research interests*: international relations, political theory and philosophy

Behning, Ute — Institute for Advanced Studies; *address*: Institute for Advanced Studies, Stumpergasse 56, A-1060 Wien, Austria; *fax*: +43-1-5999 1171; *email*: behning@his. ac.at; *research interests*: comparative politics, public policy, women and politics [EU, USA]

Bélanger, Louis — Université Laval; *address*: Bureau 5458 Pavilion Charles de Koninck, Université Laval, Québec, G1K 7P4, Canada; *fax*: +1-418-656-3634; *email*: louis. belanger@pol.ulaval.ca; *research interests*: international relations, comparative politics [Canada, US, Americas]

Belikow, Juan — Universidad de Buenos Aires; *address*: B. Encalada

3225 D8, C1428DEC Buenos Aires (CF), Argentina; *fax*: +54-11-4541 8676; *email*: jbelikow@mail.fsoc. uba.ar; *research interests*: international relations, area studies, pressure groups [Eastern Europe]

Ben Jomaa Ahmed, Fethi — International Islamic University Malaysia; *address*: B-9-6 Idaman Putera Condominium, Medan Idaman, 5300 Kuala Lumpar, Malaysia; *fax*: +60-96-669 478; *email*: fethijoma @hotmail.com; *research interests*: political theory and philosophy, comparative politics, public policy [Southeast Asia, Europe, Muslim world]

Benz, Arthur — Fern Universität Hagen; *address*: Lange Gewann 24, D-67346 Speyer, Germany; *fax*: +49-2331-987 326; *email*: Arthur.Benz@ Feruni-hagen.de; *research interests*: public policy, central government, public administration [Western Europe]

Berg, John C — Suffolk University; *address*: Department of Government, Suffolk University, Boston, MA 02108-2770, USA; *fax*: +1-617-573 8703; *email*: jberg@acad. suffolk.edu; *research interests*: legislatures, political parties, pressure groups [USA, North America]

Berg-Schlosser, Dirk — Philipps-Universität Marburg; *address*: Scheppe-Gewisse-Gasse 26, D-35039 Marburg, Germany; *fax*: +49-6421-282 8991; *email*: bergschl@ mailer.uni-marburg.de; *research interests*: comparative politics, development politics, political science methods [Europe, Africa, Latin America]

Berndtson, Erkki — University of Helsinki; *address*: Viskaalintie 5a, 00690 Helsinki, Finland; *fax*: +358-9-191 8832; *email*: erkki.berndtson@ helsinki.fi; *research interests*: US government and politics, political theory and philosophy, comparative politics

Bernik, Ivan — University of Ljubljana; *address*: Faculty of Social Sciences, University of Ljubljana, POB 2547, 1001 Ljubljana, Slovenia; *fax*: +386-61-580 5101; *email*: ivan.bernik @guest.arnes.si; *research interests*: political theory and philosophy, comparative politics [Central and Eastern Europe]

Berry, Christopher — Glasgow University; *address*: Politics Department, University of Glasgow, Adam Smith Building, Glasgow G12 8RT, UK; *fax*: +44-141-330 5071; *email*: c.j.berry@socsci.gla.ac.uk; *research interests*: political theory and philosophy

Berthet, Thierry — CERVL; *address*: CERVL- Institut d'Etudes Politiques de Bordeaux, BP 101, 33405 Talence Cedex, France; *fax*: +33-5-5684 4329; *email*: t.berthet@iep.u-bordeaux.fr; *research interests*: public policy, local and urban politics, education and training policies [France, Canada]

Bhandari, Prabha — JNV University; *address*: 397/3C Road, Sardarpura, Jodhpur - 342003, India; *email*: sat yaprabha1@yahoo.com; *research interests*: international relations, public administration

Biegelbauer, Peter — Institute for Advanced Studies; *address*: Stumpergasse 56, A-1060 Vienna, Austria; *fax*: +43-1-5999 1171; *email*: beagle @ihs.ac.at; *research interests*: political economy, comparative politics, political theory and philosophy [Central and Eastern Europe]

Bin Hadi, Abdel-Rahman — Ministry of Foreign Affairs; *address*: PO Box 3642, Sharjah, United Arab Emirates; *fax*: +971-2-665 4366; *research interests*: political science, international relations, public administration [Arab World, developing countries, Europe, USA, Southeast Asia]

Bislev, Sven — Copenhagen Business School; *address*: Dalgas Have 15, DK-2000 Frederiksberg, Denmark;

fax: +45-3815 3840; email: sb.ikl@cbs. dk; research interests: public administration, political theory and philosophy, European integration [Europe]

Biswas, Rathindra — Kalyani University; address: 22 Rabindra Sarani, PO Berhampore (WB) 742101, India; fax: +91-348-250 091; email: jtodto @dte.vsnl.net.in; research interests: international relations, women and politics, environment [USA]

Björkman, James W — Institute of Social Studies; address: Institute of Social Studies, PO Box 29776, 2502 LT The Hague, Netherlands; fax: +31-70-426 0799; email: bjorkman@ iss.nl; research interests: public policy, public administration, development politics [South Asia, developing world, Europe]

Blais, Andri — Université de Montréal; address: Département de Science Politique, Université de Montréal, CP 6128, Succ Centre-Ville, Montréal, H3C 3J7, Canada; fax: +1-514-343 2360; email: blaisa@pol. umontreal.ca; research interests: elections and voting behaviour

Blatter, Joachim — Universität Konstanz; address: Triftstrasse 53, D-13353 Berlin, Germany; email: joachim.blatter@uni-konstanz.de; research interests: international relations, public administration, local and urban politics [Europe, North America]

Blechinger, Verena — German Institute for Japanese Studies; address: German Institute for Japanese Studies, Nissei Kojimachi Bldg, 3-3-6 Kudan-Minami, Chiyoda-ku, Tokyo 102-0074, Japan; fax: +81-3-3222 5420; email: bleching@dijtokyo.org; research interests: political parties, comparative politics, area studies [Japan, Asia]

Boas, Morten — Centre for Development and the Environment; address: Centre for Development and the Environment, PO Box 1116, Blin-

dern, 0317 Oslo, Norway; fax: +47-22-858 920; email: morten.boas@ sum.uio.no; research interests: international relations, area studies, development politics [Southeast Africa, Southeast Asia, West Africa]

Bobrow, Davis B — University of Pittsburgh; address: Graduate School of Public and, International Affairs, 3J34 Forbes Quadrangle, Pittsburgh, PA 15260, USA; fax: +1-412-648 2605; email: bobrow@imdi.gspia. pitt.edu; research interests: international relations, public policy [Japan, China]

Bockmeyer, Janice — John Jay College; address: Department of Government, John Jay College - CUNY, 445 West 59th Street, Room 3230, New York, NY 10019, USA; fax: +1-212-237 8742; email: jbockmeyer@ aol.com; research interests: local and urban politics, public policy [USA, Germany]

Boehmer-Christiansen, SA — University of Hull; address: Department of Geography, Faculty of Science and the Environment, University of Hull, Hull HU6 7RX, UK; fax: +44-1482-466 341; email: sonja.b-c@geo. hull.ac.uk; research interests: international relations and global warming, environmental politics and energy policy, development politics and "green" development politics [Europe, Australia,]

Boenker, Frank — European University Viadrina; address: Department of Economics, European University Viadrina, Frankfurt Institute for Transformation Studies, PO Box 1786, Frankfurt (O), D-15207, Germany; fax: +49-335-553 4807; email: boenker@euv-frankfurt-o.de; research interests: comparative politics, post-communist countries, public policy [OECD, post-communist countries]

Bohm, Antal — Institute for Political Science HAS; address: 1026 Budapest Nyul 16, Hungary; fax: +36-1-322

1843; *email:* bohm@wtepti.hu; *research interests:* political parties, elections and voting behaviour, local and urban politics

Bokina, John — University of Texas-Pan American; *address:* 303 Austin Boulevard, Edinburg, Texas, TX 78539, USA; *fax:* +1-956-381 2180; *email:* jb83e8@panam.edu; *research interests:* political theory and philosophy, comparative politics, politics of art & mass culture [West Europe, Germany]

Bolin, Anna — National Defence College; *address:* Box 27 805, 115 93 Stockholm, Sweden; *fax:* +46-8-788 9464; *email:* Anna.Bolin@fhs.mil.se; *research interests:* central government, international relations, public administration [Nordic countries, Europe, Latin America]

Boschi, Renato R — IUPERJ; *address:* IUPERJ, Rua da Matriz, 82 Botafogo, 22260-100 Rio de Janeiro, Brazil; *fax:* +55-21-286 7146; *email:* rbos chi@iuperj.br; *research interests:* democratization, political & economic elites, social movements, political development, state & public policies

Bostedt, Göran — Mid-Sweden University; *address:* Department of Business & Public Administration, Mid-Sweden University, 85170, Sweden; *fax:* +46-60-148 783; *email:* goran.bostedt@mkv.mh.se; *research interests:* public policy, public administration, political parties [Scandinavia, Europe]

Bostock, William W — University of Tasmania; *address:* School of Government, GPO Box 252-22, Hobart, Tasmania, Australia; *email:* bostock @utas.edu.au; *research interests:* comparative politics

Bottinelli, Oscar — Universidad de la Republica; *address:* 18 de Julio 1825 Apt 501, 11200 Montevideo, Uruguay; *fax:* +598-2-409 3645; *email:* obottine@adinet.com.uy; *research interests:* elections and voting behav-

iour, public opinion, political parties [Latin America, Western Europe]

Boussard, Isabel — CEVIPOF; *address:* CEVIPOF (FNSP), 10 rue de la Chaise, F-75007 Paris, France; *fax:* +33-1-4222 0764; *email:* isabel.bous sard@cevipol.sciences-po.fr; *research interests:* elections and voting behaviour, pressure groups, public policy [France]

Bouza-Brey Villar, Luis — Barcelona University; *address:* Avda. Dels Garrofers, 57, Sitges - 08870, Spain; *email:* lbouza@retemail.es; *research interests:* comparative politics, development politics, federalism [Spain, EU, Latin America]

Bowornwathana, Bidhya — Chulalongkorn University; *address:* 634 Nakorn Chaisi Street, Bangkok 10300, Thailand; *fax:* +66-2-243 6414; *email:* bidhya.b@chula.ac.th; *research interests:* governance, administrative reform, new public management

Brams, Steven J — New York University; *address:* 4 Washington Square Village, Apartment 171, New York, NY 10012, USA; *fax:* +1-212-995 4184; *email:* steven.brams@nyu.edu; *research interests:* political science methods, international relations, elections and voting behaviour [America, Europe]

Brandao, Ana Paula LPOA — University of Minho; *address:* R da Fábrica, 259, 4710 Braga, Portugal; *fax:* +351-1253-676 375; *email:* abrandco@eeg. uminho.pt; *research interests:* international relations, security studies, European studies [EU, Portugal]

Brar, JS — Punjabi University; *address:* 37, Raghbir Marg, Patiala (Punjab) 147001, India; *fax:* +91-175-212 022; *email:* jsbrar@ernet.pbi.in; *research interests:* elections and voting behaviour, political parties, comparative politics

Braun, Dietmar — Université de Lausanne; *address:* IEPI, Université de Lausanne, BFSH, CH-1015 Lausanne, Switzerland; *email*: diet mar.braun@iepi.unil.ch; *research interests*: federalism, public policy, research policies [Europe, Switzerland, Germany, Canada]

Braungart, Richard G—Syracuse University; *address*: Deparment of Sociology, Syracuse University, Syracuse, NY 13244-1090, USA; *fax*: +1-315-443 4597; *email*: rgbraung@ maxwell.syr.edu; *research interests*: generational politics, cultural politics, political psychology

Brautigam, Deborah—American University; *address*: School of International Service, 4400 Massachusetts Avenue NW, American University, Washington, DC 20016, USA; *fax*: +1-202-885 1695; *email*: dbrauti@american.edu; *research interests*: comparative politics, development politics, public policy

Brecher, Michael—McGill University; *address*: Department of Political Science, McGill University, 855 Therbrooke Street West, Montréal H3A 2T7, Canada; *fax*: +1-514-398 1770; *email*: msbrech@pluto.mscc. huji.ac.il; *research interests*: foreign policy analysis, international systems, international conflict, crisis and war [South Asia, Middle East]

Brenninkmeijer, Olivier AJ—Université de Genève; *address*: 52, chemin des Coudriers, Appartement 34, CH-1209 Genève, Switzerland; *fax*: +41-22-346 2510; *email*: brennin3@hei.unige.ch; *research interests*: security studies, multilateral conflict prevention, international relations, international law [Europe, Asia, North America]

Bresser Pereira, Luiz Carlos—; *address*: Av Jorge Joao Saad 104, 05618-000 Sao Paulo - SP, Brazil; *fax*: +55-11-3744 6137; *email*: bresserpereira@uol.com.br; *research interests*: public administration, public policy [Brazil, Latin America]

Bressers, Hans ThA—University of Twente; *address*: POB 217, NL-7500 AE Enschede, Netherlands; *email*: J.T.A.Bressers@cstm.utwente.nl; *research interests*: public policy, public administration, environmental policy

Briggs, Philip J—East Stroudsburg University, emeritus; *address*: 173 Cherry Lane Road, East Stroudsburg, PA 18301, USA; *research interests*: international relations, war and peace studies [Europe, North America]

Bröcker, Barbara—Staatskanzlei Nordrhein-Westfalen; *address*: Eschbachweg 7, D-40625 Dusseldorf, Germany; *fax*: +49-211-238 3143; *email*: fam.broecker@t-online. de; *research interests*: political education, public administration, women and politics

Brockman, Bert A—University of Pittsburgh; *address*: Department of Political Science, 4L01 Wesley W Posvar Hall, University of Pittsburgh, Pittsburgh, PA 15260, USA; *fax*: +1-412-648 7277; *email*: brock man+@pitt.edu; *research interests*: comparative institutions, comparative elites and leadership, structure and organisation of government

Brown-John, Lloyd—University of Windsor; *address*: Department of Political Science, University of Windsor, Windsor, ON, N9B 3P4, Canada; *fax*: +1-519-973 7094; *email*: lbj@uwindsor.ca; *research interests*: federalism, public administration, public policy [Canada, Europe]

Bryner, Gary—University of Colorado; *address*: University of Colorado, School of Law, Natural Resources Law Center, Boulder, CO 80309-0401, USA; *fax*: +1-303-492 1297; *email*: gary.bryner@colorado. edu; *research interests*: public policy, international law, development politics

Buchstein, Hubertus—Greifswald University; *address*: Department of

Political Science, Greifswald University, Baderstrasse 6-7, 17487 Greifswald, Germany; email: buchst@zedat.fu-berlin.de; *research interests*: political theory and philosophy

Bukve, Oddbjörn—Sogn og Fjordane College; *address*: Department of Economics & Languages, Sogn og Fjordane College, PO Box 133, N-6851 Sogndal, Norway; *fax*: +47-57-676 301; *email*: oddbjorn.bukve@hisf.no; *research interests*: local and urban politics, public policy [Scandanavia]

Burin, Xavier—OIEC; *address*: Residence AJAX, Quai de Longdoz 17/072, B-4020 Liege, Belgium; *fax*: +32-2-230 9745; *email*: oiec@ pophost.eunet.be; *research interests*: political theory and philosophy, development politics, religion, education and politics

Burke, Charles—Baldwin Wallace College; *address*: Department of Political Science, Baldwin-Wallace College, Berea, OH 44017, USA; *fax*: +1-440-826 3396; *email*: cburke@bw.edu; *research interests*: American politics and government, constitutional law, international politics

Burke, John Francis—University of St Thomas; *address*: Department of Political Science, University of St Thomas, 3800 Montrose Boulevard, Houston, TX 77006-4696, USA; *fax*: +1-713-525 2125; *email*: jfburke@basil.stthom.edu; *research interests*: political theory and philosophy, public administration, area studies [USA, Mexico, Latin America]

Büttner, Friedemann—Freie Universität Berlin; *address*: Assmannshauser Str 12, D-14197 Berlin, Germany; *fax*: +49-30-8385 6637; *email*: fbue@zedat.fu-berlin.de; *research interests*: comparative politics, area studies, political theory and philosophy [Middle East]

Cairns, Alan—University of Waterloo; *address*: Department of Political Science, University of Waterloo, 200 University Avenue West, Waterloo, ON, N2L 3G1, Canada; *email*: acairns@atarts.waterloo.ca; *research interests*: constitutional issues, elections and voting behaviour [Canada]

Cairo, Heriberto—Universidad Com plutense de Madrid; *address*: Urb 109 Villas, casa B-10, 28224 Pozuelo, Spain; *fax*: +34-91-394 2664; *email*: sohi102@sis.ucm.es; *research interests*: political geography, area studies, local and urban politics [Latin America, Europe]

Calise, Mauro—Universita di Napoli; *address*: Via A Caccavello, 18, 80129 Napoli, Italy; *fax*: +39-81-552 1176; *email*: calise@unina.it; *research interests*: political executives, political parties, political science methods

Calvez, Jean-Yves—IEP de Paris; *address*: 35 bis rue de Sèvres, 75006 Paris, France; *fax*: +33-1-4439 7518; *email*: jycalvezsj@yahoo.com; *research interests*: comparative politics, international relations, politics and religion [Eastern Europe]

Camp, Glen D—Bryant College; *address*: Social Science Department, Bryant College, Smithfield, RI 02917-1284, USA; *fax*: +1-401-232 6319; *email*: gcamp@bryant.edu; *research interests*: comparative politics, area studies, international relations [Russia, Eastern Europe, Greece, East Mediterranean]

Candler, Gaylord George—University of Vermont; *address*: MA of Public Administration Program, Old Mill 500, University of Vermont, Burlington, VT 05405, USA; *fax*: +1-802-656 4447; *email*: gcandler @zoo.uvm.edu; *research interests*: public administration, public policy, pressure groups [Brazil, Canada, Australia, South Pacific]

Caoili, Olivia C—University of the Philippines; *address*: Department of Political Science, College of Social Sciences & Philosophy, University of the Philippines, Diliman, Quezon City, Philippines; *fax*: +63-2-924 4875; *email*: upd.polsci@pacific.net. ph; *research interests*: legislatures, public administration, public policy

Cardinal, Linda — Université d'Ott awa; *address*: 550 rue Cumberland, Ottawa, ON, K1N 6NS, Canada; *fax*: +1-613-562 5106; *email*: lcardina@uottawa.ca; *research interests*: rights and political ethniticity, area studies, political theory and philosophy [Canada, Europe]

Carnota, Walter F — Universidad de Buenos Aires; *address*: 2260 Freire Street, 2nd Floor B, (1428) Buenos Aires, Argentina; *fax*: +54-11-4541 0995; *research interests*: comparative politics, judicial systems and behaviour, pressure groups

Caro Figueroa, Ramiro Fernando — Universidad Argentina John F Kennedy; *address*: Montevideo, 958, 2°, Universidad Argentina John F Kennedy, 1019 Buenos Aires, Argentina; *fax*: +54-87-811 0989; *email*: policaro@fibertel.com.ar; *research interests*: political theory

Carrasco, Michael — *address*: 140 Normandy Hill Drive, Alexandria, VA 22304, USA; *fax*: +1-202-224 9516; *email*: mjc55@hotmail.com; *research interests*: legislatures, political executives, judicial systems and behaviour

Carrasquero, José Vicente — Universidad Simon Bolivar; *address*: Apartado Postal 81074, Prados del Este, Caracas 1080, Venezuela; *fax*: +58-2-906 3771; *email*: jcarrasq@usb.ve; *research interests*: political culture, public opinion [Latin America]

Carroll, Barbara Wake — McMaster University; *address*: Department of Political Science, McMaster University, 1280 Main Street West, Hamilton, ON L8S 4M4, Canada; *fax*: +1-905-527 3071; *email*: carrollb@mcmaster.ca; *research interests*: public administration, public policy, women and politics [Canada, Af-

rica]

Carroll, Terrance — Brock University; *address*: Department of Political Science, Brock University, St Catharines, ON L2S 3A1, Canada; *fax*: +1-905-988 9388; *email*: tcarroll@spart an.ac.brocku.ca; *research interests*: comparative politics, development politics [Africa]

Carruthers, David — San Diego State University; *address*: Department of Political Science, San Diego State University, 5500 Campanile Drive, San Diego, CA 92182-4427, USA; *fax*: +1-619-594 7302; *email*: davidc @mail.sdsu.edu; *research interests*: comparative politics, development politics, international relations [Mexico, Latin America]

Carver, Terrell — University of Bristol; *address*: Department of Politics, University of Bristol, 10 Priority Road, Bristol, BS8 1TU, UK; *fax*: +44-117-973 2133; *email*: t.carver @bris.ac.uk; *research interests*: political theory and philosophy

Castellano Christy, Ernesto — Universidad de la República; *address*: Zabala 1313 Ap 1, Montevideo CP 11000, Uruguay; *fax*: +598-2-409 2946; *email*: ecastellano@mail.antel. com.uy; *research interests*: public administration, public policy

Castillo, Hernán — Universidad Simon Bolivar; *address*: CC 90087, PO Box 025323, Miami, FL 33102-5323, USA; *fax*: +58-2-962 1308; *email*: castillh@pims.org; *research interests*: civil-military relations, legislatures, national security [third world, Latin America]

Cattoir-Jonville, Vincent — Université de Lille; *address*: 62, Avenuede Jussieu, F-59130 Lambersart, France; *fax*: +33-320-907 638; *email*: vcj@hp-sc.univ.lille2.fr; *research interests*: public administration, central government, political theory and philosophy

Cavatorta, Francisco — Trinity College Dublin; *address*: Department of

Political Science, Trinity College Dublin, Dublin 2, Ireland; *fax*: +353-1-677 0546; *email*: cavatorf@tcd.ie; *research interests*: international relations, comparative politics

Cerny, Philip — University of Manchester; *address*: Department of Government, University of Manchester, Dover Street, Manchester M13 9PL, UK; *fax*: +44-161-275 4925; *email*: philip.cerny@man.ac.uk; *research interests*: international relations, political economy, comparative politics

Chandran, S — University of Madras; *address*: Department of Politics & Public Administration, University of Madras, Chepauk, Chennai 600 005, India; *fax*: +91-44-536 6693; *email*: chand.ran@usa.net; *research interests*: political theory and philosophy, comparative politics, public policy [Asia, India]

Chang, Eugene YS — Tunghai University; *address*: PO Box 870, Department of Political Science, Tunghai Universty, Taichung 407, Taiwan; *fax*: +886-4-359 0256; *email*: ys chang@mail.thu.edu.tw; *research interests*: comparative politics, legislatures, international organisations [UK, France, Germany, Russia, USA]

Chang, Jekuk — *address*: 102 Inaki Apartment, 2-26-16 Tomigaya, Shibuya-ku, Tokyo, Japan; *fax*: +81-3-3481 6319; *email*: jchang@tkd.att.ne.jp; *research interests*: international relations, area studies, international law [Northeast Asia]

Chaques, Laura — University of Barcelona; *address*: Departament de Ciencia Polmtica, Universitat de Barcelona, Aveda. Diagonal 690, 08034 Barcelona, Spain; *fax*: +34-93-402 1294; *email*: chaques@riscd2.eco.ub.es; *research interests*: public policy, pressure groups, local and urban politics [Spain, EU, Mediterranean region]

Chaturvedi, Inakshi — University of

Rajasthan; *address*: B-41, Pink Cottage, Jyoti Nagar, Jaipur - 302005, India; *fax*: +91-141-743 238; *email*: inakshic@hotmail.com; *research interests*: women and politics, political theory and philosophy, comparative politics [Canada]

Chazan, Naomi — The Hebrew University; *address*: Department of Political Science, The Hebrew University, Mount Scopus, Jerusalem 91905, Israel; *fax*: +972-2-792 046; *email*: nchazan@knesset.gov.il; *research interests*: comparative politics [Middle East, Africa]

Cheibub, Jose — Yale University; *address*: Department of Political Science, Yale University, PO Box 208301, New Haven, CT 06520-8301, USA; *email*: cheibub@sas.upenn.edu; *research interests*: comparative politics, development politics, elections and voting behaviour [Latin America]

Chilcote, Ronald H — University of California; *address*: Department of Economics, University of California, Riverside, CA 92521, USA; *fax*: +1-909-787 5685; *email*: chilcoter@aol.com; *research interests*: comparative politics, development politics, comparative political economy [Brazil, Portugal]

Cho, Yong-Sang — Keimyung University; *address*: 101-1407 Sung-seo, Woo-bang Town, Lee-gok Dong, Dal-suh Ku, Taegu 704-140, Republic of Korea; *fax*: +82-53-580 5313; *email*: ysc@kmu.ac.kr; *research interests*: comparative politics, international relations, development politics [East Asia]

Choe, Yonhyok — Södertörns Högskola-University College; *address*: Box 4101, 141 04 Huddinge, Sweden; *fax*: +46-8-5858 8420; *email*: yonhyok.choe@sh.se; *research interests*: comparative politics, elections and voting behaviour, area studies [Korea, Baltic countries]

Choi, Jong Chul — Korea National

Defense University; *address*: Susaek-dong, Eunpyung-Gu, Seoul 122-090, Korea; *fax*: +82-2-309 9774; *email*: jcchoi@kndu.ac.kr; *research interests*: international studies, area studies, comparative politics [Northeast Asia, USA]

Choi, Mario—Columbia University; *address*: 1258 Commonwealth Avenue, Boston, MA 02134, USA; *email*: mmc191@columbia.edu; *research interests*: political executives, area studies, comparative politics [China, USA]

Choi, Sukyong—Chungnam National University; *address*: Department of Political Science, Chungnam National University, 220 Kung-dong, Yusong-ku, Taejon 305-764, Republic of Korea; *fax*: +82-42-823 6348; *email*: johhj7@nownuri. net; *research interests*: area studies, international relations, political parties [North America]

Choucri, Nazli—MIT; *address*: MIT E53-493, 77 Massachusetts Avenue, Cambridge, MA 02139, USA; *fax*: +1-617-258 7989; *email*: nchoucri@MIT.edu; *research interests*: international relations

Chowdhury, Najma—Dhaka University; *address*: Department of Political Science, University of Dhaka, Nilkhet, Dhaka, Bangladesh; *fax*: +880-2-861 5583; *email*: duregstr@bangla. net; *research interests*: legislatures, women and politics, public policy [South Asia, developing countries]

Christensen, Tom—University of Oslo; *address*: Department of Political Science, University of Oslo, PO Box 1097, Blindern, 0317 Oslo, Norway; *fax*: +47-22-854 411; *email*: tom.christensen@stv.uio.no; *research interests*: public administration, central government, comparative politics [Europe, USA, Oceania, Asia]

Chun, In-Young—Seoul National University; *address*: College of Education, Seoul National University, 56-1 Shinlim-Dong, Kwan AK-GU, Seoul 151-742, Korea; *fax*: +82-2-888 3296; *email*: iychun@plaza.snu.ac.kr; *research interests*: international relations, comparative politics, area studies [Korean peninsula]

Chun, Kyung Ock—Sookmyung Women's University; *address*: Department of Political Science, Sookmyung Women's University, 53-12 Chunpal-dong 2 ka, Yongsan-ku, Seoul, Korea; *email*: kczoom@hotmail.com; *research interests*: political theory and philosophy, women and politics, comparative politics

Chung, Carmen—University of Western Ontario; *address*: 12-461 Platt's Lane, London, ON, N6G 3H2, Canada; *fax*: +1-519-663 0940; *email*: cchung3@julian.uwo.ca; *research interests*: comparative politics, public administration, international law

Chung, Eunsook—The Sejong Institute; *address*: The Sejong Institute, Bundang PO Box 45, Sungnam 463-050, Republic of Korea; *fax*: +82-2-233 8832; *email*: chunges@sejong. org; *research interests*: comparative politics, area studies, international relations [Russia, Eastern Europe, Central Europe]

Cingranelli, David—Binghamton University, SUNY; *address*: 3149 Briarcliff Avenue, Vestal, NY 13850, USA; *fax*: +1-607-777 2675; *email*: davidc@binghamton.edu; *research interests*: international relations, comparative politics, public policy

Cioffi-Revilla, Claudio—University of Colorado; *address*: Department of Political Science, Campus Box 333, University of Colorado, Boulder, CO 80309-0333, USA; *fax*: +1-303-492 0978; *email*: cioffi@colorado.edu; *research interests*: international relations, political science methods, comparative politics

Clarkson, Stephen—University of Toronto; *address*: Department of Political Science, University of Toronto, 100 St George Street, Toronto, ON, M5S 1A1, Canada; *fax*: +1-416-971 2027; *email*: clarkson@chass.utoronto.ca; *research interests*: political economy, comparative politics, political parties [North America]

Claussen, Bernhard — Universität Hamburg; *address*: Husumer Strasse 17, D-20251 Hamburg, Germany; *research interests*: political theory and philosophy, political education, political socialisation

Claval, Paul — Université de Paris-Sorbonne Paris IV; *address*: 29 rue de Soisy, 95600 Eaubonne, France; *fax*: +33-1-3959 8383; *email*: p.claval @wanadoo.fr4; *research interests*: political theory and philosophy, political geography and geopolitics [Europe]

Close, David — Memorial University; *address*: Department of Political Science, Memorial University, St Johns, Newfoundland, A1B 3X9, Canada; *fax*: +1-709-737 4000; *email*: dclose@morgan.ucs.mun.ca; *research interests*: legislatures, area studies, international relations [Latin America]

Coakley, John — University College Dublin; *address*: UCD, Belfield, Dublin 4, Ireland; *fax*: +353-1-706 1171; *email*: john.coakley@ucd.ie; *research interests*: comparative politics, nationalism [Europe]

Coghill, Ken — Monash University; *address*: 97 Prospect Road, Newtown, Victoria 3220, Australia; *fax*: +61-3-9903 8701; *email*: kencogl@bigpond.com; *research interests*: legislatures, political theory and philosophy, comparative politics

Cohen, Edward — Westminster College; *address*: Department of Political Science, PO Box 106, Westminster College, New Wilmington, PA 16172, USA; *fax*: +1-724-946 7256; *email*: cohenes@westminster.edu; *research interests*: public policy, politi-

cal theory and philosophy, international relations

Colas, Dominique — IEP de Paris; *address*: 49 Rue de la Fontaine au Roi, Paris 75011, France; *fax*: +33-1-4544 9549; *email*: dcolas@club internet.fr; *research interests*: political theory and philosophy, comparative politics, area studies [Eastern Europe, Russia, France]

Collier, David — University of California-Berkeley; *address*: Department of Political Science, 210 Barrows Hall, University of California, Berkeley, CA 94720-1950, USA; *fax*: +1-510-642 9515; *email*: dcollier@socrates.berkeley.edu; *research interests*: comparative politics, methodology [Latin America]

Connor, Walker — Middlebury College; *address*: Box 289, Belmont, VT 05730, USA; *fax*: +1-802-259 7020; *email*: walkconnor@aol.com; *research interests*: comparative nationalism

Constantin, François-Guy — Université de Pau et des Pays de l'Adour; *address*: 25, Rue du Prof Jacques Monod, F-64000 Pau, France; *fax*: +33-5-5980 7554; *email*: francois. constantin@univ-pav.fr; *research interests*: international relations, development politics, public policy (environment) [Africa, third world]

Costa, Olivier — IEP de Bordeaux; *address*: CERVL- IEP de Bordeaux, BP 101, 33405 Talence Cedex, France; *fax*: +33-5-5684 4329; *email*: o.casta@iep.u-bordeaux.fr; *research interests*: legislatures, comparative politics, international relations [EU]

Costa, Paulo Roberto Neves — Universidade Federal do Paraná; *address*: rua Marechal Hermes 491 - ap 701, Curitiba, PR 80530-230, Brazil; *fax*: +55-41 360 5093; *email*: paulornc @coruja.humanas.ufpr.br; *research interests*: elections and voting behaviour, comparative politics, political executives [Brazil, Latin America, Europe]

Couffignal, Georges — Université

Paris 3-Sorbonne; *address*: 76, Rue des Mûres, F-92160 Antony, France; *fax*: +33-1-4548 7958; *email*: iheal@lendit.univ-paris3.fr; *research interests*: political parties, public policies, public administration [Latin America]

Courtney, John — University of Saskatchewan; *address*: Department of Political Studies, University of Saskatchewan, Saskatsoon, Saskatchewan, S7N 0W0, Canada; *fax*: +1-306-966 5250; *email*: courtney@sask.usask.ca; *research interests*: legislatures, political executives and party leaders, political parties, electoral districting [Canada, USA, Europe]

Covell, Maureen — Simon Fraser University; *address*: Political Science Department, Simon Fraser University, Burnaby, BC, V5A 1S6, Canada; *fax*: +1-604-291 4786; *email*: covell@sfu.ca; *research interests*: comparative politics, area studies, international relations [Europe]

Crete, Jean — Université Laval; *address*: Département de science politique, Université Laval, Cité Universitaire, Quèbec, G1K 7P4, Canada; *fax*: +1-418-656 7861; *email*: jean.crete@pol.ulaval.ca; *research interests*: public policy, elections and voting behaviour, political science methods [North America, Europe]

Crowley, John — FNSP; *address*: CERI, 4 rue de Chevreuse, 75006 Paris, France; *fax*: +33-1-4410 8450; *email*: john.crowley@ceri.sciences-po.fr; *research interests*: political theory and philosophy, comparative politics [UK, France]

Cullen, Dolores — Organization of American States; *address*: 2950 Van Ness Street, Apt 924 NW, Washington, DC 20008, USA; *fax*: +1-202-458 3678; *email*: dcullen@oas.org; *research interests*: elections and voting behaviour, political parties, political theory and philosophy [Latin America]

Cuntigh, Philippe — IEP de Bor-deaux; *address*: Le Verneuil, 24380 Creyssensac, France; *email*: p. cuntig h@wanadoo.fr; *research interests*: public policy [France, Europe]

Curtice, John K — University of Strathclyde; *address*: Department of Government, University of Strathclyde, 16 Richmond Street, Glasgow, G1 1XQ, UK; *fax*: +44-141-552 5677; *email*: j.curtice@strath.ac.uk; *research interests*: elections and voting behaviour [UK]

Dallmayr, Fred R — University of Notre Dame; *address*: Dee Professor of Political Theory, Department of Government & International Studies, University of Notre Dame, Notre Dame, IN 46556-0780, USA; *fax*: +1-219-631 8209; *email*: Fred.R.Dallmayr.1@nd.edu; *research interests*: political theory and philosophy, comparative political theory, development politics, globalisation theory

Daloz, Jean-Pascal — IEP de Bor-deaux; *address*: CERVL, BP 101, 33405 Talence Cedex, France; *fax*: +33-5-5684 4329; *email*: j.p.daloz@iep.u-bordeaux.fr; *research interests*: comparative politics, area studies, political executives [Nordic countries]

Danopoulos, Constantine P — San Jose State University; *address*: 6188 Northland Terrace, Fremont, CA 94555, USA; *fax*: +1-510-494 9544; *email*: danopoulos@aol.com; *research interests*: comparative politics, international law, development politics [Balkans, Eastern and Central Europe]

D'Araújo, Maria Celina — Universidad Federal Fleiminente; *address*: R Sao Salvador, 29/202 - Flamengo, Cep 22231-130, Rio de Janeiro, RJ, Brazil; *fax*: +55-21-205 2558; *email*: daraujo@fgv.br; *research interests*: democracy, political institutions [Latin America]

Davis, Laurence A — *address*: 29 Parnell Court, Harold's Cross, Dublin

12, Ireland; *research interests*: political theory and philosophy
Davis, Michael C — Chinese University of Hong Kong; *address*: GPA Department, Chinese University of Hong Kong, Shatin, Hong Kong; *fax*: +852-2603 5229; *email*: mcdavis@cuhk.edu.hk; *research interests*: international law, comparative politics, area studies [Asia]
Davis, Sue — APSA; *address*: 1527 New Hampshire Avenue NW, Washington, DC 20036, USA; *fax*: +1-202-483 2657; *email*: sdavis@apsanet.org; *research interests*: comparative politics, international relations, area studies [Russia, Ukraine, Caucasus, Central Asia]
de Almeida, Maria Herminia Tauares — University of Sao Paulo; *address*: Department of Political Science, University of Sao Paulo, Av Prof Luciano Gualberto, 315, Sao Paulo - 05508-900, Brazil; *fax*: +55-11-211 2269; *email*: mhbtdalm@usp.br; *research interests*: public policy, local politics, federalism
de Hoyos, Ruben J — University of Wisconsin-Oshkosh; *address*: 547 Hazel Street, Oshkosh, WI 54901, USA; *fax*: +1-920-424-0739; *email*: dehoyos@vbe.com; *research interests*: international relations, comparative politics [Latin America, Pacific Basin]
De Jonge Oudraat, Chantal — Carnegie Endowment for International Peace; *address*: 1779 Massachusetts Avenue, NW, Washington, DC 20007, USA; *fax*: +1-202-483 4462; *email*: coudraat@ceip.org; *research interests*: international relations, area studies, international law [UN]
De Moraes Filho, José Filomeno — Universidade Estadual do Ceara, Universidade de Fortaleza; *address*: Rua Mons Catao, 1442 Apt 1003, Aldeota, 60175-000 Fortaleza - CE, Brazil; *email*: filomeno@secrel.com.br; *research interests*: elections and voting behaviour, legislatures, po-

litical theory and philosophy
De Stubrim, Lilia Puig — Universidad Nacional del Litoral; *address*: Saavedra 2252, 3000 Santa Fe, Argentina; *email*: lipuig@arnet.com.ar; *research interests*: comparative politics, political parties, elections and voting behaviour [Europe, USA, Latin America]
Deetz, Werner — WDR; *address*: Hermeskeilerstr 7, D-50935 Köln 41, Germany; *research interests*: public administration, political theory and philosophy, media [Europe, USA]
Degtyarev, Andrei — Moscow Institute of International Relations; *address*: 1st Ostankinskaya Street 25-31, Moscow, 129515, Russia; *fax*: +7-095-434 7547; *email*: andrew@msses.ru; *research interests*: political power and policy making process, local and regional politics, sociology of public policy [Russia]
Dekker, Henk — University of Leiden, Utrecht University; *address*: Leiden University, Department of Political Science, PO Box 9555, 2300 RB Leiden, Netherlands; *fax*: +31-71-527 3815; *email*: dekkerh@fsw.leidenuniv.nl; *research interests*: political psychology, political socialisation, nationalism
Dekker, Paul — Social & Cultural Planning Offices (SCP); *address*: Beeklaan 520, 2562 BS Den Haag, Netherlands; *fax*: +31-70-340 7044; *email*: pdekker@scp.nl; *research interests*: political psychology, behaviour, attitudes, political science methods, comparative politics [Europe]
Delgado Sotillos, Irene — Universidad Nacional del Educacion a Distancia; *address*: UNED, Facultad de Ciencias Politicas y Sociologia, Dpto de Ciencia Politica, c/ Obispo Trejo s/n, 28040 Madrid, Spain; *fax*: +34-1-398 7003; *email*: Idelgado@sr.uned.es; *research interests*: elections and voting behaviour, legislatures, political parties [western democracies]

Delmartino, Frank — Leuven University; *address*: Department of Political Science, E Van Evenstraat 2B, B-3000 Leuven, Belguim; *fax*: +32-16-323 144; *email*: frank.delmartino@soc.kuleuven.ac.be; *research interests*: comparative politics, public administration, public policy [EU]

Demirel, Tanel — Hacettepe University; *address*: Kamu Yvnetimi Bvlimi, Iktisadi Idari Bilimler Fakiltesi, Hacettepe Universitesi, Beytepe, Ankara, Turkey; *fax*: +90-312-297 8740; *email*: tanel@hacettepe.edu.tr; *research interests*: comparative politics, development politics, area studies [Turkey]

Demtchouk, Artour — Moscow State University; *address*: Faculty of Philosophy, Moscow State University, Vorobjovy Gory, 119899 Moscow, Russia; *fax*: +7-095-939 2208; *email*: arthur@host.cis.lead.org; *research interests*: comparative politics, area studies, international relations [Latin America]

Derlien, Hans-Ulrich — Universität Bamberg; *address*: Universität Bamberg, Feldkirchenstr 21, D-96045 Bamberg, Germany; *fax*: +49-951-863 2627; *email*: hans-ulrich.derlien@sowi.uni-bamberg.de; *research interests*: political executives, public administration, public policy [Anglo Saxon countries]

Deschouwer, Kris — Vrije Universiteit; *address*: Vrije Universiteit Brussels, Centrum voor Politicologie, Pleinlaan 2 - 1050 Brussels, Belgium; *fax*: +32-2-629 2282; *email*: kris.deschouwer@vub.ac.be; *research interests*: political parties, comparative politics

Deshmukh, Neelima — Nagpur University; *address*: "Shirish" - 16, South Ambazari Road, Laxmi-Nagar, Nagpur 440022, Maharashtra, India; *fax*: +91-712-237 445; *email*: n-deshmukh@yahoo.com; *research interests*: public administration [India]

Deutschamnn, Alrun — Stiftung Wissenschaft und Politik, Ebenhausen; *address*: Duenzelbach 10, D-82272 Moorenweis, Germany; *fax*: +49-8146-946 745; *email*: adtmann@aol.com; *research interests*: international relations, comparative politics, political theory and philosophy [Great Britain, USA]

Diamond, Larry — Stanford University; *address*: Hoover Institution, Stanford University, Stanford, CA 94305-6010, USA; *fax*: +1-650-723 1928; *email*: diamond@hoover.stanford.edu; *research interests*: comparative politics, development politics, area studies [Africa, Asia, Latin America]

Dicklitch, Susan — Frankling & Marshall College; *address*: Department of Government, Franklin & Marshall College, PO Box 3003, Lancaster, PA 17604-3003, USA; *fax*: +1-717-291 4356; *email*: S_Dicklitch@acad.fandm.edu; *research interests*: development politics, area studies, comparative politics [Africa]

Dill, Gunter — Konrad Adenaur Foundation; *address*: Postfach 10 04 21, Konrad-Adenauer-Str 2, D-63004 Offenbach, Germany; *fax*: +49-2241-246 611; *email*: guenter.dill@inter.kas.de; *research interests*: comparative politics, new public management, local self-government [Latin America]

Dimier, Veronique — IEP de Grenoble; *address*: IEP BP 48, 28040 Cedex 9, Grenoble, France; *fax*: +33-4-8792 6098; *email*: veroniquedimier@hotmail.com; *research interests*: comparative politics, international relations, public administration [Great Britain, Frank, former British and French colonies in Africa]

Diniz, Eli Roque — Federal University of Rio de Janeiro; *address*: Rua Benjamin Batista 180, Apt 501, Jardim Botâmico, Rio de Janeiro RJ CEP22461-120, Brazil; *fax*: +55-21-220 4038; *email*: ediniz@unisys.com.

br; *research interests*: political theory, comparative politics, public policy [Latin America]

Dogan, Mattei — CNRS; *address*: Centre National De La Recherche, Scientifique, 72 Boulevard Arago, 75013 Paris, France; *fax*: +33-1-4707 1222; *research interests*: comparative politics, political executives, elections and voting behaviour [Europe]

Doherty, Roisin — University of Ulster at Jordanstown; *address*: School of Public Policy, Economics & Law, University of Ulster, Jordanstown, Newtownabbey, Co Antrim, Northern Ireland; *fax*: +44-1232-366 847; *email*: R.Doherty@ulst.ac.uk; *research interests*: international relations, public policy, public procurement, contract compliance [Ireland, UK, EU]

Donneur, André P — UQAM; *address*: Département de science politique, UQAM, CP 8888, Succ Centre-ville, Montréal, QC H3C 3P8, Canada; *fax*: +1-514-987 0218; *email*: dept.sc.politiques@uqam.ca; *research interests*: international relations, comparative politics, political parties [Europe, Asia]

Donolo, Carlo — Universita di Roma, "La Sapienza"; *address*: Via S Anselmo 14, 00153 Roma, Italy; *fax*: +39-6-4991 0720; *email*: cdonolo@uniroma1.it; *research interests*: public policy, public administration, political theory and philosophy [Europe]

Doran, Charles F — Johns Hopkins University-SAIS; *address*: 8544 Brickyard Rd, Potomac, MD 20854, USA; *fax*: +1-301-983 9270; *email*: charles.doran@worldnet.att.net; *research interests*: international relations, political theory and philosophy

Doron, Gideon — Tel Aviv University; *address*: Department of Political Science, Tel Aviv University, PO Box 39040, Tel Aviv 69978, Israel;

fax: +972-3-643 0046; [Asia]

Dotan, Yoav — The Hebrew University; *address*: Faculty of Law, The Hebrew University, Mount Scopus, Jerusalem 91905, Israel; *fax*: +972-2-582 3042; *email*: msdotan@pluto.ms cc.huji.ac.il; *research interests*: political executives, political theory and philosophy, public administration

Dowding, Keith — London School of Economics; *address*: Department of Government, London School of Economics, Houghton Street, London WC2A 2AE, UK; *fax*: +44-207-831 1707; *research interests*: political theory and philosophy, public administration, local and urban politics [UK]

Dowty, Alan — University of Notre Dame; *address*: 0313 Hesburgh Center, University of Notre Dame, Notre Dame, IN 46556, USA; *fax*: +1-219-631 6973; *email*: alan.k.dow ty.1@nd.edu; *research interests*: international relations, area studies, comparative politics [Middle East]

Draibe, Sonia M — Universidade de Campinas; *address*: R São Vincente Paulo 526, Apto 91, São Paulo 01229.010, Brazil; *fax*: +55-11-3667 0631; *email*: smdraibe@uol.com.br; *research interests*: public policy, local and urban politics, social policy [Latin America, USA, Europe]

Du Toit, Pierre — University of Stellenbosch; *address*: Department of Political Science, University of Stellenbosch, Private Bag X1, Stellenbosch 7602, South Africa; *fax*: +27-21-808 2110 *email*: pdt@maties.sun.ac.za; *research interests*: comparative politics, elections and voting behaviour, conflict studies [Africa]

Duchesne, Erick — SUNY-Buffalo; *address*: Political Science Department, SUNY, Buffalo, NY 14260, USA; *fax*: +1-716-645 2166; *email*: duchesne@acsu.buffalo.edu; *research interests*: international relations, political science methods, comparative politics [the Americas]

Dutta, Anuradha — *address*: Navagraha Path, Chenikuthi Hillside, Guwahati, Assam, PIN - 781003, India; *fax*: +91-361-570 133; *email*: digital@gw1.dot.net.in; *research interests*: area studies, women and politics, comparative politics [India]

Dwivedi, OP — University of Guelph; *address*: Department of Political Science, University of Guelph, Guelph ON, N1G 2W1, Canada; *fax*: +1-519-837 9561; *email*: odwivedi@uo guelph.ca; *research interests*: public administration, area studies, development administration [Canada, India, PNG, developing nations]

Dzhunusova, Zhanylzhan — Diplomatic Academy of the Ministry of Foreign Affairs of Kazkhstan; *address*: 480099 Almaty, Furmanov Street 229, Apt #64, Allmaty, Kazakstan; *fax*: +7-3972-506 568; *email*: zhanyl@freenet.kz; *research interests*: political parties, comparative politics, presidency [Central Asia]

Eagles, Munroe — SUNY-Buffalo; *address*: Department of Political Science, 520 Park Hall, North Campus SUNY, Buffalo, NY 14260, USA; *fax*: +1-716-645 2166; *email*: eagles@acsu. buffalo.edu; *research interests*: elections and voting behaviour, political parties, comparative politics [West Europe, Anglo-American countries]

Easton, David — University of California; *address*: Department of Politics and Society, University of California, Irvine, CA 92717, USA; *fax*: +1-949-854 5180; *email*: deaston@ uci.edu; *research interests*: political theory and philosophy, political science methods

Eberwein, Wolf-Dieter — FIB-WZB; *address*: Wissenschaftszentrum Berlin für Sozialforschung, Reichpietschufer 50, D-10785 Berlin, Germany; *fax*: +49-30-2549 1561; *email*: eberwein@medea.wz-berlin. de; *research interests*: international

relations, comparative politics

Eccles, Jeremy — Marygrove College; *address*: 8425 West McNichols Road, Detroit, MI 48221, USA; *email*: jec cles@arygrove.edu; *research interests*: public politics, public administration, local and urban politics [USA, Russia, India]

Edelman, Martin — University at Albany; *address*: Department of Political Science, University at Albany, 135, Western Avenue, Albany, NY 12222-0001, USA; *fax*: +1-518-442 5298; *email*: me354@csc.albany.edu; *research interests*: public law: courts, law and politics, political theory and philosophy [Israel, USA]

Eisenberg, Avigail — University of Victoria; *address*: Department of Political Science, PO Box 3050, University of Victoria, Victoria, BC, V8W 3P5, Canada; *fax*: +1-250-721 7485; *email*: avigaile@uvic.ca; *research interests*: political theory and philosophy, judicial systems and behaviour, women and politics [Canada, USA, Britain, Western Europe]

Eisfeld, Rainer — Universität Osnabrück; *address*: Universität Osnabruck, FB1, D-49069 Osnabruck, Germany; *fax*: +49-541-969 4600; *email*: rainer.eisfeld@uos.de; *research interests*: political theory and philosophy, pressure groups, history of discipline [Western Europe, USA]

El Amin, Nafisa Ahmed — Ahfad University, Omdurman, Sudan; *address*: Head, Documentation Unit for Women's Studies, Ahfad University for Women, PO Box 167, Omdurman, Sudan; *fax*: +249-11-553363; *email*: AHFAD@sudanmail. net; *research interests*: elections and voting behaviour, international relations, women and politics [Africa]

El Mossadeq, Rkia — Sidi Mohamed Ben Abdellah; *address*: 4, Cooperative al Makrizi, Rout Ain Chkaff, Fes, Morocco; *fax*: +212-5-64 13 04; *research interests*: women and politics, political parties, elections and voting behaviour [Morocco, Maghreb]

Elaigwu, J Isawa — Institute of Governance and Social Reform; *address*: PO Box 2687, Jos, Nigeria; *fax*: +234-73-460 894; *email*: elaigwu@infoweb. abs.net; *research interests*: comparative politics, international relations, development politics [Africa]

Eldersveld, Samuel J — University of Michigan; *address*: Political Science Department, University of Michigan, Ann Arbor, Michigan 48109, USA; *email*: sjelders@um.edu; *research interests*: political parties, comparative politics, local and urban politics [USA, Europe, India, Eastern Europe, China, Taiwan]

El-Geadi, Isheteiwi — Libyan Peoples Bureau; *address*: 4-5 Hannam-dong, Yongsan-ku, Seoul, Korea; *fax*: +82-2-797 6007; *email*: libyaemb@kornet. net; *research interests*: elections and voting behaviour, political theory and philosophy, international relations [Northeast Asia, North Africa, Middle East]

Elizondo, Carlos — Centro de Investigación y Docencia Economica (CIDE); *address*: Carretera libre México -Toluca #3655 or 16.5 km, Lomas de Santa Fé, DF 01020, Mexico; *fax*: +52-5-727 9874; *email*: elizondo@dis1.cide.mx; *research interests*: Mexican political economy, tax reform political perspective, development politics [Mexico]

El-Mikawy, Noha — Universität Bonn; *address*: Am Staute 7, D-58802 Balve, Germany; *fax*: +49-2375 4516; *email*: honert@compuserve.com; *research interests*: comparative politics, development politics, political theory [Near East, Latin America]

Elsenhaus, Hartmut — Universität Leipzig; *address*: Universität Leipzig, Institüt für Politikwisssenschaft, Burgstrasse 21, D-04109 Leipzig, Germany; *fax*: +49-341-973 5696; *email*: helsen@server1.rz.uni-leipzig.de; *research interests*: devel-

opment and politics, international relations, public administration

Elshtain, Jean Bethke — University of Chicago; *address*: 233 Swift Hall, The Divinity School, University of Chicago, 1025 E 58th Street, Chicago, IL 60637, USA; *fax*: +1-773-643 5146; *research interests*: political theory, international relations

Engelmann, Frederick C — University of Alberta; *address*: 10939-85 Avenue, Edmonton, Alberta T6G 0W3, Canada; *fax*: +1-789-439 6859; *email*: maryeng@telusplanet.net; *research interests*: political parties, Canadian politics, Austrian politics

Erasov, Boris — Institute of Oriental Studies; *address*: Rozhdestvenka 12, Institute of Oriental Studies, Moscow 103031, Russia; *fax*: +7-095-975 2396; *email*: erasov@orient.soc.msu. ru; *research interests*: political theory and philosophy, comparative politics, international relations [Russia, Eurasia]

Erickson, Lynda — Simon Fraser University; *address*: Political Science Department, Simon Fraser University, Burnaby, BC, V5A 1S6, Canada; *fax*: +1-604-291 4786; *email*: erickson@sfu.ca; *research interests*: area studies, political parties, women and politics [Canada]

Ethier, Diane — Université de Montréal; *address*: Département de science politique, Université de Montréal, PO Box 6128, Station Centre-Ville, Montréal, H3C 3J7, Canada; *fax*: +1-514-343 2360; *email*: Diane. Ethier@ere.umontreal.ca; *research interests*: comparative politics, international relations, area studies [Eastern and Southern Europe, East and Southeast Asia]

Etzioni-Halevy, Eva — Bar-Ilan University; *address*: Bar-Ilan University, Department of Sociology & Anthropology, 52 900 Ramat Gan, Israel; *fax*: +972-3-635 0995; *email*: ehzioe@mail.biv.ac.il; *research interests*: political theory and philosophy, comparative politics, elites, democracy

Evenson, Krisan—Syracuse University; *address*: Department of Political Science, 100 Egger's Hall, Maxwell School, Syracuse University, Syracuse, NY 13244-1090, USA; *fax*: +1-315-443 9204; *email*: klevenso@max well.syr.edu; *research interests*: comparative politics, area studies, political psychology [Canada, Quebec, francophone communities]

Fabbrini, Sergio—Trento University; *address*: Universita Degli Studi - Dip Sociologia, E Ricerca Sociale, Via Verdi 26, 38100 Trento, Italy; *fax*: +39-461-881 348; *email*: fabbrini@ soc.unitt.it; *research interests*: central government, political institutions, comparative politics [Western Europe, USA]

Fakiolas, Efstathios—King's College, London; *address*: 86 Xanthipou Street, Holargos 15561, Athens, Greece; *fax*: +30-1-654 5390; *research interests*: comparative politics, international relations, strategic studies [Balkans, Greece]

Falger, Vincent SE—University of Utrecht; *address*: Department of International Relations, University of Utrecht, Achter Sint Pieter 200, 3512 HT Utrecht, Netherlands; *fax*: +31-30-253 7067; *email*: v.falger@law.uu. nl; *research interests*: political theory and philosophy, international relations, women and politics [Europe]

Färber, Gisela—Deutsche Hochsch ule für Verwaltungswissenschaften *address*: Deutsche Hochschule für Verwaltungswissenschaften, Postfach 1409, D-67234 Speyer, Germany; *fax*: +49-623-265 4306; *email*: faerber@dhv-speyer.de; *research interests*: comparative politics, public finance, local and urban politics

Farnen, Russell—University of Connecticut; *address*: 5 Cypress Trail, Farmington, CT 06032, USA; *fax*: +1-860-570 9210; *email*: htfdadm2@ uconnvm.uconn.edu; *research inter-*

ests: political socialisation, democratisation, area studies, comparative politics [USA, Europe]

Faroukshin, Midkhat—Kazan State University; *address*: Apartment 9, ul Janovich 57/2, 420012 Kazan, Russia; *fax*: +7-8432-366822 sat 14000 4470; *email*: root@mfar.kcn.ru; *research interests*: comparative politics, political parties, political science methods [Russia, USA, Canada]

Farrell, David—University of Manchester; *address*: University of Manchester, Department of Government, Manchester, M13 9PL, UK; *fax*: +44-161-275 4925; *email*: david.farrell@man.ac.uk; *research interests*: political parties, elections and voting behaviour, comparative politics [Western Europe, Australia]

Faucher, Florence—University of Stirling; *address*: Department of Politics, University of Stirling, FK9 4LA, Stirling, UK; *fax*: +44-1786-466 266; *email*: florence.faucher@stir.ac. uk; *research interests*: political parties, comparative politics, green politics

Feldman, Ofer—Naruto University of Education; *address*: Social Science Education, Naruto University of Education, Naruto, Takashima, Tokushima 772-8502, Japan; *fax*: +81-886-876 375; *email*: hatani@naruto-u. ac.jp; *research interests*: elections and voting behaviour, comparative politics, area studies [Japan]

Fernandez, Arturo Aquilino—Universidad de Buenos Aires; *address*: Borges 2308, Po 1o, (1425) Buenos Aires, Argentina; *fax*: +54-11-953 9853; *email*: postmaster@piettefer nan.ar; *research interests*: development and politics, pressure groups, political parties

Fernández Ramil, María de los Angeles S—Universidad Central de Chile; *address*: Universidad Central de Chile, Calle Lucas Sierra 2412, Santiago, Chile; *fax*: +56-2-687 4271; *email*: ramil@ctcinternet.cl; *research*

interests: globalisation and governance, the study of political science as a discipline, advances in political science at the year 2000

Ferreira Filho, Manoel — University of Sao Paulo; address: Rua Hungria, 644 Sao Paulo, CEP 01455-904, Brazil; fax: +55-11-814 0278; email: mgff@uol.com.br; research interests: political theory and philosophy, comparative politics, political parties

Fields, A Belden — University of Illinois-Urbana; address: Department of Political Science, University of Illinois, 361 Lincoln Hall, 702 S Wright Street, Urbana, Il 61801, USA; fax: +1-217-244 5712; email: a-fields@uiuc.edu; research interests: political theory and philosophy, comparative politics, human rights [USA, France, Africa, Central America]

Finifter, Ada W — Michigan State University-East Lansing; address: Department of Political Science, 303 South Kedzie Hall, Michigan State University, East Lansing, Michigan 48824-1032, USA; fax: +1-517-432 1091; email: finifter@msu.edu; research interests: elections and voting behaviour, comparative politics, political science methods [USA, former Soviet Union, Australia]

Fisher, David — North Central College; address: Department of Philosophy, North Central College, 30 N Brainard Street, PO Box 3063, Naperville, IL 60566, USA; fax: +1-630-637 5610; email: dhf@noctrl.edu; research interests: political theory and philosophy, judicial systems and behaviour, philosophy of law, ethics, aesthetics [Macedonia, Balkans]

Fitzgerald, Rona — University of Strathclyde; address: 28 Ancaster Drive, Glasgow GL3 1NB, Scotland; fax: +44-141-548 4898; email: r.n.fitzgerald@strath.ac.uk; research interests: regional policy at national and European level, gender equal-

ity in the EU [Ireland, EU]

Fleming, James S — Rochester Institute of Technology; address: 99 Bonnie Brae Avenue, Rochester, New York, NY 14618, USA; fax: +1-716-475 7120; email: jsfgSS@rit.edu; research interests: legislatures, political executives, public policy [global, especially USA]

Fletcher, Christine — Australian National University; address: North Australian Research Unit, ANU, PO Box 41321, Casuarina, NT 0811, Australia; fax: +61-89-220 055; email: christine.fletcher@anu.edu.au; research interests: federalism, public policy, development and politics [Australia, North America, Africa]

Floria, Carlos A — University of Buenos Aires, University of San Andres; address: Juez Tedin 2935, Buenos Aires (1425), Argentina; fax: +54-11-801 8752; email: cfloria@inf oria.com.ar; research interests: political executives, comparative politics, international relations [Latin America, Europe]

Florig, Dennis — Hanyang University; address: Graduate School of Asia-Pacific Studies, Hanyang University, Seoul, 133-791, Korea; email: dennis@email.hanyang.ac.kr; research interests: area studies, public policy, media studies [USA, Asia Pacific]

Fortescue, Stephen — University of New South Wales; address: School of Political Science, University of New South Wales, Sydney, NSW 2052, Australia; fax: +61-2-9385 1555; email: s.fortescue@unsw.edu.au; research interests: area studies, public administration [Russia]

Fossum, John — University of Bergen; address: Department of Administration &, Organisation Theory, University of Bergen, Christies Gate 17, 5007 Bergen, Norway; fax: +47-55-589 890; email: john.fossum@aorg.uib.no; research interests: political theory and philosophy, comparative politics, European integration [Europe, Canada]

Franz, John B — *address*: PO Box 10568, Pompano Beach, FL 33061-6568, USA; *research interests*: political psychology [USA]

Fraschini, Angela — University of Eastern Piedmont; *address*: Via Simonetta 2, 27100 Pavia, Italy; *email*: angela.fraschini@sp.unipmon.it; *research interests*: fiscal federalism, public expenditures, public debt [Italy]

Freeman, Michael — University of Essex; *address*: Department of Government, University of Essex, Wivenhoe Park, Colchester CO4 3SQ, UK; *fax*: +44-1206-873 598; *email*: freema@essex.ac.uk; *research interests*: political theory and philosophy, international relations, comparative politics

Freire, Andre — ISCTE; *address*: ISCTE, Av das Forgas Armadas, 1600 Lisboa, Portugal; *fax*: +351-21-796 4953; *email*: andre.freire@iscte. pt; *research interests*: elections and voting behaviour, political science methods, political parties [Europe, Portugal, EU]

Freyberg-Inan, Annette — University of Bucharest; *address*: University of Bucharest, National School of Political Studies, CP 54-86, Bucuresti, Romania; *email*: Freyberg-Inan@btr. ro; *research interests*: international relations, comparative politics, political theory and philosophy [EU, Romania, Turkey, Germany, USA]

Friedland, Elaine A — *address*: 89 Forest Green, Staten Island, New York, NY 10312, USA; *email*: elaine3@ mindspring.com; *research interests*: political economy, development politics, international relations [Africa]

Friedman, Edward — University of Wisconsin-Madison; *address*: Political Science Department, Bascom Mall 1050, North Hall, Madison, WI 53707-1389, USA; *fax*: +1-608-265

2663; *email*: friedman@polisci.wisc. edu; *research interests*: comparative politics, area studies (EA), international relations (IPE) [China, Asia]

Fry, Earl H — Brigham Young University; *address*: Department of Political Science, 114 SWKT, Brigham Young University, Provo, UT 84602, USA; *fax*: +1-801-378 5730; *email*: earl_ fry@byu.edu; *research interests*: area studies, international relations, public policy [Canada]

Fuchs, Gerhard — Centre for Technology Assessment; *address*: Akademie für Technikfolgenabschätzung, Industriestr 5, D-70565 Stuttgart, Germany; *fax*: +49-711-906 3175; *email*: gerhard.fuchs@taakademie.de; *research interests*: comparative politics, international relations, public policy [German, Western Europe]

Fuhr, Harald — Universität Potsdam; *address*: International Relations Chair, Faculty of Economics and Social Sciences, Universität Potsdam, PO Box 900327, D-14439 Potsdam, Germany; *fax*: +49-331-977 3429; *email*: hfuhr@rz.uni-potsdam.de; *research interests*: public administration, international relations, local and urban politics [Latin America, Eastern Europe]

Fukui, Haruhiro — Nanzan University; *address*: Yamzato Haimu I-7, 103 Yamzato-cho, Nagoya 466 0824, Japan; *fax*: +81-52-834 3886; *email*: fukui@ic.nanzan-u.ac.jp; *research interests*: comparative politics, international relations, political parties [Asia, Japan]

Fukuju, Yukio — Kokushikan University (Retired); *address*: 5-8-62, Koyanagi-Cho, Fuchu-Shi, Tokyo, Japan; *research interests*: legislatures, elections and voting behaviour, comparative politics

Fukushima, Shingo — Senshu University (Professor Emeritus); *address*: 2-9-1 Dai'ta, Setagaya Ku, Tokyo 155-0033, Japan; *research inter-*

ests: international relations, military systems and policies, central government, comparative politics [East Asia, Japan]

Funes de Rioja, Daniel CL — Universidad Católica Argentina; *address*: Alsina 495 piso 11, Buenos Aires, (CP 1087), Argentina; *fax*: +54-11-331 1167; *email*: jfr@funes.com.ar; *research interests*: federalism and regionalism, pressure groups, comparative politics

Gabriel, Jürg Martin — Swiss Federal Institute of Technology; *address*: Centre for International Studies, Swiss Federal Institute of Technology, Seilergraben 49, 8092 Zürich, Switzerland; *fax*: +41-1-632 1945; *email*: gabriel@ir.gess.eth2.ch; *research interests*: international relations, comparative politics, political theory and philosophy [Africa, Europe, USA]

Galligan, Yvonne — University College Cork; *address*: Department of Government, University College Cork, Western Road, Cork, Ireland; *fax*: +353-21-903 135; *email*: y.galligan@ucc.ie; *research interests*: public policy, women and politics, political parties [Ireland]

Garcia-Zamor, Jean-Claude — Florida International University; *address*: 6039 Collins Avenue, Apt 717, Miami Beach, FL 33140, USA; *fax*: +1-305-919 5848; *email*: garciaz@fiu.edu; *research interests*: public policy and administration [Latin America, Africa]

Garon, Lise — Université Laval; *address*: Department of Communication & Information Studies, Laval Université, 5419 Pavillion Louis-Jacques, Quèbec City, Caseault G1K 7PR, Canada; *fax*: +1-418-656 7807; *email*: lise.garon@com.ulaval.ca; *research interests*: comparative politics, political communication, democracy [North Africa]

Garreton, Manuel A — University of Chile; *address*: Sociology Depart-ment, University of Chile, Ignacio Carrera Pinto 1045, 3er piso, Ñuñoa, Santiago, Chile; *fax*: +56-2-678 7777; *email*: marret@uchile.cl; *research interests*: political parties, elections and voting behaviour, political theory and philosophy [Chile, Latin America, Europe]

Gebhardt, Jürgen — Universität Erlangen-Nurnberg; *address*: Institüt für Politische Wissenschaft, Kochstr 4, D-91054 Erlangen, Germany; *fax*: +49-91-31852 2371; *email*: Ingebhar@phil.uni-erlangen. de; *research interests*: political theory and philosophy, comparative politics [Europe, USA, Near East]

Geller, Daniel S — University of Mississippi; *address*: 711 Manor Drive, Oxford, MS 38655, USA; *fax*: +1-662-915 7808; *email*: psgeller@olmiss.edu; *research interests*: international relations, peace and conflict studies

Genckaya, Ömer Faruk — Bilkent University; *address*: Department of Political Science & Public Administration, Bilkent University, 06533 Ankara, Turkey; *fax*: +90-312-266 4960; *email*: genckaya@bilkent.edu.tr; *research interests*: legislatures, political parties, comparative politics [Europe]

Genovese, Michael A — Loyola Marymount University; *address*: Political Science Department, Loyola Marymount University, Loyola Blvd and W 80th, Los Angeles, CA 90045, USA; *fax*: +1-310-338 1950; *email*: mgenoves@lmu.edu; *research interests*: political leadership, political executives [USA, Great Britain]

George, Robley E — Center for the Study of Democratic Societies; *address*: Center for the Study of Democratic Societies, Box 475, Manhattan Beach, CA 90267-0475, USA; *fax*: +1-310-374 0440; *email*: georgecsds@aol.com; *research interests*: quantitative democracy, political theory and philosophy, elections and voting behaviour

Gerace, Michael — Northeastern University; *address*: 7 Liberty Street #3, Worcester, MA 01605, USA; *email*: mger@concentric.net; *research interests*: international relations, political science methods, comparative politics

German, Daniel B — Appalachian State University; *address*: Department of Political Science, Appalachian State University, Boone, NC 28608, USA; *fax*: +1-828-262 2947; *email*: germandb@appstate.edu; *research interests*: political culture, area studies, comparative politics [Central and Eastern Europe]

Ghio, José María — Universidad Torcuato Di Tella; *address*: Universidad Torcuato Di Tella, Minones 2159/77, (1428) Capital Federal, Buenos Aires, Argentina; *fax*: +54-11-784 0089; *email*: ghio@utdt.edu. ar; *research interests*: institutions, political economy, religion [Latin America, Europe]

Giadone, Dante — *address*: Avda. de Mayo 1460, 3o, 15, (1085) Buenos Aires, Argentina; *fax*: +54-11-383 7635; *email*: giadoneycosta@ciudad. com.ar; *research interests*: public administration, political parties [Latin America]

Gibbons, Kenneth M — University of Winnipeg; *address*: Department of Political Science, University of Winnipeg, 515 Portage Avenue, Winnipeg, Manitoba, R3B 2E9, Canada; *fax*: +1-204-774 4134; *email*: k.gibbons@uwinnipeg.ca; *research interests*: public administration, public policy, political science methods [North America, Western Europe]

Gibson, Edward — Northwestern University; *address*: 601 University Place, Evanston, IL 60208, USA; *fax*: +1-847-491 8985; *email*: egibson@northwestern.edu; *research interests*: comparative politics, area studies [Latin America]

Gibson, Rachel — Australian National University; *address*: Research School of Social Sciences, Australian National University, ACT 0200, Canberra, Australia; *fax*: +61-2-6249 3051; *email*: rachelg@coombs.anu. edu.au; *research interests*: political parties, elections and voting behaviour, political communication [Western Europe]

Gills, Barry Keith — University of Newcastle; *address*: Department of Politics, University of Newcastle, Newcastle-upon-Tyne, NE1 7RU, UK; *fax*: +44-191-222 5069; *email*: b.k.gills@ncl.ac.uk; *research interests*: area studies, international relations, development politics [Korea, East Asia]

Gills, Dong-Sook — University of Sunderland; *address*: 28 Mountfield Gardens, Kenton, Newcastle-upon-Tyne, NE3 3DB, UK; *fax*: +44-191-515 2229; *email*: dong-sook.gills@ sunderland.ac.uk; *research interests*: international political economy, women and development, development politics [Korea, Southeast Asia]

Girard, Michel — Université Paris 1; *address*: 18 rue Paul Couderc, 92330 Sceaux, France; *fax*: +33-1-4702 2302; *email*: mgirard@univ-paris1.fr; *research interests*: international relations, political science methods [EU]

Girvin, Brian — University of Glasgow; *address*: Department of Politics, University of Glasgow, Glasgow, G12 8RT, UK; *fax*: +44-141-330 5071; *email*: b.girvin@socsci.gla.ac. uk; *research interests*: nationalism, comparative politics [Ireland, Europe, USA, India]

Glad, Betty — University of South Carolina; *address*: GINT Department, Gambrell Hall, University of South Carolina, Columbia, SC 29208, USA; *fax*: +1-803-777 8255; *email*: glad@garnet.cla.sc.edu; *research interests*: political psychology [USA, Russia, South Africa]

Glassberg, Andrew — University of Missouri-St Louis; address: Public Policy Administration, University of Missouri-St Louis, St Louis, MI 63121, USA; fax: +1-314-516 5210; email: glassberg@umsl.edu; research interests: public administration, public policy, local and urban politics [USA, EU, UK]

Gleditsch, Nils Petter — International Peace Research Institute; address: PRIO, Fuglehauggata 11, 0260 Oslo, Norway; fax: +47-22-547 701; email: npg@prio.no; research interests: international relations, peace, conflict, democracy

Godt, Paul — The American University of Paris; address: 32 rue d'Yerres, 91800 Brunoy, France; fax: +33-1-4555 1789; email: pgodt@easy net.fr; research interests: comparative politics, public policy [Europe, France, UK, Germany]

Goetz, Anne Marie — University of Sussex; address: 107 Beaconsfield Villas, Brighton BN1 6HF, UK; fax: +44-1273-621 202; email: a.m.goetz@ids.ac.uk; research interests: women and politics, development politics, public administration [Bangladesh, Uganda, South Africa, India]

Göhler, Gerhard — Freie Universität Berlin; address: Freie Universität Berlin, FB Politik Wissenschaft, Ihnestr 21, D-14195 Berlin, Germany; fax: +49-30-8385 2345; email: goehler @zedat.fu-berlin.de; research interests: political theory and philosophy

Goldsmith, Michael — University of Salford; address: Department of Politics and Government History, University of Salford, Salford M5 4W5, UK; fax: +44-161-295 5545; email: mjfgoldsmith@pch.salford.ac.uk; research interests: comparative politics, public administration, local and urban politics

Goodin, Robert E — Australian National University; address: Philosophy, RSSS, Australian National University, Canberra, ACT 0200, Australia; fax: +61-2-6249 3294; email: goodinb@coombs.anu.edu.au; research interests: political theory and philosophy, public policy

Gottlieb, Stephen — Albany Law School; address: Albany Law School, 80 New Scotland Avenue, Albany, NY 12208, USA; fax: +1-518-445 2315; email: stevegot@alumni.prince ton.edu; research interests: comparative politics, judicial systems and behaviour, political theory and philosophy [USA]

Goverde, Henri J — University of Nijmegen; address: Reestraat 39, 6531 JJ Nijmegen, Netherlands; fax: +31-24-361 2379; email: hjgoverde@ bw.kun.nl; research interests: political theory and philosophy, comparative politics, public policy [Europe]

Graham, George J, Jnr — Vanderbilt University; address: 4400 Belmont Park Terrace, Unit 145, Nashville, TN 37215, USA; fax: +1-615-343 6003; email: grahamgj@ctrvax.van derbilt.edu; research interests: political theory and philosophy, public policy, political science methods

Graham, Lawrence S — University of Texas-Austin; address: Department of Government, Main Building 101, University of Texas at Austin, Austin, TX 78712, USA; fax: +1-512-471 3090; email: l.graham@mail.utexas.edu; research interests: comparative politics, public policy, comparative federalism [Latin America]

Grant, WP — University of Warwick; address: Department of Politics and International Studies, University of Warwick, Coventry, CV4 7AL, UK; fax: +44-1203-524 221; email: porcb@ titanic.csv.warwick.ac.uk; research interests: public policy, pressure groups, comparative politics

Graziano, Luigi — Universita di Torino; address: Universita di Torino, Dipartimento di Scienze Sociali, Via S. Ottavio 50, I-10124 Torino, Italy; fax: +39-11-670 2612; email:

s_graziano@hotmail.com; *research interests*: European integration, political theory, comparative politics

Greenwood, Justin — Robert Gordon University; *address*: School of Public Administration and Law, Robert Gordon University, Garthdee Road, Aberdeen AB10 7QE, UK; *fax*: +44-1224-263 434; *email*: j.greenwood@rgu.ac.uk; *research interests*: interest representation, public policy [EU]

Gress, Franz — JW Goethe-Univers ität; *address*: JW Goethe University; FB03, Robert-Mayer-Str 5, D-60054 Frankfurt-am-Main, Germany; *fax*: +49-607-461   658; *email*: gress@soz.uni-frankfurt.de; *research interests*: comparative politics, legislatures, area studies

Gribanova, Galina — Herzen Pedagogical University; *address*: Shuvalovsky pr 63-2-5, St Petersburg, Russia; *fax*: +7-812-343 9853; *email*: gribanov_@chat.ru; *research interests*: comparative politics, public administration, local and urban politics [Russia, developed democracies]

Grofman, Bernard — UCL Irvine; *address*: School of Social Sciences, UCL, Irvine, CA 92717, USA; *fax*: +1-714-8248762; *email*: bgroman@ucf.edu; *research interests*: elections and voting behaviour, comparative politics, legislatures [USA, Western Europe, Japan]

Guelke, Adrian B — Queen's University, Belfast; *address*: School of Politics, Queen's University, Belfast BT7 1PA, Northern Ireland; *fax*: +44-28-90 235 373; *email*: a.guelke@queen-belfast.ac.uk; *research interests*: comparative politics, international relations, development politics [Northern Ireland, South Africa]

Guetzkow, Harold — Northwestern University (retired); *address*: Monterey 8, 1660 Gaton Drive, San Jose, CA 95125-4534, USA; *research interests*: international relations, political theory and philosophy

Guillorel, Hervé — Université de Paris 10-Nanterre, CNRS; *address*: 130 rue Raymond Barbet, 92000 Nanterre, France; *fax*: +33-1-4097 7643; *email*: herveg@u-paris10.fr; *research interests*: elections and voting behaviour, comparative politics, political science methods [Western Europe, Celtic countries]

Guimaraes, Roberto P — United Nations Econ Commission for Latin America & the Caribbean; *address*: United Nations - ECLAC, Casilla 179-D, Santiago, Chile; *fax*: +56-2-208 0252; *email*: rguimaraes@eclac. cl; *research interests*: public policy, development politics, environmental politics [Latin America, Brazil]

Guizzi, Vincenzo — Universita di Napoli; *address*: Via Capodistria 4, 00198 Roma, Italy; *fax*: +39-6-6760 4995; *email*: guizzi@mclink.it; [Europe]

Gundapuneni, Koteswara Prasad — University of Madras; *address*: Department of Politics and Public Administration, University of Madras Chepauk, Madras 600 005, India; *fax*: +91-44-566 693; *email*: gkp@nd3.vsnl.net.in; *research interests*: political theory and philosophy, public policy, political science methods [India]

Gunnell, John G — SUNY-Albany; *address*: Department of Political Science, SUNY, Albany, NY 12222, USA; *fax*: +1-518-442 5298; *email*: jgg@csc.albany.edu; *research interests*: political theory and philosophy, political science methods, history of political science

Gunther, Magnus — Trent University; *address*: 508 Gilmour Street, Ottawa, ON, K1R 5L4, Canada; *fax*: +1-613-237 4563; *email*: magnus@inrtanet. ca; *research interests*: comparative politics, conflict, violence [South Africa, Russia, China]

Gupta, Asha — Bharati College; *address*: BQ2, Shalimar Bagh, Ring

Road, Delhi - 110052, India; *fax*: +91-11-747 4104; *email*: ashagupta@ vsnl.com; *research interests*: comparative politics, women and politics, third world politics [North America, third world, Germany]

Gupta, Inder Mohini—University College of Cape Breton; *address*: 297 Newlands Avenue, Sydney NS, B1S 1Y9, Canada; *fax*: +1-902-567 6452; *email*: jgupta@ns.sympatico.ca; *research interests*: comparative politics, international relations, development politics [Europe, South Asia, China]

Gupta, Sanjay—Lucknow University; *address*: 8-B Faizabad Road, Near Central Bank, Lucknow 226007 (UP), India; *email*: sanjay-gupta_66@hotmail.com; *research interests*: development and politics, international relations, area studies

Gupta, Surendra K—Pittsburgh State University; *address*: 321 Sharon Drive, Lawrence, KS 66049, USA; *fax*: +1-800-881 9938; *email*: sgupta@sunflower.com; *research interests*: international relations, area studies [Russia, Asia]

Gurr, Ted Robert—University of Maryland; *address*: CIDCM, Tydings Hall, University of Maryland, College Park, MD 20742-7231, USA; *fax*: +1-301-314 9256; *email*: tgurr@cid cm.umd.edu; *research interests*: comparative politics, ethnic conflict, conflict theory [global and Africa]

Gustafsson, Gunnel—University of Umeå; *address*: Department of Political Science, University of Umeå, SE-901 87 Umeå, Sweden; *fax*: +46-90-7816 6681; *email*: gunnel.gustaf sson@pol.umu.se; *research interests*: governance, political culture, local government

Habegger, Helga—Universidad Nacional del Nordeste; *address*: Gutnisky 3089, 3400 Corrientes, Argentina; *email*: mihel@espacio.com.ar; *research interests*: international relations, pressure groups, develop-

ment politics

Habib, Adam—University of Durban-Westville; *address*: School of Governance, University of Durban-Westville, Private Bag X5400I, Durban 4001, South Africa; *fax*: +27-31-204 4340; *email*: habib@pixie.udw. ac.za; *research interests*: political parties, comparative politics, international relations [Africa, Latin America]

Hagevi, Magnus—Göteborg University; *address*: Center for Public Sector Research, Göteborg University, Box 720, SE-416 73 Göteborg, Sweden; *fax*: +46-31-773 4480; *email*: magnus.hagevi@cefos.gu.se; *research interests*: elections and voting behaviour, legislatures, political parties

Hahm, Chaibong—Yonsei University; *address*: Department of Political Science, Yonsei University, 134 Shinchon-dong, Seoul 120-749, Korea; *fax*: +82-2-363 5769; *email*: cbhahm@yonsei.ac.kr; *research interests*: political theory and philosophy, comparative politics, area studies [East Asia, Korea]

Hakansson, Nicklas—Göteborg University; *address*: Department of Political Science, University of Göteborg, Box 711, SE 405 30 Göteborg, Sweden; *fax*: +46-31-773 4599; *email*: Nicklas.Hakansson@pol.gu.se; *research interests*: elections and voting behaviour, comparative politics, political communication

Hakovirta, Harto—University of Turku; *address*: Department of Political Science, University of Turku, 20500 Turku, Finland; *fax*: +358-2-333 5090; *research interests*: political theory and philosophy, international relations, political science methods

Halligan, John—University of Canberra; *address*: School of Management and Policy, University of Canberra, Belconnen ACT 2601, Australia; *fax*: +61-2-6201 5237;

email: jah@management.canberra. edu.au; *research interests*: public administration, political executives, central government

Haluani, Makram — Universidad Simon Bolivar; *address*: Quinta Magia, Calle Costa Rica, Las Acacias, Caracas 1040, Venezuela; *fax*: +58-2-906 3801; *email:* mhaluani@ usb.ve; *research interests*: comparative politics, area studies, international relations [Europe, Middle East, Latin America]

Hamel, Pierre — Université de Montréal; *address*: Institut d'urbanisme, Université de Montréal, CP 6128, Succ Centre-ville, Montréal, Quèbec H3C 3J7, Canada; *fax*: +1-514-343 2338; *email:* pierre.hamel@umon treal.ca; *research interests*: political theory and philosophy, public policy, local and urban politics [North America]

Hamm, Keith E — Rice University; *address*: Department of Political Science, Rice University, PO Box 1892, Houston, TX 77251, USA; *fax*: +1-713-348 5273; *email:* hamm@rice. edu; *research interests*: legislatures, local and urban politics, pressure groups [USA]

Han, Kee Soo — National Intelligence Educational and Research Institute; *address*: 1205 Anam Apartments, 90-27 Haweolgok-dong, Sông Buk-Gu, Seoul, Korea; *email:* keesohn@han mail.net; *research interests*: political theory and philosophy, comparative politics, area studies [Northeast Asia]

Hanley, David — Cardiff University; *address*: School of European Studies, PO Box 908, Cardiff University, Cardiff CF10 3YQ, UK; *fax*: +44-2920-874 946; *email:* hanleydl@car diff.ac.uk; *research interests*: political parties, comparative politics [Western Europe, France]

Hanson, Elizabeth — University of Connecticut; *address*: Political Science Department U-1024, 341 Mans-field Rd, Room 137, University of Connecticut, Storrs, CT 06269-1024, USA; *fax*: +1-860-486 3347; *email:* hanson@uconnvm.uconn.edu; *research interests*: area studies, international relations [South Asia]

Haque, Shamsul — National University of Singapore; *address*: Department of Political Science, National University of Singapore, 10 Kent Ridge Cresent, Singapore 119260, Singapore; *fax*: +65-779 6815; *email:* polhaque@nus.edu.sg; *research interests*: comparative politics, public administration, development politics [South and Southeast Asia]

Harbeson, John W — City University of New York; *address*: 5 Valley Trail, Croton-on-Hudson, New York, NY 10520-2213, USA; *fax*: +1-914-271 7915; *email:* jwharbeson@aol.com; *research interests*: comparative politics, development politics, international relations

Harles, John — Messiah College; *address*: Department of Politics, Messiah College, Grantham, PA 17027, USA; *email:* jharles@messiah.edu; *research interests*: comparative politics, racial and ethnic politics [USA, Canada, UK]

Harrington, Jonathan — Troy State University; *address*: Troy State University, PSC 80, Box 10,000, APO, AP 96367, USA; *email:* jianan11@cs. com; *research interests*: international relations, comparative politics, development politics [China]

Haugaard, Mark — National University of Ireland, Galway; *address*: Department of Political Science & Sociology, National University of Ireland, Galway, Ireland; *fax*: +353-91-525 700; *email:* Mark.Haugaard@nui galway.ie; *research interests*: political theory and philosophy, power and democracy

Hawkesworth, Mary — Rutgers University; *address*: Center for American Women and Politics, Eagleton Institute of Politics, Rutgers University, 191 Ryders Lane, New Brunswick, NJ, USA; *fax*: +1-732-932 0014; *email*: mhawkes@rci.rutgers.edu; *research interests*: political theory and philosophy, women and politics

Hayler, Barbara J — University of Illinois-Springfield; *address*: University of Illinois at Springfield, Criminal Justice Department, BRK 330, PO Box 19243, Springfield, IL 62794-9243, USA; *fax*: +1-217-206 7188; *email*: hayler.barbara@uis.edu; *research interests*: law and courts, women and politics, comparative politics [Europe - EC, Central and Eastern Europe]

Hazan, Reuven — The Hebrew University; *address*: Department of Political Science, The Hebrew University, 91905 Jerusalem, Israel; *fax*: +972-2-588 1333; *email*: mshazan@mscc.huji.ac.il; *research interests*: legislatures, elections and voting behaviour, political parties [Israel, Western Europe]

Hazarika, Niru — Gauhati University; *address*: 8 GU Campus, Gopinath Bardoloi Nagar, Guwahati - 781014, District Kamrup, State Assam, India; *fax*: +91-361-561 067; *email*: kkhlgu@gw1.dot.net.in; *research interests*: public administration, area studies [Northeast India]

He, Baogang — University of Tasmania; *address*: Department of Government, University of Tasmania, GPO Box 252-22, Hobart, Tasmania 7001, Australia; *fax*: +61-3-6224 0973; *email*: b.he@utas.edu.au; *research interests*: political theory, democratisation, Chinese politics [East Asia, China]

Hector, Cary — Université Notre-Dame d'Haiti; *address*: Faculté des Sciences Administrative/UDER-CAP, Université Notre-Dame d'Haiti, Rues 18 et B, PO Box 13, Cap-Haitien, Haiti; *fax*: +509-262 1178; *email*: caryhector@hotmail.com; *research interests*: comparative politics, international relations, development politics [Latin America, Caribbean]

Hefron, Peter — Troy State University; *address*: 400 Franklin Street, Wrentham, MA 02093, USA; *email*: +su_7 @hotmail.com; *research interests*: international relations, area studies, development politics [East and Southeast Asia]

Heidenheimer, Arnold — Washington University; *address*: Political Science Department, Washington University, Campus Box 1063, St Louis, MO 63130, USA; *fax*: +1-314-935 5856; *email*: heidenhe@artsci.wustl.edu; *research interests*: comparative politics, public policy, political finance and corruption

Hentz, James — Virginia Military Institute; *address*: Department of International Studies, Virginia Military Institute, Lexington, VA 24450, USA; *fax*: +1-540-464 7763; *email*: hentzjj@vmi.edu; *research interests*: international relations, IPE [Africa, Brazil]

Heo, Man-ho — Kyungpook National University; *address*: Department of Political Science & Diplomacy, College of Social Sciences, Kyungpook National University, 1370 Sankyuk-dong Pook-ku, Taegu, Republic of Korea; *fax*: +82-53-950 6206; *email*: mhheo@bh.kyungpook.ac.kr; *research interests*: international relations, area studies, comparative politics [North Korea]

Hepburn, Mary — Carl Vinson Institute of Government, University of Georgia; *address*: 215 Los Tree Trail, Athens, GA 30605, USA; *fax*: +1-706- 542 9301; *email*: MHepburn@cviog.uga.edu; *research interests*: political socialisation, political education, media literacy [USA, world trends]

Hermann, Tamar — The Open University, Tel Aviv University; *address*: 16 Zafririm Street, Givatayim, 53485, Israel; *email*: tamarhe@open umail.ac.il; *research interests*: elections and voting behaviour, comparative politics

Herz, Dietmar — Universität Erfurt; *address*: Staatswissenschaftliche Fakultät der Universität Erfurt, Nordhäuser Strasse 63, 99089 Erfurt, Germany; *email*: dietmar.herz@uni-erfurt.de; *research interests*: political theory and philosophy, international relations, comparative politics [Germany, Europe, USA, Middle East]

Hey, Hilde — Center for Development Research; *address*: Am Botanischen Garten 7, 40225 Dusseldorf, Germany; *fax*: +49-228-731 972; *email*: h.hey@uni-bonn.de; *research interests*: human rights, international relations, development politics [Central America]

Higley, John — University of Texas-Austin; *address*: Department of Government, University of Texas, Burdine Hall 536, Austin, TX 78712-1087, USA; *fax*: +1-512-471 1061; *email*: jhigley@mail.la.utexas.edu; *research interests*: comparative politics, elites, development politics [Australasia, Eastern Europe, Latin America]

Hirano, Hiroshi — Meijigakuin University; *address*: 3-4-10 Katase-Kaigan, Fujisawa, Kanagawa 251, Japan; *fax*: +81-3-5421 5597; *email*: hirano@law.meijigakuin.ac.jp; *research interests*: elections and voting behaviour, comparative politics, political communication [Japan]

Hirosawa, Takayuki — Matsuyama University; *address*: 3-4-15-4 Yamagoe, Matsuyama Ehime, 791-8013, Japan; *fax*: +81-89-922 5415; *email*: hirosawa@cc.matsuyama-u.ac.jp; *research interests*: comparative politics, local and urban politics [France]

Hirschl, Ran — University of Toronto; *address*: Department of Political Science, University of Toronto, 100 St George Street, Toronto, M5S 3G3, Canada; *fax*: +1-416-978 5566; *email*: ran.hirschl@utoronto.ca; *research interests*: judicial systems and behaviour, comparative politics, international law

Hisschemoller, Matthijs — Vrije Universiteit; *address*: Vrije Universiteit, Institute of Environmental Studies, 1081 HV Amsterdam, Netherlands; *fax*: +31-20-444 9553; *email*: matthijs.hisschemoller@ivm.vu.nl; *research interests*: public policy, public administration, international relations

Hjartardottir, G Lilja — The Reykjavik Academy; *address*: Hrefnugata2, 105 Reykjavik, Iceland; *fax*: +354-561 8528; *email*: thorlilja@heimsnet.is; *research interests*: international relations, comparative politics, human rights

Hocking, Brian — Coventry University; *address*: School of International Studies & Law, Coventry University, Priory Street, Coventry CV1 5FB, UK, *fax*: +44-24-76 888 256; *email*: g.hocking@coventry.ac.uk; *research interests*: international relations

Hoetjes, Bernard JS — Institute Clingendael, Leiden; *address*: Waterruit 54, 2804 PD Gouda, Netherlands; *fax*: +31-70-328 2002; *email*: bhoetjes@clingendael.nl; *research interests*: comparative politics, public administration, public policy analysis [Europe, EU]

Hofferbert, Richard I — SUNY-Binghamton; *address*: Department of Political Science, SUNY, Binghamton, NY 13902-6000, USA; *fax*: +1-607-7772675; *email*: rhofferb@binghamton.edu; *research interests*: comparative politics, public policy, political parties [Europe]

Hofnung, Menachem — The Hebrew University; *address*: Department of Political Science, The Hebrew University, Jerusalem 91905, Israel; *fax*: +972-2-322 545; *email*: msmm@mscc.huji.ac.il; *research interests*: legislatures, judicial systems and behaviour, political finance

Holmes, Jennifer — University of Texas-Dallas; *address*: School of Social Sciences, University of Texas at Dallas, GR31, PO Box 830688, Richardson, TX 75080-0688, USA; *email*: j.holmes@utdallas.edu; *research interests*: comparative politics, area studies, international relations [Latin America, Southern Europe]

Holsti, Kalevi J — University of British Columbia; *address*: Department of Political Science, University of British Columbia, Vancouver, BC, V6T 1Z1, Canada; *fax*: +1-604-822 5540; *email*: golsti@interchange.ubc. ca; *research interests*: international relations

Holtz-Bacha, Christina — Universität Mainz; *address*: Arndtstrasse 7, 65185 Wiesbaden, Germany; *fax*: +49-613-392 4586; *email*: christina. holtz-bacha@uni-mainz.de; *research interests*: elections and voting behaviour, women and politics, comparative politics [Europe, USA]

Holzinger, Katharina — Max-Planck-Project Group on Common Goods; *address*: Max-Planck-Project on Common Goods, Poppelsdorfer Allee 45, D-53115 Bonn, Germany; *fax*: +49-228-914 1675; *email*: holzinger@mpp-rdg.mpg.de; *research interests*: political theory and philosophy, political science methods, public policy [EU, Germany, USA]

Honap, Shrikant — University of Pune; *address*: 55/10 Shagun Ashokpath, Erandware, Pune 411004, India; *email*: lalitahonap@ hotmail.com; *research interests*: public administration, public policy, human resource development [India]

Hori, Masaharu — Ritsumeikan University; *address*: Sunstage-Kinugasa #312, 5-2 Okitayama-Hase, Kita, Kyoto 603-8488, Japan; *fax*: +81-75-465 8294; *email*: hori@law.ritsumei. ac.jp; *research interests*: public administration, public policy [Japan,

OECD]

Hottinger, Julian — Institute of Federalism; *address*: Institute of Federalism, University of Fribourg, Route d'Englisberg 7, CG-1763 Granges-Paccot, Switzerland; *fax*: +41-26-300 9724; *email*: juan.hottinger@unifr.ch; *research interests*: political parties, elections and voting behaviour, development politics [Europe, Africa, South America]

Hrbek, Rudolf — Universität Tübingen; *address*: Melanchthonstrasse 36, D-72074 Tübingen, Germany; *fax*: +49-7071-292 417; *email*: rudolf. hrbek@uni-tuebingen.de; *research interests*: European integration and EU politics, federalism, political parties [Europe]

Hsieh, John Fuh-sheng — University of South Carolina; *address*: Department of Government & International Studies, Gambrell Hall, Room 408, University of South Carolina, Columbia, SC 29208, USA; *fax*: +1-803-777 0568; *email*: hsieh@sc.edu; *research interests*: comparative politics, elections and voting behaviour, political parties [Taiwan, China]

Huberts, LWJC — Vrije Universiteit; *address*: Mgr Nolenslaan 6, 1181 VM Amstelveen, Netherlands; *email*: lwjc.huberts@scw.vu.nl; *research interests*: public administration, public policy, ethics, police and criminology

Hudon, Raymond — Université Laval; *address*: Département de science politique, Université Laval, Cité Universitaire, Quèbec, G1K 7P4, Canada; *fax*: +1-418-656 7861; *email*: raymond.hudon@pol.ulaval.ca; *research interests*: political behaviour, interest groups and lobbying, comparative politics [Quebec, North America, Europe]

Hufty, Marc — Graduate Institute of Development Studies; *address*: 24 rue Rothschild, CP 136, 1211 Geneva 21, Switzerland; *fax*: +41-22-906 5947; *email*: marc.hufty@iued.

unige.ch; *research interests*: international relations, comparative politics, political science methods [South America, Madagascar]

Hughes, Colin — University of Queensland; *address*: Department of Government, University of Queensland, QLD 4072, Australia; *fax*: +61-7-3365 1388; *email*: colin.hughes @mailbox.uq.edu.au; *research interests*: elections and voting behaviour, political parties

Hughes, David — University of British Columbia; *address*: 47 East 22nd Avenue, Vancouver, BC, V5V 1T3, Canada; *email*: davhug@hotmail. com; *research interests*: political theory and philosophy, comparative politics

Hui, Tin-Bor V — Columbia University; *address*: 24 Tai Wu Kok, Tui Min Hoi, Sai Kung, Hong Kong; *email*: TVH2@columbia.edu; *research interests*: international relations, comparative politics, development politics [East Asia, China, Europe]

Hunold, Christian — Drexel University; *address*: Department of History & Politics, 5010 MacAlister Hall, Drexel University, Philadelphia, PA 19104, USA; *fax*: +1-215-895 6614; *email*: hunoldc@drexel.edu; *research interests*: environmental policy, comparative politics, public administration [OECD]

Hunt, Wayne — Mount Allison University; *address*: Department of Political Science, Mount Allison University, Sackville, NB, E4L 1A7, Canada; *fax*: +1-506-364 2625; *email*: whunt@mta.ca; *research interests*: international relations, comparative politics, political theory and philosophy [North America, Western Europe]

Hurtig, Serge — International Political Science Abstracts; *address*: International Political Science Abstracts, Fondation nationale des sciences politiques, 27 rue Saint-Guillaume, 75337 Paris, Cedex 07, France; *fax*:

+33-1-4549 0149; *email*: ipsa-aisp@ sciences-po.fr; *research interests*: comparative politics, scientific information [USA, Western Europe]

Hyden, Göran S — University of Florida-Gainesville; *address*: Department of Political Science, 3324 Turlington Hall, University of Florida, Gainesville, FL 32611-7325, USA; *fax*: +1-352-392 8127; *email*: ghyden@polisci.ufl.edu; *research interests*: comparative politics, development politics, public policy [Africa, Europe, Latin America]

Hyvärinen, Matti — University of Tampere, RISS; *address*: Sotkankatu 17-19 B 34, FIN-33230 Tampere, Finland; *fax*: +358-31-215 6502; *email*: Matti.Hyvarinen@uta.fi; *research interests*: political theory and philosophy, history of political concepts, politics and the arts

Ibeanu, Okechukwu O — University of Nigeria; *address*: Department of Political Science, PO Box 3106, University of Nigeria, Nsukka, Enugu State, Nigeria; *fax*: +234-42-771198; *email*: ibeanu@cddnig.org; *research interests*: political theory and philosophy, elections and voting behaviour, political science methods [Africa]

Icduygu, Ahmet — Bilkent University; *address*: Department of Political Science, Bilkent University, 06533 Bilkent-Ankara, Turkey; *fax*: +90-312-266 4960; *email*: icduygu@bil kent.edu.tr; *research interests*: comparative politics, area studies, ideology politics

Ido, Masanobu — Ibaraki University; *address*: 2-4-18-601 Mita, Minato-ku, Tokyo 108, Japan; *fax*: +81-3-3451 4609; *email*: ed5m-id@asahi-net.or. jp; *research interests*: comparative politics [Italy, Japan]

Igarashi, Takeshi — University of Tokyo; *address*: 7-3-1 Hongo, Bunkyo-ku, Tokyo 113-0033, Japan; *fax*: +81-3-5841 3239; *email*: igarashi@j.u-tokyo.ac.jp; *research interests*: central government, public policy, international relations [USA]

Ignazi, Piero — Universita della Calabria; *address*: Via Ca' Selvatica 1, 40123 Bologna, Italy; *fax*: +39-51-239 548; *email*: ignazi@planet.it; *research interests*: political parties, comparative politics [Western Europe]

Iida, Fumio — Kobe University; *address*: c/o Faculty of Law, Kobe University, Rokkodai, Nada, Kobe 657-8501, Japan; *fax*: +81-78-803 6735; *email*: fumoiida@rokkodai.kobe-u.ac.jp; *research interests*: political theory and philosophy, women and politics, political science methods [USA, Europe, Japan]

Ikeda, Ken'ichi — University of Tokyo; *address*: 2-10-14 Hiroo, Shibuya-ku, Tokyo, 150, Japan; *fax*: +81-3-3815 6673; *email*: ikeken@l.u-tokyo.ac.jp; *research interests*: elections and voting behaviour, comparative politics [Japan, USA, UK, Germany]

Im, Hyug Baeg — Korea University; *address*: Olympic Sunsoochon, Apt #217-504, Songpa-ku, Seoul, Korea; *fax*: +82-2-923 4661; *email*: hyugim@kuccnx.korea.ac.kr; *research interests*: political theory and philosophy, comparative politics, area studies [East Asia]

Inoguchi, Takashi — University of Tokyo; *address*: Institute of Oriental Culture, University of Tokyo, 7-3-1-Hongo, Bunkyo-ku, Tokyo 113-0033, Japan; *fax*: +81-3-5684 5197; *email*: inoguchi@ioc.u-tokyo.ac.jp; *research interests*: political theory and philosophy, comparative politics, international relations

Ippolito, Dennis S — Southern Methodist University; *address*: Department of Political Science, Southern Methodist University, Dallas, TX 75275-0117, USA; *fax*: +1-214-768 3469; *email*: ippolito@mail.smu.edu

Irwin, Galen — Leiden University; *address*: PO Box 9555, Department of Political Science, Leiden University, 2300 RB Leiden, Netherlands; *fax*: +31-71-527 3815; *email*: galen_irwin@hotmail.com; *research interests*: elections and voting behaviour, comparative politics, political science methods [Europe, America]

Ishida, Atsushi — Tokyo Metropolitan University; *address*: Faculty of Law, Tokyo Metropolitan University, 1-1 Minami-Ohsawa, Hachioji-shi, Tokyo 192-0397, Japan; *fax*: +81-42-677 2260; *email*: aishida@bcomp.metro-u.ac.jp; *research interests*: international relations

Ito, Youichi — Keio University at Shonan Fujisawa; *address*: 253-0054 Chigasaki-shi, Higashikaigan, Minami 2-7-17, Japan; *fax*: +81-446-475 041; *email*: ito3045@sfc.keio.ac.jp; *research interests*: influence of mass media on policy making and decisions

Iwasaki, Masahiro — Kyorin University; *address*: Faculty of Social Sciences, Kyorin University, 476 Miyashita-cho, Hachioji, Tokyo 192-8508, Japan; *fax*: +81-42-691 5899; *email*: miwasaki@msn.com; *research interests*: political parties, comparative politics, development politics [Japan, Europe]

Jacek, Henry — McMaster University; *address*: Department of Political Science, McMaster University, 1280 Main Street West, Hamilton, ON, L8S 4M4, Canada; *fax*: +1-905-527 3071; *email*: jacekh@mcmaster.ca; *research interests*: elections and voting behaviour, public policy, comparative politics [OECD]

Jackson, Donald W — Texas Christian University; *address*: Department of Political Science, Texas Christian University, TCU Box 297021, Fort Worth, TX 76129, USA; *fax*: +1-817-257 7397; *email*: d.w.jackson@tcu.edu; *research interests*: political executives, international law, comparative judicial parties

Jacobs, Jörg — Frankfurter Institut für

Transformationsstudien; *address:* Europa Universität-Viadrima, Frankfurter Institut für Transformationsstudien, Postfach 1786, D-15207 Frankfurt (Ode), Germany; *fax:* +49-335-553 4807; *email:* jacobs@euv-frankfurt-o.de; *research interests:* elections and voting behaviour, comparative politics, political science methods [Central and Eastern Europe, EU]

Jacobson, Harold K — University of Michigan; *address:* Center for Political Studies, ISR, University of Michigan, Ann Arbor, MI 48106-1248, USA; *fax:* +1-734-764 3341; *email:* hkj@umich.edu; *research interests:* international relations, international law, international organisations

Jaime, Oscar — Universidad de Burgos; *address:* C/ Pradoluengo 11, 1:-Izq, 09001 Burgos, Spain; *fax:* +34-94-725 8702; *email:* ojaime@ubu.es; *research interests:* public policy, political parties

Jain, Purnendra C — University of Adelaide; *address:* Centre for Asian Studies, University of Adelaide, Adelaide, SA 5005, Australia; *fax:* +61-8-303 4388; *email:* purnendra. jain@adelaide.edu.au; *research interests:* area studies, international relations, public policy [Japan, Asia Pacific]

Jain, Randhir B — University of Delhi; *address:* 102 DDA Mukherji Apartments, East of Mukherji Nagar, Delhi - 110009, India; *fax:* +91-11-765 4794; *email:* rbjain@ndf.vsnl.net. in; *research interests:* comparative politics, public administration, legislatures [North America, South Asia, Germany, UK]

Jain, Sharda — Kalindi College, University of Delhi; *address:* S-U/77, Pitampura, Delhi - 110034, India; *fax:* +91-11-723 5150; *email:* jainsh arda@hotmail.com; *research interests:* political theory and philosophy, international relations, women and

politics [Asia, North America, Europe]

Jakobsen, Uffe — University of Copenhagen; *address:* Institute of Copenhagen, University of Political Science, University of Copenhagen, Rosenborggade 15, DK-1130 Copenhagen, Denmark; *fax:* +45-3532 3399; *email:* UJ@ifs.ku.dk; *research interests:* political theory and philosophy, comparative politics, political science methods [Baltic Sea region]

James, Carolyn — Iowa State University; *address:* IITAP, 108 Office and Lab Link, Iowa State University, Ames, IA 50011-3160, USA; *fax:* +1-515-294 1003; *email:* cjames@iastate. edu; *research interests:* international relations, comparative politics, civil-military relations [Middle East]

James, Patrick — Iowa State University; *address:* Department of Political Science, Iowa State University, 521 Ross Hall, Ames, IA 50011-1204, USA; *fax:* +1-515-294 1003; *email:* pjames@iastate.edu; *research interests:* international relations, comparative politics, political science methods [Canada]

Jancar-Webster, Barbara — State University of New York Central Administration; *address:* 282 Atateka Drive, Chestertown, NY 12817, USA; *fax:* +1-518-494 3036; *email:* bjancar@brockport.edu; *research interests:* comparative politics, area studies, comparative environmental politics

Janda, Kenneth — Northwestern University; *address:* Department of Political Science, Northwestern University, 601 University Place, Evanston, IL 60208, USA; *fax:* +1-847-491 2634; *email:* k-janda@north western.edu; *research interests:* political parties, comparative politics, elections and voting behaviour

Jang, Dong-Jin — Yonsei University; *address:* Department of Political Science and Diplomacy, Yonsei University, Seoul 120-749, Korea; *fax*: +82-2-393 7642; *email*: jang@bubble. yonsei.ac.kr; *research interests*: political theory and philosophy

Jaquette, Jane — Occidental College; *address*: 1343 Luna Vista, Pacific Palisades, CA 90272, USA; *email*: jsjaquet@oxy.edu; *research interests*: comparative politics, women and politics, international relations [Latin America]

Jasiewicz, Krzysztof — Washington & Lee University; *address*: Department of Sociology, Washington & Lee University, Lexington, VA 24450-0303, USA; *fax*: +1-540-463 8498; *email*: jasiewiczk@wlu.edu; *research interests*: elections and voting behaviour, area studies [Poland, Europe]

Jee, Byung-Moon — Chonnam National University; *address*: Department of Political Science, Chonnam National University, 300 Yong-bong Don, Kwang Ju, Seoul, Korea; *fax*: +82-62-530 0051; *email*: bmjee@ chonnam.ac.kr; *research interests*: political parties, elections and voting behaviour, local and urban politics

Jefferson, Kurt W — Westminster College; *address*: Department of Political Science, Westminster College, Fulton, MO 6251-1299, USA; *fax*: +1-573-592 5291; *email*: jefferk@jaynet. wcmo.edu; *research interests*: comparative politics, area studies, political parties [Europe]

Jenkins, Robert — Birbeck College; *address*: 107 Beaconsfield Villas, Brighton BN1 6HF, UK; *fax*: +44-207-631 6787; *email*: rjenksin@bea consfield.u-net.com; *research interests*: comparative politics, international relations, area studies [India, South Africa, Uganda]

Jentleson, Bruce W — Duke University; *address*: Terry Sanford Institute of Public Policy, Duke University, Box 90239, Durham, NC 27708-

0239, USA; *fax*: +1-919-681 8288; *email*: bwj@pps.duke.edu; *research interests*: area studies, international relations [Middle East, Europe]

Jinadu, L Adele — Lagos State University; *address*: 262B Corporation Drive, LSDPC Dolphin Estate, Osborne Road, Ikoyi-Lagos, Nigeria; *fax*: +234-1-269 4413; *email*: ashoka@rel.nig.com; *research interests*: political theory, comparative politics, federalism [Africa, third world, Europe, USA]

Jo, Yukiko — Bunka Women's University; *address*: 30-82 Gakuen Higashi-cho, Kodaira-shi, Tokyo 187-0043, Japan; *fax*: +81-42-346 9863; *email*: yjo@tky.3web.ne.jp; *research interests*: international relations, comparative politics, area studies [Canada]

Johansson, Karl Magnus — University College of Southern Stockholm; *address*: University College of Southern Stockholm, PO Box 4101, SE-141 04 Huddinge, Sweden; *fax*: +46-8-5858 8010; *email*: karl.mag nus.johansson@sh.se; *research interests*: European integration, international relations, political parties [Europe]

John, Peter — Birbeck College; *address*: School of Politics and Sociology, Birkbeck College, Malet Street, London WC1E 7HX, UK; *fax*: +44-207-631 6787; *email*: p.john@pol-soc. bbk.ac.uk; *research interests*: local and urban politics, public policy, political science methods [UK]

Johnston, Michael — Colgate University; *address*: Department of Political Science, Colgate University, Hamilton, NY 13346, USA; *fax*: +1-315-228 7883; *email*: mjohnston@mail. colgate.edu; *research interests*: comparative politics, public policy, development politics

Jonasdottir, Anna G — Örebro University; *address*: Borgallén 2, S-702 17 Örebro, Sweden; *fax*: +46-19-303 484; *email*: anna.jonasdottir@sam.

oru.se; *research interests*: political theory and philosophy, women and politics

Jones, GW — London School of Economics; *address*: Department of Government, London School of Economics, Houghton Street, London WC2A 2AE, UK; *fax*: +44-207-831 1707; *email*: g.w.jones@lse.ac.uk; *research interests*: central government, public administration, local and urban politics [Europe, USA]

Jones, Mark P — Michigan State University-East Lansing; *address*: Department of Political Science, Michigan State University, 303 S Kedzie, East Lansing, MI 48824-1032, USA; *fax*: +1-517-432 1091; *email*: mark.jones@ssc.msu.edu; *research interests*: elections and voting behaviour, legislatures, women and politics [Latin America]

Jönsson, Christer — University of Lund; *address*: Department of Political Science, Box 52, S-221 00 Lund, Sweden; *fax*: +46-46-222 4006; *email*: christer.jonsson@svet.lu.se; *research interests*: international relations, comparative politics [EU]

Jorrat, Jorge Raul — Universidad de Buenos Aires; *address*: Alsina 711, Apto 10, Buenos Aires 1087, Argentina; *email*: jorrat@mail.retina.ar; *research interests*: elections and voting behaviour, political parties

Journes, Claude R — Université Lyon 2; *address*: 4 Avenue Berthelot, 69007 Lyon, France; *fax*: +33-4-7869 7093; *email*: claude.journes@univ-lyon2.fr; *research interests*: comparative politics, public administration, policing in western democracies [western democracies]

Joye, Dominique — SIDOS; *address*: SIDOS, 13 ruelle Vaucher, 2000 Neuchâtel, Switzerland; *fax*: +41-32-721 2074; *email*: dominique.joye@sidos.unine.ch; *research interests*: local and urban politics, elections and voting behaviour, political science methods [Europe]

Jung, Tai-hyun — Chosun University; *address*: Anam Apt 101-1013, 676-1 Hak-dong, Dong-gu, Gwang-ju 501-190, Republic of Korea; *research interests*: area studies, international relations, international law [Japan]

Jung, Yong-duck — Seoul National University; *address*: Graduate School of Public Administration, Seoul National University, Seoul 151-742, Korea; *fax*: +82-2-882 3998; *email*: ydjung@plaza.snu.ac.kr; *research interests*: public administration, public policy, political executives [East Asia]

Jupp, James — Australian National University; *address*: CIMS Building 70, Australian National University, Canberra, ACT 0200, Australia; *fax*: +61-2-6249 0771; *email*: jupp@coombs.anu.edu.au; *research interests*: immigration and ethnicity, comparative politics, political parties [Australia]

Kaase, Max — WZB; *address*: Wissenschaftszentrum Berlin für Sozialforschung, Reichpietschufer 50, 10785 Berlin, Germany; *fax*: +49-30-2549 1318; *email*: maka@medea.wz-berlin.de; *research interests*: comparative politics, elections and voting behaviour, political science methods [Europe, North America]

Kabashima, Ikuo — University of Tokyo; *address*: Faculty of Law, University of Tokyo, Hongo 7-3-1, Bunkyo-ku 113-0033, Japan; *fax*: +81-3-5841 3174; *email*: kabashim@j.u-tokyo.ac.jp; *research interests*: elections and voting behaviour, political parties

Kacowicz, Arie M — The Hebrew University; *address*: Department of International Relations, The Hebrew University, Mount Scopus, Jerusalem 91905, Israel; *fax*: +972-2-588 2989; *email*: mskaco@mscc.huji.ac.il; *research interests*: international relations theories, international ethics, area studies, comparative politics [Latin America]

Kanet, Roger E — University of Miami; *address*: School of International Studies, University of Miami, PO Box 248123, Coral Gables, FL 33124-3010, USA; *fax*: +1-305-284 6883; *email*: rkanet@sis.miami.edu; *research interests*: area studies, international relations, comparative politics [Russia, Central and Eastern Europe]

Kang, Jong Il — Institute of Korean Peninsula Neutralization; *address*: 1405 10-Dong, Kyongnam Apt, Kaepo-dong, Kangnam-gu, Seoul, 135-240, Korea; *fax*: +82-2-739 2104; *email*: jungrip@unitel.co.kr; *research interests*: international relations [South and North Korea, USA]

Kang, Myung-Goo — Ajou University; *address*: College of Social Sciences, Wonchon Dong, Paldal Ku, Suwon, Kyung-gi Do 442-749, Republic of Korea; *fax*: +82-331-219 2195; *email*: mgkmgk@madang.ajou.ac.kr; *research interests*: local and urban politics, development politics, comparative politics [Latin America, Korea]

Kang, Sung-Hack — Korea University; *address*: Department of Political Science, Korea University, 1 Anam-dong, Seoul 136-701, Korea; *fax*: +82-2-929 9164; *research interests*: political theory and philosophy, area studies, international relations [Northeast Asia]

Kapsch, Stefan — Reed College; *address*: Reed College, Portland, OR 97202-8199, USA; *fax*: +1-503-777 7776; *email*: stefan.kapsch@reed.edu; *research interests*: public policy, judicial systems and behaviour [Yugoslavia]

Karal, H Ibrahim — Middle East Technical University, Ankara (retired); *address*: Nergis Sokak 12-9, Cankaya, 06680 Ankara, Turkey; *research interests*: political theory and philosophy, comparative politics, political sociology [Turkey]

Karklins, Rasma — University of Illinois-Chicago; *address*: Department of Political Science, University of Illinois, 1007 W Harrison, Chicago, IL 60608, USA; *fax*: +1-312-413 0440; *email*: karklins@uic.edu; *research interests*: comparative politics, area studies, ethnopolitics [Baltic States, former USSR]

Karvonen, Lauri A — Åbo Akademi; *address*: Department of Political Science, Åbo Akademi, FIN-20500, Åbo, Finland; *fax*: +358-2-215 4585; *email*: lauri.karvonen@abo.fi; *research interests*: comparative politics, political parties, central government

Kashikar, Mohan S — Nagpur University; *address*: 113, Park Corner, Shivaji Nagar, Nagpur-440010, India; *email*: mohan_vinaya@hotmail.com; *research interests*: international relations, area studies, public policy [South Asia, Europe, South East Asia]

Kasper, WS — *address*: 466 Campus View Drive, Riverside, CA 92507, USA; *email*: wkasper@msn.com; *research interests*: comparative politics, political science methods, political theory and philosophy [Western Europe, Germany]

Kato, Junko — University of Tokyo; *address*: 3-8-1 Komaba, Meguro, Tokyo 153-8902, Japan; *fax*: +81-3-5454 4339; *email*: katoj@waka.c.u-tokyo.ac.jp; *research interests*: comparative politics, public policy, political science methods [North America, Western Europe, Japan]

Kato, Tetsuro — Hitotsubashi University; *address*: Graduate School of Social Sciences, Hitotsubashi University, 2-1, NAKA Kunitachi, Tokyo 186-8601, Japan; *fax*: +81-42-327 9262; *email*: cs00231@srv.cc.hit-u.ac.jp; *research interests*: political theory and philosophy, comparative politics, central government [Europe, USA, Japan]

Katz, Ellis — Center for the Study of Federalism; *address*: 1084 Sherman Avenue, Huntingdon Valley, PA

19006, USA; *fax*: +1-215-663 1062; *email*: elliskatz@home.com

Kaufer-Barbe, Pablo — Universidad de Buenos Aires; *address*: Calle Arcos 1865, 1428 Buenos Aires, Argentina; *fax*: +54-11-372 7732; *email*: kbiv@satlink.com; *research interests*: political corruption, financing of political parties, international relations

Kaufmann, Eric — University of Southampton; *address*: 156 Heythorp Street, London, UK; *fax*: +44-2380-593 276; *email*: epk@socsci.soton.ac.uk; *research interests*: comparative politics, international relations, area studies [Northern Ireland, Canada, USA]

Kazancigil, Ali — UNESCO; *address*: 22, Rue Edouard Manet, 78370 Plaisir, France; *fax*: +33-1-4568 5724; *email*: a.kazancigil@unesco.org; *research interests*: comparative politics, international relations, political theory and philosophy [Europe, Turkey]

Kazemi, Farhad — New York University; *address*: Department of Politics, New York University, New York, NY 10003, USA; *fax*: +1-212-995 4184; *email*: farhad.kazemi@nyu.edu; *research interests*: comparative politics, area studies, international relations [Middle East]

Keck, Otto — Universität Potsdam; *address*: Universität Potsdam, Wirtschafts-und Sozialwissenschaftliche Fakultät, Postfach 90 03 27, D-14439 Potsdam, Germany; *fax*: +49-331-977 4673; *email*: keck@rz.uni-potsdam.de; *research interests*: international relations, political theory and philosophy, public policy

Kellow, Aynsley — University of Tasmania; *address*: School of Government, University of Tasmania, Box 252-22, Hobart 7001, Australia; *fax*: +61-3-6226 2895; *email*: akellow@utas.edu.au; *research interests*: public policy, pressure groups, international relations

Kelly, Rita Mae — University of Texas-Dallas; *address*: School of Social Sciences, GR3.104, University of Texas at Dallas, Richardson, TX 75083, USA; *fax*: +1-972-883 6234; *email*: rmkelly@utdallas.edu; *research interests*: women and politics, public administration, political executives [USA, NAFTA, EU, Asia]

Keman, Hans — Vrije Universiteit; *address*: Department of Political Science, Vrije Universiteit, De Bodelaan 1081 C, 1081 HV Amsterdam, Netherlands; *fax*: +31-20-444 6820; *email*: keman@scw.vu.nl; *research interests*: comparative politics, political executives, public policy [OECD-Europe]

Kemmet, Lynndee — Levy Economics Institute; *address*: Levy Economics Institute, Bard College, Blithewood, Annadale-on-Hudson, NY 1250, USA; *fax*: +1-914-758 1149; *email*: kemmet@levy.org; *research interests*: local and urban politics, comparative politics, federalism

Kemp, Donna R — California State University-Chico; *address*: Department of Political Science, California State University, Chico, CA 95929-0455, USA; *fax*: +1-530-898 5301; *email*: dkemp@csuchico.edu; *research interests*: public administration, public policy [Baltic, South Pacific]

Kevenhörster, Paul — Universität Münster; *address*: Goethestr 16, D-48341 Altenberge, Germany; *fax*: +49-251-832 4372; *email*: kevenho@Uni-Muenster.de; *research interests*: comparative politics, area studies, public policy [Japan]

Keymen, Fuat — Bilkent University; *address*: Department of Poltical Science, Bilkent University, 06533 Ankara, Turkey; *fax*: +90-312-266 4960; *research interests*: comparative politics, international relations, globalisation

Khaddar, M Moncef — *address*: 10 Wendell Street, North Providence,

RI 02911, USA; *fax*: +90-392-365 2028; *email*: moncef@benet.de.emu. edu.tr; *research interests*: political theory, comparative politics, human rights [North Africa, Middle East]

Khadiagala, Gilbert — Johns Hopkins University-SAIS; *address*: 1001 N Randolph Street, Apt no 502, Arlington, VA 22201, USA; *fax*: +1-202-663 5683; *email*: gkhadiag@mail. jhuwash.jhu.edu; *research interests*: international relations, comparative politics, development politics [Africa]

Khan, Haroan A — Henderson State University; *address*: HSU Box 7864, Arkadelphia, AR 71923, USA; *fax*: +1-870-230 5144; *email*: khanh@holly.hsu.edu; *research interests*: political executives [Bangladesh]

Khan, Zillur — University of Wisconsin-Oshkosh; *address*: Department of Political Science, University of Wisconsin, Oshkosh, WI 54901, USA; *fax*: +1-920-424 0739; *email*: Khan@uwosh.edu; *research interests*: development and politics, political executives, public administration

Khare, Brij B — California State University at San Bernardino; *address*: Department of Political Science, California State University, 5500 University Parkway, San Bernardino, CA 92407, USA; *fax*: +1-909-880 7081; *email*: bkhare@csusb. edu; *research interests*: comparative politics, development politics, area studies [Asia]

Khator, Renu — University of South Florida; *address*: Government & International Affairs, University of South Florida, Tampa, FL 33620-8100, USA; *fax*: +1-813-974 2184; *email*: khator@chuma1.cas.usf.edu; *research interests*: comparative politics, public policy, environmental policy [Asia, Brazil]

Khoshkish, A — *address*: 186 Riverside Drive, New York, NY 10024, USA; *fax*: +1-212-721 3149; *email*: ak@akim.com; *research interests*: inter-

national political economy, international relations, international law

Kienle, Eberhard — School of Oriental and African Studies; *address*: SOAS, Department of Politics, Thornhaugh Street, London WC1H 0XG, UK; *fax*: +44-207-898 4759; *email*: ek@soas.ac. uk; *research interests*: development and politics, comparative politics, international relations, international political economy [Middle East, Mediterranean]

Kihm, Hong-Chul — Hanyang University; *address*: 42-46 6GA Bomoun-Dong, Seongbouk-ku, Seoul 136-086, Korea; *research interests*: international relations, international law, war and peace

Kilgour, D Marc — Wilfrid Laurier University; *address*: Department of Mathematics, Wilfrid Laurier University, Waterloo, ON, N2L 3C5, Canada; *fax*: +1-519-886 5057; *email*: mkilgour@wlu.ca; *research interests*: international relations, elections and voting behaviour

Kili, Suna — Bogazici University; *address*: Bogazici University, Bebek 80815, Istanbul, Turkey; *fax*: +90-212-262 3635; *email*: kili@boun.edu. tr; *research interests*: political theory, political culture, the military

Kim, Cheon Bong — Jean Ju University; *address*: 53-3 Kyung Won Dong 2 Ka, Wan Sanku Jeon Ju, 560-020, Republic of Korea; *fax*: +82-63-286 8887; *email*: cbk@jeondrs.jeonju.ac. kr; *research interests*: central government, public administration [developed countries, USA]

Kim, Dalchoong — The Sejong Institute; *address*: Department of Political Science, Yonsei University, 134 Shinchon-dong, Seodaemoon-ku, Seoul, Korea; *fax*: +82-2-741 4567; *email*: dkim@sejong.org; *research interests*: international relations [East Asia]

Kim, Hee Min — Florida State University; *address*: Department of Political Science, Florida State University, Tallahassee, FL 32306-2230, USA; *fax*: +1-850-644 1367; *email*: hkim@garnet.acns.fsu.edu; *research interests*: elections and voting behaviour, comparative politics, political parties [western democracies, Northeast Asia]

Kim, Hong Woo—Seoul National University; *address*: Department of Politics, Seoul National University, Seoul 151-742, Korea; *fax*: +82-2-887 4375; *email*: wjdgns1@snu.ac.kr; *research interests*: political theory and philosophy, comparative politics, area studies

Kim, Jong-Myung—Hyo Sung Catholic University; *address*: 103-702 Young Nam Apt, Gi San Dong, Tae Gu, Republic of Korea; *fax*: +82-53-850 3302; *email*: jmkim1@cuth.cat aegu.ac.kr; *research interests*: area studies, international relations, public administration [Russia]

Kim, Joonho—Tokyo International University; *address*: Yamadai Mansion 408, Minamidai 3-2-10, Kawagoe, Saitama, Japan; *email*: joonho@tiu.ac.jp; *research interests*: international relations, political theory and philosophy, globalism [global, Europe]

Kim, Pan Suk—Yonsei University; *address*: Department of Public Administration, Yonsei University, Wonjoo, Kangwon-do 220-710, Republic of Korea; *fax*: +82-371-766 2341; *email*: pankim@dragon.yonsei.ac.kr; *research interests*: public administration, public policy, comparative politics

Kim, Soung Chul—Sejong Institute; *address*: 25-503 Walkerhill Apt, Kwangjang-dong, Kwangjin-ku, Seoul, Korea; *fax*: +82-342-723 6508; *email*: soung@sejong.org; *research interests*: comparative politics, international relations, political economy [Japan, Korea, China]

Kim, Sung-Han—Institute of Foreign Affairs & National Security; *address*: 1376-2 Socho 2-Dong, Socho-Gu,

Seoul 137-072, Korea; *fax*: +82-2-575 5245; *email*: ksunghan@chollian.net; *research interests*: international relations, area studies, comparative politics [USA]

Kim, Sunhyuk—University of Southern California; *address*: Department of Political Science, University of Southern California, Los Angeles, CA 90089-0044, USA; *fax*: +1-213-740 8893; *email*: sunhyukk@usc.edu; *research interests*: comparative politics, international relations, area studies [East Asia, Korea]

Kincaid, John—Lafayette College; *address*: Meyner Center for State & Local Government, 002 Kirby Hall of Civil Rights, Lafayette College, Easton, PA 18042-1785, USA; *fax*: +1-610-559 4048; *email*: meynerc@la fayette.edu; *research interests*: public administration, local and urban politics, federalism [USA]

King, Preston—Lancaster University; *address*: Department of Politics & International Relations, Cartmel College, Lancaster University, Lancaster LA1 4YL, UK; *fax*: +44-1524-594 238; *email*: p.king@lancaster.ac.uk; *research interests*: political theory and philosophy, comparative politics, development politics [Africa, EU, USA]

Kirchner Baliu, Mercè—EIPA Antenna Catalunya; *address*: Pau Claris 109, 3-2, 08009 Barcelona, Spain; *fax*: +34-93-402 4063; *email*: m.kirchner@eipa-ecr.com; *research interests*: international relations, comparative politics, area studies [Europe, Southeast Asia]

Kiss, Rosemary—University of Melbourne; *address*: Centre for Public Policy, University of Melbourne, 234 Queensberry Street, Carlton, Victoria 3053, Australia; *email*: r.kiss@politics.unimelb.edu.au; *research interests*: local and urban politics, public policy, comparative politics

Kissler, Leo—Universität Marburg; *address*: Tückingstr 28, D-58135

Hagen, Germany; *fax*: +49-6421-282 6642; *email*: kissler@mailer.uni-marburg.de; *research interests*: comparative politics, public administration, local and urban politics
Kitamaru, Kaoruko — United Nations, Iraq; *address*: 11 Hanazono Enjyoji-cho, Ukyo-ku, Kyoto 616-8027, Japan; *fax*: +81-75-463 7722; *email*: rkitamar@mba.sphere.ne.jp; *research interests*: international relations [Japan]
Kleinberg, Raymonde — University of North Carolina-Wilmington; *address*: Department of Political Science, University of North Carolina, 601 South College Road, Willmington, NC 28403, USA; *fax*: +1-910-962 3284; *email*: kleinberg@uncwil.edu; *research interests*: development politics, international relations, international law [Latin America, Mexico, developing world]
Klesner, Joseph L — Kenyon College; *address*: 102 W Woodside Drive, Gambier, OH 43022, USA; *fax*: +1-740-427 5306; *email*: klesner@kenyon.edu; *research interests*: comparative politics, elections and voting behaviour, area studies [Latin America]
Klingemann, Hans-Dieter — WZB; *address*: Wissenschaftszentrum Berlin für Sozialforschung, Berlin, Reichpietschufer 50, D-10785 Berlin, Germany; *fax*: +49-30-2549 1345; *email*: klingem@medea.wz-berlin.de; *research interests*: comparative politics, elections and voting behaviour, political parties
Klöti, Ulrich — University of Zürich; *address*: University of Zürich, Institut für Politikwissenschaft, Karl-Schmid-Str 4, CH 8006 Zürich, Switzerland; *fax*: +41-1-634 4925; *email*: ukloeti@pwi.unizh.ch; *research interests*: government, federalism, public policy [Europe]
Knight, Kelvin — University of North London; *address*: 67 Dunlace Road,

London E5 0NF, UK; *email*: k.knight@unl.ac.uk; *research interests*: political theory and philosophy
Kobayashi, Yoshiaki — Keio University; *address*: 1-12-9 Todoroki, Setagaya-ku, Tokyo 158-0082, Japan; *fax*: +81-3-3705 4530; *email*: cpskobayasi@msn.com; *research interests*: elections and voting behaviour, political science methods, comparative politics
Koen, Carla Irene — University of Tilburg; *address*: Department of Organisation & Strategy, Tilburg University, Warandelaan 2, PO Box 30 153, 5000 LE, Netherlands; *fax*: +31-13-466 2875; *email*: c.i.koen@kub.nl; *research interests*: comparative political economy, comparative management [Germany, Japan]
Kogure, Kentaro — Tokai University; *address*: 1-20-11 A201 Minami-Ogikubo, Suginami-ku, Tokyo 167-0052, Japan; *email*: kogure@mua.biglobe.ne.jp; *research interests*: political parties, comparative politics, area studies [Canada]
Kohler-Koch, Beate — Universität Mannheim; *address*: Jean Monnet Chair of European Integration, University of Mannheim, D-68131 Mannheim, Germany; *fax*: +49-621-181 2072; *email*: bkohler@rumms.uni-mannheim.de; *research interests*: international relations, governance [Europe, OECD]
Koji, Junichiro — McGill University; *address*: 3647 rue University #13, Montréal, Quèbec, H3A 2B3, Canada; *email*: junichiro_koji@hotmail.com; *research interests*: comparative politics, area studies, international relations [Quebec, Canada]
Kolodziej, Edward A — University of Illinois-Urbana-Champaign; *address*: 711 West University Avenue, Champaign, Illinois, IL 61820, USA; *email*: edkoloj@uiuc.edu; *research interests*: global governance, international security [Europe]
Korsmo, Fae — University of Alaska;

address: National Science Foudation, University of Alaska, 4201 Wilson Boulevard, Arlington, VA 22230, USA; *fax*: +1-703-306 0648; *email*: fkorsmo@nsf.gov; *research interests*: comparative politics, political executives [Artic, Canada, Sweden, Norway]

Kotze, Dirk — University of South Africa; *address*: Department of Political Sciences, University of South Africa, PO Box 392, Unisa, 0003, South Africa; *fax*: +27-12-429 3221; *email*: kotzedj@unisa.ac.za; *research interests*: development and politics, public policy, conflict resolution [Southern and South Africa]

Kotzé, Hennie — University of Stellenbosch; *address*: Department of Political Science, University of Stellenbosch, Private Bag XI, 7602 Stellenbosch, South Africa; *fax*: +27-21-808 4336; *email*: hjk@akad.sun.ac.za; *research interests*: legislatures, political parties, public policy [Africa]

Kowalik, Tadeusz — Polish Academy of Sciences; *address*: Al Niedpodleglosci 161/13, 02-555 Warszawa, Poland; *fax*: +48-22-629 5897; *email*: tkowalikdws@iz.edu.pl; *research interests*: comparative economics and politics, public policy, development politics [North America, Europe]

Krasteva, Anna — New Bulgarian University; *address*: Department of Political Science, New Bulgarian University, 21 Montevideo, 1635 Sofia, Bulgaria; *fax*: +359-2-279 874; *email*: akrasteva@diana.nbu.bg; *research interests*: ethnicity and politics, political discourse, post-communist transition

Krisch, Henry — University of Connecticut; *address*: Department of Political Science, U-24, University of Connecticut, Storrs, CT 06269-1024, USA; *fax*: +1-860-486 3347; *email*: henry.2.krisch@uconn.edu; *research interests*: political parties, comparative politics, area studies [Russia, Germany]

Kristof, Ladis KD — Portland State University; *address*: 23050 NW Roosevelt Drive, Yamhill, OR 97148, USA; *fax*: +1-503-662 4273; *email*: kristofj@pdx.edu; *research interests*: political theory and philosophy, international relations, geopolitics [East Europe, Eurasia]

Kuan, Hsin-Chi — Chinese University of Hong Kong; *address*: Department of Government & Public Administration, Chinese University of Hong Kong, Shatin, NT, Hong Kong; *fax*: +852-2603 5229; *email*: hckuan@cuhk.edu.hk; *research interests*: comparative politics, international politics [Hong Kong, China, Asia]

Kuersten, Ashlyn — Western Michigan University; *address*: Department of Political Science, 1201 Oliver Street, Kalamazoo, MI 49008, USA; *fax*: +1-616-387 3999; *email*: kuersten@wmich.edu; *research interests*: comparative judicial studies [USA, Germany]

Kuhn, Katja — Schiller International University; *address*: Mühlenweg 61, 68549 Ihvesheim, Germany; *email*: kuhn@rumms.uni-mannheim.de; *research interests*: comparative politics, political parties, international relations [EU, ECE]

Kuhnle, Stein — University of Bergen; *address*: Department of Comparative Politics, University of Bergen, Christiesgt 15, N-5007 Bergen, Norway; *fax*: +47-55-589 425; *email*: stein.kuhnle@isp.uib.no; *research interests*: comparative politics, public policy [Scandanavia, Europe, West and Southeast Asia]

Kumar, Devendra — Rajdhani College, University of Delhi; *address*: ND-68 Pitampura, Delhi - 110034, India; *fax*: +91-11-710 3932; *email*: drdkumar@ftnetwork.com; *research interests*: public policy, international business [India]

Kuwabara, Itoko — Japanese Political Science Association; *address*: 5-1-201

Takamori, Isehara, Kanagawa, 259-1114, Japan; *fax*: +81-463-949 122; *research interests*: political theory and philosophy, women and politics

Kwak, Jin-Young—Ewha Women's University; *address*: 85-7 Yunhee Dong, Suhdaemun-ku, Seoul 120-112, Korea; *fax*: +82-2-336 5183; *email*: jykwak@chollian.net; *research interests*: political parties, comparative politics, area studies [Japan, Korea, USA]

Lachapelle, Guy—Concordia University; *address*: Département de Science Politique, Université Concordia GS-333, 1455 rue Sherbrooke Ouest, Montréal QC, H3G 1M8, Canada; *fax*: +1-514-848 4072; *email*: lachape@alcor.concordia.ca; *research interests*: public policy, elections and voting behaviour, comparative politics [Quebec, Canada]

Laenen, Ria—University of Leuven, Belgium; *address*: Harriman Institute (Visiting scholar), Columbia University, 420 West 118th Street, New York, NY 10027, USA; *email*: ria.laene@hotbot.com; *research interests*: area studies, international relations [Russia, CIS]

Laferriere, Eric—John Abbott College; *address*: 67 Fairwood Avenue, Pointe-Claire, QC H9R 5R9, Canada; *email*: eric@mail.johnabbott.qc.ca; *research interests*: international relations, political theory and philosophy, ecological thought

Lafferty, William M—University of Olso; *address*: ProSus/SUM, Post Box 1116 Blindern, University of Oslo, 0317 Oslo, Norway; *fax*: +47-22-858 920; *email*: william.lafferty@prosus.uio.no; *research interests*: environmental development, policy implementation, democratic governance [Western Europe]

Lahneman, William—University of Maryland; *address*: 6283 McKendree Road, Dunkirk, MD 20754, USA; *fax*: +1-301-403 8107; *email*: WL74@ umail.umd.edu; *research interests*: international relations, political theory and philosophy, public policy

Lall, Marie-Carine—New Policy Institute; *address*: Flat 833, William Goodenough House, Mecklenburgh Square, London WC1N 2AN, UK; *fax*: +44-207-219 2695; *email*: marie. lall@btinternet.com; *research interests*: international relations, area studies, development politics [India]

Lamson, Robert W—*address*: 4020 North Stuart Street, Arlington, VA 22207, USA; *fax*: +1-203-533 2167; *email*: rlamson@erols.com; *research interests*: public policy, international relations, political theory and philosophy

Lancaster, Thomas D—Emory University; *address*: Department of Political Science, Emory University, Atlanta, GA 30322, USA; *fax*: +1-404-727 4586; *email*: polstdl@emory. edu; *research interests*: comparative politics, elections and voting behaviour, legislatures [Western Europe, Spain, Germany]

Landry, Rejean—Université Laval; *address*: Département de science politique, Université Laval, Quèbec G1K 7P4, Canada; *fax*: +1-418-656 7861; *email*: rejean.landry@pol. ulaval.ca; *research interests*: public policy

Langenberg, Susan—Academie Leo Beyers voor Kunsten en Leefwetenschappen; *address*: Gelbergenstraat 54, 3471 Hoeleden-Kortenaken, Belgium; *fax*: +32-16-770 060; *email*: s.langenberg@project21.be; *research interests*: political theory and philosophy, women and politics, citizenship

Langhelle, Oluf—RF-Rogaland Research; *address*: RF- Rogaland Research, PO Box 2503 Ullandhaug, 4091 Stavanger, Norway; *fax*: +47-51-875 200; *email*: oluf.langhelle@rf. no; *research interests*: political theory and philosophy, environmental politics, development politics

Laponce, Jean — University of British Columbia, Université d'Ottawa; *address*: Department of Political Science, University of British Columbia, Vancouver 8, V6T 1W5, Canada; *fax*: +1-604-822 5540; *email*: jlaponce@interchange.ubc.ca; *research interests*: ethnicity, comparative government, political geography

Launius, Michael — Central Washington University; *address*: 1202 Vuecrest, Ellensburg, WA 98926, USA; *fax*: +1-509-963 1134; *email*: launiusm@cwu.edu; *research interests*: comparative politics, area studies, international relations [East Asia, Korea]

Lawrence, Ralph — University of Natal; *address*: Centre for Government & Policy Studies, School of Human & Social Studies, Private Bag XO1, University of Natal, Scottsville 3209, South Africa; *fax*: +27-331-260 5599; *email*: lawrencer@politics.unp.ac.za; *research interests*: area studies, development politics, citizenship education [South Africa, Brazil, Nigeria, USA]

Lawson, Kay — San Francisco State University; *address*: 389 Gravatt Drive, Berkeley, CA 94705, USA; *fax*: +1-510-883 9624; +33-3-8096 1786; *email*: klawson@sfsu.edu; *research interests*: political parties, comparative politics, pressure groups [France, USA]

Lawson, Stephanie — University of East Anglia; *address*: School of Economics and Social Studies, University of East Anglia, Norwich NR4 7TJ, UK; *fax*: +44-1603-250 434; *email*: s.lawson@uea.ac.uk; *research interests*: comparative politics, area studies, international relations [Southeast Asia]

Laycock, David — Simon Fraser University; *address*: Department of Political Science, Simon Fraser University, Burnaby, BC, V5A 1S6, Canada; *fax*: +1-604-291 4786; *email*: laycock@sfu.ca; *research interests*: political theory and philosophy, area studies, comparative studies [Canada]

Lazin, Fred — Ben Gurion University; *address*: Department of Behavioural Sciences, Ben Gurion University, Beer Sheva 84105, Israel; *fax*: +972-7-647 2932; *email*: lazin@bgumail.bgu.ac.il; *research interests*: public administration, public policy, local and urban politics [Middle East, USA, Europe]

Lazzarich, Eduardo Felix — Argentine Academy of International Affairs; *address*: Esmeralda 3422, 1605 Munro, Buenos Aires, Argentina; *fax*: +54-11-4761 5094; *email*: Dr_Lazzarich@ciudad.com.ar; *research interests*: political behaviour, territorial politics [South America]

Le Duc, Lawrence — University of Toronto; *address*: Department of Political Science, University of Toronto, 100 St George Street, Toronto, ON, M5S 3G3, Canada; *fax*: +1-416-978 5566; *email*: leduc@chass.utoronto.ca; *research interests*: comparative politics, elections and voting behaviour, political parties [North America, Western Europe]

Le Gales, Patrick — CEVIPOF; *address*: CEVIPOF (Sciences-Po/CNRS), Maison des Sciences de l'Homme, 54 Boulevard Raspail, 75006 Paris, France; *fax*: +33-1-9984 3902; *email*: legales@msh-paris.fr; *research interests*: local and urban politics, public policy, comparative politics [Western Europe]

Leca, Jean — IEP, Paris; *address*: Institut d'Etudes Politiques Paris, 27 rue Saint Guillaume, 75341 Paris Cedex 07, France; *fax*: +33-1-4422 4026; *email*: jean.leca@sciences-po.fr; *research interests*: political theory, comparative politics, public policy [Middle East, Western Europe]

Lee, In-Sung — Yonsei University;

address: 1008 Bangbae-Dong, Socho-ku, SORA Apt #Ka-806, Seoul 137-063, Korea; *fax*: +82-371-763 4324; *email*: inslee@dragon.yonsei.ac.kr; *research interests*: comparative politics, area studies, development politics [Russia, post-communist states]

Lee, Song-Hee — Korea National Defense University; *address*: Eun Pyong-Ku, Susaek-Dong, Seoul 122-090, Korea; *fax*: +82-2-309 9774; *email*: shlee@kndu.ac.kr; *research interests*: international relations, area studies, security and defence affairs [Russia, CIS states, Northeast Asia]

Lee, Yong Sun — Kookmin University; *address*: 2-1 BANPO 2-dong, apt 10-105, Seochogu, Seoul 137-042, Republic of Korea; *fax*: +82-2-537 2686; *email*: infnet@kmu.kookmin.ac.kr; *research interests*: comparative politics, public policy, political theory and philosophy

Lee, Young A — Dankook University; *address*: 29 Anseo-dong, Chonan City, Dankook University, Choongnam 330-714, Republic of Korea; *fax*: +49-4171-550 1814; *email*: younglee@anseo.dankook.ac.kr; *research interests*: political theory and philosophy, area studies, women and politics

Legault, Albert — Laval University; *address*: Institut Québécois des Hautes Etudes Internationales, Pavillion Charles-de-Koninck, Québec G1K 7P4, Canada; *fax*: +1-418-656 3634; *email*: albert.legault@pol.ulaval.ca; *research interests*: international relations, area studies

Lehman-Wilzig, Sam — Bar-Ilan University; *address*: Department of Political Studies, Bar-Ilan University, 52900 Ramat Gan, Israel; *fax*: +972-3-923 4511; *email*: wilzis@mail.biu.ac.il; *research interests*: political communication, pressure groups [Middle East]

Lehning, Percy B — Erasmus University; *address*: Onstein 40, 1082 KL Amsterdam, Netherlands; *fax*: +31-20-644 8533; *email*: lehning@fsw.eur.nl; *research interests*: political theory and philosophy, public administration, public policy

Leloup, Lance — Washington State University; *address*: Department of Political Science, Washington State University, 801 Johnson Tower, Pullman, WA 99164-4880, USA; *fax*: +1-509-335 7990; *email*: leloup@wsu.edu; *research interests*: public policy, legislatures, comparative politics

Leng, Tse-Kang — National Cheng-Chi University; *address*: 64 Wan-Shou Road, Wenshan, Taipei, 116, Taiwan; *email*: tkleng@nccu.edu.tw; *research interests*: international relations, comparative politics, development politics [China, Taiwan]

Lentner, Howard H — City University of New York; *address*: PhD Program in Political Science, City University of New York Graduate School, 365 Fifth Avenue, New York, NY 10016, USA; *fax*: +1-212-387 1662; *email*: howardh.lentner@worldnet.att.net; *research interests*: international relations, area studies, political theory and philosophy [East Asia]

Leonardy, MA, Uwe — Bundestrat Secretariat; *address*: Servatisstrasse 12, D-53604 Bad Honnef, Germany; *fax*: +49-228-228 3237; *research interests*: legislatures, political parties, federalism

Leslie, Peter M — Queen's University; *address*: Political Studies Department, Queen's University, Kingston, ON, K7L 3N6, Canada; *fax*: +1-613-533 6848; *email*: lesliepm@qsilver.queensu.ca; *research interests*: political economy, political integration, public policy [Canada, EU]

Leston-Bandeira, Cristina — University of Hull; *address*: Department of Politics, University of Hull, Cottingham Road, Hull, HU6 7RX, UK; *fax*: +44-1482-466 208; *email*: c.c.leston-bandeira@pol-as.hull.ac.uk; *research interests*: legislatures, comparative politics, elections and voting behaviour [South, Central and Eastern Europe, Portugal]

Levi, Margaret — University of Washington; *address*: Department of Political Science, Box 353530, University of Washington, Seattle, WA 98195, USA; *fax*: +1-206-685 2146; *email*: mlevi@u.washington.edu; *research interests*: comparative politics, political theory and philosophy

LeVine, Victor T — Washington University in St Louis; *address*: Department of Political Science, Box 1063, Washington University, One Bookings Drive, St Louis, MO 63130, USA; *fax*: +1-314-935 5856; *email*: vlevine@artsci.wustl.edu; *research interests*: comparative politics, area studies, international relations [Africa, Middle East]

Li, Linda Chelan — City University of Hong Kong; *address*: Department of Public & Social Administration, City University of Hong Kong, Tai Chee Avenue, Kowloon, Hong Kong; *fax*: +852-2788 8926; *email*: salcli@cityu.edu.hk; *research interests*: legislatures, comparative politics, central-local relations [China]

Liao, Da-Chi — National Sun Yat-sen University; *address*: Institute of Political Science, National Sun Yat-sen University, Kaohsiung, Taiwan; *fax*: +886-7-525 5540; *email*: dcliao@mail.nsysu.edu.tw; *research interests*: legislatures, comparative politics, local elite studies

Lieber, Robert J — Georgetown University; *address*: Department of Government, Georgetown University, Washington, DC 20057-1034, USA; *fax*: +1-202-338 1406; *email*: lieberr@georgetown.edu; *research interests*: international relations [Europe, Middle East]

Liebowitz, Debra — Drew University; *address*: Department of Political Science, Drew University, Smith House, Madison, NJ 07940, USA; *fax*: +1-973-408 3143; *email*: dliebowi

@drew.edu; *research interests*: women and politics, international relations [Latin America]

Lieverdink, Harm J — Supervisory Board for Health Care Insurance; *address*: Supervisory Board for Health Care Insurance, PO Box 459, 1180 AL Arstelveen, Netherlands; *email*: h.lieverdink@ctu.nl; *research interests*: public administration, public policy, judicial systems and behaviour

Lijphart, Arend — University of California-San Diego; *address*: Department of Political Science, University of California, San Diego, 9500 Gilman Drive, La Jolla, CA 92093-0521, USA; *fax*: +1-858-534 7130; *email*: alijphar@ucsd.edu; *research interests*: comparative politics

Lim, Haeran — Ewha Women's University; *address*: 1406-904 Chunggu-apt, Ilsan-dong, Ilsan-Ku, Koyang City, Kyunggi-do, Korea; *fax*: +82-344-913 0008; *email*: hrlim@hananet.net; *research interests*: comparative politics, area studies, political economy [East Asia]

Lim, Hyun-Chin — Seoul National University; *address*: Department of Sociology, College of Social Sciences, Seoul National University, Seoul 151-742, Korea; *fax*: +82-2-873 3799; *email*: hclim@plaza.snu.ac.kr; *research interests*: comparative politics, area studies, international relations [Asia, Latin America]

Lin, Wan-huei — National Taiwan University; *address*: 2F, No 3, Alley 10, Lane 60, Chao-chou Street, 106 Taipei, Taiwan; *fax*: +886-2-2391 3309; *email*: kflee@ms9.hinet.net; *research interests*: public policy, area studies, women and politics [PRC, Taiwan]

Lindahl, Rutger — Göteborg University; *address*: Tjädergatan 32, SE-426 69, Västra Frölunda, Sweden; *fax*: +46-31-773 4599; *email*: rutger.lindahl@pol.gu.se; *research interests*: international relations, EU affairs

[Europe]

Lindgren, Lena—Göteborg University; *address*: PO Box 750, University of Göteborg, SE 405 30 Göteborg, Sweden; *fax*: +46-31-773 4719; *email*: lena.lindgren@spa.gu.se; *research interests*: public administration, public policy

Linz, Juan—Yale University; *address*: Department of Sociology, Yale University, PO Box 208265, New Haven, CT 06520-8265, USA; *fax*: +1-203-432 6976; *research interests*: political parties, elections and voting behaviour, comparative politics [Spain, Europe, Latin America]

Lo, Man Keung (Jack)—Hong Kong Polytechnic University; *address*: School of Professional & Executive Development, Hong Kong Polytechnic University, Hung Hom, Kowloon, Hong Kong; *fax*: +852-2363 0540; *email*: spjacklo@inet.polyu.edu.hk; *research interests*: public administration, local and urban governance, development politics [East Asia]

Loaeza, Soledad—El Colegio de Mexico; *address*: Camino Al Ajusco 20, Pedregal de Santa Teresa, MEXICO DF, CP 0 1000, Mexico; *fax*: +52-5-645 0464; *email*: maloa@colmex.mx; *research interests*: political parties, comparative politics, elections and voting behaviour [Mexico, Latin America, Western Europe]

Loftsson, Elfar—Södertörns University College; *address*: Box 4101, SE-141 04 Huddinge, Sweden; *email*: Elfar.Loftsson@sh.se; *research interests*: political theory and philosophy, area studies, development politics [Baltic Sea region]

Longley, Lawrence D—Lawrence University; *address*: Department of Government, Lawrence University, Appleton, WI 54912, USA; *fax*: +1-414-832 6962; *email*: powerldl@aol.com; *research interests*: legislatures, comparative politics, central government [USA, East and Central Europe]

Lopez-Nieto, Lourdes—UNED; *address*: Cardenal Herrera Oria, 173, 28034 Madrid, Spain; *fax*: +34-91-398 7003; *email*: llopez@poli.uned.es; *research interests*: legislatures, political parties, local and regional politics [Europe]

Lopez-Pintor, Rafael—Universidad Autonóma de Madrid; *address*: C/Recoletos 7, 1 DCHA 28001 Madrid, Spain; *fax*: +34-1-397 4259; *email*: lpintor@bitmailer.net; *research interests*: elections and voting behaviour, comparative politics, area studies [Spain, Latin America]

Losco, Joseph—Ball State University; *address*: Department of Political Science, Ball State University, Muncie, IN 47306, USA; *email*: 00jalosco@bsuvc.bsu.edu; *research interests*: political theory and philosophy, public policy

Lovelace, Leopoldo G—Ohio State University; *address*: Mershon Center, Ohio State University, 1501 Neil Avenue, Columbus, OH 43201, USA; *fax*: +1-614-292 2407; *email*: lovelace.12@osu.edu; *research interests*: international law, international relations, central government

Lowi, Theodore J—Cornell University; *address*: Department of Government, Cornell University, 105 McGraw Hall, Ithaca, NY 14853, USA; *fax*: +1-607-255 4530; *email*: TJL7@cornell.edu; *research interests*: political parties, public policy, public administration

Luksic, Igor—University of Ljubljana; *address*: Faculty of Social Science, Kardeljeva Place 5, 1001 Ljubljana, Slovenia; *fax*: +386-61-580 5102; *email*: igor.luksic@uni-lj.si; *research interests*: political theory and philosophy, legislatures, elections and voting behaviour [Europe]

Lumumba-Kasongo, Tukumbi—Cornell University; *address*: Department of City & Regional Planning, 106 W Sibley Hall,

Sibley Hall, Cornell University, Ithaca, NY 14853, USA; *email*: tl25@cornell.edu; *research interests*: comparative politics, international relations, development politics [Africa, Europe, South America]

Lundstrom, Mats — Uppsala University; *address*: Uppsala University, Department of Government, PO Box 514, SE-75120 Uppsala, Sweden; *fax*: +46-18-471 3409; *email*: mats.lundstrom@statsvet.uu.se; *research interests*: political theory and philosophy, theories of democracy, international law, women and politics

Maarek, Philippe J — Université Paris 12; *address*: 41 rue du Colisée, 75008 Paris, France; *fax*: +33-1-4359 5703; *email*: maarek@univ-paris12.fr; *research interests*: pressure groups, comparative politics, area studies [Western Europe, ISA]

Mabuchi, Masaru — Kyoto University; *address*: 59-7 Sumiyoshi-dai, Sasayama City, Hyogo Prefecture, 669-2231, Japan; *fax*: +81-795-944 186; *email*: masaru-mabuchi@msn.com; *research interests*: public administration [Japan]

Mace, Gordon — Université Laval; *address*: Département de Science Politique, Pavillon De Koninck, Université Laval, Québec, G1K 7P4, Canada; *fax*: +1-418-656 7861; *email*: gordon.mace@pol.ulaval.ca; *research interests*: international relations, comparative politics, political science methods [Canada, Americas]

MacLennan, Gregory Alexander — *address*: 8806 Nora Lane, Indianapolis, IN 46240, USA; *fax*: +1-317-846 5158; *email*: gmaclen@att.globalnet

MacLeod, Michael — George Washington University; *address*: 14 Lambton Avenue, Ottawa, K1M 0Z5, Canada; *fax*: +1-613-741 5894; *email*: mrm@gwu.edu; *research interests*: international relations, international law

MacMillan, Michael — Mount St Vincent University; *address*: Political & Canadian Studies Department, Mount St Vincent University, 166 Bedford Highway, Halifax, NS, B3M 2J6, Canada; *fax*: +1-902-457 6455; *email*: michael.macmillan@msvu.ca; *research interests*: political theory and philosophy, public policy, language conflicts in society

Magara, Hideko — University of Tsukuba; *address*: 2-4-18-601 Mita, Minato-ku, Tokyo 1080073, Japan; *fax*: +81-3-3451 4509; *email*: hmagara@msn.com; *research interests*: comparative politics, political parties, pressure groups [Italy, Japan]

Magnusson, Warren — University of Victoria; *address*: Department of Political Science, University of Victoria, PO Box 3050, Victoria, BC V8W 3P5, Canada; *fax*: +1-250-721 7485; *email*: wmagnus@uvic.ca; *research interests*: political theory and philosophy, local and urban politics, comparative politics [North Atlantic]

Mahon, James — William College; *address*: Stetson Hall, William College, Williamstown, MA 01267, USA; *fax*: +1-413-597 4305; *email*: jmahon@williams.edu; *research interests*: comparative politics, political economy, judicial systems and behaviour [Latin America]

Mahon, Rianne — Carleton University; *address*: 245 Fifth Avenue, Ottawa, ON, K1S 2N1, Canada; *fax*: +1-613-520 2255; *email*: rmahon@ccs.carleton.ca; *research interests*: comparative politics, unions, women's movements [Western Europe, North America]

Mahtab, Nazmunnessa — University of Dhaka; *address*: House No 1, Road No 34, Green Heritage (3rd Floor), Gulshn, Dhaka - 1212, Bangladesh; *fax*: +880-2-832 749; *email*: mahtab@bangla.net; *research interests*: women and politics, public administration, area studies [South

Asia, Southeast Asia]

Mainwaring, Scott — University of Notre Dame; *address*: Kellog Institute, University of Notre Dame, Notre Dame, IN 46556-5677, USA; *fax*: +1-219-631 6717; *research interests*: political executives, political parties, comparative politics [Latin America]

Maioni, Antonia — McGill University; *address*: Department of Political Science, McGill University, 855 Sherbrooke West, Montreal, Quebec, H3A 2T7, Canada; *fax*: +1-514-398 1770; *email*: maioni@leacock.lan.mc gill.ca; *research interests*: comparative politics, public policy, political parties [Canada, USA, Europe]

Makasiar Sicat, Loretta — University of the Philippines; *address*: UP PO Box 371, University of the Philippines, Diliman, Quezon City 1101, Philippines; *fax*: +63-2-929 1532; *email*: maksicat@info.com.ph; *research interests*: political science methods, international relations, political theory and philosophy [Asia-Pacific (including North America), western world]

Mälkiä, Matti — The Police College of Finland; *address*: The Police College of Finland, PO Box 13, FIN-02151 Espoo, Finland; *fax*: +358-9-8388 3500; *email*: malkia@uta.fi; *research interests*: central government, public administration, public policy [EU]

Mandeville-Briot, Anne — Université de Toulouse I; *address*: IEP - CERSA, 2 ter, rue des Puits Creusés, 31000 Toulouse, France; *email*: anmaderi@ aol.com; *research interests*: political executives, comparative politics, security police studies [UK, Ireland, Israel, USA]

Mansfeldova, Zdenka — Czech Academy of Sciences; *address*: Insititute of Sociology, Czech Academy of Sciences, Jilska 1, 11000, Prague 5, Czech Republic; *fax*: +420-2-2222 0143; *email*: mansfeld@soc.cas.cz; *research interests*: political parties,

legislatures, civil society [Central Europe]

Maor, Moshe — The Hebrew University; *address*: Department of Political Science, The Hebrew University, Mount Scopus, Jerusalem 91905, Israel; *fax*: +972-2-588 3454; *email*: msmaor@mscc.huji.ac.il; *research interests*: political parties, public administration

Marantzidis, Nicos — University of Macedonia; *address*: Papafi 36, 54639 Thessaloniki, Greece; *fax*: +30-31-852 195; *email*: nikosm@ uom.gr; *research interests*: elections and voting behaviour, political parties, ethnicity [Europe]

Margolis, Michael — University of Cincinnati; *address*: Department of Political Science, University of Cincinnati, PO Box 210375, Cincinnati, OH 45221-0375, USA; *fax*: +1-513-556 2314; *email*: michael.margolis@ uc.edu; *research interests*: political parties, political science methods, political communication [industrialized countries]

Markovits, Andrei — University of Michigan; *address*: Department of Sociology, University of Michigan, 3110 Modern Language Building, 812 East Washington Street,, Ann Arbor, MI 48109-1275, USA; *fax*: +1-734-763 6557; *email*: andymark@ umich.edu; *research interests*: comparative politics [Europe, North America]

Markowski, Radoslaw — Collegium Civitas; *address*: ul. Tylzycka 11/125, 01656 Warszawa, Poland; *fax*: +48-22-825 2146; *email*: rmark@ ispppan.waw.pl; *research interests*: elections and voting behaviour, political parties, comparative politics [transitional countries]

Marques-Pereira, Bérangère — Université libre de Bruxelles; *address*: 54 rue Dautzenberg (boite 2), B-1050 Bruxelles, Belgium; *fax*: +32-2-646 2378; *email*: bmarques@ulb.ac.be; *research interests*: women and politics, political sociology, area studies [Latin America, West Europe]

Martin, James — University of London; *address*: Department of Social Policy & Politics, Goldsmith College, University of London, New Cross, London SE14 6NW, UK; *research interests*: political theory and philosophy [Italy, Europe]

Martinez, Jose Roberto — Luis Munoz-Marin Foundation; *address*: 20 Calle Delcassé, Apt 1001, San Juan, Puerto Rico 00907-1680, USA; *fax*: +1-787-755 0240; *email*: citi7@hot mail.com; *research interests*: elections and voting behaviour, political parties, comparative politics [Western Europe, Caribbean]

Martinez, Rafael C — Universitat de Barcelona; *address*: Departamento de Ciencia Politica, Universitat de Barcelona, Avda Diagonal 690, 08034 Barcelona, Spain; *fax*: +34-93-402 4409; *email*: rafael@riscd2.eco.ub.es; *research interests*: comparative politics, elections and voting [Europe, Latin America]

Martinez de Luna, Iñaki — Gobierno Vasco; *address*: Navarra 2, 01006 Vitoria-Gasteiz, País Vasco, Spain; *fax*: +34-45-188 157; *email*: mtzdeluna@ej-gv.es; *research interests*: elections and voting behaviour, public administration, political science methods

Martiniello, Marco — Université de Liège; *address*: Université de Liège, Faculté de Droit, Science Politique, Centre d'Etude de l'Ethnicité et des Migrations, Bâtiment 31, Boite 38, 7, Boulevard du Rectorat, 4000 Liège (Sart-Tilman), Belgium; *fax*: +32-4-366 4557; *email*: m.martiniello@ulg.ac.be; *research interests*: local and urban politics, pressure groups, migration, ethnicity, citizenship [Belgium, EU, USA]

Marvick, Elizabeth Wirth — *address*: 10499 Wilkins Avenue, Los Angeles, CA 90024, USA; *fax*: +1-310-474 3618; *email*: dmarv@ucla.edu; *re-search interests*: political psychology, political executives [North Europe, USA]

Masare, Johannes — Skyline College; *address*: 5016 Lyng Drive, San Jose, CA 95111-2720, USA; *fax*: +1-408-224 7613; *email*: akoirmi@aol.com; *research interests*: central government, political theory and philosophy, local and urban politics [USA]

Massicotte, Louis — Université de Montréal; *address*: Département de Science Politique, Université de Montréal, CP 6128, Succ "A", Montréal H3C 3J7, Canada; *fax*: +1-514-343 2360; *research interests*: comparative politics, legislatures, elections and voting behaviour

Mathur, Prakash Chand — University of Rajasthan; *address*: B-87 Ganesh Marg, Bapunagar, Jaipur - 302015, India; *fax*: +91-141-510 880; *email*: sfourti@jp1.dot.net.in; *research interests*: public administration, local and urban politics, comparative politics [South Asia, India]

Mathur, Subhaschandra — JNV University; *address*: 354/4th C Road, Sardarpura, Jodhpur - 342003, India; *fax*: +91-291-438 266; *email*: sumit@yahoo.com; *research interests*: elections and voting behaviour, public administration [USA]

Maurer, Andreas — Universität Cologne; *address*: Forschung Iinstitut für Politische, Wissenschaft und Europäische, Gottfried Keller Str 6, D-50931 Cologne, Germany; *fax*: +49-221-940 2542; *email*: maurer_andre@yahoo.com; *research interests*: international relations, comparative politics, legislatures [EU]

Mawhood, Philip N — University of Exeter; *address*: Department of Politics, Amory Building, University of Exeter, Exeter EX4 4RJ, UK; *fax*: +44-1392-263 305; *research interests*: public administration, comparative politics, development politics [Africa]

Mayer, Margit — Freie Universität;

address: Freie Universität Berlin, Kennedy-Institut, Lansstr 7-9, 14195 Berlin, Germany; fax: +49-30-8385 2875; email: mayer@zedat.fu-berlin. de; research interests: comparative politics, local and urban politics, public policy [North America, Europe]

McAllister, Ian — Australian National University; address: RSSS, Australian National University, Canberra, ACT 0200, Australia; fax: +61-2-6247 8522; email: ian.mcallister@anu.edu. au; research interests: elections and voting behaviour, comparative politics, political science methods

McClain, Paula — Duke University; address: Department of Political Science, Duke University, 214 Perkins Library, PO Box 90204, Durham, NC 22708-0204, USA; fax: +1-919-660 4330; email: pmcclain@duke. edu; research interests: local and urban politics, public policy, racial and ethnic minority politics

McCoy, Elaine — Kent State University; address: 302 Bowman Hall, Department of Political Science, Kent State University, OH, 44240, USA; fax: +1-330-672 3362; email: emccoy @kent.edu; research interests: political theory and philosophy, comparative politics, public policy [North America, Western Europe, Australasia]

McDougall, AK — University of Western Ontario; address: Department of Political Science, University of Westen Ontario, London, ON, N6A 5C2, Canada; fax: +1-810-982 3181; email: akmcdll@julian.uwo.ca; research interests: area studies, public policy, discourse and power [North America]

McLeay, Elizabeth — Victoria University of Wellington; address: School of Political Science and International Relations, Victoria University of Wellington, PO Box 600, Wellington, New Zealand; fax: +64-4-463 5414; email: Elizabeth.McLeay@

vuw.ac.nz; research interests: political representation, cabinet and policy process, electoral system change [New Zealand, Britain, Germany]

McRae, Kenneth D — Carleton University; address: Department of Political Science, Carleton University, 1125 Colonel By Drive, Ottawa K1S 5B6, Canada; fax: +1-613-520 4064; research interests: political theory and philosophy, comparative politics [North America, Western Europe]

McRoberts, Kenneth — York University; address: Office of the Principal, Glendon College, York University, C203 YH, 2275 Bayview Avenue, Toronto, ON M4N 3M6, Canada; fax: +1-416-487 6786; email: kmc roberts@glendon.yorku.ca; research interests: comparative politics, public policy, central government [North America, Western Europe]

Meadowcroft, James — University of Sheffield address: Department of Politics, University of Sheffield, Elmfield Building, Northumberland Road, Sheffield, S10 2TU, UK

Medhi, Kunja — Gauhati University; address: 101, Gauhati University Campus, Gauhati - 781 014, Assam, India; fax: +91-361-570 133; email: kkhlgu@gwi.vsnl.net.in; research interests: human rights, women's issues, political studies

Mehra, Ajay K — Centre for Public Affairs; address: Swasti, D-104, Sector 27, Noida 201 301, UP, India; email: drmehra@vsnl.com; research interests: local and urban politics, legislatures, political parties [South Asia]

Meintjes, Sheila — University of Witwatersrand; address: Department of Political Studies, University of Witwatersrand, Postal Bag 3, PO Wits, 2050 Johannesburg, South Africa; fax: +27-11-403 7482; email: 064 smm@muse.wits.ac.za; research interests: women and politics, political theory and philosophy, elections and voting behaviour [South Africa]

Meisel, John—Queen's University; *address*: Department of Political Studies, Queen's University, Kingston, ON, K7A 3N6, Canada; *fax*: +1-613-533 6848; *email*: meiselj@politics.queensu.ca; *research interests*: parties and elections, ethnic politics, cultural politics [Canada, Europe]

Melone, Albert P—Southern Illinois University-Carbondale; *address*: Department of Political Science, Southern Illinois University, Carbondale, IL 6290-4501, USA; *fax*: +1-618-453 3163; *email*: melone@siu.edu; *research interests*: political executives, legislatures, comparative judicial studies [Eastern Europe, Bulgaria]

Melville, Andrei—Moscow State Institute of International Relations; *address*: 76 Prospect Vernadskogo, Moscow, Russia; *fax*: +7-095-434 9179; *email*: melville@mgimo.ru; *research interests*: comparative politics, area studies, international relations [Russia, CIS, third wave democracies]

Mendes, Candido—Universidade Candido Mendes; *address*: Sociedade Brasileira de Instrucao, Praca XV de Novembro, 101 Rio de Janeiro, Brazil; *fax*: +55-21-533 4782; *email*: cmendes@candidomendes.br

Merrien, François-Xavier—Université Lausanne; *address*: BFSH2, Faculté des Sciences Sociales et Politiques, Institut des Sciences Sociales et Pedagogoques, Université de Lausanne, Switzerland; *fax*: +41-21-692 32 35; *email*: francoisxavier.merrien@issp.unil.ch; *research interests*: public policy, comparative politics, public administration [Europe, USA, developing countries]

Merritt, Richard L—University of Illinois-Urbana-Champaign; *address*: Institute of Communications Research, University of Illinois, 228 Gregory Hall, 810 S Wright Street, Urbana, IL 61801, USA; *fax*: +1-217-244 7695; *email*: richmerr@uiuc.edu; *research interests*: international communication, political sociology, international relations [Germany]

Mertin, Manuel—Mount Royal College; *address*: Department of Policy Studies, Mount Royal College, 4825 Richard Road SW, Calgary, AB, T3E 6K6, Canada; *fax*: +1-403-240 6815; *email*: mmertin@mtroyal.ab.ca; *research interests*: comparative politics, public policy [Canada, EU]

Midlarsky, Manus I—Rutgers University; *address*: Department of Political Science, Rutgers University, 89 George Street, New Brunswick, NJ 08903-0270, USA; *fax*: +1-732-932 7170; *email*: midlarsk@rci.rutgers.edu; *research interests*: international relations, comparative politics

Migdal, Joel—University of Washington; *address*: Box 353650, Seattle, WA 98195-3650, USA; *fax*: +1-206-658 0668; *email*: migdal@u.washington.edu; *research interests*: comparative politics, development politics, area studies [Middle East]

Milly, Deborah—Virginia Tech; *address*: Deparment of Political Science, Virginia Tech, Blacksburg, VA 24061-0130, USA; *fax*: +1-540-231 6078; *email*: djmilly@vt.edu; *research interests*: comparative politics, public policy, international migration [Japan, Asia]

Mina, José A—Ministry of Foreign Affairs; *address*: Anchorena 1751 - 7 "A", 1425 Buenos Aires, Argentina; *fax*: +54-11-4819 7713; *email*: min@mrecic.gov.ar; *research interests*: area studies, comparative politics, central government [North America, Europe, Asia (Pacific), Middle East]

Mironesco, Christine—Université de Genève; *address*: Département de science politique, Université de Genève, 102 Boulevard Carl Vogt, 1211 Genève 4, Switzerland; *email*: christine.mironesco@politic.unige.

ch; *research interests*: science, technology and politics [EU]

Mishra, Rajalakshmi – GM College, Sambalpur University; *address*: Modipara, Sambalpur - 768002, (Orissa), India; *fax*: +91-663-403 468; *email*: rajalakshmi_mishra@hotmail. com; *research interests*: local and urban politics, public administration, development politics [South Asia]

Mishra, Ramesh – York University; *address*: 24 Market Street North, Dundas, ON, L9H 2Y3, Canada; *fax*: +1-905-628 9697; *email*: mishra@globalserve.net; *research interests*: comparative politics, public policy, development politics

Mitchell, Charles – Grambling State University; *address*: 301 East Reynolds Drive 10C, Ruston LA 71270, USA; *fax*: +1-318-274 2310; *email*: cmitc@linknet.idt.net; *research interests*: public administration, political science methods, comparative politics

Mohabbat Khan, Mohammad – Bangladesh Public Service Commission; *address*: Bangladesh Public Service Commission, Old Airport Building, Tejgaon, Dhaka 1215, Bangladesh; *fax*: +880-2-861 5583; *email*: cdrb@dhaka.agni.com; *research interests*: public administration, central government, area studies [South Asia, USA, Western Europe]

Mohanty, Bijoyini – Utkal University; *address*: N/6-18, Nayapalli, Bhubaneswar, Orissa, PIN 751 015, India; *fax*: +91-674-509 237; *research interests*: local and urban politics, public administration, women and politics

Molina, José – Universidad del Zulia; *address*: Institutio de Estudios Politicos, Fac de Ciencias Juridicias y Politicas, Universidad del Zulia, Maracaibo, Venezuela; *fax*: +58-61-596 676; *email*: jmolina@iamnet.com; *research interests*: electoral systems, political behaviour [Latin America]

Montero, José Ramón – Universidad Autonóma de Madrid; *address*: Valle de la Fuenfria 8, 1°A, 28034 Madrid, Spain; *fax*: +34-91-576 3420; *email*: montero@ceacs.march.es; *research interests*: elections and voting behaviour, political parties, comparative politics [Western Europe]

Montialverne Barreto Lima, Martonio – Universidade de Fortaleza-UNIFOR; *address*: Rua Fco. Farias Filho, 100/702, 60810-110 Fortaleza - CE, Brazil; *fax*: +55-85-273 1546; *email*: barreto@ultranet.com.br; *research interests*: courts and democracy, legislatures, elections and voting behaviour [Brazil, Latin America, Russia]

Moreira Monteiro, Geraldo Tadeu – State University of Rio de Janeiro; *address*: Praia do Flamengo no 176/401, CEP: 22.210-030, Rio de Janeiro (RJ), Brazil; *fax*: +55-21-556 1592; *email*: gtmm@infolink.com.br; *research interests*: elections and voting behaviour, political parties, comparative politics

Moreno, Luis – Instituto de Estudios Sociales Avanzados; *address*: CSIC, Inst de Estudios, Sociales Avanzados, c/Alfonso XII, no. 18 - 5 piso, E-28104 Madrid, Spain; *fax*: +34-91-521 8103; *email*: lmorfer @iesam.csic.es; *research interests*: public policy, federalism, nationalism [Europe]

Morgan, John David – Warwick University, Open University; *address*: 232 Spinney Hill Road, Parklands, Northampton, NN3 6DR, UK; *fax*: +44-1203-524 304; *email*: j.d. morgan@warwick.ac.uk; *research interests*: legislatures, comparative politics [UK, Europe, USA]

Morlino, Leonardo – University of Florence; *address*: Via St Marta No 31, I-50139 Firenze, Italy; *fax*: +39-55-503 2426; *email*: morlino@unifi.it; *research interests*: comparative politics, political parties, pressure groups [Southern Europe, Italy]

Morris, Michael — Clemson University; *address*: Department of Political Science, Brackett Hall 232, Clemson University, Clemson, SC 29634-1534, USA; *fax*: +1-864-656 0690; *email*: morrism@clemson.edu; *research interests*: area studies, international relations, development politics

Mostov, Julie — Drexel University; *address*: Department of History and Politics, Institute for the Humanities, Drexel University, Philadelphia, PA 19104, USA; *fax*: +1-215-895 6614; *email*: mostovj@drexel.edu; *research interests*: political theory and philosophy, women and politics, international relations [Balkans, Eastern Europe]

Moul, William — University of Waterloo; *address*: Department of Political Science, University of Waterloo, Waterloo, ON, N2L 3G1, Canada; *email*: wbmoul@watarts.uwaterloo.ca; *research interests*: international relations, development politics, political science methods

Mouritzen, Poul Erik — Odense University; *address*: Department of Political Science and Public Management, SDU-Odense University, Campusvej 55, 5230 Odense, Denmark; *fax*: +45-6619 2577; *email*: pem @sam.sdu.dk; *research interests*: local and urban politics, comparative politics, public administration

Mozaffar, Shaheen — Bridgewater State College; *address*: Department of Political Science, Bridgewater State College, Bridgewater, MA 02323, USA; *fax*: +1-508-531 6186; *email*: smozaffar@bridgew.edu; *research interests*: comparative politics, area studies, development politics [Africa]

Mpondo-Epo, Bruno — United Nations; *address*: DPKO/Fald UNOB, PO Box 4884, New York, NY 10163, USA; *fax*: +1-212-963 2839; *email*: brunom@un.org; *research interests*: political executives, elections and voting behaviour, political science methods [Africa]

Mudgerikar, Pratibha — Tilak Maharashtra Vidyapeedh; *address*: Saideep 65, Tulsibagwale Colony, Pune 9, MS, India; *fax*: +91-20-422 1321; *email*: mudgerikarpc@hotmail.com; *research interests*: public administration, local and urban politics [India, Canada, Latin America, Europe, Africa]

Mukandala, Rwekaza S — University of Dar es Salaam; *address*: Department of Political Science, University of Dar es Salaam, PO Box 35042, Dar es Salaam, Tanzania; *fax*: +255-51-410 084; *email*: rwekaza@udsm.ac.tz; *research interests*: public administration, development politics, elections and voting behaviour [Africa]

Mukherjee, Subrata — University of Delhi; *address*: I 1689 Chittaranjan Park, New Delhi 110019, India; *fax*: +91-11-544 0916; *email*: polybins@ndb.vsnl.net.in; *research interests*: comparative politics, political theory and philosophy, area studies [Asia Pacific]

Muller, Pierre — CEVIPOF; *address*: Maison des Sciences de l'Homme, 54 Boulevard Raspail, 75006 Paris, France; *fax*: +33-1-4954 2025; *email*: muller@msh-paris.fr; *research interests*: public policy, public administration, central government [Europe]

Müller-Rommel, Ferdinand — Universität Düsseldorf; *address*: Gutshof 1, D-21394 Heiligenthal, Germany; *fax*: +49-4131-781 093; *email*: muero @uni-duesseldorf.de; *research interests*: central government, political parties, comparative politics [Western and Central Europe]

Murai, Hiroshi — University of Shimane; *address*: 2433-2 Nobara-Cho, Hamada-Shi Schimane-Ken, 697-0016, Japan; *fax*: +81-855-242 317; *email*: h-murai@u-shimsne.ac.jp; *research interests*: political theory and philosophy, central government [Europe]

Muramatau, Michio — Kyoto University; *address*: Faculty of Law, Kyoto University, Sakyo-ku, Kyoto 606 8501, Japan; *fax*: +81-75-753 3290; *email*: muramatu@law.kyoto-u.ac.jp; *research interests*: political executives, public administration, local and urban politics [Asia, USA, Europe]

Murphy, Irene L — *address*: 2005 37th St NW, Washington, DC 20007, USA; *fax*: +1-202-342 6434; *email*: imurph@aol.com; *research interests*: environmental issues, international relations, development and politics [Central and Eastern Europe]

Murphy, Walter F — Princeton University; *address*: 1533 Eagle Ridge Drive NE, Albuquerque, NM 87122, USA; *fax*: +1-505-828 3587; *email*: WFMurphy@flash.net; *research interests*: constitutional theory, comparative politics, political theory and philosophy [North America, Western Europe, Japan]

Mutimer, David — York University; *address*: YCISS, 3rd Floor York Lanes, York University, 4700 Keele Street, Toronto, ON, M3J 1P3, Canada; *fax*: +1-416-736 5752; *email*: dmutimer@yorku.ca; *research interests*: international relations

Mydske, Per Kristen — University of Oslo; *address*: Department of Political Science, University of Oslo, PO Box 1097, N-0317 Oslo, Norway; *fax*: +47-22-854 411; *email*: p.k.mydske@stv.uio.no; *research interests*: public administration, local and urban politics, development politics [Baltic]

Myers, James — University of South Carolina; *address*: Center for Asian Studies, University of South Carolina, Columbia, SC 29204, USA; *fax*: +1-803-252 6272; *email*: jmyers7462@aol.com; *research interests*: area studies, comparative politics, international relations [Chinese policies]

Myrvold, Trine Monica — NIBR; *address*: NIBR, PO Box 44 Blindern, N-0313 Oslo, Norway; *fax*: +47-22-607 774; *email*: trine.myrvold@nibr.no; *research interests*: local and urban politics, elections and voting behaviour, political executives

Nam, Kim Yu — Dankook University; *address*: Hanyang Apt 1-305, Socho-Dong, Sooho-ku, Seoul, Korea; *fax*: +82-2-790 6866; *research interests*: comparative politics, area studies, international relations [USA, Russia]

Naor, Arye — Ben Gurion University; *address*: Department of Public Policy & Administration, School of Management, Ben Gurion University, Beer Sheva, Israel; *fax*: +972-2-563 1344; *email*: arien@nihul.bgu.ac.il; *research interests*: central government, public administration, public policy [Israel]

Napel, Hans-Martien ten — University of Leiden; *address*: Thérèse Schwartzestraat 132, 2597 XM Den Haag, Netherlands; *fax*: +31-71-527 3815; *email*: tennapel@fsw.leiden univ.nl; *research interests*: political parties, religion and politics [Western Europe]

Narang, Amarjit S — Indira Gandhi National Open University; *address*: 192 Madanlal Block, Asian Games Village, New Delhi - 110049, India; *fax*: +91-11-685 9197; *email*: amarjitnarang@hotmail.com; *research interests*: comparative politics, development politics, local self-government and politics [India, South Asia, North America]

Nasri Messarra, Antoine — Lebanese University; *address*: 56, rue Abd el-Wahab el-Inglizi-Sodeco, Rés Messarra, BP 16-5738, Beyrouth, Lebanon; *fax*: +961-1-219 613; *email*: ames sarra@kleudge.com; *research interests*: plural societies, civic education, public administration [Arab countries]

Nassmacher, Karl H — Carl-Von-

Ossietzky University; *address*: 14 Alma-Rogge Str, D-26131 Oldenburg, Germany; *fax*: +49-441-504 0842; *email*: karl.h.nassmacher@uni-oldenburg.de; *research interests*: political parties, comparative politics, local and urban politics [Western Europe, North America]

Natalicchi, Giorgio — University of Florence; *address*: Via P Mascagni 12, I-50019 Sesto Fiorentino, Firenze, Italy; *email*: ggnatali@syr.fi.it; *research interests*: international relations, public policy, EU studies [Europe]

Naveh, Chanan — Tel Aviv University; *address*: 14, Nahage Hapredot Street, Jerusalem 97890, Israel; *email*: msnaveh@pluto.mscc.huji.ac.il; *research interests*: international relations, political communication [Middle East]

Nayak, Pandav — Indira Gandhi National Open University; *address*: 827 Asian Village, New Delhi, 110049, India; *fax*: +91-11-686 2312; *email*: ignouhrp@del3.vsnl.net.in; *research interests*: comparative politics, development politics [third world, South Asia]

Nelson, John — University of Iowa; *address*: Department of Political Science, University of Iowa, Iowa City, IA 52242, USA; *fax*: +1-319-335 3400; *email*: john-nelson@uiowa.edu; *research interests*: political theory and philosophy, political communication, political science methods

Nemni, Max — Laval University; *address*: 6150 ave du Boisé, apt 7L, Montreal, QC H3S 2V2, Canada; *fax*: +1-514-738 5516; *email*: max.nemni@pol.ulaval.ca; *research interests*: political theory and philosophy, comparative politics [Canada]

Neuberger, Benyamin — The Open University of Israel; *address*: Department of Sociology & Political Science, The Open University of Israel, 16 Klausner Street, Ramat-Aviv, Tel Aviv 61392, Israel; *fax*:

+972-3-646 0755; *email*: bennyn@oumail.openu.ac.il; *research interests*: political theory and philosophy, comparative politics, area studies [Africa]

Neunreither, Karlheinz — University of Heidelberg; *address*: Bei der Aarnescht 1, L-6969 Oberanven, Luxembourg; *fax*: +352-341 394; *email*: KhNeunreither@compuserve.com; *research interests*: European integration, international relations, political theory and philosophy

Neves Costa, Paulo Roberto — Universidade Federal do Parana; *address*: Rua Marechal Hermes 491, ap 801, Centro Civico, Curitiba, Brazil; *fax*: +55-41-360 5093; *email*: paulornc@humanas.ufpr.br; *research interests*: pressure groups, legislatures, political science methods [Brazil, Latin America, Europe, USA]

Nevitte, Neil — University of Toronto; *address*: Department of Political Science, University of Toronto, 100 St George Street, 3rd Floor, Toronto, ON M5S 3G3, Canada; *fax*: +1-416-978 5566; *email*: nnevitte@chass.utoronto.ca; *research interests*: comparative politics, elections and voting behaviour, political science methods

Newman, Saul — Macquarie University; *address*: Department of Sociology, SCMP, Macquarie University, NSW 2109, Australia; *fax*: +61-2-9850 9355; *email*: snewman@scmp.mq.edu.au; *research interests*: political theory and philosophy

Nezami, M A — King Saud University; *address*: King Saud University, PO Box 60846, Riyad 11555, Saudi Arabia; *fax*: +966-1-468 2084; *email*: mnezami@ksu.edu.sa; *research interests*: political theory and philosophy, judicial systems and behaviour, comparative politics

Niemi, Richard G — University of Rochester; *address*: Department of Political Science, University of Rochester, Rochester, NY 14627-

0146, USA; *fax*: +1-716-271 1616; *email*: niemi@mail.rochester.edu; *research interests*: elections and voting behaviour, political education

Ninsin, Kwame — African Association of Political Science; *address*: PO Box MP1100, Mt Pleasant, Harare, Zimbabwe; *fax*: +263-4-730 403; *email*: aaps@samara.co.zw; *research interests*: comparative politics [Africa]

Nisbet, Robert J — University of Pennsylvania; *address*: PO Box 218, Trexlertown, PA 18087, USA; *fax*: +1-610-820 3615; *email*: nisbetr@sas.upenn.edu; *research interests*: comparative politics, pressure groups, area studies [former USSR, Europe]

Nishizawa, Yoshitaka — Doshisha University; *address*: Karasuma Imadegawa, Kamigyo, Kyoto 602-8580, Japan; *fax*: +81-75-251 3060; *email*: ynishiza@mail.doshisha.ac.jp; *research interests*: elections and voting behaviour, political science methods [Japan]

Noelle-Neumann, Elisabeth — Institut für Demoskopie Allensbach; *address*: Institut für Demoskopie Allensbach, Radolfzeller Str 8, D-78472 Allensbach, Germany; *fax*: +49-753-3048; *email*: enoelle-neumann@ifd-allensbach.de; *research interests*: elections and voting behaviour, political theory and philosophy, political science methods

Norderval, Ingunn — Molde College; *address*: Kirkeveien 79A, 0364 Oslo, Norway; *fax*: +47-71-214 100; *research interests*: comparative politics, political parties, women and politics [Nordic countries]

Norris, Pippa — Harvard University; *address*: Kennedy School of Government, Harvard University, Cambridge, MA 02138, USA; *fax*: +1-617-495 8696; *email*: pippa_norris @harvard.edu; *research interests*: comparative politics, elections and voting behaviour, women and politics

Norton of Louth, Lord P — University of Hull; *address*: Department of Politics, University of Hull, Hull HU6 7RX, UK; *fax*: +44-1482-466 208; *email*: p.norton@pol-as.hull.ac.uk; *research interests*: legislatures, political executives, political parties [UK]

Nouhoume, BA — *address*: 16 rue des Carriéres d'Amérique, 75019 Paris, France; *research interests*: international law, public policy, political parties [West Africa, Europe]

Nurmi, Hannu — University of Turku; *address*: Department of Political Science, University of Turku, FIN-20014 Turku, Finland; *fax*: +358-2-333 5090; *email*: hnurmi@utu.fi; *research interests*: comparative politics, political science methods, formal theory

O'Brien, David M — University of Virginia; *address*: 916 Tilman Road, Charlottesville, VA 22901, USA; *fax*: +1-804-979 6318; *email*: dmo2y@virginia.edu; *research interests*: law and courts [Europe, Asia]

O'Donnell, Guillermo — University of Notre Dame; *address*: Kellogg Institute, University of Notre Dame, Notre Dame, IN 46556-5677, USA; *fax*: +1-219-631 6717; *email*: odonnell.1@nd.edu; *research interests*: comparative politics, democratisation, Latin American politics [Latin America]

Offerdal, Audun — University of Bergen; *address*: University of Bergen, Department of Administration and Organisation Theory, Christiesgt 17, N-5007 Bergen, Norway; *fax*: +47-55-589 890; *email*: audun. offer dal@aorg.uib.no; *research interests*: political parties, public administration, local and urban politics

Ohkoshi, Yasuo — Tokyo International University; *address*: 1-5-4 Yotsuya, City Fuchu, Tokyo 183, Japan; *fax*: +81-492-327 477; *email*: ohkoshi@tiu.ac.jp; *research interests*: political executives, elections and

voting behaviour, area studies [USA, Germany, EU, Canada]
O'Kane, Rosemary HT — University of Keele; *address*: Department of Politics, University of Keele, Keele, Staffs, ST5 5BG, UK; *fax*: +44-1782-583 452; *email*: r.h.t.o'kane@pol.keele.ac.uk; *research interests*: comparative politics, development politics, political sociology
Okuda, Kazuhiko — International University of Japan; *address*: Graduate School of International Relations, International University of Japan, Yamato-machi, Niigata, 949-72, Japan; *fax*: +81-257-794 442; *email*: okuda@iuj.ac.jp; *research interests*: political theory and philosophy, area studies, international relations [North America]
O'Leary, Brendan — London School of Economics; *address*: Department of Government, London School of Economics, Houghton Street, London WC2 2AE, UK; *fax*: +44-207-955 6549; *email*: b.o'leary@lse.ac.uk; *research interests*: nationalism and ethnic conflict regulation, theories of democracy, theories of the state [UK, Ireland, Canada, Western Europe, Africa]
Olgers, Ton — Vrije Universiteit; *address*: Lambert Rimastraat 48, NL 1106 ZT Amsterdam, The Netherlands; *fax*: +31-20-444 6862; *email*: aaj.olgers@scw.vu.nl; *research interests*: political education, political socialisation
Oliveira, Isabel — Federal University at Rio de Janeiro; *address*: rua Redentor 60/301, Ipanema, Rio de Janeiro, 22421-030, Brazil; *email*: isabel@ifcs.ufrj.br; *research interests*: political theory and philosophy, comparative politics, public policy
Oliveira Rocha, José A — Universidade do Minho; *address*: R. Pinheiro Manso 22, 4710 Braga, Portugal; *email*: jarocha@eeg.uminho.pt; *research interests*: public policy, judicial systems and behaviour, public

administration [Europe]
Onu, Godwin — Nnamdi Azikiwe University; *address*: Department of Political Science, Nnamdi Azikiwe University, PMB 5025, Awka, Anambra State, Nigeria; *email*: go mach@infoweb.abs.net; *research interests*: public bureaucracies, ethnic studies, local government studies [developing countries, Africa]
Oppenheim, Lois Hecht — University of Judaism; *address*: Political Science Department, University of Judaism, 15600 Mulholland Drive, Los Angeles, CA 90077, USA; *fax*: +1-310-471 1278; *email*: loppenheim@uj.edu; *research interests*: comparative politics, area studies, women and politics [Latin America]
Orlansky, Dora — Instituto de Investigaciones Gino Germani (UBA); *address*: Instituto de Investigaciones Gino Germani, Facultad de Ciencias Sociales (UBA), Junin 1431 9/A, 1113 Buenos Aires, Argentina; *fax*: +54-11-806 7327; *email*: orlansky@mail.retina.ar; *research interests*: public policy, public administration, government [Argentina]
Ortiz, Marco — Universidad de Los Andes; *address*: Apartado Postal 614, Mérida, Estado Mérida, 5101-A, Venezuela; *email*: ortizmar@telcel.net.ve; *research interests*: elections and voting behaviour, political parties, political science methods [Venezuela]
Ostiguy, Pierre — Concordia Université; *address*: 1455 de Maisonneuve Boulevard W, Montréal, Quèbec, Canada; *fax*: +1-514-848 4072; *email*: postiguy@vax2.concordia.ca; *research interests*: comparative politics, elections and voting behaviour [Latin America]
Ostrom, Elinor — Indiana University; *address*: Workshop in Political Theory & Policy Analysis, Indiana University, 513 N Park, Bloomington, IN 47408-3895, USA; *fax*: +1-812-855 3150; *email*: ostrom@indiana.edu;

research interests: political theory and philosophy, public policy, biodiversity and sustainable development

Ostrom, Vincent — Indiana University; address: Workshop in Political Theory & Policy Analysis, Indiana University, 513 N Park, Bloomington, IN 47408-3895, USA; fax: +1-812-855 3150; email: ghiggins @indiana.edu; research interests: political theory and philosophy, public administration, development politics

Ostrowski, Krzysztof — Pultusk School of Humanities; address: Elegijna 29, 02-787 Warszawa, Poland; fax: +48-22-643 3537; email: ostrow@ wsh.edu.pl; research interests: comparative politics, local and urban politics, political science methods [Central Europe, Russia]

Osttveiten, Helle — NIBR; address: NIBR, PO Box 44, Blindern, N-0313 Oslo, Norway; fax: +47-22-607 774; email: helge.s.osttveiten@nibr.no; research interests: local and regional politics, health policy

Otake, Hideo — IEPde Paris; address: 28 rue Vauguelin, Escalier C, 75005 Paris, France; fax: +33-1-4549 5390; email: hiotake@ibm.net; research interests: political parties, comparative politics, public policy [Japan, France, Germany]

Ottaway, Marina — Carnegie Endowment for International Peace; address: Carnegie Endowment for International Peace, 1779 Massachusetts Avenue NW, Washington, DC 20036, USA; fax: +1-202-483 4462; email: ottawaym@ceip.org; research interests: comparative politics, area studies, development politics [Africa]

Ouchi, Minoru — Shumei University; address: 5-29-26 Narashino-Dai, Funabashi-shi, Chiba-ken 274, Japan; fax: +81-474-888 290; research interests: development and politics, area studies, international relations

[South and Southeast Asia]

Ougaard, Morten — Copenhagen Business School; address: 1KL Copenhagen Business School, Dalgas Have 15, 2000 Frederiusberg, Denmark; fax: +45-3815 3815; email: mo. ikl@cbs.dk; research interests: international political economy [USA, global issues]

Øyen, Else — University of Bergen; address: Gamle Kalvedalsveien 34, N-5019 Bergen, Norway; fax: +47-55-589 745; email: else.oyen@helsos. uib.no; research interests: social policy, poverty, comparative studies, international politics

Padia, Chandrakala — Banaras Hindu University; address: New G7, Hyderabad Colony, Banaras Hindu University, Varanasi 221005, India; fax: +91-54-231 774; email: cpadia@ banaras.ernet.in; research interests: political theory and philosophy, women and politics, human rights

Paehlke, Robert — Trent University; address: Political Studies Department, Trent University, Peterborough, ON, K9J 7B8, Canada; fax: +1-705-748 1715; email: rpaehlke@ trentu.ca; research interests: public policy, international relations, environmental politics

Paige, Glenn D — Center for Global Nonviolence; address: Center for Global Nonviolence, 3653 Tantalus Drive, Honolulu, HI 96822-5033, USA; fax: +1-808-524 8501; email: cgnv@hawaii.rr.com; research interests: nonkilling global political science, political leadership

Pakulski, Jan — University of Tasmania; address: Department of Sociology and Social Work, University of Tasmania, GPO Box 252-17, Hobart, Tasmania 7001, Australia; fax: +61-3-6226 2279; email: jan.pakulski@ utas.edu.au; research interests: elites, post-communism

Palard, Jacques — IEP de Bordeaux; address: CERVL, BP 101, 22405 Talence, France; fax: +33-5-5684

4329; *email:* j.palard@iep.u-bor deaux.fr; *research interests*: local and urban politics, politics and religion [Canada, France, Europe]

Palecki, Krzysztof — Jagiellonian University; *address*: Faculty of Law & Administration, Jagiellonian University, Bracka 12, 31-005 Kraków, Poland; *fax*: +48-12-422 3742; *email*: palecki@adm.uj.edu.pl; *research interests*: general theory of power, political philosophy, political sociology

Pallares, Francesc — Universitat Pompeu Fabra; *address*: c/Santa Maria, 27-29, B, 7-4, ES-08290 Cerdanyola del Valles, Barcelona, Spain; *fax*: +34-93-542 1654; *email*: francesc.pallares@cpis.upf.es; *research interests*: elections and voting behaviour, political parties, comparative politics [Europe, North and Latin America]

Palonen, Kari — University of Zyväskylä; *address*: Sturenkatu 31 B 17, FIN-00550 Helsinki, Finland; *fax*: +358-14-602535; *email*: kpalonen@cc.jyu.fi; *research interests*: political theory and philosophy, political rhetoric, history of political concepts

Paltiel, Jeremy — Carleton University; *address*: Department of Political Science, Carleton University, Ottawa, K1S 5B6, Canada; *fax*: +1-613-520 4064; *email*: jpaltiel@ccs.carleton.ca; *research interests*: comparative politics, international relations, area studies [East Asia, China]

Pammett, Jon H — Carleton University; *address*: Department of Political Science, Carleton University, 1125 Colonel By Drive, Ottawa, ON, K1S 5B6, Canada; *fax*: +1-613-520 4064; *email*: jpammett@ccs.carleton.ca; *research interests*: central government, elections and voting behaviour, comparative politics [Canada]

Pandit, Vijay L — Delhi University, Maitreyi College; *address*: B-24 Radhey Puri, Krishna Nagar, Delhi - 110051, India; *fax*: +91-11-687 2746;

email: j_l_sharma@hotmail.com; *research interests*: political executives, local and urban politics, women and politics

Papadopoulos, Ioannis — Université de Lausanne; *address*: Institut d'etudes politiques et internationales, Université de Lausanne, BFSH2-Dorigny, CH-1015 Lausanne, Switzerland; *fax*: +41-21-692 3145; *email*: ipapadop@iepi.uuil.ch; *research interests*: institutional analysis (direct democracy), governance, democratic theory [Europe, USA]

Park, Chan Wook — Seoul National University; *address*: Department of Political Science, Seoul National University, Seoul 151-742, Korea; *fax*: +82-2-887 4375; *email*: chwpark @snu.ac.kr; *research interests*: comparative politics, legislatures, elections and voting behaviour [Korea, USA, UK]

Park, Hee-Bong — Daejin University; *address*: School of International Area Studies, Daejin University, Pocheon-Gun, Gyonggi-Do 487-800, Republic of Korea; *fax*: +82-357-539 1089; *email*: hbpark@road.daejin.ac.kr; *research interests*: political theory and philosophy, public administration, local and urban politics [USA, Korea]

Park, Jong-chul — Korea Institute for National Unification; *address*: Korea Institute for National Unification, SL Tobong PO Box 22, Seoul 142-600, Korea; *fax*: +82-2-901 2533; *email*: pjc@ku-kinu.or.kr; *research interests*: comparative politics, international relations, development politics [Northeast Asia, North and South Korea]

Parkin, Andrew — Flinders University of South Australia; *address*: School of Political & International Studies, Flinders University, GPO Box 2100, Adelaide SA 5001, Australia; *fax*: +61-8-8201 5111; *email*: Andrew.Parkin@flinders.edu.au; *research interests*: public policy, political executives, comparative politics [Australia, Southeast Asia, North America]

Pastusiak, Longin — Gdansk University; *address*: Al Niepodleglosci 151 Apt 21, 02-555 Warsaw, Poland; *fax*: +48-22-849 5044; *email*: Longin. Pastusiak@sejm.gov.pl; *research interests*: international relations, comparative politics, area studies [North America]

Pateman, Carole — UCLA; *address*: Department of Political Science, University of California, LA, 4289 Bunche Hall, Box 951472, Los Angeles, CA 90095-1472, USA; *fax*: +1-310-825 0778; *email*: pateman@ucla. edu; *research interests*: modern political theory, women and politics, political economy

Pathak, Saroj — University of Delhi; *address*: Apt No 1B/16B, Ashok-Vihar-Phase I, Delhi, PIN 110052, India; *research interests*: area studies, international relations, women and politics [Southeast Asia, Indonesia]

Patterson, Samuel C — Ohio State University; *address*: Department of Political Science, Ohio State University, 2140 Derby Hall, 154 North Oval Mall, Columbus, OH 43210-1373, USA; *fax*: +1-614-292 1146; *email*: patpat851@aol.com; *research interests*: legislatures, political parties, elections and voting behaviour [Europe, North America]

Pavlov, Yuri — Moscow State University; *address*: Political Science Department, Faculty of Philosophy, Moscow State University, Moscow, Russia; *fax*: +7-095-939 2208; *research interests*: political theory and philosophy, international relations, global policy

Pedler, Robin H — Templeton College; *address*: Templeton College, Oxford OX1 5NY, UK; *fax*: +44-1865-422 501; *email*: pedler_r@ templeton.oxford.ac.uk; *research interests*: central government, legislatures, pressure groups

Peeler, John — Bucknell University; *address*: Department of Political Science, Bucknell University, Lewisburg, PA 17837, USA; *fax*: +1-570-577 3533; *email*: peller@bucknell. edu5491; *research interests*: comparative politics, area studies [Latin America]

Peleg, Ilan — Lafayette College; *address*: Department of Government & Law, Lafayette College, Easton, PA 18042-1780, USA; *fax*: +1-610-330 5397; *email*: pelegi@lafayette.edu; *research interests*: comparative politics, international relations, human rights [Middle East, Europe]

Pellet Lastra, Arturo — Universidad de Buenos Aires; *address*: Paraguay 1847, 2o D, (1121) Buenos Aires, Argentina; *fax*: +54-11-666 3549; *research interests*: legislatures, comparative politics [Latin America]

Pelletier, Réjean — Université Laval; *address*: Departément de Science Politique, Université Laval, Ste-Foy, QC, G1K 7P4, Canada; *fax*: +1-418-656 7861; *email*: rejean.pelletier@pol. ulaval.ca; *research interests*: legislatures, political parties, comparative politics, federalism [Canada, Quebec, federal states]

Perez Nieves, José C — *address*: Guayra 2215, 1429 Buenos Aires, Argentina; *email*: pereznieves@mix mail.com; *research interests*: legislatures, political theory and philosophy, comparative politics

Peréz Sosto, Guillermo — Universidad Nacional del Nord Este; *address*: Costa Rica 4550 Loft 3, C14144BSH Ciudad Autónoma de Buenos Aires, Argentina; *fax*: +54-11-4833 0585; *email*: gperezsosto@ arnet.com.ar; *research interests*: international relations, legislatures, comparative politics [Mercosur]

Perrotti, Luisa — INSEAD; *address*: INSEAD, Boulevard de Constance, 77300 Fontainebleau - Cedex, France; *fax*: +33-1-6074 5500; *email*: perrotti@insead.fr; *research interests*:

public policy, comparative politics, EU integration [EU, Italy]

Peters, Ronald M — University of Oklahoma; *address*: Carl Albert Center, University of Oklahoma, 630 Parrington Oval, Room 101, Norman, OK 73019-0275, USA; *fax*: +1-405-325 6419; *email*: peters@uou.edu

Petersen, Thomas — Institut für Demoskopie Allensbach; *address*: Radolfzellerstr 8, D-78476 Allensbach, Germany; *fax*: +49-753-33048; *email*: tpetersen@ifd-allensbach.de

Peterson, Steven A — Penn State University; *address*: School of Public Affairs, Penn State University, 777 W Harrisburg Pike, Middletown, PA 17057, USA; *fax*: +1-717-948 6320; *email*: sap12@psu.edu; *research interests*: public policy, elections and voting behaviour, biology and politics [USA]

Petrarú, Augusto J — Universidad Católica de la Plata, Universidad de Moron; *address*: Moreno 998, (1878) Quilmes (BA), Argentina; *fax*: +54-11-4253 0471; *email*: apetraru@ciudad.com.ar; *research interests*: political theory and philosophy, comparative politics, political science methods

Petrusevska, Tatiana — Law School, Skopje; *address*: Vladimir Komharov, 33, 10-II/S, Skopje 91000, Macedonia; *fax*: +389-91-117 244; *email*: tapet@pf.ukim.edu.mk; *research interests*: international relations, international law, comparative politics [Europe]

Pfeifenberger, Werner — Universität Bielefeld; *address*: Von Esmarch str 157, D-48149 Münster, Germany; *fax*: +49-251-864 352; *research interests*: international relations, international law

Philippart, André — Université Libre de Bruxelles, honoraire; *address*: Avenue des Naïades, 11, 1170 Bruxelles, Belgium; *fax*: +32-2-675 8563; *email*: a_philippart@hotmail.

com; *research interests*: science policy and politics in education

Picard, Elizabeth — CNRS; *address*: 3, rue de Moscou, 75008 Paris, France; *fax*: +33-1-4387 6676; *research interests*: comparative politics, area studies, international relations [Middle East]

Pinkney, Robert — University of Northumbria; *address*: 4 Shaftesbury Avenue, Whitley Bay, Tyne & Wear NE26 3TF, UK; *fax*: +44-191-227 4654; *email*: bob.pinkney@unn.ac.uk; *research interests*: development and politics, area studies, comparative politics [Africa]

Pinto Paiva, Maria Arair — Universidade Federal Fluminense; *address*: Rua Baronesa de Poconé 71/701, Lagoa, 22471-270 Rio de Janeiro - RJ, Brazil; *fax*: +55-21-620 3236; *email*: mappaiva@uol.com.br; *research interests*: legislatures, elections and voting behaviour, political theory and philosophy [Brazil, South America]

Pires Lucas, Joco Ignacio — Universidade de Cazias do Sul; *address*: Rua Governado Roberto Silveira, 1190/402 Bairro Santa Catarina, CEP: 95032-390, Brazil; *fax*: +55-54-212 2171; *email*: jiplucas@ucs.tche.br; *research interests*: political parties, pressure groups, political socialisation [Latin America]

Plasser, Fritz — University of Innsbruck; *address*: Dannebergplatz 14-6, A-1030 Vienna, Austria; *research interests*: comparative politics, elections and voting behaviour, area studies [USA, Western and Central Europe]

Plattner, Marc F — Journal of Democracy; *address*: Journal of Democracy, 1101 15th Street NW, Washington, DC 20005, USA; *fax*: +1-202-293 0258; *email*: marc@ned.org; *research interests*: comparative politics, political theory and philosophy

Pohoryles, Ronald J — Interdisciplinary Centre for Comparative Research in the Social Sciences (ICCR); address: ICCR-IFS-CIR, Schottenfeldgasse 69/1, A-1070 Vienna, Austria; fax: +43-1-524 1393 200; email: r.pohoryles@iccr-internation al.org; research interests: social science, transport, environment [EU]

Polanco, Jacqueline J—John Jay College of Criminal Justice (CUNY); address: 435 Central Park West, Apartment 4R, New York, NY 10025, USA; fax: +1-212-237 8742; email: jjpolanco@aol.com; research interests: women and politics, comparative politics, political parties [Latin America, Caribbean, Dominican Republic]

Poirier, Christian—IEP de Bordeaux; address: 88 Avenue Charles de Gaule, 3320 Bordeaux, France; email: cpoirier@rsiep.iep.u-bord eaux.fr; research interests: political theory and philosophy, local and urban politics, politics and the arts [Canada, Europe]

Pradetto, August M—Universität der Bundeswehr Hamburg; address: Universität der Bundeswehr Hamburg, Fachbereich Wirtschafts- und Organisationwissenschaften, Holstenhofweg 85, 22043 Hamburg, Germany; fax: +49-40-65412726; email: august.predetto@unibw.ham burg.de; research interests: international relations, area studies (post communist countries), comparative politics [Central and Eastern Europe, Europe, Germany, USA - Europe]

Preciado Coronado, Jaime Antonio—University of Guadalajara; address: Calle Guanajuato 1045, Sector Hidalgo, Guadalajara, Jalisco 44600, Mexico; fax: +52-3-854 2195; email: japreco@hotmail.com; research interests: international relations, elections and voting behaviour, area studies [Latin America, Mexico]

Pross, Harry—Freie Universität Berlin, emeritus; address: Weissen No 4, D-88171 Weiler-simmberberg 1,

Germany; fax: +49-30-8387 2529; research interests: political theory and philosophy, mass media

Prud'homme, Jean-Francois—El Colegio de Mexico; address: Centro de Estudios Sociologicos, El Colegio de Mexico, Camino al Ajusco 20, 01740 DF, Mexico; fax: +52-5-645 0464; email: jfprud@colmex.mx; research interests: comparative politics, political parties, political theory and philosophy [Mexico, Latin America]

Pugliese, Elizabeth—Rosetta Research; address: PO Box 684643, Austin, TX 78768-4643, USA; fax: +1-512-326 9733; email: rosettars@ aol.com; research interests: international relations, international law, area studies [Eastern Europe]

Puhle, Hans Jürgen—Johann Wolfgang Goethe-Universität; address: Johann Wolfgang Goethe-Universi tät, Fachbereich Gesellschaftswissen schaften/Inst II, D-60054 Frankfurt-am-Main, Germany; fax: +49-69-7982 2881; email: puhle@soz.uni-frankfurt.de; research interests: comparative politics, political parties, political theory and philosophy [Europe, USA, Latin America]

Quermonne, Jean-Louis—IEP, Grenoble; address: 6, Allée de la Rose-raie, 38240 Meylan, France; fax: +33-1-4548 9945; research interests: comparative politics, European integration, central government

Rajput, Pam—Panjab University; address: Professor of Political Science, Panjab University, Chandigarh-160014, India; fax: +91-172-545 425; research interests: political executives, women and politics, international law [Asia Pacific, Africa, Latin America]

Rakhimkulov, Edward—Indiana University; address: 104 Banta Apartments, Bloomington, IN 47408, USA; fax: +1-812-855 0269; email: erakhimk@indiana.edu; research interests: comparative politics, public policy, public administration

[Central and Eastern Europe]
Ramaswamy, Sushila—Jesus and Mary College; *address*: 39C, Pocket A, Siddarth Extension, New Delhi - 110014, India; *fax*: +91-11-544 0916; *email*: polybins@ndb.vsnl.net.in; *research interests*: political theory and philosophy, women and politics, comparative politics [Asia Pacific]

Rappa, Antonio—National University of Singapore; *address*: Department of Political Science, National University of Singapore, 10 Kent Ridge Crescent, 119260, Singapore; *fax*: +65-779 6815; *email*: polar@nus.edu.sg; *research interests*: political theory and philosophy, comparative politics, public policy [Southeast Asia, Europe]

Ratan, Nil—AN Sinha Institute of Social Sciences; *address*: 56 Patliputra Colony, Patna-800013, Bihar, India; *email*: mlratan@dte.vsnl.net.in; *research interests*: area studies, development politics, dalit politics in India [India]

Rattan, Ram—University of Delhi; *address*: C-4/2, Rana Pratap Bagh, Delhi - 110007, India; *research interests*: Gandhian politics, Afro-American politics, modern Indian politics [India, America, Canada, South Africa]

Ravenal, Earl C—Cato Institute; *address*: 4439 Cathedral Avenue NW, Washington, DC 20016, USA; *fax*: +1-202-362 5414; *research interests*: international relations, political science methods, US foreign policy and military strategy [USA]

Ravenhill, John—University of Edinburgh; *address*: Department of Politics, University of Edinburgh, 31 Buccleuch Place, Edinburgh, EH8 9JT, UK; *fax*: +44-131-650 6546; *email*: john.ravenhill@ed.ac.uk; *research interests*: international relations, comparative politics [East Asia]

Reed, Steven R—Chuo University; *address*: 742-1 Higashinakano, Ha-chioji City, Tokyo 192-0933, Japan; *fax*: +81-42-669 0386; *email*: sreed@fps.chuo-u.ac.jp; *research interests*: comparative politics, elections and voting behaviour, political parties [Japan, Western Europe]

Reilly, Ben—International IDEA; *address*: Stromsborg, S-103 34, Stockholm, Sweden; *fax*: +46-8-202 422; *email*: b.reilly@idea.int; *research interests*: elections and voting behaviour, comparative politics [Asia Pacific]

Reinares, Fernando—University of Burgos; *address*: Reyes Católicos 17 (Casa 2), 28280 El Escorial, Madrid, Spain; *fax*: +34-91-896 1593; *email*: freinar@ubu.es; *research interests*: comparative politics, pressure groups, political violence [Western Europe, Latin America]

Reis, Elisa P—Federal University of Rio de Janeiro; *address*: Rua Conselheiro Lafayette, N° 4, apt 501, Rio de Janeiro, RJ - 22081-020, Brazil; *fax*: +55-21-286 7146; *email*: epreis@omega.cncc.br; *research interests*: political theory and philosophy, comparative politics, political sociology

Rendel, Margherita—University of London (reader emerita); *address*: 71, Clifton Hill, London NW8 OJN, UK; *fax*: +44-207-624 9626; *research interests*: women and politics, human rights, equality, control of arbitrary power [UK, Europe]

Resnick, Philip—University of British Columbia; *address*: Department of Political Science, University of British Columbia, Vancouver, V6T 1Z1, Canada; *fax*: +1-604-822 5540; *email*: resnick@interchange.ubc.ca; *research interests*: political theory and philosophy, comparative politics, political economy

Reuter, Lutz R—Bundeswehr Universität; *address*: Gartenholz 15, D-22926 Ahrensburg, Germany; *fax*: +49-40-6541 2762; *email*: lutz.reuter@unibw-hamburg.de; *research interests*: comparative politics, area

studies [Europe, USA, Southern Africa, PR of China]
Reutter, Werner M — Humboldt-Universität zu Berlin; *address*: Philosophische Fakultat III, Institut Sozialwissenschaften, Unter den Linden 6, 10099 Berlin, Germany; *fax*: +49-30-2093 1429; *email*: werner. reutter@rz.hu-berlin.de; *research interests*: elections and voting behaviour, comparative politics, public policy [Western Europe, USA]
Reyes, Socorro L — Centre for Legislative Development; *address*: Rm 217, Phillipine Social Science Centre, Commonwealth Ave, Quezon City, Philippines; *fax*: +63-2-927 2936; *email*: cld@info.com.ph; *research interests*: legislatures, public policy, women and politics
Rhee, Jong-Chan — Kookmin University; *address*: 2-506, Sunkyung Apartment, Daechi Dong, Gangnam Gu, Seoul 135-280, Korea; *fax*: +82-2-564 6289; *email*: jcrhee@kmu.kook min.ac.kr; *research interests*: comparative politics, development politics, international relations [East Asia]
Rhodes, Roderick AW — University of Newcastle; *address*: Department of Politics, University of Newcastle, Newcastle-upon-Tyne, NE1 7RU, UK; *fax*: +44-191-222 5069; *email*: r.a.w.rhodes@ncl.ac.uk; *research interests*: central government, public administration [UK, Western Europe (Denmark), Westminster system]
Rial, Juan — Peitho/Sociedad de Analisis Politico; *address*: 300 East 40th Street, AP 14B, New York, NY 10016-2149, USA; *fax*: +598-2-711 2384; *email*: peitho@adinet.com.uj; *research interests*: political parties, central government, comparative politics
Riccamboni, Gianni — *address*: Via del Santo 28, 35123 Padova, Italy; *fax*: +39-49-827 4029; *email*: gr@ux1. unipd.it; *research interests*: political

culture, elections and voting behaviour, area studies [Italy]
Rich, Paul — University of the Americas; *address*: University of the Americas, Sta Catrina Martir, Cholula, Puebla, 72820, Mexico; *fax*: +52-22-292 488; *email*: rich@hoover. stanford.edu; *research interests*: elections and voting behaviour, comparative politics, international relations [Mexico]
Riggs, Fred W — University of Hawai; *address*: 3920 Lurline Drive, Honolulu, HI 96316, USA; *fax*: +1-808-956 6877; *email*: fredr@hawaii.edu; *research interests*: comparative politics, public administration [Global interest]
Ringdal, Kristen — Norwegian University of Science & Technology; *address*: Department of Sociology & Political Science, Norwegian University of Science & Technology, N-7491 Trondheim, Norway; *fax*: +47-73-591 564; *email*: kristen.ringdal@ svt.ntnu.no; *research interests*: elections and voting behaviour, political science methods, organisational studies [Norway]
Rioux, Jean-Sebastien — Vrije Universiteit Brussel; *address*: Vesalius College - VUB, Pleinlaan 2, 1-5-Brussels, Belgium; *fax*: +32-2-629 3637; *email*: jrioux@vub.ac.be; *research interests*: international relations
Rittberger, Volker — Universität Tübingen; *address*: Centre for International Relations, University of Tübingen, Melanchthostr 36, D-72074 Tübingen, Germany; *fax*: +49-7071-292 417; *email*: volker.ritt berger@uni-tuebingen.de; *research interests*: international relations, comparative politics, political theory and philosophy [Europe]
Robins, Robert S — Tulane University; *address*: Department of Political Science, Tulane University, New Orleans, LA 70118, USA; *email*: robins@tulane.edu; *research interests*:

political psychology, biology and politics, political science methods [India]

Robinson, Lucy — Sage Publications; *address*: Sage Publications Limited, 6 Bonhill Street, London EC2A 4PU, UK; *fax*: +44-207-374 8741; *email*: lucy.robinson@sagepub.co.uk; *research interests*: international relations, political theory and philosophy, comparative politics

Rocha Valencia, Alberto — University of Guadalajara; *address*: Av De los Maestros y Av. Alcade, Puerta 1, Sector Hidalgo, CP 44260 Guadalajara, Jalisco, Mexico; *fax*: +52-3-854 2195; *email*: alrova@mail.udg.mx; *research interests*: international relations, regional integration [Latin America]

Rochtus, Dirk — Handelshogeschool, Centrum voor Duitslandstudiën; *address*: Handelshogeschool, Korte Nieuwstraat 33, B-2000 Antwerpen, Belgium; *fax*: +32-3-226 4404; *email*: dirk.rochtus@hha.be; *research interests*: international relations, comparative politics, political theory and philosophy [Germany, South Africa, Canada, Turkey]

Rodriguez, Mario Edgardo — Universidad Nacional de la Plata; *address*: Avda 51, nro 1087, piso 8 pato "D", 1900 La Plata, Argentina; *fax*: +54-221-429 1034; *email*: mariorod@net verk.com.ar; *research interests*: central government, public administration, development politics [America, Europe]

Rogerson, Kenneth — Duke University; *address*: DeWitt Wallace Center for Communications & Journalism, Box 90241, Duke University, Durham, NC 27708, USA; *fax*: +1-919-684 4279; *email*: rogerson@pps.duke.edu; *research interests*: international communications and media, international relations, comparative politics [Europe]

Rohdewohld, Rainer — German Agency for Technical Cooperation; *address*: GTZ/Support for Decentralisation Measures (SfDM), PO Box 4813, Jakarta 10048, Indonesia; *fax*: +62-21-386 8167; *email*: rainer.rohdewohld@ciptanet.com; *research interests*: public administration, development politics, area studies [Southeast Asia]

Rohr, John A — Virginia Tech; *address*: Centre for Public Administration and Policy, Virginia Tech, Blacksburg, VA 24061, USA; *fax*: +1-540-231 7067; *email*: jrohr@vt.edu; *research interests*: public administration, judicial systems and behaviour, comparative politics [France, Canada, UK]

Röiseland, Asbjörn — Bodö Regional University; *address*: Nordland Research Centre, N-8049 Bodö, Norway; *fax*: +47-75-517 234; *email*: asb joern.Roeiseland@hibo.no; *research interests*: public policy, local and urban politics, area studies

Rokkan, Elizabeth — *address*: 7 Maynard Court, Fairwater Road, Llandaff, Cardiff CF5 2LS, UK; *fax*: +44-2920-562 666; *research interests*: central government, area studies [Celtic nations and devolution]

Roman, Mikael — MIT; *address*: Center for International Studies, MIT, E38-264, Cambridge, MA 02139, USA; *fax*: +1-617-253 9330; *email*: mroman@mit.edu; *research interests*: comparative politics, public policy, environmental politics [South America, Europe]

Rommetvedt, Hilmar — Rogaland Research; *address*: Rogaland Research, PO Box 2503 Ullandhaug, N-4091 Stavanger, Norway; *fax*: +47-51-875 200; *email*: hilmar.rom metvedt@rf.no; *research interests*: legislatures, political executives, pressure groups

Ronen, Dov — Harvard University; *address*: 85 Griggs Road, Brookline, MA 02446, USA; *fax*: +1-617-232 7415; *email*: dov_ronen@hms.har vard.edu; *research interests*: comparative politics, area studies, international relations [Central Europe, Middle East, Africa]

Rosales, José Maria – University of Malaga; *address*: Departamento de Filosofia, Universidad de Malaga, Campus de Teatinos, Malaga 29071, Spain; *email*: jmrosales@uma.es; *research interests*: political theory and philosophy, comparative politics [Europe]

Rose, Lawrence E – University of Oslo; *address*: Department of Political Science, University of Oslo, PO Box 1097 Blindern, N-0317 Oslo, Norway; *fax*: +47-22-854 411; *email*: l.e.rose@stv.uio.no; *research interests*: democratic citizenship, political theory and philosophy, political science methods [Europe, North America]

Rose, Richard – University of Strathclyde; *address*: CSPP, University of Strathclyde, Glasgow G1 1XH, UK; *fax*: +44-141-552 4711; *research interests*: comparative politics, elections and voting behaviour, public policy

Rosenau, James – George Washington University; *address*: Apartment #901, 955 26th Street NW, Washington, DC 20037, USA; *fax*: +1-202-994 0792; *email*: jnr@gwu.edu; *research interests*: international relations, globalisation, comparative politics

Rothchild, Donald – University of California-Davis; *address*: Department of Political Science, University of California, Davis, CA 95616, USA; *fax*: +1-916-752 8666; *email*: dsrothchild@ucdavis.edu; *research interests*: ethnic conflict and conflict management, comparative politics, international relations [Africa]

Rothstein, Bo – Göteborg University; *address*: Department of Political Science, Box 711, SE 405 30 Göteborg, Sweden; *fax*: +46-31-773 4599; *email*: Bo.Rothstein@pol.qu.se; *research interests*: comparative politics, political theory and philosophy, public

policy [Europe]

Rouban, Luc – FNSP-CNRS; *address*: CEVIPOF, 10 rue de la Chaise, 75007 Paris, France; *fax*: +33-1-4222 0764; *email*: luc.rouban@cevipof. sciences-po.fr; *research interests*: central government, political executives, public administration [Europe]

Rubio, Luis – CIDAC; *address*: P O Box 60326 - AP 218, Houston, TX 77205, USA; *fax*: +52-5-395 9174; *email*: lfrubio@compuserve.com; *research interests*: political economy [Mexico, USA]

Rudder, Catherine E – APSA; *address*: APSA, 1527 New Hampshire Ave NW, Washington, DC 20036, USA; *fax*: +1-202-483 2657; *email*: rudder@ apsnet.org; *research interests*: legislative politics, non-profit organisations, public policy [USA, Europe]

Rukavishnikov, Vladimir – Russian Academy of Sciences; *address*: Marshala Zakharova str 13-36, Moscow 115569, Russia; *fax*: +7-095-938 1886; *email*: rukavish@matrix.ru; *research interests*: comparative politics, area studies, elections and voting behaviour [Russia, Europe, CIS]

Rule, Wilma – University of Nevada; *address*: 14 Hawkside Court, Markleeville, CA 96120, USA; *fax*: +1-530-694 2460; *email*: wilmarule@ gbis.com; *research interests*: legislatures, comparative politics, women and politics

Rush, Mark – Washington & Lee University; *address*: Department of Politics, Washington & Lee University, Lexington, VA 24450, USA; *fax*: +1-540-463 8639; *email*: rushm@ wlu.edu; *research interests*: elections and voting behaviour, political parties, judicial systems and behaviour [North America, Western Europe]

Russell, Peter H – University of Toronto; *address*: 21 Dale Avenue, Apartment 508, Toronto, ON, M4W 1K3, Canada; *fax*: +1-416-923 4446; *email*: phruss@aol.com; *research in-*

terests: judicial systems and behaviour, indigenous people [Canada, Australia]

Rutgers, Mark — Leiden University; *address*: Calslaan 18, 2314 GJ Leiden, Netherlands; *fax*: +31-71-527 3979; *email*: rutgers@fsw.leidenuniv.nl; *research interests*: public administration, political theory and philosophy, administrative history

Rydell, Randy — Department for Disarmament Affairs, United Nations; *address*: 5 Tudor City Place #1906, New York, NY 10017, USA; *fax*: +1-212-963 4066; *email*: rydell@un.org; *research interests*: international relations, public administration, public policy [South and East Asia]

Ryoo, Jae-Kap — Kyonggi University; *address*: College of Law & Political Science, Kyonggi University, Yuidong, Paldalku, Suwon, Kyonggi do 442-760, Republic of Korea; *fax*: +82-331-254 9695; *email*: sjbada@ kruie.kyonggi.ac.kr; *research interests*: comparative politics, area studies, international relations [USA, China, Korea]

Ryuen, Ekiji — Department of Jurisprudence; *address*: Otuka 359, Hachiaji-shi, Tokyo 192-0395, Japan; *fax*: +81-42-676 0388; *email*: eryuen@ main.teikyo-u.ac.jp; *research interests*: public policy, comparative politics, international relations [Japan]

Safran, William — University of Colorado; *address*: Department of Political Science, University of Colorado, Campus Box 333, Boulder, CO 80309, USA; *fax*: +1-303-492 0978; *email*: safran@colorado.edu; *research interests*: comparative politics, area studies, ethnic politics [Western Europe, France]

Sala de Davies, Celia Amanda — *address*: Brown 183, Trelew - Chubut, CP 9100, Argentina; *fax*: +54-29-6542 2745; *email*: celiaamandasala @topmail.com.ar; *research interests*: women and politics, political science methods, development politics

Sala-Porras, Alejandra — UNAM; *address*: Buhos 33 Col Lomas de Guadalupe, Delegacio Alvaro Obregon, Mexico, DF 01720, Mexico; *fax*: +52-5-665 1786; *email*: asalas porras@hotmail.com; *research interests*: international relations, policy networks, business interest intermediation [Mexico, Latin America]

Samaras, Athenassios — Sigma Multimedia, IOM; *address*: Str Syndesmon 14A, PO: 15669 Kolonaki, Athens, Greece; *fax*: +30-1-361 8693; *email*: a.samaras@sussex.ac.uk; *research interests*: elections and voting behaviour, political parties, political science methods [Greece, USA]

Samoff, Joel — Stanford University; *address*: 3527 South Court, Palo Alto, CA 94306, USA; *fax*: +1-650-856 2326; *email*: joel.samoff@ stanford.edu; *research interests*: comparative politics, area studies, development politics [Africa]

Sanchez-Ruiz, Enrique — Universidad de Guadalajara; *address*: Circunvalacion Norte 187-8, Col Las Fuentes, Zapopan, Jal, 45070, Mexico; *email*: rock@foreigner.class.udg. mx; *research interests*: international relations, comparative politics, mass media and political culture [NAFTA]

Sandberg, Siv — Åbo Akademi; *address*: Åbo Akademi, Department of Public Administration, Biskopsgatan 15, FIN-20500 ÅBO, Finland; *fax*: +358-2-215 4585; *email*: siv. sandberg@abo.fi; *research interests*: local and urban politics, public administration, public policy

Sankhdher, Madan M — University of Delhi; *address*: 89 Vaishali, Pitampura, Delhi - 110034, India; *fax*: +91-11-744 1284; *email*: sankh@hot mail.com; *research interests*: political theory and philosophy, area studies, public policy [India]

Sankhdher, Mandakini — Poona University; *address*: 89 Vaishali, Pitampura, Delhi - 110034, India; *fax*: +91-11-744 1284; *email*: sankh@hot mail.com; *research interests*: art journalism, broadcast, musicology [India]

Santa Cruz, Arturo — Universidad de Guadalajara; *address*: Montenegro 1907, Guadalajaca, Jac, 44100, USA; *fax*: +52-3-853 3318; *email*: jas116@cornell.edu; *research interests*: international relations, comparative politics, development politics [Mexico]

Sargent, Lyman T — University of Missouri-St Louis; *address*: Department of Political Science, University of Missouri-St Louis, 8001 Natural Bridge Road, St Louis, MO 63121, USA; *fax*: +1-314-516 5268; *email*: lyman.sargent@umsl.edu; *research interests*: political theory and philosophy

Satineau, Maurice — *address*: Gratta Paille 13, 1018 Lausanne Vaud, Switzerland; *fax*: +41-21-648 6533; *research interests*: political communication

Sauer, Birgit — Universität Wien; *address*: A-1090 Wien, Wahringer Strasse 17, Austria; *fax*: +43-1-4277 47719; *email*: brigit.sauer@univie.ac. at; *research interests*: political theory and philosophy, comparative politics, women and politics [Europe]

Saunders, Cheryl — University of Melbourne; *address*: Faculty of Law, University of Melbourne, Victoria 3010, Australia; *email*: saunders@law.unimelb.edu.au; *research interests*: constitutions, comparative constitutions, federalism [Australia, Asia]

Sawshilya, Archana — Delhi University; *address*: c/o Dr Shalini, K-10 Model Town, Delhi - 110009, India; *research interests*: public administration, women and politics, political theory and philosophy [India, USA]

Sbragia, Alberta — University of Pittsburgh; *address*: 4G38 Wesley W Posvar Hall, University of Pitts-

burgh, Pittsburgh, PA 15260, USA; *fax*: +1-412-648 2199; *email*: sbragia@ucis.pitt.edu; *research interests*: comparative politics, area studies, public policy [EU]

Schachter, Hindy L — New Jersey Institute of Technology; *address*: 420 East 64 Street, New York, NY 10021, USA; *fax*: +1-973-596 3074; *email*: schachterh@admin.njit.edu; *research interests*: public administration, public policy

Schaefer, Guenther F — European Institute of Public Administration; *address*: European Institute of Public Administration, PO Box 1229, NL-6201 BE Maastricht, Netherlands; *fax*: +31-43-329 6296; *email*: g.schaefer@eipsa-nl.com; *research interests*: public policy, comparative politics, European system of governance especially committees and comitology [Europe]

Schedler, Andreas — FLACSO; *address*: Facultad Latinoamericana de Ciencias Sociales (FLACSO), Camino al Ajusco 377, Col Heroes de Padierna, Delegacion Alvaro Obregón, CP 14200 Mexico, DF, Mexico; *fax*: +52-5-631 6609; *email*: andreas@flasco.flacso.edu.mx; *research interests*: elections and voting behaviour, comparative politics, political science methods [Latin America]

Schemeil, Yves — IEP de Grenoble; *address*: Institut d'Etudes Politiques de Grenoble, BP 48, 38040 Grenoble, Cedex 9, France; *fax*: +33-4-7689 4372; *email*: schemeil@cidsp.upmf-grenoble.fr; *research interests*: comparative politics [Europe, Middle East]

Schild, Veronica — University of Western Ortario; *address*: Department of Political Science, Faculty of Social Science, University of Western Ontario, London, Ontario N6A 5C2, Canada; *fax*: +1-519-661 3904; *email*: vschild@julian.uwo.ca; *research interests*: comparative politics, area studies, political theory and philosophy [Latin America, Chile]

Schlager, Edella — University of Arizona; *address*: 2200 E Edison Street, Tucson, AZ 85719, USA; *fax*: +1-520-626 5549; *email*: bluff2u@aol.com; *research interests*: public administration, public policy

Schlichte, Klaus — Universität Hamburg; *address*: Institut für Politische Wissenschaft, Universität Hamburg, Allende-Platz 1, D-20146 Hamburg, Germany; *fax*: +49-40-42838 2460; *email*: kschlichte@yahoo.com; *research interests*: international relations, political theory and philosophy, comparative politics [third world]

Schmidhauser, John R — University of Southern California; *address*: 726 Arbol Verde Street, Carpinteria, CA 93013, USA; *email*: jschmidhau@aol.com; *research interests*: judicial politics, comparative legal systems and politics

Schmidt, Gustav F — Ruhr Universität Bochum; *address*: Am Ossenbrink 2a, D-58313 Herdecke, Germany; *fax*: +49-234-322 532 ext 112; *email*: gustav.schmidt@ruhr-uni-bochum.de; *research interests*: comparative politics, area studies, international relations [USA, Europe, Asia Pacific]

Schmidt, Manfred — Universität Bremen; *address*: Zentrum für Sozial politik, Universität Bremen, Park allee 39, 28209 Bremen, Germany; *fax*: +49-421-218 4052; *email*: mgs@zes.uni-bremen.de; *research interests*: public policy, comparative politics

Schmidt, Vivien — Boston University; *address*: 205 Beacon Street, Boston, MA 02116, USA; *fax*: +1-617-353 9290; *email*: vschmidt@bu.edu; *research interests*: area studies, comparative politics, political theory and philosophy [Europe, France]

Schneider, Eberhard — Bundesinstitut für Ostwissen, University of Inter-

national Studies; *address*: Wichterstrasse 25, D-50937 Köln, Germany; *fax*: +49-221-468 0821; *email*: mail@eberhardt.schneider.de; *research interests*: area studies, political parties, elections and voting behaviour [Russia]

Schneider, Gerald — Universität Konstanz; *address*: Faculty of Public Policy & Management, Universität Konstanz, PO Box D86, D-78457 Konstanz, Germany; *fax*: +49-7531-88 2774; *email*: gerald.schneider@uni-ko-stanz.de; *research interests*: international relations, political theory and philosophy, political science methods [OECD, Europe]

Schneider, Hans-Peter — Universität Hannover; *address*: Universität Hannover, Fachbereich Rechtswissenschaften, Koenigsworther Platz 1, D-30167 Hannover, Germany; *fax*: +49-511-762 8173; *email*: nhjchps@rrzn-user.uni-hannover.de; *research interests*: political parties, comparative politics, international law

Schneier, Edward — City College, CUNY; *address*: 1284 Lakeview Road, Copake, NY 12516, USA; *fax*: +1-212-650 5468; *email*: neds@taconic.net; *research interests*: legislatures, public policy, comparative politics [USA, Iceland]

Schoenberg, Hans W — *address*: Postfach 101322, D-80087 Munich, Germany; *fax*: +49-89-335 583

Schrecker, Ted — *address*: 450 rue de la Congregation, Montréal, Quèbec, H3K 2H7, Canada; *email*: tschrecker@sympatico.ca; *research interests*: political theory and philosophy, public policy, globalisation [North America]

Schröter, Eckhard — Humboldt-Universität zu Berlin; *address*: Humboldt-Universität zu Berlin, Institut für Sozialwissenschaft, Unter den Linden 6, D-10099 Berlin, Germany; *fax*: +49-30-2093 1500; *email*: eckhard.schroeter@rz.hu-berlin.de; *research interests*: public administration, public policy, comparative politics [Europe]

Schüttemeyer, Suzanne S — Universität Potsdam; *address*: Haupt Strasse 40, D-25497 Prisdorf, Germany; *fax*: +49-331-977 3291; *email*: sschnett@rz.uni-potsdam.de; *research interests*: legislatures, political parties, comparative politics

Schwartz, Mildred A — New York University; *address*: 326 Prospect Avenue, Apt 5F, Hackensack, NJ 07601, USA; *email*: Mildred@uic.edu; *research interests*: political parties, elections and voting behaviour, comparative politics [Canada, USA]

Scienceman, David M — *address*: c/o Australian Rural Group Limited, PO Box 307, Bathurst, New South Wales 2795, Australia; *fax*: +61-63-311 513; *research interests*: political parties, political theory and philosophy, public policy

Segbers, Klaus — Freie Universität Berlin; *address*: Institute for East European Studies, Freie Universität Berlin, Garirstr 55, D-14195 Berlin, Germany; *fax*: +49-30-8385 3616; *email*: segbers@zedat.fu-berlin.de; *research interests*: international relations, transformation of Eastern Europe [Eastern Europe]

Seidle, F Leslie — Privy Council Office; *address*: Director General, Policy and Research, Privy Council Office, 2144-66 Slater Street, Ottawa, K1A 0A3, Canada; *fax*: +1-613-947 7581; *email*: lseidle@pco-bcp.gc.ca

Seliger, Martin — The Hebrew University; *address*: 3 Guatemala Street, 96704 Jerusalem, Israel; *fax*: +972-2-643 9535; *email*: mseli@mscc.huji.ac.il; *research interests*: political philosophy

Senese, Paul — SUNY-Buffalo; *address*: 520 Park Hall, Department of Political Science, SUNY, Buffalo, NY 14214, USA; *fax*: +1-716-645 2166; *email*: pdsenese@acsu.buffalo.edu; *research interests*: international relations, political science methods

Seroka, Jim — Auburn University; *address*: Director, Center for Governmental Services, 2236 Haley Center, Auburn University, AL 36849-5225, USA; *fax*: +1-334-844 4781; *email*: jseroka@auburn.edu; *research interests*: comparative politics, area studies, local and urban politics [East and Central Europe]

Sevgilier, Ulkem O — University of London; *address*: 1 Penton Rise, B142, London WC1X 9EH, UK; *email*: ulkem1@excite.com; *research interests*: elections and voting behaviour, political parties, area studies [Turkey]

Shamir, Michal — Tel Aviv University; *address*: Department of Political Science, Tel Aviv University, Tel Aviv 69978, Israel; *fax*: +972-3-640 9515; *email*: m3600@post.tau.ac.il; *research interests*: elections and voting behaviour, comparative politics, political science methods

Shanley, Mary L — Vassar College; *address*: Department of Political Science, Box 455, Vassar College, Poughkeepsie, NY 12604-0455, USA; *fax*: +1-914-437 7599; *email*: shanley@vassar.edu; *research interests*: political theory and philosophy, women and politics, area studies [USA]

Shapiro, Ovadia — University of Haifa; *address*: Department of Sociology, University of Haifa, 31905 Haifa, Israel; *fax*: +972-4-824 0819; *research interests*: political parties, elections and voting behaviour, comparative politics [Israel]

Sharan, Sarojini — Patna University; *address*: c/o Mrs Shambhu Sharan, Salimpur Ahra Road, Lane-1, Patna 800003, India; *email*: dt@mecon.nic.in; *research interests*: political sociology, women and politics, comparative politics [South Asia]

Sharma, Deepak — Khalsa College, University of Delhi; *address*: H-19/130 Sector-VII, Rohini, Delhi - 110085, India; *email*: sharmad@ndb.

vsnl.net.in; *research interests*: public administration, public policy, development politics [Canada, Britain, USA]

Sharma, Om P – University of Delhi, Bhagat Singh (Eye) College; *address*: B-24 Radhey Puri, Krishna Nagar, Delhi - 110051, India; *fax*: +91-11-687 2746; *email*: cpr@giasdlOl.vsnl. net.in; *research interests*: public administration, public policy, comparative politics

Sharma, RD – Institute of Policy Research & Analysis; *address*: Institute of Policy Research & Analysis, Summer Resort, near Luxmi Naranyan Temple, Sanjauli-Shimla, India; *fax*: +91-177-241 245; *research interests*: political executives, public administration, public policy making [India, France, Germany, UK, USA, Canada]

Sharp, Andrew – University of Auckland; *address*: Department of Political Science, University of Auckland, Private Bag 92019, Auckland, New Zealand; *fax*: +64-9-360 2386; *email*: a.sharp@aukland. ac.nz; *research interests*: political theory and philosophy, area studies, indigenous politics [New Zealand, USA, Europe]

Shaw, Timothy M – Dalhousie University; *address*: Department of Political Science, Dalhousie University, Halifax, Nova Scotia, B3H 4H6, Canada; *fax*: +1-902-494 3825; *email*: tshaw@is.dal.ca; *research interests*: international relations, development politics, comparative politics [Africa]

Shestopal, Helen – Moscow State University; *address*: Stroitelei 4-2-8, 117311 Moscow, Russia; *fax*: +7-095-939 2208; *email*: shestop@aha.ru; *research interests*: elections and voting behaviour, political psychology, transition to democracy

Shin, Doh C – University of Missouri; *address*: Department of Political Science, 113 Professional Building, University of Missouri, Columbia, MO 65211, USA; *fax*: +1-573-884 5131; *email*: shind@missouri.edu; *research interests*: comparative politics, development politics, elections and voting behaviour

Shin, Myungsoon – Yonsei University; *address*: 2091-6 Daehwa-Dong, Ilsan-Gu, Koyang City, Kyongki-Do, Republic of Korea; *fax*: +82-2-393 7642; *email*: msshin@ellie. yonsei.ac.kr; *research interests*: comparative politics, political parties, elections and voting behaviour [Korea, third world]

Shinkawa, Toshimitsu – Hokkaido University; *address*: Kita 9, Nishi 7, Kita-ku, Sapporo Hokkaido 060-0809, Japan; *fax*: +11-81-706 4948; *email*: shinkawa@juris.hokudai.ac. jp; *research interests*: comparative politics, central government, political parties [Japan, Canada, USA]

Shiraishi, Masaki – Soka University; *address*: 2-14-11-1104 Kasuga-cho, Iruma-shi, 3580006 Saitama-ken, Japan; *fax*: +81-42-691 8507; *email*: siraisi@mail.s.soka.ac.jp; *research interests*: political theory and philosophy, comparative politics, area studies [Asia, France]

Shiratori, Hiroshi – Shizuoka University; *address*: 3-1-5-502 Yahata, Shizuoka-shi, Shizuoka 422-8076, Japan; *fax*: +81-54-282 9755; *email*: hiro_shiratori@msn.com; *research interests*: comparative politics, political parties, development politics [Japan]

Shrivastava, Rashmi – Vikram University; *address*: D-2, Vikram University Campus, Dewas Road, Ujjain-456010, India; *email*: mayank 444@aol.com; *research interests*: legislatures, political parties, elections and voting behaviour [USA, India, UK]

Shukla, Surinder K – Panjab University; *address*: 62, Sector 11-A, Chandigarh 160 011, India; *fax*: +91-172-747 525; *email*: surindershukla

@usa.net; *research interests*: international relations, comparative politics, area studies [Western and South Asia]

Siaroff, Alan — University of Lethbridge; *address*: Department of Political Science, University of Lethbridge, 4401 University Drive, Lethbridge, Alberta, T1K 3M4, Canada; *fax*: +1-403-382 7148; *email*: alan.siaroff@uleth.ca; *research interests*: comparative politics, elections and voting behaviour, political executives [Europe]

Sidjanski, Dusan — Université de Genève; *address*: 16, chemin de la Rippaz, 1223 Cologny-Genève, Switzerland; *fax*: +41-22-752 4324; *research interests*: European integration, federal future of Europe, pressure groups, comparative politics [Europe, Latin America, UAE]

Siedschlag, Alexander — Humboldt-Universität zu Berlin; *address*: Eisenzahnstr 16, D-10709 Berlin, Germany; *fax*: +49-30-891 5618; *email*: alexander.siedschlag@rz.hu-berlin.de; *research interests*: international relations, comparative politics, political theory and philosophy [Europe, Transatlantic]

Siemienska, Renata — University of Warsaw; *address*: Institute of Sociology, University of Warsaw, Karowa 18, 00-324 Warsaw, Poland; *fax*: +48-22-826 5591; *email*: siemiens@optimus.waw.pl; *research interests*: elections and voting behaviour, local and urban politics, women and politics [EU, Central and Eastern Europe, North America]

Sigel, Roberta — Rutgers University; *address*: Department of Political Science, Douglass College, Rutgers University, New Brunswick, NJ 08903, USA; *fax*: +1-609-466 8011; *email*: rsigel@aol.com; *research interests*: public opinion, gender attitudes, political psychology [USA, Western Europe]

Simone, Vera — California State University-Fullerton; *address*: 1849 Greenfield #105, Los Angeles, CA 90025, USA; *fax*: +1-310-473 1934; *email*: vsimone@ix.netcom.com; *research interests*: comparative politics, area studies, development politics [China, Asia Pacific]

Sinclair, Barbara — University of California-Los Angeles; *address*: Department of Political Science, Box 951472, University of California, Los Angeles, CA 90095-1472, USA; *fax*: +1-310-825 0778; *email*: sinclair@polisci.ucla.edu; *research interests*: legislatures, political parties, women and politics [USA]

Sing, Ming — City University of Hong Kong; *address*: Department of Public & Social Administration, City University of Hong Kong, Tat Chee Avenue, Kowloon Tong, Hong Kong; *fax*: +852-2788 8926; *email*: sasing@cityu.edu.hk; *research interests*: comparative politics; comparative democratisation, legislatures, political parties [Asia, Hong Kong]

Singer, J David — University of Michigan; *address*: Department of Political Science, University of Michigan, Ann Arbor, MI 48109-1045, USA; *fax*: +1-734-764 3522; *email*: jdsinger@umich.edu; *research interests*: international relations, public policy, political science methods

Singh, Jagpal — Indira Gandhi National Open University; *address*: Faculty of Political Science, School of Social Sciences, Indira Gandhi National Open University, Maidan Garhi, New Delhi 110068, India; *fax*: +91-11-686 2312; *email*: jagpal9@hotmail.com; *research interests*: development and politics, area studies, agrarian politics and identity politics [India, South Asia]

Singh, Lekh Raj — University of Pune; *address*: Teachers Quarters Block F/2, University of Pune, Pune 411 007, India; *fax*: +91-20-565 3899;

email: lekhraj@unipune.ernet.in; *research interests:* area studies, international relations, public policy [China]

Singleton, Gwynneth — University of Canberra; *address:* Faculty of Management & Technology, University of Canberra, ACT 2601, Australia; *fax:* +61-2-5201 5239; *email:* gms@management.canberra.edu.au; *research interests:* political parties, pressure groups, trade unions

Sinha, Niroj — Patna University; *address:* 49-B, SK Puri, Patna - 800001, Bihar, India; *fax:* +91-612-229 189; *email:* nirojsinha@hotmail.com; *research interests:* elections and voting behaviour, local and urban politics, women and politics [India, South Asia]

Sixto, Peraza Padron — University de la Laguna; *address:* Camino la Hornera Sn, Facultad de Ciencias Economicas y Empresariales, La Laguna 38071, Tenerife, Spain; *research interests:* public policy, public administration, legislatures [EU, Latin America]

Sjöblom, Gunnar — Institute of Political Science; *address:* Institute of Political Science, Rosenborggade 15, DK-Copenhagen, Denmark; *fax:* +45-35-323 3399

Skach, Cindy — Yale University; *address:* 549 W 123rd Street, Apart 14H, New York, NY 10027, USA; *email:* cls13@columbia.edu; *research interests:* comparative politics, political executives, political parties [Europe]

Škaloud, Jan — University of Economics; *address:* Taussigova 1169, 182 00 Praha 8, Czech Republic; *fax:* +420-724-220 657; *email:* skaloud@vse.cz; *research interests:* political executives, political parties, political theory and philosophy

Sklar, Richard L — UCLA; *address:* Department of Political Science, University of California, Los Angeles, CA 90095-1472, USA; *fax:* +1-

310-825 0778; *email:* sklar@polisci.ucla.edu; *research interests:* comparative politics, area studies, development politics [Africa]

Skuhra, Anselm — University of Salzburg; *address:* Rudolfskai 42, A-5020 Salzburg, Austria; *fax:* +43-662-6389 6614; *email:* anselm.skuhra@sbg.ac.at; *research interests:* international relations

Slomczynski, Kazimierz M — Ohio State University; *address:* Department of Sociology, Ohio State University, 300 Bricker Hall, 190 N Oval Hall, Columbus, OH 43210, USA; *fax:* +1-614-292 6687; *email:* slomczynski.i@osu.edu; *research interests:* comparative politics, development politics, political science methods [East-Central Europe]

Smith, Andrew — Université Bordeaux IV; *address:* CERVL IEP de Bordeaux, BP 101 Domaine Universitaire, 33405 Talence Cedex, France; *fax:* +33-5-5684 4329; *email:* a.smith@iep.u-bordeaux.fr; *research interests:* comparative politics, international relations, pressure groups

Smith, Rand — Lake Forest College; *address:* 1110 Madison Street, Evanston, IL 60202, USA; *fax:* +1-847-735 6292; *email:* rsmith@lfc.edu; *research interests:* comparative politics, public policy, comparative political economy [Western Europe, Latin America]

Smorgunov, Leonid — St Petersburg State University; *address:* 199034, St Petersburg, Mendeleevskayailinia 5, Faculty of Philosophy, Russia; *fax:* +7-812-328 0871; *email:* Leonid@LS2502.spb.edu; *research interests:* comparative politics, public administration, political theory and philosophy

Sohn, Bong Scuk — Center for Korean Women & Politics; *address:* 256-13 Gpongduk-dong, Jaeil Bldg #906, Mapo-ku, Seoul 121-020, Republic of Korea; *fax:* +82-2-706 6765; *email:*

ckwp@www.feminist.or.kr; *research interests*: comparative politics, women and politics [Korea, Asia Pacific]
Soler, Silvestre Segarra—*address*: Licenciado en Derecho y, Ciencas Economicas UCD, Plaza Santo Angel 12, 12600 Vall de UXO, Castellon, Spain; *research interests*: elections and voting behaviour, public administration, public policy [Spain, Europe]
Solingen, Etel—University of California-Irvine; *address*: 2927 Woodwardia Drive, Los Angeles, CA 90077, USA; *fax*: +1-310-441 0056; *email*: esolinge@uci.edu; *research interests*: international relations, comparative politics, development politics [Middle East, East Asia, Latin America]
Somit, Albert—Southern Illinois University-Carbondale; *address*: Room 256, Lesar Law Building, Southern Illinois University, Carbondale, IL 62901-6804, USA; *fax*: +1-618-453 8728; *research interests*: political theory and philosophy, political science methods
Somjee, Geeta—Simon Fraser University; *address*: Department of Political Science, Simon Fraser University, Burnaby, BC CSA 156, Canada; *email*: somjee@sfu.ca; *research interests*: health policy in Asia and women's participation, women and politics, development politics
Sonenshein, Raphael—California State University-Fullerton; *address*: Department of Political Science, California State University, Fullerton, CA 92634, USA; *fax*: +1-714-278 3524; *email*: rsonenshein@fullerton.edu; *research interests*: local and urban politics, public policy, elections and voting behaviour [USA]
Soni, Vidu—Central Michigan University; *address*: Central Michigan University, Department of Political Science, 235 Anspach, Mount Pleas-

ant, MI 48858, USA; *fax*: +1-517-774 1136; *email*: vidu.soni@cmich.edu
Sorbets, Claude—CNRS, IEP; *address*: CERVL - IEP, Domaine Universitaire Talence, BP 101, 33405 Talence, France; *fax*: +33-5-5684 4329; *email*: c.sorbets@iep.u-bordeaux.fr; *research interests*: local and urban politics, political science methods, public policy [France, Europe]
Sotiropoulos, Dimitri A—University of Athens; *address*: 22 Dorylaiou Street, Plateia Mavili, Athens GR-115 21, Greece; *fax*: +30-1-645 9937; *email*: dsotirop@cc.uoa.gr; *research interests*: comparative politics, public administration, area studies [Southern Europe, the Balkans]
Souza Jnr, Cezar Saldanha—Universidade Federal do Rio Grande do Sul; *address*: Rua Riachuelo 1305, ap. 1401, 90.010-271 Porto Alegre/rs, Brazil; *fax*: +55-51-316 3987; *email*: souzajr@vortex.ufrgs.br; *research interests*: political executives, political parties, political theory and philosophy [South America]
Sprinz, Detlef—Potsdam Institute for Climate Impact Research; *address*: c/o Potsdam Institute for Climate Impact Research, Global Change & Social, Systems, PO Box 601203, D-14412 Potsdam, Germany; *fax*: +49-331-288 2600; *email*: dsprinz@pik-potsdam.de; *research interests*: international relations, comparative politics, environmental politics [Europe]
Sridharan, Eswaran—University of Pennsylvania, Institute for the Advanced Study of India; *address*: University of Pennsylvania Institute, for the Advanced Study of India, India Habitat Center, Lodi Road, New Delhi 110003, India; *fax*: +91-11-469 8201; *email*: upiasi@del2.vsnl.net.in; *research interests*: comparative politics, international relations, elections and voting behaviour [India, East Asia]

Srivastava, Renu—*address*: N-9/31 A-19 Brij Enclave Extn II, PO Bajardiha, Varanasi 221109, India; *research interests*: public administration [Asia, India]

Stahel, Albert A—University of Zurich, Swiss Military College of Zurich; *address*: MFS-FTHZ, Steinacherstr. 101b, 8804 An/Wädensee 1, Switzerland; *fax*: +41-11-781 3077; *email*: stahel@mfs.ethz.ch; *research interests*: peace science, strategic studies, game theory [Russia, China, Afghanistan]

Starr, Harvey—University of South Carolina; *address*: Department of Government & International Studies, University of South Carolina, Columbia, SC 29208, USA; *fax*: +1-803-777 8255; *email*: starr-harve@sc.edu; *research interests*: international relations, political science methods, international law

Statham, E Robert, Jr—University of Guam; *address*: University of Guam, Division of Social & Behavioural Sciences, UOG Station, Mangilao, Guam 96923, USA; *fax*: +1-671-734-5255; *email*: estatham@uog9.uog.edu; *research interests*: political theory and philosophy, judicial systems and behaviour, area studies [Asia Pacific, USA]

Steen, Anton—University of Oslo; *address*: Department of Political Science, PO Box 1097, University of Oslo, 0317 Oslo, Norway; *fax*: +47-22-854 411; *email*: anton.steen@stv.uio.no; *research interests*: public policy, political elites, comparative politics [Nordic countries, Baltic states, Russia]

Stein, Michael B—McMaster University; *address*: Department of Political Science, McMaster University, Hamilton, ON, L8S 4M4, Canada; *fax*: +1-905-527 3071; *email*: steinm@mcmaster.ca; *research interests*: comparative politics, political parties, comparative federalism [Canada]

Steinbauer, Franz—Institute for Advanced Studies; *address*: Stumperg. 56, A-1060 Wien, Austria; *fax*: +43-1-5999 1171; *email*: steinbau@his.ac.at; *research interests*: comparative politics, international relations, women and politics [Europe]

Still, Edward—*address*: Lawyers' Committee for Civil Rights Under Law, 1401 New York Avenue NW, Suite 400, Washington, DC 20005-2124, USA; *fax*: +1-202-783 5130; *email*: still@votelaw.com; *research interests*: elections and voting behaviour, judicial systems and behaviour, legislatures

Stoerker, CF—City University of New York, emeritus; *address*: 567 Mayflower Road, Claremont, CA 91711, USA; *research interests*: American constitution, public opinion, politics and religion

Stokke, Olav Schram—The Fridtjof Nansen Institute; *address*: The Fridtjof Nansen Institute, PB 326, 1326 Lysaker, Norway; *fax*: +47-67-111 910; *email*: olav.s.stokke@fni.no; *research interests*: international relations, comparative politics, political science methods [Polar, Europe]

Story, Jonathan—INSEAD; *address*: INSEAD, Boulevard de Constance, 77305 Fontainebleau, France; *fax*: +33-60-745 500; *email*: jonathan.story@insead.fr; *research interests*: european integration, transition economics, international and comparative political economy [EU]

Subirats, Joan—Universitat Autonoma Barcelona; *address*: Vallirana 57, ES-08006 Barcelona, Spain; *fax*: +34-93-581 2439; *email*: joan.subirats@uab.es; *research interests*: public policy, public administration, local and urban politics [Europe, Spain, Latin America]

Sud, Usha—University of Delhi (retired); *address*: A8A Friends Colony (East), New Delhi - 65, India; *fax*: +91-11-684 6632; *email*: psud@aol.com; *research interests*: international relations, women and politics

Sundberg, Jan—University of Helsinki; *address*: Department of Political Science, PO Box 54, SF-00014 University of Helsinki, Finland; *fax*: +358-9-191 8832; *email*: jan.sundberg @helsinki.fi; *research interests*: political parties, comparative politics [Scandanavia, Europe]

Suzuki, Teruji—Tokai University; *address*: Chiba, Mihama-ku, Utase 1-4, Patios 8-202, Japan; *fax*: +81-43-211 6836; *research interests*: political theory and philosophy, comparative politics, area studies

Svåsand, Lars—University of Bergen; *address*: Department of Comparative Politics, University of Bergen, Christiesgt 15, N-5007 Bergen, Norway; *fax*: +47-55-589 425; *email*: lars.svasand@isp.uib.no; *research interests*: political parties, comparative politics, elections and voting behaviour [Europe, USA, Africa]

Svensson, Torsten—Uppsala University; *address*: Department of Government, Research Programme "The Swedish Model in Change", Kyrkogerdsgatan 2B, 753 12 Uppsala, Sweden; *fax*: +46-18-471 6326; *email*: Torsten.Svensson@ statsvet.uu.se; *research interests*: industrial relations, comparative politics, political science methods

Swarup, Hem Lata—Kanpur University; *address*: 111/98 A, Ashok Nagar, Kanpur 208012, India; *fax*: +91-512-559 042; *research interests*: women and politics, political theory and philosophy, sustainable development, gender politics [developing countries]

Swyngedouw, Marc—Catholic University of Brussels; *address*: Vrijheidslaan 17, 1081 Bruxelles, Belgium; *fax*: +32-2-412 4200; *email*: marc.swyngedouw@soc.kuleuven.a c.be; *research interests*: elections and voting behaviour, comparative politics, political science methods [Belgium, France, USA]

Sylla, Lancine—Université de Co-

cody - Abidjan; *address*: 06 BP 425 Cedex 1, Abidjan 06, Ivory Coast; *fax*: +225-441 407; *research interests*: political parties, comparative politics, development politics [Africa, third world]

Sznajder, Mario S—The Hebrew University; *address*: Department of Political Science, The Hebrew University, Mount Scopus, 91905 Jerusalem, Israel; *fax*: +972-2-588133; *email*: msmarios@mscc.huji.ac.il; *research interests*: comparative politics, political theory and philosophy [Latin America, Chile, Italy]

Szyliowicz, Joseph—Denver University; *address*: 5450 S Newport Circle, Englewood, CO 80111, USA; *fax*: +1-303-871 2456; *email*: jszyliow@ du.edu; *research interests*: public policy (transportation), comparative politics, area studies [Turkey, Middle East]

Taber, Charles S—SUNY-Stony Brook; *address*: Department of Political Science, SUNY, Stony Brook, NY 11794-4392, USA; *fax*: +1-631-632 4116; *email*: chuck@datalab2.sbs. sunysb.edu; *research interests*: international relations, political psychology, political science methods

Talcott, Paul—Harvard University; *address*: 1737 Cambridge Street, Room 502, Cambridge, MA 02138, USA; *fax*: +1-617-495 4921; *email*: talcott@fas.harvard.edu; *research interests*: comparative politics, pressure groups, elections and voting behaviour

Talekar, Vandana—HPT Arts & RYK Science College; *address*: Smita, 40/2 Erandavan, Bhonde Colony, Kasve Road, Pune 411 004, Maharashtra, India; *research interests*: local and urban politics, women and politics [India]

Tanaka, Yasumasa—Gakushuin University; *address*: 1-5-1 Mejiro, Toshima-ku, Tokyo 171-8588, Japan; *fax*: +81-3-5992 1006; *email*: yas umasa.tanaka@gakushuin.ac.jp; *re-*

search interests: elections and voting behaviour, international relations

Taniguchi, Masaki — University of Tokyo; *address*: Graduate School of Law, 7-3-1- Hongo, Bunkyo-ku, Tokyo 113-0033, Japan; *fax*: +81-3-5841 3291; *email*: masaki@j.u-tokyo.ac.jp; *research interests*: political parties, comparative politics, area studies [Japan]

Tate, C Neal — University of North Texas; *address*: Robert B Toulouse School of Graduate Studies, University of North Texas, PO Box 5459, Denton, TX 76203-5459, USA; *fax*: +1-517-369 7486; *email*: ntate@unt.edu; *research interests*: judiciaries, comparative politics, development politics [Asia]

Tehranian, Majid — Toda Institute for Global Peace and Policy Research; *address*: Toda Institute for Global Peace and Policy Research, 1600 Kapiolani Boulevard, Suite 1111, Honolulu, HI 96814, USA; *fax*: +1-808-955 6476; *email*: majid@hawaii.edu; *research interests*: political theory and philosophy, international relations, development politics [Middle East]

Teune, Henry — University of Pennsylvania; *address*: Department of Political Science, University of Pennsylvania, H/A 6100 Henry Avenue 6F, Philadelphia, PA 19128, USA; *email*: hteune@mail.sas.upenn.edu; *research interests*: comparative politics, local and urban politics, political science methods

Thoenig, Jean-Claude — CNRS-GAPP, INSEAD; *address*: INSEAD, Boulevard de Constance, 77300 Fontainbleau, France; *fax*: +33-1-4740 2959; *email*: thoenig@gapp.rus.cachon.fr; *research interests*: central government, comparative politics, public policy [Europe]

Thomas, D Paul — University of California-Berkeley; *address*: 1337 Martin Luther King Jr Way, Berkeley, CA 94709-1912, USA; *fax*: +1-510-

642 9515; *email*: pt@socrates.berkeley.edu; *research interests*: political theory and philosophy

Thomas, Elaine R — University of Chicago; *address*: 2374 Park Row West, Montréal, Quèbec H4B 2G4, Canada; *email*: er-thomas@uchicago.edu; *research interests*: political theory and philosophy, comparative studies, area studies [Western Europe]

Thompson, Elfi — University of Nevada; *address*: PO Box 374, Reno, NV 89504, USA; *fax*: +1-209-396 3501; *email*: elfithompson@yahoo.com; *research interests*: development and politics, women and politics, political science methods [USA, Africa, China]

Thränhardt, Dietrich — Universität Münster; *address*: Institut für Politikwissenschaft, Westfälische Wilhelms-Universität Münster, Platz der Weißen Rose, 48151 Münster, Germany; *fax*: +49-251-839 356; *email*: thranh@uni-muenster.de; *research interests*: comparative politics, migration, local and urban politics [Europe]

Tiilikainen, Teija — University of Helsinki; *address*: University of Helsinki, Department of Political Science, Box 54 1 00014, University of Helsinki, Finland; *fax*: +358-9-191 8832; *email*: teija.tiilikainen@helsinki.fi; *research interests*: political theory and philosophy, international relations, European integration [Europe]

Tomat, Olivier — IEP d'Aix en Provence; *address*: La Tour d'Aygosi bat 8, 67/69 cours Gambetta, 13100 Aix en Provence, France; *fax*: +33-4-4217 0542; *email*: olivier.tomat@wanadoo.fr; *research interests*: public policy, political science methods, local and urban politics [Western Europe, North America]

Topan, Angelina — Hochschule für Wirtschaft und Politik; *address*: Hochschule für Wirtschaft und

Politik, Von-Melle Park 9, D-20146 Hamburg, Germany; *fax*: +49-40-42838 6134; *email*: TopanA@HWP-Hamburg.de; *research interests*: international relations, development politics, area studies

Torrecillas Ramos, Dircêo — Fundação Getulio Vargas; *address*: Rua Otto Bender, 162, Sâo Paulo - SP, CEP 02418, Brazil; *fax*: +55-11-220 0308; *email*: unid@mandic.com.br; *research interests*: central government, federalism, environmental policy

Tóth, Rastislav — Department of Comparative Politics, UMB; *address*: Ivana Bukoucana 4, 841 08 Bratislava, Slovak Republic; *email*: ratislavt@hotmail.com; *research interests*: central government, comparative politics, political theory and philosophy

Totten, George Oakley, III — University of Southern California; *address*: 5129 Village Green, Los Angeles, California, CA 90016-5205, USA; *fax*: +1-323-299 1064; *email*: totten@usc.edu; *research interests*: comparative politics, political theory and philosophy, area studies [East Asia, China, Japan, Korea]

Tournon, Jean P — Université Pierre Mendes France, Grenoble; *address*: 5 rue de la Madeleine, Grenoble 38000, France; *fax*: +33-4-7682 6098; *email*: jean.tournon@upmf-grenoble.fr; *research interests*: ethnicity and nationalism, political theory and philosophy, local and urban politics [North America (especially French-speaking Canada), Europe]

Tremblay, Gaetan — University of Quebec; *address*: CP 8888, Succ centre-ville, Montréal, Quèbec, H3C 3P8, Canada; *fax*: +1-514-987 7804; *email*: tremblay.gaetan@uqam.ca; *research interests*: public policy, comparative politics, area studies [Americas]

Trent, John E — University of Ottawa; *address*: 11 Williamson Road, Chelsea, QC, J9B 1Z4, Canada; *fax*: +1-613-562 5106; *email*: jtrent@uottawa.ca; *research interests*: ethnicity, development of the discipline, global governance [Canada]

Tsai, Chi-ching — Tunghai University; *address*: 22 Tunghai Road, Tunghai University, Taichung, 407, Taiwan; *fax*: +886-4-359 4653; *email*: cctsai@mail.thu.edu.tw; *research interests*: comparative politics, elections and voting behaviour, area studies [Taiwan, Japan, America]

Tummala, Krishna K — Kansas State University; *address*: Department of Political Science, Kansas State University, Manhattan, KS 66506, USA; *fax*: +1-785-532 2339; *email*: tummala@ksu.edu; *research interests*: public administration, comparative politics, development politics [South Asia, South Africa]

Turan, Ilter — Istanbul Bilgi University; *address*: Istanbul Bilgi University, Indnu Cad No 28, Kustepe 80310, Istanbul, Turkey; *fax*: +90-212-216 2414; *email*: ituran@bilgi.edu.tr; *research interests*: comparative politics

Turhan, Ayse Bahar — Atilim University; *address*: Zekai Apaydin Sokak, Orman Sitesi No 21, 06450 Or-An Sehri, Ankara, Turkey; *fax*: +90-312-439 4123; *email*: bturhan@tr-net.net.tr; *research interests*: elections and voting behaviour, area studies, international relations

Turkmen, A Fusun — Galatasaray University; *address*: Cemil Topuzlu cad, s Bankas, Dalyan Sitesi, D Blok, Daire 8, Fenerbahce 81030 Istanbul, Turkey; *email*: nuriye@turk.net; *research interests*: international relations, area studies [USA, Middle East, Central Asia, Balkans]

Turpin, Pierre — CNRS; *address*: Laboratoire Travail et Mobilités, Université Paris X, 200 Avenue de la République, 92000 Nanterre, France; *fax*: +33-1-4097 7135; *email*: pierre.turpin@u-paris10.fr; *research inter-*

ests: political parties, political science methods, political theory and
philosophy

Uchida, Takeo — Chuo University;
address: Faculty of Economics, Chuo
University, 742-1 Higashi Nakano,
Hachioji-shi, 192-0393, Japan; fax:
+81-3-3707 9315; email: uchidat@
tanass.chuo-u.ac.jp; research interests: international public policy, international organisation

Ume, Gabriel — Palo Alto College;
address: 7706 Gallant Ridge Drive,
San Antonio, TX 78239, USA; fax:
+1-210-921 5050; email: gume@accd.
com; research interests: public policy,
international relations, international
law [USA, West Africa]

Unekis, Joseph K — Kansas State
University; address: 221 Waters Hall,
Kansas State University, Manhattan, KS 66506, USA; fax: +1-785-532
2339; email: jku@ksu.edu; research
interests: legislatures, political parties, elections and voting behaviour
[USA]

Uriarte, Edurne — Universidad del
Pais Vasco; address: Universidad del
Pais Vasco, Fac CCSS y de la Inf,
Dpto de Ciencia Politica, 48940 Lejona, Vizcaya, Spain; fax: +34-94-601
5140; email: zipurbee@lg.ehu.es; research interests: comparative politics,
political executives, legislatures
[Western countries, Latin America]

Urushadze, Levan Z — International
Association "CAUCASUS: Ethnic
relations, human rights, geopolitics"; address: Giorgi Tsabadze St 3-
32, 380012 Tbilisi, Republic of
Georgia; fax: +995-32-348651; email:
lur@lycosmail.com; research interests: political parties, human rights,
area studies [CIS, Caucasus]

Vajpeyi, Dhirendra — University of
Northern Iowa; address: 1913 Four
Winds Drive, Cedar Falls, IA 50613,
USA; fax: +1-319-273 7108; email:
dhirendra.vajpeyi@uni.edu; research
interests: comparative politics, local
and urban politics, environmental

technology [South Asia, third
world]

Valavanis, Tassos — World Affairs
Organisation; address: PO Box 3039,
Aiolos Street, 100, Athens 102-10,
Greece; fax: +30-1-412 0986; email:
comm@strategy.gr; research interests:
international relations

Vallanadu, Viswanathan — Presidency College; address: 1114 Paces
Avenue, Matthews, NC 28105, USA;
email: visu_v_n@hotmail.com; research interests: area studies, comparative politics, international relations [South Asia]

Van Apeldoorn, Bastiaan — Max
Planck Institute for the Study of Societies; address: Paulstrasse 3, D-
50676 Cologne, Germany; fax: +49-
221-276 7555; email: apeldoorn@
mpi-fg-koeln.mpg.de; research interests: international relations, comparative politics, international political economy [EU]

Van Der Made, MA, Jan — University
of Maastricht; address: Department
of Health Organisation, Policy &
Economics, University of Maastricht, PO Box 616, 6200 MD Maastricht, Netherlands; email: jan.vand
ermade@beoz.unimaas.nl; research
interests: health policy, comparative
politics, public administration
[Europe]

Van Gunsteren, Herman — Leiden
University; address: Department of
Political Science, Leiden University,
PO Box 9555, 2300 RB Leiden, The
Netherlands; fax: +31-71-527 3815;
email: gunstere@fsw.leidenuniv.nl;
research interests: public administra-
tion, public policy, citizenship

Van Holsteyn, Joop — Leiden University; address: Department of Political
Science, Leiden University, PO Box
9555, 2300 RB Leiden, The Netherlands; fax: +31-71-527 3815; email:
holsteyn@fsw.leidenuniv.nl; research interests: elections and voting
behaviour, political science methods, political parties

Van Schendelen, MPCM — Erasmus University; *address*: Political Science Department, Room M 7-4, Erasmus University, PO Box 1738, 3000 DR Rotterdam, Netherlands; *fax*: +31-10-408 9106; *email*: vanSchendelen@ fsw.eur.nl; *research interests*: pressure groups, legislatures, area studies [EU]

Van Schuur, WH — University of Groningen; *address*: Groenestraat 43, 6531 HB Nijmegen, Netherlands; *fax*: +31-50-3636226; *email*: h.van. schuur@ppsw.rug.nl; *research interests*: political science methods, political parties, elections and voting behaviour

Vanags, Edvins — Latvian Statistical Institute; *address*: Maskavas Str 268/2-27, Riga, LV 1063, Latvia; *fax*: +371-7-286 876; *email*: lsi@latnet.lv; *research interests*: local and urban politics, public administration, central government [Europe]

Vanhanen, Tatu — University of Helsinki; *address*: Suopolku 4 D, 01800 Klaukkala, Finland; *fax*: +358-9-191 8832; *email*: tatu4@saunalahti.fi; *research interests*: comparative politics, elections and voting behaviour, biopolitics

Vankovska, Biljana — University of Skopje; *address*: 'Praska' 80a, Skopje, Macedonia; *fax*: +389-91-118 143; *email*: biljanav@osi.net.mk; *research interests*: peace studies, security studies, international relations [Europe, Balkans]

Varhelyi, Tamas — COMPUDOC; *address*: Gyimes 10, Debrecen, H 4032, Hungary; *fax*: +36-52-340 103; *email*: optonet@mail.datanet.hu; *research interests*: local and urban politics, information society

Vecchiarelli Scott, Joanna — Eastern Michigan University; *address*: 1525 Harding Road, Ann Arbor, MI 48104, USA; *fax*: +1-734-662 9952; *email*: PLS_Scott@online.emich.edu; *research interests*: political theory and philosophy, comparative politics and continiental political thought, women and politics [Western Europe, Great Britain, USA]

Vedung, Evert — Uppsala University; *address*: Uppsala University, Institute for Housing Research, PO Box 785, HSE-80129 Gävle, Sweden; *fax*: +46-26-147 802; *email*: evert.vedung @ibf.uu.se; *research interests*: public administration, public policy, political science methods [Scandinavia, Korea, USA, Austria]

Verba, Sidney — Harvard University; *address*: Littauer Centre, Department of Government, Havard University, Cambridge, MA 02138, USA; *fax*: +1-617-495 0438; *email*: sverba@harvard.edu; *research interests*: American and comparative government

Vernardakis, George — Middle Tennessee State University; *address*: 1442 Kensington Drive, Murfreesboro, TN 37127, USA; *fax*: +1-615-898 5460; *email*: guernard@mtsu. edu; *research interests*: comparative politics, public administration, public policy [USA, UK, France, Greece]

Verney, Douglas V — University of Pennsylvania; *address*: 104 Pine Street, Philadelphia, PA 19106-4312, USA; *fax*: +1-215-592 1418; *email*: dverney@sas.upenn.edu; *research interests*: comparative politics, development politics [Canada, India]

Vianello, Mino — University of Rome; *address*: Via Brennero 36, Rome 00141, Italy; *fax*: +39-6-4991 0720; *email*: vianello@uniroma1.it; *research interests*: women and politics, political theory and philosophy, comparative politics

Vigevani, Tullo — UNESP, CEDEC; *address*: Rua Havai 533, Apto 2A, 01259-000 San Paulo, Brazil; *fax*: +55-11-3871 2123; *email*: vigevani@ unesp.br; *research interests*: international relations, political theory and philosophy [Brazil, Argentina,

USA, world]

Vilanova, Pere — University of Barcelona; *address*: Department of Constitutional Law & Political Science, University of Barcelona, Diagonal 684, Barcelona 08034, Spain; *fax*: +34-93-414 6999; *email*: pvilat@eco.ub.es; *research interests*: comparative politics, international relations, area studies [Europe, Mediterranean, Middle East]

Vile, Maurice — University of Kent; *address*: Little Cob, Garlinge Green, Petham, Canterbury CT4 5RT, UK; *email*: mjcvile@hotmail.com; *research interests*: comparative politics, judicial systems and behaviour, political theory and philosophy

Viola, Eduardo — University of Brasilia; *address*: Department of International Relations, University of Brasilia, CP 04359 Brasilia, DF 70919-970, Brazil; *fax*: +55-61-344 5684; *email*: eduviola@linkexpress.com.br; *research interests*: comparative politics, international relations [Latin America]

Vogel, Ursula — University of Manchester; *address*: Department of Government, University of Manchester, Manchester, M13 9PL, UK; *fax*: +44-161-275 4925; *email*: ursula.vogel@man.ac.uk; *research interests*: political theory, history of political thoughts, gender in political thoughts

Vohra, Ranbir — Trinity College, Conneticut; *address*: 282 Sector 17, Gurgaon, Haryana 122001, India; *email*: rvohra@satyam.net.in; *research interests*: area studies, development politics, international relations [modern China, modern India]

Voich, Dan, Jr — Florida State University; *address*: College of Business, Florida State University, Tallahassee, FL 32306, USA; *fax*: +1-850-644 7843; *email*: dvoich@cob.fsu.edu; *research interests*: cultural politics, political economy

Volcansek, Mary L — Texas Christian University; *address*: Addran College of Humanities & Social Sciences, Texas Christian University, Fortworth, TX 76129, USA; *email*: m.volvansek@tcu.edu; *research interests*: judicial politics, comparative politics, area studies [Western Europe, USA]

Von Beyme, Klaus — Institut für Politische Wissenschaft; *address*: Institut für Politische Wissenschaft, Universität Heidelberg, Marstallstr 6, D-69117 Heidelberg, Germany; *fax*: +49-6221-542 896; *email*: w21@ix.urz.uni-heidelberg.de; *research interests*: comparative politics, political theory [West and East Europe]

Von Sydow, Björn — University of Stockholm, Ministry of Defence, Sweden; *address*: Infanterig. 1, S-17159 Solna, Sweden; *fax*: +46-8-730 3617; *email*: mvs@home.se; *research interests*: central government, legislatures, political parties [Europe, USA]

Vowles, Jack — University of Waiican; *address*: Department Political Science & Public Policy, University of Waiican, Private Bag 3105, Hamilton, New Zealand; *fax*: +64-7-838 4203; *email*: j.vowles@wailcato.ac.nz; *research interests*: elections and voting behaviour, comparative politics, political parties [New Zealand, democracies in general]

Vullierme, Jean Louis — *address*: 194, rue de Rivoli, F-75001 Paris, France; *email*: jlv@hightel.com; *research interests*: political theory and philosophy, political science methods

Waelti, Sonja — Université de Lausanne; *address*: Institute of Political and International Studies, IEPI BFSH 2, 1015 Lausanne, Switzerland; *fax*: +41-21-692 3145; *email*: sonja.walti@iepi.unil.ch; *research interests*: public policy, comparative politics, public administration [Europe, North America]

Wahlke, John C — University of Arizona; *address*: 5462 N Entrada Catorce, Tucson, AZ 85718, USA; *fax*: +1-520-621 5151; *email*: wahlke@u. arizona.edu; *research interests*: legislatures, political theory and philosophy, political science methods

Wallace, Helen — University of Sussex; *address*: Sussex European Institute, University of Sussex, Falmer, Brighton BN1 9QN, UK; *fax*: +44-1273-678 571; *email*: h.wallace@sussex.ac.uk; *research interests*: area studies, public policy, comparative politics [Europe]

Walters, Robert S — University of Pittsburgh; *address*: Department of Political Science, 4L01 Forbes Quadrangle, University of Pittsburgh, Pittsburgh, PA 15260, USA; *fax*: +1-412-648 7277; *email*: rsw2+@pitt.edu; *research interests*: international relations, international political economy

Wang, Hongying — Syracuse University; *address*: 204 Brattle Road, Syracuse, NY 13203, USA; *fax*: +1-315-443 9082; *email*: hwang04@syr.edu; *research interests*: international relations, international political economy, area studies [Asia]

Ward, James — University of Massachusetts Boston; *address*: University of Massachusetts, Boston, MA 02125, USA; *fax*: +1-508-520 0834; *email*: jfward@ncounty.net; *research interests*: political theory and philosophy, public policy, elections and voting behaviour

Warries, Garth — Kitakyushu University; *address*: 2-6-25-1005 Kitagata, Kokuraminami-ku, Kitakyushu-shi, Fukuoka-ken, 802 0841, Japan; *fax*: +81-93-964 4236; *email*: liberate@kitakyu-u.ac.jp; *research interests*: political theory and philosophy, international relations, ethics, human rights

Waugh, William L — Georgia State University; *address*: Department of Public Administration and Urban Studies, Andrew Young School of Policy Studies, Georgia State University, Atlanta, GA 30303, USA; *fax*: +1-404-651 1378; *email*: wwaugh@gsu.edu; *research interests*: public administration, public policy, local and urban politics

Weare, Christopher — University of Southern California; *address*: Annenberg School for Communication, University of Southern California, Los Angeles, CA 90089-0821, USA; *fax*: +1-213-740 0014; *email*: weare@usc.edu; *research interests*: political communication, public administration, local and urban politics

Weber, Ronald E — University of Wisconsin-Milwaukee; *address*: Department of Political Science, Bolton Hall 640, 3210 N Maryland Avenue, Milwaukee, WI 53201-0413, USA; *fax*: +1-414-229 5747; *email*: rweber@uwm.edu; *research interests*: legislatures, political parties, elections and voting behaviour [USA]

Weede, Erich — Universität Bonn; *address*: Seminar für Soziologie, Adenauerallee 98a, 53113 Bonn, Germany; *fax*: +49-228-738 430; *email*: e.weede@uni-bonn.de; *research interests*: international relations, development politics, comparative politics [Asia]

Weinberg, Leonard — University of Nevada; *address*: Department of Political Science, University of Nevada, Reno, NV 89557-0060, USA; *fax*: +1-735-784 1473; *email*: wqeinbrl@gcg.unr.edu; *research interests*: right wing extremism, political violence [Europe]

Welsch, Friedrich — Universidad Simon Bolivar; *address*: Apartado 61.728, Caracas 1060-A, Venezuela; *fax*: +58-2-906 3700; *email*: fwelsch@usb.ve; *research interests*: political culture, public opinion

Werlin, Herbert — *address*: 5910 Westchester Park Drive, College Park, MD 20740-2802, USA; *fax*: +1-301-474 5278; *email*: werlin@crosslink.net; *research interests*: comparative politics, public administration, development politics

Wessels, David—Sophia University; *address*: Sophia University, 7-1 Kioicho, Chiyoda-ku, Tokyo 102-8554, Japan; *fax*: +81-3-3238 3592; *email*: wessels@hoffman.cc.sophia.ac.jp; *research interests*: international relations, comparative politics, political theory and philosophy [East Asia, USA, Europe]

White, Graham—University of Toronto; *address*: Department of Political Science, University of Toronto, 100 St George Street, Toronto, ON, M5S 3E3, Canada; *fax*: +1-416-978 5566; *email*: gwhite@chass.utoronto.ca; *research interests*: area studies, politics of indigenous peoples, legislatures, cabinets [Canada]

White, Stephen—University of Glasgow; *address*: Department of Politics, University of Glasgow, Glasgow, G12 8RT, UK; *fax*: +44-141-330 5071; *email*: s.white@socsci.gla.ac.uk; *research interests*: area studies, elections and voting behaviour, comparative politics [Russia, CIS]

Whitehead, Laurence—Nuffield College; *address*: Nuffield College, Oxford OX1 1NF, UK; *fax*: +44-1865-278 557; *email*: laurence.whitehead@nuf.ox.ac.uk; *research interests*: comparative politics, area studies, development politics [Latin America]

Whitman, Kurt—Santa Barbara Business College; *address*: 2301 June Avenue, Bakersfield, CA 93304, USA; *email*: kurtwhitman@hotmail.com; *research interests*: international relations, development politics, elections and voting behaviour [East Asia]

Wiatr, Jerzy J—University of Warsaw; *address*: Sosnowskiego 2 apt 1, 02784 Warsaw, Poland; *fax*: +48-22-278 599; *research interests*: political sociology [Europe, Asia, America]

Wiberg, Håkan—Copenhagen Peace Research Institute; *address*: Islands Brygge 27, 5, DK-2300 København S, Denmark; *fax*: +45-3345 5060; *email*: hwiberg@copri.dk; *research interests*: international relations, peace research [Southeast Europe]

Wilensky, Harold L—University of California; *address*: 210 Barrows Hall, Department of Political Science, University of California, Berkeley, CA 94720, USA; *fax*: +1-510-642 9515; *email*: hwilensk@socrates.berkley.edu; *research interests*: comparative politics, public policy, comparative political economy

Willems, Ulrich—Universität Hamburg; *address*: Institut für Politische Wissenschaft, Allende Platz 1, D-20146 Hamburg, Germany; *fax*: +49-40-42838 6818; *email*: willems@sozialwiss.uni-hamburg.de; *research interests*: political theory and philosophy, pressure groups, public policy [Germany, Europe]

Wilson, Graham K—University of Wisconsin-Madison; *address*: La Follette Institute for Public Policy, University of Wisconsin-Madison, 125 Observatory Drive, Madison, WI 53706, USA; *fax*: +1-608-265 3223; *email*: wilson@lafollette.wisc.edu; *research interests*: central government, pressure groups, public policy [North America, UK, Europe, Australia, New Zealand, Japan]

Wiltshire, Kenneth—University of Queensland; *address*: AO, Centre for Public Administration, University of Queensland, Ackroyd Building, St Lucia, Brisbane 4072, Australia; *fax*: +61-7-3365 8581; *email*: k.wiltshire@mailbox.uq.edu.au; *research interests*: public administration, public policy, legislatures [Europe, North America, Asia-Pacific]

Winer, Frederico M—Universidad de Buenos Aires; *address*: Delgado 811, (1426) Buenos Aires, Argentina; *fax*: +54-11-4551 0982; *email*: winer@overnet.com.ar; *research interests*: international relations, political theory and philosophy, interna-

tional politics
Winham, Gilbert — Dalhousie University; *address*: Department of Political Science, Dalhousie University, Halifax, Nova Scotia B3H 4H6, Canada; *fax*: +1-902-494 3825; *email*: winham@is.dal.ca
Wise, Lois — Indiana University; *address*: School of Public & Environmental Affairs, Indiana University, 1315 E 10th Street, Bloomington, IN 47405-2100, USA; *fax*: +1-812-855 7802; *email*: wisel@indiana.edu; *research interests*: public administration, public policy, central government [Scandinavia, USA]
Wollmann, Hellmut — Humboldt-Universität zu Berlin; *address*: Humboldt Universität zu Berlin, Institut für Sozialwissenschaften, Unter den Linden 6, D-10099 Berlin, Germany; *fax*: +49-30-2093 1500; *email*: hellmut.wollmann@rz.hu- berlin.de; *research interests*: local and urban politics, public administration, comparative politics [Western and Central Eastern Europe]
Woo, Chul-Koo — Yeungnam Universrity; *address*: Department of Political Science, Yeungnam University, 214-1 Dae-Dong Gyongsan, 712-749, Republic of Korea; *fax*: +82-2-594 4607; *email*: gkwoo@ynucc.yeungnam.ac.kr; *research interests*: international relations, comparative politics, area studies [USA, Europe, Asia Pacific]
Woolstencroft, Peter — University of Waterloo; *address*: Department of Political Science, University of Waterloo, Waterloo, ON, N2L 3G1, Canada; *fax*: +1-519-746 3956; *email*: pwool@watarts.uwaterloo.ca; *research interests*: political parties, elections and voting behaviour, federalism [Canada]
Worcester, Robert — MORI/LSE; *address*: MORI/LSE, 32 Old Queen Street, London, SW1 H9HP, UK; *fax*: +44-207-227 0404; *email*: worc@mori.com; *research interests*: elec-

tions and voting behaviour, political parties [Great Britain]
Wring, Dominic — Loughborough University; *address*: Department of Social Sciences, Loughborough University, Leicestershire, LE11 3TU, UK; *fax*: +44-1509-223 944; *email*: d.j.wring@lboro.ac.uk; *research interests*: political communication, political parties, elections [Britain, Europe]
Wu, Yu-Shan — National Taiwan University; *address*: Department of Political Science, National Taiwan University, 21 Hsu-chou Road, Taipei, Taiwan; *fax*: +886-2-341 2806; *email*: ziyu@ccms.ntu.edu.tw; *research interests*: comparative politics, area studies, public policy [PRC, Taiwan, Russia, Eastern Europe]
Wyatt, Andrew — University of Bristol; *address*: Department of Politics, University of Bristol, 10 Priory Road, Bristol, BS8 1TU, UK; *fax*: +44-117-973 2133; *email*: a.k.j.wyatt @bristol.ac.uk; *research interests*: political parties, development politics, elections and voting behaviour [South Asia]
Xu, Mingxu — The Center for the Tibet Question; *address*: 362 Centre Street, #16, Quincy, MA 02169, USA; *fax*: +1-617-984 0935; *email*: britexu@hotmail.com; *research interests*: area studies, political theory and philosophy, international relations [Sino-US relationship, Tibet question, China]
Yamada, Masahiro — Kwansei Gakuin University; *address*: 11-17-201 Nakaya-cho, Nishinomiya-shi, Hyogo-ken, Japan; *fax*: +81-798-546 415; *email*: myamada@kwansei.ac.jp; *research interests*: elections and voting behaviour, political parties, local and urban politics [Japan]
Yang, Oh Suk — Warwick University; *address*: Department of PAIS, University of Warwick, Coventry, CV4 7AL, UK; *fax*: +44-1203-524 221;

email: osyang30@hotmail.com; *research interests*: international relations, area studies, international political economy [EU]

Yoon, Bang-Soon — Central Washington University; *address*: 1202 Vuecrest, Ellensburg, WA 98962, USA; *fax*: +1-509-963 1134; *email*: yoonb@cwu.edu; *research interests*: women and politics, comparative politics, area studies [Korea]

Yoon, Jong-Ho — National Defence University; *address*: National Defence University, Susaek-dong, Eunpyung-ku, Seoul 122-090, Korea; *fax*: +82-2-309 9774; *email*: jhyoon@kndu.ac.kr; *research interests*: peace, area studies, international relations [Asia Pacific, USA, Japan]

Yoon, Young-Kwan — Seoul National University; *address*: Department of International Relations, College of Social Sciences, Seoul National University, Kwanak-gu, Sinrim-dong, Seoul 151-742, Korea; *fax*: +82-2-872 4115; *email*: ykyoon@plaza.snu.ac.kr; *research interests*: international relations, political economy [East Asia]

Young, Ken — University of London; *address*: Department of Politics, Queen Mary and Westfield College, University of London, London E1 4NS, UK; *email*: k.g.young@qmw.ac.uk; *research interests*: public administration, public policy, local and urban politics

Young, M Crawford — University of Wisconsin-Madison; *address*: Department of Political Science, University of Wisconsin-Madison, North Hall, 1050 Bascom Mall, Madison, WI 53706, USA; *fax*: +1-608-265 2663; *email*: young@polisci.wisc.edu; *research interests*: comparative politics, area studies, development politics [Africa]

Zajc, Drago — University of Ljubljana; *address*: Podlimbarskega 13, 1000 Ljubljana, Slovenia; *fax*: +386-61-580 4101; *email*: drago.zajc@uni-lj.si; *research interests*: legislatures, political parties, elections and voting behaviour [Central and Eastern Europe]

Zartman, I William — Johns Hopkins University-SAIS; *address*: 713 Quaint Acres, Silver Spring, MD 20904, USA; *fax*: +1-202-663 5683; *email*: tsimmons@mail.jhuwash.jhu.edu; *research interests*: international relations, comparative politics [Africa, Middle East]

Zaverucha, Jorge — Universidade Federal de Pernambuco; *address*: Rua Quimico Antonio Victor 211, 54450-010 Jaboatao - Pernambuco, Brazil; *fax*: +55-81-469 2885; *email*: zav@npd.ufpe.br; *research interests*: armed forces and police, comparative politics, judicial systems and behaviour [Latin America]

Zaznaev, Oleg — Kazan State University; *address*: Department of Political Science, Kazan State University, 18 Kzemlyovskaya Street, 420008 Kazan, Russia; *fax*: +7-8432-387418; *email*: Oleg.Zaznaev@ksu.ru; *research interests*: comparative politics, area studies, central government [Russia]

Zha, Daojiong — International University of Japan; *address*: Yamatomachi, Minami Uonuma-gun, Niigata 949-7277, Japan; *fax*: +81-257-791 187; *email*: zha@iuj.ac.jp; *research interests*: international relations, area studies, development politics [Asia Pacific, China]

Zink, Allan — *address*: 11, allée Carl, F-67120 Molsheim, France; *fax*: +33-3-8838 2722; *email*: allan.zink@wanadoo.fr; *research interests*: comparative politics, international relations, political culture [Greece, Middle East]

Zirker, Daniel — Montana State University-Billings; *address*: College of Arts and Sciences, Montana State University-Billings, 1500 N 30th Street, Billings, MT 59101, USA; *fax*:

+1-406-657 2187; *email*: dzirker@
msubillings.edu; *research interests*:
comparative politics, development
politics, area studies [Latin Amer
ica, Africa]

9 / POLITICAL SCIENCE JOURNALS

9.1 OVERVIEW

The following list of journals is based on that of the *International political science abstracts*, the most comprehensive abstracting service within the discipline. It may be instructive to compare this list with that of the Social Science Citation Index (SSCI). In 1997, the latter cited 2,384 journals spanning a wide disciplinary range. Of these, only 73 were classified as political science journals, but 52 journals were classified as international relations and 24 as public administration in 1998. Because of overlap arising from multiple classifications, the SSCI listed a total of 137 journals in these three categories.

Most (but by no means all) of these journals were also abstracted in the *International political science abstracts*. The exceptions were periodicals containing large numbers of short articles (such as the *Nation* and the *New Republic*), and journals which, though carrying a "political science" tag in the SSCI database, seem to fall outside the conventional boundaries of the discipline (such as the *Scottish journal of political economy*). But, though excluding periodicals of this kind, the *Abstracts* include very many more. Indeed, of 974 journals covered in whole or in part by the *Abstracts* in 1999, only 262 were also covered by the SSCI. The regional breakdown of these journals is indicated in table 9.1

Table 9.1: Political science journals abstracted in
International political science abstracts, 1999

Continent	Abstracts *only*	Abstracts+*SSCI*	Total
Africa	14	.	14
America, North	174	139	313
America, South	19	.	19
Asia	64	8	72
Europe, C. and E.	23	.	23
Europe, Western	410	110	520
Oceania	8	5	13
Total	712	262	974

The following pages present a listing of all of these journals. Those which are covered by SSCI are italicised. Those which are journals of national political science associations, where known, are bolded. Some new journals, such as those lauched recently by the Spanish and UK associations, are not included. It may be of interest to review the consider the "impact factor" of major political science journals as measured by the extent to which each jounal has been cited by other journals in the database during a particular. The top 20 "political science" journals are listed in table 9.2. It should be noted that this list excludes a number of "international relations" journals such as *World politics* (impact factor: 2.943) which are not given a political science tag by SSCI.

Table 9.2: Top 10 political science journals by impact factor, 1997

Journal	Country	Impact factor
American Political Science Review	USA	2.078
American Journal of Political Science	USA	1.476
British Journal of Political Science	United Kingdom	1.228
Comparative Political Studies	USA	1.137
New Left Review	United Kingdom	1.031
Comparative Politics	USA	1.028
Political Geography	United Kingdom	0.987
Human Rights Quarterly	USA	0.902
Party Politics	United Kingdom	0.810
Europe-Asia Studies	United Kingdom	0.771
Journal of Politics	USA	0.758
Political Studies	United Kingdom	0.724
Politics and Society	USA	0.676
Policy and Politics	United Kingdom	0.638
Political Research Quarterly	USA	0.566
Political Communication	United Kingdom	0.545
International Political Science Review	United Kingdom	0.532
Public Opinion Quarterly	USA	0.490
Electoral Studies	United Kingdom	0.489
Canadian Journal of Political Science	Canada	0.452

9.2 LISTING OF JOURNALS

AFRICA

Algeria
Revue algérienne des Sciences juridiques économiques et politiques (Alger)

Egypt
Cairo Papers in Social Science (Cairo)
Egypte (L') contemporaine (Le Caire)

Ethiopia
African Review (Dar es Salaam)

Kenya
African Urban Quarterly (Nairobi)

Morocco
Cahiers africains d'Administration publique (Tanger)

Nigeria
African Journal of International Affairs and Development (Ile-Ife)
Nigerian Journal of International Affairs (Lagos)

South Africa
African Studies (Johannesburg)
Politeia (Pretoria)
Politikon (Florida, South Africa)
South Africa International (Johannesburg)
South African Journal on Human Rights (Johannesburg)

Tunisia
Revue tunisienne de Sciences sociales (Tunis)

AMERICA, NORTH

Canada
Canada Among Nations (Ottawa, ON)
Canadian Issues (Ottawa, ON)

Canadian Journal of African Studies (Toronto, ON)
Canadian Journal of Development Studies (Ottawa, ON)
Canadian Journal of Political and Social Theory (Montréal, QC)
Canadian Journal of Political Science (Waterloo, ON)
Canadian Public Administration (Toronto, ON)
Canadian Public Policy (North York, ON)
Canadian Review of Sociology and Anthropology (Calgary, AB)
Canadian Review of Studies in Nationalism (Charlottetown, PE)
Canadian Yearbook of International Law (Vancouver, BC)
Études internationales (Québec, QC)
International History Review (Burnaby, BC)
International Journal (Toronto)
International Journal of Canadian Studies (Ottawa, ON)
Lien social et Politiques - RIAC (Montréal, QC)
Optimum (Ottawa, ON)
Pacific Affairs (Vancouver, BC)
Politique et Societés (Montréal, QC)
Queen's Quarterly (Kingston, ON)
Recherches sociographiques (Québec, QC)
Revue d'Intégration européenne (Montréal, QC)
Sociologie et Societés (Montréal, QC)
Studies in Political Economy (Ottawa, ON)
Tocqueville Review (Toronto, ON)

Mexico
Acta sociologica (México)
Boletín mexicano de Derecho comparado (Mexico)

Cuadernos americanos (Mexico)
Estudios latinoamericanos (Mexico)
Estudios políticos (Mexico)
Foro internacional (Mexico)
Gestión y política pública (Mexico)
Iztapalapa (Iztapalapa)
Metapolítica (Mexico)
Política y Gobierno (Mexico)
Relaciones internacionales (México)
Revista de Ia Facultad de Derecho de
Mexico (Mexico)
Revista mexicana de Ciencias políti-
cas (Mexico)
Revista mexicana de Sociología
(Mexico)

USA

*Administration and Society (Thousand
Oaks, CA)*
*Administrative Science Quarterly
(Ithaca, NY)*
Africa Today (Denver, CO)
African Studies Review (East Lans-
ing, MI)
Alternatives (Boulder, CO)
*American Anthropologist (Arlington,
VA)*
*American Behavioral Scientist (Thou-
sand Oaks, CA)*
American Enterprise (Washington,
DC)
*American Historical Review (New York,
NY)*
American Journal of Criminal Justice
(Cincinnati, OH)
*American Journal of Economics and So-
ciology (New York, NY)*
*American Journal of International Law
(Washington, DC)*
American Journal of Islamic Social
Sciences (Silver Spring, MD)
*American Journal of Political Science
(Madison, Wis.)*
*American Journal of Sociology (Chicago,
IL)*

*American Political Science Review
(Washington, D.C.)*
*American Politics Quarterly (Thousand
Oaks, Cal.)*
*American Review of Public Administra-
tion (Kansas City, MO)*
American Scholar (Washington, DC)
*American Sociological Review (Washing-
ton, DC)*
American Sociologist (The) (New
Brunswick, NJ)
*Annals of the American Academy of Po-
litical and Social Science (Thousand
Oaks, CA)*
*Annals of the Association of American
Geographers (Cambridge, MA)*
*Annual Review of Anthropology (Stan-
ford, CA)*
*Annual Review of Sociology (Palo Alto,
CA)*
Arab Studies Quarterly (Washington,
DC)
Armed Forces and Society (Buffalo, NY)
Asian Affairs : An American Review
(New York, NY)
Asian Survey (Berkeley, CA)
Asian Thought and Society (Oneonta,
NY)
Berkeley Journal of Sociology (Ber-
keley, CA)
Brassey's Mershon American Defense
Annual (Columbus, 0H)
Brookings Review (The) (Washing-
ton, DC)
Campaigns and Elections (Washing-
ton, DC)
Caribbean Studies (Puerto Rico)
Cato Journal (Washington, DC)
*Chinese Law and Government (White
Plains, NY)*
*Columbia Journal of Transnational Law
(New York, NY)*
Columbia Law Review (New York, NY)
Commentary (New York, NY)
*Comparative Political Studies (Thousand
Oaks, Cal.)*

Comparative Politics (New York, N.Y.)
Comparative Strategy (Washington, DC)
Comparative Studies in Society and History (Ann Arbor, MI)
Congress and the Presidency (Washington, DC)
Contemporary French Civilization (Bozeman, MO)
Critical Review (Danbury, CT)
Cross-Cultural Research (Thousand Oaks, CA)
Cuban Studies (Pittsburgh, PA)
Current Anthropology (Chicago, IL)
Daedalus (Cambridge, MA)
Demokratizatsiya (Washington, DC)
Denver Journal of International Law and Policy (Denver, CO)
Désarmement (New York, NY)
Diplomatic History (Cambridge, MA)
Disarmament (New York, NY)
Dissent (New York, NY)
Drugs and Society (New York, NY)
Duke Journal of Comparative and International Law (Durham, NC)
East Asia : an International Quarterly (New Brunswick, NJ)
East European Politics and Societies (Seattle, WA)
East European Quarterly (Boulder, CO)
Economic Development and Cultural Change (Chicago, IL)
Economic Geography (Worcester, MA)
Employee Responsibilities and Rights Journal (New York, NY)
Ethics (Chicago, IL)
Ethics and International Affairs (New York, NY)
Ethnology (Pittsburgh, PA)
Fletcher (The) Forum of World Affairs (Medford, MA)
Foreign Affairs (New York, N.Y.)
Foreign Policy (Washington, D.C.)
Forum for Applied Research and Public Policy (Knoxville, TN)

French Politics and Society (Cambridge, MA)
General Systems (Gainesville, FL)
Geographical Review (New York, NY)
Global Governance (Boulder, CO)
Governance (Cambridge, MA)
Government Information Quarterly (Greenwich, CT)
Growth and Change (Cambridge, MA)
Harvard Educational Review (Cambridge, MA)
Harvard International Journal of Press/Politics (Cambridge, MA)
Harvard Law Review (Cambridge, MA)
History and Theory (Middletown, CT)
Howard Journal of Communications (Washington, DC)
Human Organization (New York, NY)
Human Rights Quarterly (Baltimore, MD)
Independent Review (Oakland, CA)
Indonesia (Ithaca, NY)
Industrial and Labor Relations Review (Ithaca, NY)
Industrial Relations (Berkeley, CA)
International Environmental Affairs (Hanover, NH)
International Journal of Political Economy (White Plains, NY)
International Journal of Politics, Culture and Society (New York, NY)
International Journal of Public Administration (Monticello, NY)
International Journal of Urban and Regional Research (Monticello, NY)
International Organization (Cambridge, Mass.)
International Regional Science Review (Morgantown, WV)
International Security (Cambridge, MA)
International Social Science Review (Winfield, KS)

International Studies Quarterly (Cambridge, Mass.)
Israel Studies (Bloomington, IN)
Jewish Social Studies (New York, NY)
Journal of Applied Behavioral Science (New York, NY)
Journal of Asian Studies (Ithaca, NY)
Journal of Black Studies (Los Angeles, CA)
Journal of Communication (Austin, TX)
Journal of Community Practice (New York, NY)
Journal of Conflict Resolution (Thousand Oaks, CA)
Journal of Contemporary China (Princeton, NJ)
Journal of Democracy (Washington, DC)
Journal of Developing Areas (Macomb, IL)
Journal of Environment and Development (Thousand Oaks, CA)
Journal of Global Marketing (New York, NY)
Journal of Health and Social Policy (Binghamton, NY)
Journal of Health Politics, Policy and Law (Durham, NC)
Journal of Interamerican Studies and World Affairs (Coral Gables, FL)
Journal of International Affairs (New York, NY)
Journal of Japanese Studies (Seattle, WA)
Journal of Law and Economics (Chicago, IL)
Journal of Law and Politics (Charlottesville, VA)
Journal of Legal Studies (Chicago, IL)
Journal of Libertarian Studies (New York, NY)
Journal of Interdisciplinary History (Medford, MA)
Journal of Interdisciplinary Studies (Santa Monica, CA)

Journal of Managerial Issues (Pittsburgh, PA)
Journal of Modern History (Chicago, IL)
Journal of Northeast Asian Studies (Washington, DC)
Journal of Palestine Studies (Berkeley, CA)
Journal of Policy Analysis and Management (New York, NY)
Journal of Policy Modeling (New York, NY)
Journal of Political and Military Sociology (Dekalb, IL)
Journal of Political Economy (Chicago, IL)
Journal of Politics (Gainesville, Fla.)
Journal of Psychology (Washington, DC)
Journal of Public Administration Research and Theory (Lawrence, KS)
Journal of Public and International Affairs (Princeton, NJ)
Journal of Regional Science (Cambridge, MA)
Journal of Social Issues (New York, NY)
Journal of Social Psychology (Washington, DC)
Journal of Social, Political and Economic Studies (Washington, DC)
Journal of South Asian and Middle Eastern Studies (Villanova, PA)
Journal of the American Planning Association (Chicago, IL)
Journal of the Hellenic Diaspora (New York, NY)
Journal of the History of Ideas (New York, NY)
Journal of the History of Sexuality (Chicago, IL)
Journal of the Third World Spectrum (Washington, DC)
Journal of Third World Studies (Americus, GA)
Journal of Urban Affairs (Greenwich, CT)
Journalism and Mass Communication Quarterly (Washington, DC)

Knowledge and Policy (New Brunswick, NJ)

Labor Studies Journal (Morgantown, WV)

Language Problems and Language Planning (Philadelphia, PA)

Latin American Perspectives (Riverside, CA)

Latin American Research Review (Albuquerque, NM)

Law and Contemporary Problems (Durham, NC)

Law and Society Review (Amherst, MA)

Legislative Studies Quarterly (Iowa City, Iowa)

Liberian Studies Journal (Sewanee, TN)

Lituanus (Chicago, IL)

Mediterranean Quarterly (Durham, NC)

Mershon International Studies Review (Cambridge, MA)

Mexican Studies (Berkeley, CA)

Middle East Journal (Washington, DC)

Middle East Policy (Washington, DC)

Middle East Quarterly (Philadelphia, PA)

Middle East Studies Association Bulletin (Washington, DC)

Military Review (Fort Leavenworth, KS)

Modern Age (Chicago, IL)

Modern China (Los Angeles, CA)

Muslim World (Hartford, CT)

National Interest (Shrub Oak, NY)

National Tax Journal (Columbus, OH)

Naval War College Review (Newport, RI)

Negotiation Journal (New York, NY)

New Politics (Brooklyn, NY)

New York University Law Review (New York, NY)

Nomos (New York, NY)

Non (The) Proliferation Review (Monterey, CA)

Nonprofit and Voluntary Sector Quarterly (Camden, NJ)

Occasional Papers/Reprints Series in Contemporary Asian Studies (Baltimore, MD)

Orbis (Greenwich, CT)

Organization Studies (New York, NY)

Pacific Studies (Laie, HI)

Peace and Change (Kent, OH)

Peace and Conflict (Mahwah, NJ)

Perspectives on Political Science (Washington, DC)

Philosophical Forum (New York, NY)

Philosophy and Public Affairs (Princeton, NJ)

Philosophy of the Social Sciences (Thousand Oaks, CA)

Policy Review (Washington, DC)

Policy Studies Journal (Urbana, IL)

Policy Studies Review (Lawrence, KS)

Policy Studies Review Annual (New Brunswick, NJ)

Polish Review (New York, NY)

Political Psychology (Cambridge, MA)

Political Analysis (Ann Arbor, MI)

Political Anthropology (New Brunswick, NJ)

Political Behavior (New York, NY)

Political Power and Social Theory (Greenwich, CT)

Political Research Quarterly (Salt Lake City, U.)

Political Science Quarterly (New York, N.Y.)

Political Science Reviewer (Bryn Mawr, PA)

Politics and Society (Thousand Oaks, CA)

Polity (Amherst, Mass.)

Presidential Studies Quarterly (New York, NY)

PS-political science and politics (Washington, DC)

Psychology (Bowling Green, KY)

Public Administration Review (Washington, DC)
Public Budgeting and Finance (New Brunswick, NJ)
Public Culture (Chicago, IL)
Public Interest (The) (Washington, DC)
Public Manager (The) (Washington, DC)
Public Opinion Quarterly (Chicago, IL)
Publius (Easton, PA)
Research in Micropolitics (Greenwich, CT)
Research in Organizational Behavior (Greenwich, CT)
Review (F. Braudel Center) (Binghamton, NY)
Review of Politics (Notre Dame, IN)
Review of Radical Political Economics (Cambridge, MA)
Revista de Ciencias sociales (Rio Piedras, Puerto Rico)
Rural Sociology (University Park, PA)
Russian Politics and Law (New York, NY)
Saint Louis University Public Law Review (St Louis, MO)
SAIS Review (Washington, DC)
Science & Society (New York, NY)
Science, Technology and Human Values (Troy, NY)
Scientific American (New York, NY)
Signs (Stanford, CA)
Simulation and Gaming (Thousand Oaks, CA)
Slavic Review (New York, NY)
Social Forces (Chapel Hill, NC)
Social Philosophy and Policy (Bowl. Green, OH)
Social Policy (New York, NY)
Social Problems (Spencer, IN)
Social Psychology Quarterly (New York, NY)
Social Research (New York, NY)
Social Science History (Durham, NC)

Social Science Journal (Greenwich, CT)
Social Science Quarterly (Austin, TX)
Social Theory and Practice (Tallahassee, FL)
Socialism and Democracy (New York, NY)
Socialist Review (San Francisco, CA)
Society (New Brunswick, NJ)
Sociological Inquiry (Austin, TX)
Sociological Methodology (Washington, DC)
Sociological Perspectives (Greenwich, CT)
Sociological Quarterly (Berkeley, CA)
Sociology of Religion (Washington, DC)
Southeastern Political Review (Statesboro, GA)
Southern California Law Review (Los Angeles, CA)
Stanford Journal of International Law (Stanford, CA)
State and Local Government Review (Athens, GA)
Strategic Review (Washington, DC)
Studies in Comparative Communism (Los Angeles, CA)
Studies in Comparative International Development (Ypsilanti, MI)
Studies in GDR Culture and Society (Lanham, MD)
Supreme Court Review (Chicago, IL)
Telos (St Louis, MO)
Transafrica Forum (Washington, DC)
Transnational Corporations (New York, NY)
Urban Affairs Annual Review (Beverly Hills, CA)
Urban Affairs Review (Thousand Oaks, CA)
Urban and Social Change Review (Chestnut Hill, MA)
Urban Geography (Columbia, MD)
Washington Quarterly (Washington, DC)
Women and Politics (Binghamton, NY)

World Affairs (Washington, DC)
World Development (Washington, DC)
World Policy Journal (New York, NY)
World Politics (Princeton, N.J.)
Yale Journal of International Law
    (New Haven, CT)
Yale Law Journal (New Haven, CT)
Yale Review (Cambridge, MA)
Youth and Society (Thousand Oaks, CA)

AMERICA, SOUTH

Argentina
Desarrollo económico (Buenos Aires)
Brazil
Contexto internacional (Rio de Janeiro)
Dados (Rio de Janeiro)
Estudos feministas (Rio de Janeiro)
Perspectivas (São Paulo)
Revista brasileira de Ciências sociais
    (São Paulo)
Revista brasileira de Estudos políticos
    (Belo Horizonte)
Revista de sociologia e politica (Rio
    de Janeiro)
Tempo social (São Paulo)
Chile
Estudios internacionales (Santiago)
Estudios públicos (Santiago)
Revista de Ciencia política (Santiago)
Revista de Derecho público (Santiago)
Colombia
Análisis político (Bogota)
Estudios de Derecho (Antioquía)
Peru
Socialismo y Participación (Lima)
Venezuela
Cuestiones políticas (Maracaibo)
Politeia (Caracas)
Revista venezolana de Ciencia
    política (Mérida)

ASIA

Bangaldesh
BIISS Journal (Dhaka)
Politics Administration and Change
    (Dhaka)
China
Asian Journal of Public Administration (Hong Kong)
Asian Profile (Hong Kong)
Chinese Social Sciences Year Book
    (Hong Kong)
Hong Kong Public Administration
    (Hong Kong)
India
Administrative Change (Jaipur)
Africa Quarterly (New Delhi)
China Report (New Delhi)
*Contributions to Indian Sociology
    (Delhi)*
Eastern Anthropologist (Lucknow)
Economic and Political Weekly (Bombay)
India International Centre Quarterly
    (New Delhi)
India Quarterly (New Delhi)
Indian Journal of Political Science
    (Calcutta)
Indian Journal of Politics (Aligarh)
Indian Journal of Social Science (New
    Delhi)
Indian Political Science Review
    (Delhi)
International Journal of Contemporary Sociology (New Delhi)
International Journal of Punjab Studies (New Delhi)
International Studies (New Delhi)
Journal of Constitutional and Parliamentary Studies (New Delhi)
Journal of the Society for Study of
    State Governments (Varanasi)
Punjab Journal of Politics (Amritsar)

Revue des Institutions politiques et administratives du Sénégal (Dakar)
Seminar (New Delhi)
South Asian Studies (Jaipur)
South Asian Survey (New Delhi)
Strategic Analysis (New Delhi)
Strategic Digest (New Delhi)

Indonesia
Indonesian Quarterly (Jakarta)

Iran
Amu Darya Journal (Tehran)
Iranian Journal of International Affairs (Tehran)

Israel
Israel Law Review (Jerusalem)
Israel Yearbook on Human Rights (Tel Aviv)
Jewish Political Studies Review (Jerusalem)
Middle Eastern Lectures (Tel Aviv)

Japan
Cahiers du Japon (Tokyo)
Ebisu (Tokyo)
Hitotsubashi Journal of Law and Politics (Tokyo)
Japan Quarterly (Tokyo)
Japanese Annual of International Law (Tokyo)
Journal of International Studies (Tokyo)
Kobe University Law Review (Kobe)
Waseda Political Studies (Tokyo)

Korea
Asian Perspective (Seoul)
Journal of East Asian Affairs (Seoul)
Korea and World Affairs (Seoul)
Korea Journal (Seoul)
Korean Journal of Defense Analysis (Seoul)
Korean Journal of International Studies (Seoul)
Korean Review of Public Administration (Seoul)

Korean Social Science Journal (Seoul)
Vantage Point (Seoul)

Kuwait
Journal of the Social Sciences (Kuwait)

Pakistan
Journal of European Studies (Karachi)
Pakistan Horizon (Karachi)
Regional Studies (Islamabad)
Strategic Studies (Islamabad)

Philippines
Journal of Contemporary Asia (Manila)
Philippine Studies (Manila)

Singapore
Asian Journal of Political Science (Singapore)
Contemporary Southeast Asia (Singapore)
Journal of Southeast Asian Studies (Singapore)
Southeast Asian Affairs (Singapore)
Southeast Asian Journal of Social Science (Singapore)

Sri Lanka
Ethnic Studies Report (Colombo)

Taiwan
Chinese Political Science Review (Taipei)
Chinese Public Administration Review (Taipei)
Chinese Yearbook of International Law and Affairs (Taipei)
Études et Documents (Taipei)
Issues and Studies (Taipei)

EUROPE, CENTRAL AND EASTERN

Croatia
Politicka Misao (Zagreb)
Revija za Sociologiju (Zagreb)

Czech Republic
Mezinàrodni Vztahy (Praha)

Politologicka Revue (Prague)

Hungary
Acta juridica hungarica (Budapest)
Allam-Es Jogtudomány (Budapest)
Hungarian Quarterly (Budapest)

Poland
Annales Universitatis Mariae Curie-
Sklodowska (Lublin)
Panstwo i Pravo (Wassawa)
Polish Political ScienceYearbook
(Warsaw)
Polish Quarterly of International Af-
fairs (Warsaw)
Polish Round Table (Warsaw)
Polish Sociological Review (Warsaw)
Studia Nauk Politycznych (Warsaw)
Yearbook of Polish Foreign Policy
(Warsaw)

Romania
Revue roumaine des Sciences juridiques (Bucarest)
Revue roumaine d'Études internationales (Bucarest)
Romanian Journal of Sociology (Bucharest)

Slovenia
Public Enterprise (Ljubljana)
Teorija in Praksa (Ljubljana)

Yugoslavia
Medunarodni Problemi (Beograd)
Review of International Affairs (Bel-
grade)
Socioloski Pregled (Beograde)

EUROPE, WESTERN

Austria
Donauraum (Vienna)
Europäische Rundschau (Wien)
*Österreichische Zeitschrift für Poli-
tikwissenschaft (Wien)*
Österreichisches Jahrbuch für inter-
nationale Politik (Wien)
Peace and Security (Wien)

Wirtschaft und Gesellschaft (Wien)
Zeitschrift für Öffentliches Recht (Vienna)

Belgium
Annales de Droit de Louvain (Brus-
sels)
Cahiers de Droit européen (Bruxelles)
Civilisations (Bruxelles)
Res Publica (Brussels)
Réseaux (Mons)
Revue belge de Droit international
(Brussels)
Revue de l'Institut de Sociologie
(Bruxelles)
Revue des Affaires européennes
(Gand)
Revue générale (Bruxelles)
Revue internationale de Politique
comparée (Louvain)
Revue internationale des Sciences
administratives (Bruxelles)
Revue nouvelle (La) (Bruxelles)
Transitions (Bruxelles)

Cyprus
Cyprus Review (Nicosia)

Denmark
Acta sociologica (Copenhagen)
Copenhagen Papers in East and
Southeast Asian Studies (Copen-
hagen)
Danish Foreign Policy Yearbook (Co-
penhagen)
Grus (Aalborg)
Nordisk administrativt Tidsskrift
(København)
Økonomi og Politik (København)
Politica (Aarhus)

Finland
Hallinnon Tutkimus (Helsinki)
Northern Dimensions (Helsinki)
Politiikka (Helsinki)

France
*Actes de la Recherche en Sciences sociales
(Paris)*

Administration (Paris)
Afrique contemporaine (Paris)
Afrique politique (L') (Paris)
Annales (Les) (Paris)
Annales de l'Université des Sciences
  sociales de Toulouse (Toulouse)
Année sociologique (Paris)
Annuaire de l'Afrique du Nord (Aix-
  en-Provence)
Annuaire des Collectivités locales
  (Paris)
Annuaire des Pays de l'Océan indien
  (Aix-en-Provence)
Annuaire européen d'Administration
  publique (Paris)
Annuaire français de Droit interna-
  tional (Paris)
Archipel (Paris)
Archives de Philosophie (Paris)
Archives de Philosophie du Droit
  (Paris)
Archives de Sciences sociales des
  Religions (Paris)
Archives européennes de Sociologie
  (Paris)
Arès (Grenoble)
Austriaca (Rouen)
Balkanologie (Paris)
Cahiers de l'Orient (Paris)
Cahiers des Amériques latines (Paris)
Cahiers d'Études africaines (Paris)
Cahiers d'Études sur la Méditerran-
  née orientale et le Monde turco-
  iranien (Paris)
Cahiers d'Histoire, Espace Marx
  (Paris)
Cahiers du Conseil constitutionnel
  (Paris)
Cahiers du Monde russe (Paris)
Cahiers français (Paris)
Cahiers internationaux de Sociologie
  (Paris)
Commentaire (Paris)
Communications (Paris)
Communisme (Paris)

Cultures et Conflits (Paris)
Débat (Le) (Paris)
Défense nationale (Paris)
Diogène (Paris)
Droit social (Paris)
Droits (Paris)
Espaces et Societé (Paris)
Esprit (Paris)
Études (Paris)
Futuribles (Paris)
Genèses (Paris)
Hermès (Paris)
Hérodote (Paris)
Histoire et Mesure (Paris)
Homme (L') (Paris)
Homme (L') et Ia Société (Paris)
Human Rights Law Journal (Stras-
  bourg)
Irlande (L') politique et sociale (Paris)
Journal du Droit international (Paris)
Langages (Paris)
Lusotopie (Paris)
Mathématiques, Informatique et Sci-
  ences Humaines (Paris)
Metra (Paris)
Monde arabe Maghreb-Machrek
  (Paris)
Mondes en Développement (Paris)
Mots (Paris)
Mouvement (Le) social (Paris)
Notes et Études documentaires
  (Paris)
Penant (Le Vésinet)
Pensée (La) (Paris)
Peuples méditerranéens (Paris)
Philosophie politique (Paris)
Pôle Sud (Montpellier)
Politique africaine (Paris)
Politique étrangère (Paris)
Politique internationale (Paris)
Politiques et Management public
  (Paris)
Politix (Paris)
Pouvoirs (Paris)
Problèmes d'Amérique latine (Paris)

Projet (Paris)
Regards sur l'Actualité (Paris)
Relations internationales et straté-
giques (Paris)
Revue administrative (Paris)
Revue d'Allemagne (Paris)
Revue d'Etudes comparatives Est-
Ouest (Paris)
Revue d'Etudes palestiniennes (Paris)
Revue d'Histoire moderne et contem-
poraine (Paris)
Revue du Droit public et de la Science
politique (Paris)
Revue du Marché commun et de
l'Union europénne (Paris)
Revue du Monde musulman et de la
Mediterranée (Aix-en-Provence)
Revue économique (Paris)
Revue française d'Administration
publique (Paris)
Revue française de Droit adminis-
tratif (Paris)
Revue française de Droit constitu-
tionnel (Paris)
Revue française de Science politique
(Paris)
Revue française de Sociologie (Paris)
Revue française des Affaires sociales
(Paris)
Revue française d'Etudes américaines
(Paris)
Revue générale de Droit international
public (Paris)
Revue internationale de Droit com-
paré (Paris)
Revue internationale des Sciences
sociales (Paris)
Revue juridique et politique, Indé-
pendance et Coopération (Paris)
Revue philosophique de la France et
de l'Etranger (Paris)
Revue politique et parlementaire
(Paris)
Revue trimestrielle de Droit européen
(Paris)

Sociologie du Travail (Paris)
Strategiques (Paris)
Temps modernes (Les) (Paris)
Tiers-Monde (Paris)
Transeuropéennes (Paris)
Trimestre (le) du Monde (Paris)
Vingtième Siècle, Revue d'Histoire
(Paris)
Germany
Afrika Spectrum (Hamburg)
Archiv des öffentlichen Rechts
(Tübingen)
Archiv des Völkerrechts (Tübingen)
Archiv für Rechts- und Sozialphi-
losophie (Budenheim bei Mainz)
Aus Politik und Zeitgeschichte
(Bonn)
Aussenpotitik (Hamburg)
Blätter für deutsche und internation-
ale Politik (Bonn)
Documents, Revue des Questions
allemandes (Cologne)
Europäische Grundrechte Zeitschrift
(Kehl am Rhein)
Forschungsjournal Neue soziale
Bewegungen (Opladen)
Frankreich Jahrbuch (Opladen)
Friedens Warte (Die) (Berlin)
Gegenwartskunde (Leverkusen)
German Yearbook of International
Law (Kiel)
Historical Social Research (Köhln)
Internationale Politik (Bonn)
Internationale Politik und Gesell-
schaft (Bonn)
Internationales Asienforum (Köln)
Jahrbuch des öffentlichen Rechts der
Gegenwart (Tübingen)
Jahrbuch für Sozialwissenschaft
(Göttingen)
Jahrbuch. Bundesinstitut für ostwis-
senschaftliche und internationale
Studien (Köln)
Journal of Institutional and Theoreti-
cal Economics (Tübingen)

Kölner Zeitschrift für Soziologie und
soziale Psychologie (Cologne)
Kritische Justiz (Köln)
Kyklos (Bern)
Leviathan (Opladen)
Merkur (Stuttgart)
Öffentliche Verwaltung (Die) (Stuttgart)
Ordo (Stuttgart)
Ordo politicus (Köln)
Orient (Opladen)
Österreichische Zeitschrift für
Soziologie (Opladen)
Osteuropa (Stuttgart)
Politische Studien (Munich)
Politische Studien Sonderheft (Munich)
Politische Vierteljahresschrift
(Opladen)
Publizistik (Wiesbaden)
Recht und Politik (Berlin)
Sociologia internationalis (Berlin)
Sociologus (Berlin)
Soziale Welt (Göttingen)
Staat (Der) (Berlin)
Südost-Europa (München)
Südosteuropa-Mitteilungen
(München)
Verfassung und Recht in Übersee
(Baden-Baden)
Verwaltung (Die) (Berlin)
Vierteljahreshefte für Zeitgeschichte
(Munich)
WeltTrends (Berlin)
Zeitschrift für ausländisches öffentliches Recht und Völkerrecht (Heidelberg)
Zeitschrift für Geschichtswissenschaft
(Berlin)
Zeitschrift für internationale Beziehungen (Darmstadt)
Zeitschrift für Parlamentsfragen
(Opladen)
Zeitschrift für Politik (Cologne)

Zeitschrift für Politikwissenschaft
(Baden-Baden)
Zeitschrift für Soziologie (Stuttgart)
Zeitschrift für Wirtschafts- und sozial
Wissenschaften (Berlin)

Greece
Revue hellénique de Droit international (Athènes)
Southeast European Yearbook (Athens)

Ireland
Administration (Dublin)
Economic and Social Review (Dublin)
Irish Political Studies (Limerick)

Italy
Affari esteri (Rome)
Africa (Rome)
Aggiornamenti sociali (Milano)
Amministrare (Milan)
Annali della Fondazione Luigi Einaudi (Torino)
Biblioteca della Libertà (Turin)
Civiltà cattolica (Rome)
Civitas (Rome)
Comunità internazionale (Rome)
Critica marxista (Rome)
Critica sociologica (Rome)
Democrazia e Diritto (Rome)
Est-Ovest (Trieste)
International Spectator (The) (Rome)
MicroMega (Rome)
Mulino (Il) (Bologna)
Nord e Sud (Napoli)
Oriente moderno (Rome)
Parolechiave (Roma)
Pensiero politico (Il) (Firenze)
Polis (Bologna)
Politica del Diritto (Bologna)
Politica internazionale (Rome)
Politico (Il) (Pavia)
Quaderni dell'Osservatorio elettorale
(Firenze)
Quaderni di Scienza politica (Milano)
Quaderni di Scienza sociali (Genova)

Rassegna italiana di Sociologia (Bologna)
Rivista di Matematica per le Scienze economiche e sociali (Milan)
Rivista di Studi politici internazionali (Florence)
Rivista internazionale di Scienze economiche e commerciali (Padova)
Rivista internazionale di Scienze sociali (Milan)
Rivista italiana di Scienza politica (Bologna)
Rivista militare (Rome)
Rivista trimestrale di Diritto pubblico (Milano)
Rivista trimestrale di Scienza dell'Amministrazione (Roma)
Sociologia (Rome)
Stato e Mercato (Bologna)
Storia e Politica (Milan)
Studi parlamentari e di Politica costituzionale (Rome)
Teoria politica (Turin)
Terzo Mondo (Milano)

Netherlands
Acta politica (Meppel)
Annuaire européen/European Yearbook (The Hague)
Beleidswetenschap (Alphen)
China Information (Leiden)
Common Market Law Review (Dordrecht)
Constitutional Political Economy (Dordrecht)
Continental Philosophy Review (Dordrecht)
Crime, Law and Social Change (Dordrecht)
Economics of Planning (Dordrecht)
Environmental Policy and Law (Amsterdam)
European Foreign Affairs Review (Dordrecht)

European Journal of Political Economy (Amsterdam)
European Journal of Political Research (Dordrecht)
Gazette (Dordrecht)
Group Decision and Negotiation (Dordrecht)
Information Economics and Policy (Amsterdam)
International Journal of Comparative Sociology (Leiden)
International Journal on Minority and Group Rights (Dordrecht)
International Negotiation (Dordrecht)
International Politics (Dordrecht)
Journal of Asian and African Studies (Leiden)
Journal of Developing Societies (Leiden)
Man and World (Dordrecht)
Minerva (Dordrecht)
Netherlands Journal of Social Sciences (Amsterdam)
Netherlands Yearbook of International Law (The Hague)
Philosophical Studies (Dordrecht)
Policy Sciences (Dordrecht)
Population Research and Policy Review (Dordrecht)
Public Choice (Dordrecht)
Research Policy (Amsterdam)
Review of Central and East European Law (Dordrecht)
Review of Economics and Statistics (Amsterdam)
Sociologia ruralis (Assen)
Studies In East European Thought (Dordrecht)
Theory and Decision (Dordrecht)
Theory and Society (Dordrecht)

Norway
Forum for Development Studies (Oslo)
Inquiry (Oslo)
Internasjonal Politikk (Oslo)

Norsk Statsvitenskapelig Tidsskrift (Oslo)

Scandinavian Political Studies (Oslo)

Portugal

Análise social (Lisbon)

Russia

Gosudarstvo i Pravo (Moscow)

Mirovaja Ekonomika i Mezdunarodnye Otnosenija (Moscow)

Polis (Moskva)

SSA (Moscow)

Voprosi Filosofii (Moskva)

Vostok (Moskva)

Spain

América latina hoy (Madrid)

Anuario de Derecho constitucional y parlamentario (Murcia)

Anuario internacional CIDOB (Barcelona)

Boletín informativo del Seminario de Derecho político (Salamanca)

Cuadernos constitucionales (Valencia)

Cuadernos de Realidades sociales (Madrid)

Ecología política (Barcelona)

Meridiano CERI (Madrid)

Pensamiento Iberoamericano (Madrid)

Política exterior (Madrid)

Política y Sociedad (Madrid)

Revista CIDOB d'Afers internacionals (Barcelona)

Revista de Administración pública (Madrid)

Revista de Derecho comunitario europeo (Madrid)

Revista de Derecho político (Madrid)

Revista de Estudios de la Administración local y autonómica (Madrid)

Revista de Estudios políticos (Madrid)

Revista española de Derecho constitucional (Madrid)

Revista española de Derecho internacional (Madrid)

Revista española de Investigaciones sociológicas (Madrid)

Revista internacional de Filosofía política (Madrid)

Revista internacional de Sociología (Madrid)

Síntesis (Madrid)

Sistema (Madrid)

Sweden

Economic and Industrial Democracy (Stockholm)

Scandinavian Journal of Development Alternatives (Stockholm)

Statsvetenskaplig Tidskrift (Lund)

Switzerland

Relations internationales (Genève)

Review - International Commission of Jurists (Geneva)

Revue économique et sociale (Lausanne)

Revue européenne des Sciences sociales (Genève)

Revue internationale du Travail (Geneva)

Schweizerische Zeitschrift für Politische Wissenschaft (Geneva)

Schweizerische Zeitschrift für Soziologie (St-Saphorin)

Schweizerische Zeitschrift für Volkswirtschaft und Statistik (Basel)

United Kingdom

Africa (London)

African Affairs (London)

Ageing and Society (Cambridge)

Asia Pacific Viewpoint (Oxford)

Asian Affairs (London)

Australian Journal of International Affairs (Abingdon)

British Elections and Parties Year-
   book (London)
*British Journal of Industrial Relations
   (London)*
*British Journal of Political Science (Cam-
   bridge, U.K.)*
British Journal of Sociology (London)
British Yearbook of International Law
   (London)
Central Asian Survey (Abingdon)
China Quarterly (Oxford)
Citizenship Studies (Abingdon)
Coexistence (Glasgow)
*Communist and Post-Communist Stud-
   ies (Oxford)*
Community Development Journal
   (Oxford)
Conflict Studies (London)
Constellations (Oxford)
Contemporary British History (Lon-
   don)
Contemporary Politics (London)
Contemporary Security Policy (Lon-
   don)
Contemporary South Asia (Abing-
   don)
Cooperation and Conflict (London)
Current Sociology (Coventry)
Cybernetics and Systems (Basing-
   stoke)
Debatte (Abingdon)
Defense Analysis (London)
Democratization (London)
Development (Oxford)
Development and Change (Oxford)
Development in Practice (Abingdon)
Development Policy Review (Oxford)
Diplomacy and Statecraft (Birming-
   ham)
Disasters (London)
Discourse and Society (London)
Econometrica (Oxford)
Economic Policy (Oxford)
Economica (London)
Economics and Politics (Oxford)

Economy and Society (London)
Electoral Studies (Oxford)
Environmental Politics (London)
Ethnic and Racial Studies (London)
European History Quarterly (Lon-
   don)
*European Journal of Communication
   (London)*
European Journal of Development
   Research (London)
European Journal of International
   Relations (London)
European Journal of Women's Stud-
   ies (London)
European Law Journal (Oxford)
European Planning Studies (Abing-
   don)
European Security (London)
European Sociological Review (Oxford)
European Union ..., Annual Review
   of Activities (Oxford)
European Urban and Regional Stud-
   ies (Durham)
Europe-Asia Studies (Abingdon)
Geographical Journal (London)
Geopolitique and International
   Boundaries (London)
German Politics (London)
Global Society (Abingdon)
Government and Opposition (London)
Green Globe Yearbook of Interna-
   tional Cooperation on Environ-
   ment and Development (Oxford)
Higher Education Quarterly (Oxford)
History (Oxford)
History of European Ideas (Oxford)
History of Political Thought (Exeter)
History of the Human Sciences (London)
Immigrants and Minorities (London)
Innovation (Abingdon)
International Affairs (London)
International and Comparative Law
   Quarterly (London)
International Journal of Human
   Rights (London)

International Journal of Information Management (Sheffield)

International Journal of Middle East Studies (Cambridge)

International Journal of Public Opinion Research (Oxford)

International Journal of Refugee Law (Oxford)

International Peacekeeping (London)

International Political Science Review (London)

International Relations (London)

International Review of Administrative Sciences (London)

International Review of Sociology (Abingdon)

International Social Science Journal (Oxford)

International Sociology (London)

Islam and Christian-Muslim Relations (Abingdon)

Israel Affairs (London)

Italian Politics: A Review (London)

Japan Forum (Oxford)

Jewish Journal of Sociology (London)

Journal for the Theory of Social Behaviour (Oxford)

Journal of African Law (London)

Journal of American Studies (Cambridge)

Journal of Common Market Studies (Oxford)

Journal of Commonwealth and Comparative Politics (London)

Journal of Communist Studies and Transition Politics (London)

Journal of Contemporary African Studies (Abington)

Journal of Contemporary History (London)

Journal of Contingencies and Crisis Management (Oxford)

Journal of Development Studies (London)

Journal of Ethnic and Migration Studies (Abingdon)

Journal of European Public Policy (London)

Journal of Latin American Studies (Cambridge)

Journal of Law and Society (Oxford)

Journal of Legislative Studies (London)

Journal of Management Studies (Oxford)

Journal of Modern African Studies (Cambridge)

Journal of Modern Italian Studies (London)

Journal of Peace Research (London)

Journal of Peasant Studies (London)

Journal of Political Ideologies (Abingdon)

Journal of Political Philosophy (Oxford)

Journal of Public Policy (Cambridge)

Journal of Refugee Studies (Oxford)

Journal of Slavic Military Studies (London)

Journal of Social Policy (Cambridge)

Journal of Southern African Studies (London)

Journal of Strategic Studies (London)

Journal of the Royal Statistical Society (London)

Journal of Theoretical Politics (London)

Kantian Review (Aberystwyth)

Land Use Policy (Guildford)

Law and Policy (Oxford)

Intelligence and National Security (London)

Local Government Studies (London)

Low Intensity Conflict and Law Enforcement (London)

Maghreb (The) Review (London)

Media, Culture and Society (London)

Mediterranean Politics (London)

Middle Eastern Studies (London)

Millennium (London)

Modern and Contemporary France (London)

Modern Asian Studies (London)

Modern Law Review (Oxford)
Nationalism and Ethnic Politics (London)
Nationalities Papers (Abingdon)
Nations and Nationalism (Cambridge)
New Community (Abingdon)
New Left Review (London)
New Political Economy (Abingdon)
Ocean Development and International Law (London)
Organization (London)
Pacific Review (London)
Pacifica Review (Abingdon)
Parliamentarian (The) (London)
Parliamentary Affairs (London)
Party Politics (London)
Peace Review (Abingdon)
Philosophy and Social Criticism (London)
Polar Record (Cambridge)
Policy and Politics (Bristol)
Policy Studies (Abingdon)
Political Communication (London)
Political Geography (Oxford)
Political Quarterly (London)
Political Studies *(Oxford)*
Political Theory (London)
Politics (Oxford)
Politics and the Life Sciences (Guildford)
Public Administration (London)
Public Administration and Development (Chichester)
Public Law (London)
Rationality and Society (London)
Regional and Federal Studies (London)
Religion, State and Society (Oxford)
Review of African Political Economy (Abingdon)
Review of International Political Economy (London)
Review of International Studies (Leicester)
Review of Social Economy (London)

Revolutionary Russia (London)
Round Table (The) (Abingdon)
Security Dialogue (London)
Security Studies (London)
SIPRI Yearbook (Oxford)
Small Wars and Insurgencies (London)
Social Compass (London)
Social Identities (Abingdon)
Social Science Information (London)
Social Science Information Studies (Sheffield)
Social Studies of Science (London)
Socialist Register (The) (London)
Sociological Review (Keele)
Sociology (Oxford)
South European Society and Politics (London)
Southeast Asia Research (London)
Statute Law Review (Oxford)
Studies in American Political Development (Cambridge)
Survival (Oxford)
Systems Research and Behavioral Science (Lincoln)
Terrorism and Political Violence (London)
Theory, Culture and Society (London)
Thesis Eleven (London)
Third World Quarterly (London)
Time and Society (London)
Urban Studies (Glasgow)
West European Politics (London)
World (The) Economy (London)
World Today (The) (London)
Yearbook of Social Policy (London)

OCEANIA

Australia
AQ [Australian Quarterly] (Balmain, NSW)
Australia and New Zealand Journal of Sociology (Victoria)

Australian Journal of Political Science (Canberra)
Australian Journal of Politics and History (Brisbane)
Australian Journal of Public Administration (Melbourne)
China Journal (Canberra)
Pacific Research (Canberra)
Political Expressions (Clayton, Victoria)
Review of Indonesian and Malayan Affairs (Sydney)

New Zealand
New Zealand International Review (Wellington)
Pacific Viewpoint (Wellington)
Political Science (Wellington)
Public Sector (Wellington)